THE
COMPLETE
IDIOT'S
GUIDE® TO

Classic Movies

W9-ASQ-420

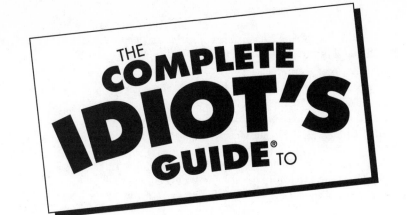

THE COMPLETE IDIOT'S GUIDE® TO

Classic Movies

by Lee Pfeiffer

A member of Penguin Group (USA) Inc.

To my daughter Nicole, the best person I know (even if she doesn't appreciate the merits of On the Beach *and* Thunderball)*. I hope to be just like her when I grow up.*

ALPHA BOOKS

Published by the Penguin Group

Penguin Group (USA) Inc., 375 Hudson Street, New York, New York 10014, U.S.A.

Penguin Group (Canada), 10 Alcorn Avenue, Toronto, Ontario, Canada M4V 3B2 (a division of Pearson Penguin Canada Inc.)

Penguin Books Ltd, 80 Strand, London WC2R 0RL, England

Penguin Ireland, 25 St. Stephen's Green, Dublin 2, Ireland (a division of Penguin Books Ltd)

Penguin Group (Australia), 250 Camberwell Road, Camberwell, Victoria 3124, Australia (a division of Pearson Australia Group Pty Ltd)

Penguin Books India Pvt Ltd, 11 Community Centre, Panchsheel Park, New Delhi—110 017, India

Penguin Group (NZ), cnr Airborne and Rosedale Roads, Albany, Auckland 1310, New Zealand (a division of Pearson New Zealand Ltd)

Penguin Books (South Africa) (Pty) Ltd, 24 Sturdee Avenue, Rosebank, Johannesburg 2196, South Africa

Penguin Books Ltd, Registered Offices: 80 Strand, London WC2R 0RL, England

Copyright © 2006 by Lee Pfeiffer

All rights reserved. No part of this book shall be reproduced, stored in a retrieval system, or transmitted by any means, electronic, mechanical, photocopying, recording, or otherwise, without written permission from the publisher. No patent liability is assumed with respect to the use of the information contained herein. Although every precaution has been taken in the preparation of this book, the publisher and author assume no responsibility for errors or omissions. Neither is any liability assumed for damages resulting from the use of information contained herein. For information, address Alpha Books, 800 East 96th Street, Indianapolis, IN 46240.

THE COMPLETE IDIOT'S GUIDE TO and Design are registered trademarks of Penguin Group (USA) Inc.

International Standard Book Number: 1-59257-557-9
Library of Congress Catalog Card Number: 2006927531

08 07 06   8 7 6 5 4 3 2 1

Interpretation of the printing code: The rightmost number of the first series of numbers is the year of the book's printing; the rightmost number of the second series of numbers is the number of the book's printing. For example, a printing code of 06-1 shows that the first printing occurred in 2006.

Printed in the United States of America

Note: This publication contains the opinions and ideas of its author. It is intended to provide helpful and informative material on the subject matter covered. It is sold with the understanding that the author and publisher are not engaged in rendering professional services in the book. If the reader requires personal assistance or advice, a competent professional should be consulted.

The author and publisher specifically disclaim any responsibility for any liability, loss, or risk, personal or otherwise, which is incurred as a consequence, directly or indirectly, of the use and application of any of the contents of this book.

Most Alpha books are available at special quantity discounts for bulk purchases for sales promotions, premiums, fundraising, or educational use. Special books, or book excerpts, can also be created to fit specific needs.

For details, write: Special Markets, Alpha Books, 375 Hudson Street, New York, NY 10014.

Publisher: *Marie Butler-Knight*

Editorial Director: *Mike Sanders*

Managing Editor: *Billy Fields*

Acquisitions Editor: *Michele Wells*

Development Editor: *Jennifer Moore*

Senior Production Editor: *Janette Lynn*

Copy Editor: *Sarah Cisco*

Cartoonist/Cover Designer: *Bill Thomas*

Book Designers: *Trina Wurst/Kurt Owens*

Indexer: *Brad Herriman*

Layout: *Ayanna Lacey*

Proofreader: *Aaron Black*

Contents

3   Animated Films: "Mirror, Mirror, On the Wall ... Who Is the Fairest One of Them All?"   43

4 Musicals: "You're Going Out There a Youngster, But You've Got to Come Back a Star!"　　53

9 Thrillers: "We All Go a Little Mad Sometimes"   197

10 Horror: "It's Alive! It's Alive!"   215

14   Westerns: "When the Legend Becomes Fact, Print the Legend"   271

Introduction

Welcome to *The Complete Idiot's Guide to Classic Movies*. I suspect the common consensus is "We need another guide to classic movies like we need sequels to *Ishtar* and *Howard the Duck*." However, the fact that you are reading this means *you* certainly have a desire to familiarize yourself with great movies. Perhaps you simply have a passion for Hollywood's heyday, or perhaps your new boss is a movie fanatic and you don't want to sidetrack your career if you are asked at the next Christmas party to name all of *The Magnificent Seven*. (Note: The one guy you can't think of is Brad Dexter.) Although the format of this *Complete Idiot's Guide* differs from most others, the overall objective is the same: to provide a wealth of facts in an interesting and entertaining way. It's the perfect companion for those of us who always found Cliff Notes to be too intense and hoped someone would come out with an abbreviated version.

This book covers movies produced between 1915 and 1969. Why end the listings in 1969? My publisher's theory is that films dating from these eras have indisputably withstood the test of time and can rightfully claim their place among the true classics of the cinema. I initially disagreed and argued that there are plenty of films dating from later years whose pedigree would be beyond reproach. I was then informed that if this book is successful, we would then do a second guide to more recent films. As a devoted capitalist with the backbone of a caterpillar, I immediately folded like a cheap camera in the hope that this book shall beget *Son of The Complete Idiot's Guide to Classic Movies*.

One of the fascinating aspects of modern society is people's pre-occupation with lists. We love them—indeed, it seems as though there is a list made for every conceivable interest. Generally speaking, these lists that people obsess over apply to rather inconsequential subject matters (for example, The Top 100 Moments in Sports, the 100 Sexiest Movie Stars, Elizabeth Taylor's Top 100 Husbands, and so on). You rarely find those nifty daily tear-away desk calendars devoted to "Albert Einstein's Favorite Mathematical Equations" or "The Classic Campaign Quotes of Walter Mondale." It's rather ironic that in an age in which many people can't form opinions about the people making life-and-death decisions at the federal government level, you can cause a near riot among men in a bar by debating who was the coolest cast member in the original *Ocean's Eleven*.

Marlon Brando often derided the medium of cinema and the notion that *any* film could be considered a work of art. Despite his genius as an actor, Brando was certainly proven wrong on this issue. (After all, he *did* star in that remake of *The Island of Dr. Moreau.*) Film can most certainly be considered art. More than any other medium, it has the ability to affect the emotions of untold millions of people, making them laugh, cry, or jump with fear. A great movie transcends its status as an entertainment vehicle for mass audiences and can affect individuals on a deeply personal basis. Each of us can recall the movies that matter most to us. They bring back specific memories of times long gone, some happy, some sad, and many bittersweet. Many of us not only recall with whom we saw a certain film but where we saw it as well.

Many years ago, film criticism seemed to be relegated to the upper crust, lifted pinky crowd. That largely changed in 1979 when film critics Roger Ebert and Gene Siskel began to broadcast what would be their long-running weekly TV show devoted to critiquing new film releases. Ebert and Siskel reflected populist sentiments in the films they chose to review. Important movies were analyzed but so was every "dead teenager" horror film. With the arrival of the Internet age, countless people have become de facto film critics, posting their opinions on websites and blogs, some professionally and many more simply for personal satisfaction. This has brought a liberating aspect to film criticism and has allowed for more discussion of films that were often ignored because mainstream critics did not consider them worthy of attention.

Thus, we come to the contents of *this* book. There is no such thing as a standard listing of classic films, nor should there be. The greatest challenge I had was trying to decide on the titles for inclusion. There are certain films that one would reasonably expect to find in any book relating to classic cinema. However, as I decided to break the book down by genre, I found it necessary to give significant representation to films in each category—a process that was more difficult than I had expected. I was not concerned if certain directors, producers, or stars appeared with disproportionate frequency. I judged the films on their individual merits and did not look to include or exclude any specific personalities. Thus, certain legendary names in movie history are not represented in this book. As I limited the listings to actual feature films, this excluded The Three Stooges, whose best work was seen in short films. Similarly, greats like Abbott and Costello were omitted simply because I did not feel any of their individual films merited inclusion. I also did not include documentary films because few have enjoyed widespread exposure from the eras covered.

Some well-regarded titles still rank as good movies, but somehow seem to not resonate with the importance they once did. Others were excluded because their vast success and popularity still doesn't mitigate their status as bad movies (for example, Demille's 1956 knee-slapping remake of *The Ten Commandments*). If all critics agreed on the same basic choices for classic films, there wouldn't be a need for more than one book analyzing them. Therefore, I have tried to think outside the box and include a number of quirky, less obvious choices. The omission of a film does not mean I do not see merit in it. Is Kurosawa's *Ikiru* a more important film than Frank Perry's little-seen *The Swimmer?* Undoubtedly, yes. However, as the latter film has few defenders, I was swayed by the desire to champion it here. I did not include any film simply because it might be *expected* to be found here. Some movies deemed as classics are the equivalent of taking a dose of medicine—they may be good for you, but somehow they're not much fun to experience. Thus, I offer no apologies for excluding the admirable but glacially paced *A Man For All Seasons* at the expense of including Jerry Lewis' wacky-but-inspired *The Nutty Professor.*

By breaking the films into genres, it has allowed me to recognize films that stood out within their individual subject matters. In the case of the horror and science fiction categories, this allowed me to include films that were derided as schlock during their initial release but have proven to withstand the test of time and have influenced many other films that followed. Thus, the presence of *The Blob* and several of the horror movies made by Britain's Hammer Studios. You can take me to task on this, but if you're willing to be brutally honest with yourself, you *know* you're more often in the mood to watch *The Abominable Snowman of the Himilayas* than *Hiroshima, Mon Amour.*

In researching this book and viewing many films that I had not seen for a number of years, the major point that struck me was the vast difference between the films of these eras and present day Hollywood. There's a reason theater attendance is plummeting, and it goes beyond factors such as having to take out a second mortgage to buy the tickets, sitting through brain-numbing commercials that were the reason you left your house for the evening in the first place, and listening to screaming babies and guys named Rocco blabbing into their cell phones during the movie. No, the overriding reason for the decline in the film business is this: few stars today can compare with those of the past. There have been no suitable replacements for the likes of John Wayne, Cary Grant, Katherine Hepburn, and Clark Gable. We're reaching a point where there are no suitable replacements for the likes of Schwarzeneggar and Stallone for God's sake! Thus, instead of having Kirk Douglas as Alexander the Great, we have Colin Farrel. Instead of Burt Lancaster in *Troy* we have Brad Pitt. Can you imagine these surf dudes starring in films like *High Noon* and *From Here to Eternity*?

The other factors I became cognizant of in my search for classic cinema is the inestimable contributions of another vanishing specie: the supporting actor. So many of the classic films have recognizable faces that greet you like old friends. Can anyone imagine giants of the cinema like Charles Laughton or Walter Brennan even making it past the studio gates today? Yet, where would so many legendary films be without the enormous contributions of great personalities like these? Similarly, I was impressed with how often the same names came up in terms of great film composers. Musical directors like Dimitri Tiomkin, Henry Mancini, Elmer Bernstein, John Barry, Lalo Schifrin, and Jerry Goldsmith created some of the greatest film themes of all time. Most of these artists are gone today, and those who are still with us are rarely employed by an industry that has an eye on a video tie-in with MTV rather than a classic film score.

Lastly, there is the overall question: "What defines a classic film?" The answer is as subjective as the films listed in this book. However, I did give it some thought and came up with the following simple criteria:

- It must have an enduring legacy that has extended long beyond its initial release, and perhaps have influenced subsequent films or the movie industry itself.

- Its merits should be appreciated internationally, not just provincially.

- It must succeed in resonating with its intended audience.

- Its appeal should be such that audiences want to experience repeated viewings over many years.

- It will undoubtedly resurface as a vastly inferior remake, most likely starring Mark Wahlberg.

The goal of any film critic is to inspire readers to experience movies they may have overlooked. I hope this book has that result. I welcome reader's comments, suggestions, and corrections. Please feel free to write to me at cinemaretro@hotmail.com or at P.O. Box 152, Dunellen, NJ 08812. I will take all comments into consideration for future updates of this book.

Now fast-forward to the good stuff—and here's looking at you, kid.

How to Use This Book

Films have been broken down by genres. Within each section, movies have been listed in order of release date, not alphabetically. This is due to the fact that listing them in sequential order allows the reader to more fully appreciate the impact a film may have had in terms of influencing other movies in that genre or perhaps inspiring a sequel.

The movie studio credited with a film pertains to its original theatrical release in the United States. Over time, rights to films might have been transferred to a new company, thus these credits don't imply who owns the present-day rights to the movies listed. The original production companies are cited in order to show the reader the impact specific studios had during any particular era. In some cases, studios that produced some of the major movies of their time no longer exist, such as RKO Radio Pictures.

Oscar nominations for each film are listed with an asterisk (*) denoting those categories that actually won the award.

For films from the silent era and early sound era, many times key contributors, such as producers or composers, did not receive screen credit. Where possible, we have indicated who those individuals were with a notation that they did not actually receive credit on screen.

Running times listed are chosen on the basis of the most recent version of the film to be released. For example, over the years, films that had been edited for reasons of censorship or running time have had footage restored. In most cases, the running times indicate the restored version if that is the version most prevalent on home video today.

About the Sidebars

The book features the following sidebars that are designed to inform you of additional interesting facts about specific films.

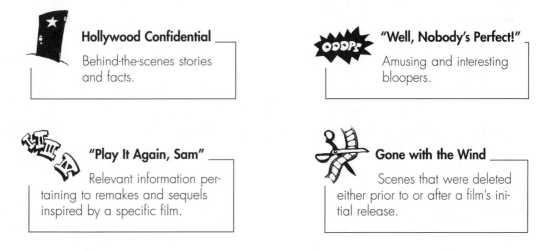

Hollywood Confidential

Behind-the-scenes stories and facts.

"Well, Nobody's Perfect!"

Amusing and interesting bloopers.

"Play It Again, Sam"

Relevant information pertaining to remakes and sequels inspired by a specific film.

Gone with the Wind

Scenes that were deleted either prior to or after a film's initial release.

Acknowledgments

My sincere thanks to:

My lovely, long-suffering wife Janet, who endured months of isolation while I embedded myself in endless screenings of classic movies. Hopefully, there will come a time when I won't be waking her up by reciting dialogue in my sleep from *True Grit* or *The Maltese Falcon*.

My partner at *Cinema Retro* magazine, Dave Worrall, as well as staff writers Mike Dainard, Mike Thomas, Mark Cerulli, Gary Giblin, and Mike Lewis. Thanks also to Richard Ashton of 20th Century Fox, Ronnee Sass of Warner Brothers, Jason Allen,

Nick Sheffo, Derek and Rita Elms, Ray Donohue, James Page, Vipul Patel, Navin Jain, and my longtime friend Ron Plesniarski. Special appreciation to my friends and colleagues at The Players club in New York and at NYU (especially Dean Williamson) for their interest and encouragement, as well as Rich Skillman, Bob Collins, Tom Stroud, Jim Sieff, Alan Laboseur, George Koodray, and Dan Willis. Thanks also to my brother Ray for getting me hooked on great movies at an early age.

I'd also like to extend my sincere appreciation to my wonderful editors, Michele Wells and Jennifer Moore, for their constant encouragement. Very special thanks to my agent Marilyn Allen. Here's looking at you, kid.

Special Thanks to the Technical Reviewer

The Complete Idiot's Guide to Classic Movies was reviewed by an expert who double-checked the accuracy of what you'll learn here, to help us ensure that this book gives you everything you need to know about classic movies. Special thanks are extended to Doug Mendini.

Trademarks

All terms mentioned in this book that are known to be or are suspected of being trademarks or service marks have been appropriately capitalized. Alpha Books and Penguin Group (USA) Inc. cannot attest to the accuracy of this information. Use of a term in this book should not be regarded as affecting the validity of any trademark or service mark.

~ Chapter 1 ~
The Pre-Sound Era
Silents Are Golden

Motion pictures existed for years prior to the premiere of D.W. Griffith's legendary *The Birth of a Nation*. However, most of the movies released during this relatively prehistoric era of filmmaking consisted of experimental works of varying lengths. Georges Mieles' landmark film *La Voyage dans La Lune* (*A Journey to the Moon*), released in 1902, was not only the first attempt to tell a science fiction story on film, but it also boasted incredible production values. Similarly, the first major western story told onscreen, *The Great Train Robbery* (1903) also contained many impressive elements that were extremely innovative in their day. However, these were short films running less than 15 minutes. I have limited the silent movies included in this book to actual feature films shot during a period in which the industry had matured to the point of telling sophisticated stories.

There has always been a small but loyal audience for silent films. For many years, however, enthusiasts had to savor them at art house showings or small screenings hosted by private collectors. The birth of the home video industry has made them far more accessible. I confess that I had not seen many of the films listed here for many years and, in reviewing them again, I was even more impressed by their merits. I hope that in reading about them, your appetite might be similarly whetted and you may give them a try.

And by all means, try to expose younger movie fans to the merits of these great films. It may be an arduous task to convince kids who consider the first *Matrix* film a golden oldie, but the work of the great directors and actors who made these landmark productions will have a timeless appeal for all who are willing to experience them.

The Birth of a Nation (1915)

D.W. Griffith Productions

Director and Producer: D.W. Griffith; **Writers:** D.W. Griffith and Frank E. Woods; **Music:** Joseph Carl Breil and D.W. Griffith; **Running time:** 165 minutes

Cast: Lillian Gish (Elsie); Mae Marsh (Flora); Henry B. Walthall (Col. Ben Cameron); Miriam Cooper (Margaret Cameron); Mary Alden (Lydia)

While undeniably a masterpiece in terms of pure cinematic aspects, *The Birth of a Nation* has long posed dilemmas for sociologists and film historians alike. Director D.W. Griffith revolutionized the young art of movie making with this big-budget ($100,000), highly ambitious recreation of the Civil War years. At 165 minutes, it was the longest movie ever released, and its magnificent battle recreations and large-scale action set pieces must have been marvels to behold when audiences first viewed the film. However, the movie's reputation has always carried the burden of its overt racism. Griffith, a staunch white supremacist, portrays blacks as the root of all evil—running amok, spreading crime, and lusting after white women. Most disturbingly, the KKK are presented as heroes, and lynchings are depicted as acts of civic duty. The message may be repulsive, but the film's historical impact cannot be ignored. From a technical standpoint, it remains an early masterpiece of the American cinema.

Hollywood Confidential

The Birth of a Nation was the first film to be shown in The White House. President Woodrow Wilson proclaimed it to be "history written in lightning."

Intolerance (1916)

Triangle Distributing Corporation

Director, Producer, and Writer: D.W. Griffith; **Running time:** 197 minutes

Cast: Mae Marsh (The Dear One); Lillian Gish (Woman Who Rocks the Cradle); Fred Turner (Her Father); Robert Harron (The Boy); Sam De Grasse (Arthur Jenkins)

D.W. Griffith's ambitious epic is the film Pauline Kael called "perhaps the greatest movie ever made and perhaps the greatest folly in movie history." Set in four different time periods of history, *Intolerance* shows the human race's propensity for … well, intolerance through the ages. There is irony in the fact that the director who made the race-baiting *Birth of a Nation* would later oversee a critique of intolerant attitudes in society. A wildly inconsistent—but highly impressive—film, it was lauded by other filmmakers as a profound influence on their works. Its visual splendor, especially in the ancient Babylon segment, still impresses viewers even in the era of CGI effects. Although the film received a weak reception from the public and critics alike, from a technical standpoint, it has become a landmark in film history. Griffith's obsession with re-editing his films has resulted in the surviving prints having different scenes and running times, though there is no complete version of the original presentation.

Tarzan of the Apes (1918)

First National Pictures

Director: Scott Sidney; **Producer:** William Parsons; **Writers:** Fred Miller and Lois Weber; **Running time:** 55 minutes

Cast: Elmo Lincoln (Tarzan); Enid Markey (Jane); True Boardman (John Clayton); Kathleen Kirkman (Alice Clayton)

Although its merits as a film are debatable, the relevance of *Tarzan of the Apes* to motion picture history is not. This crudely made film was ironically the most literal screen version of the Edgar Rice Burroughs story until Hugh Hudson's ambitious 1984 film *Greystoke*. The biggest detriment to the film is the casting of Elmo Lincoln as Tarzan. With his flabby physique, it would appear that Lincoln's man of the jungle is only a few vine swings away from the nearest White Castle. Still, the first screen appearance of Tarzan helped establish the character as a timeless cinematic hero.

The Cabinet of Dr. Caligari (1919)

Decla-Bioscop AG (Germany)

Director: Robert Wiene; **Producers:** Erich Pommer and Rudolf Meinert; **Writers:** Hans Janowitz and Carl Mayer; **Music:** Peter Schirmann; **Running time:** 67 minutes

Cast: Werner Krauss (Dr. Caligari); Conrad Veidt (Cesare); Fredrich Feher (Francis); Lil Dagover (Jane); Hans Heinrich V. Twardowski (Alan); Rudolf Lettinger (Dr. Olson)

The first film to use surrealistic production design in a major way, *Caligari* actually inspired the Expressionist movement in post-WWI Germany, influencing architecture, films, art, and the literary world in a way no other movie had. The bizarre set pieces provide a quasi-surrealistic world that always keeps the viewer off-kilter. Shadows shroud much of the action, giving a nightmarish quality to the story that concerns a mysterious doctor who arrives in a village with a somnambulist (a man in an eternal state of sleep who can be commanded to perform his master's commands). The populace is skeptical—until a series of gruesome murders lead some to believe the doctor and his strange "assistant" may well be to blame. *Caligari* gave a giant boost to the German cinema in the wake of the devastating consequences of the first World War. In doing so, it impacted the fledgling motion picture industry in a way few other films have. A remake was released in 1962 starring actress Glynis Johns, but it bore little resemblance to the original.

The Kid (1921)

First National Pictures

Director, Producer, and Writer: Charles Chaplin; **Running time:** 68 minutes

Cast: Charles Chaplin (The Little Tramp); Jackie Coogan (The Kid); Edna Purviance (The Mother)

Chaplin's first feature length film demonstrated the sensitivity and compassion that would be a hallmark of his future works. A tramp reluctantly rescues a baby abandoned by an unwed mother and successfully raises him for a number of years. When the mother eventually attempts to retrieve the child, the tramp and his young protégé embark on a desperate attempt to escape. *The Kid* made Jackie Coogan (best known to the next generation for his hilarious portrayal of Uncle Fester in *The Addams Family* TV series) one of the first child superstars. He and Chaplin would remain in touch through their lives. Like most Chaplin projects, this one was fraught with drama as he almost lost possession of the negative in a nasty divorce battle!

Nosferatu (1922)

Prana-Film GMBH

Director: F.W. Murnau; **Producers:** Enrico Dieckmann and Albin Grau; **Writer:** Henrik Galeen; **Running time:** 81 minutes

Cast: Max Schreck (Orlof); Gustav v. Wangenheim (Hutter); Greta Schroeder (Ellen Hutter); Alexander Granach (Knock)

F.W. Murnau's classic (and unapproved) adaptation of Bram Stoker's *Dracula* is, ironically, perhaps the most faithful adaptation of the original book. Nonetheless, the film didn't sit well with Stoker's widow, who filed a high-profile copyright infringement suit that greatly diminished Murnau's ability to present this amazing film to the widest international audiences. Over the years, however, prints of various lengths have appeared, and the home video boom has made the film accessible to millions. Murnau, as much as any other director, advanced the German cinema's obsession with Expressionistic production design, which utilized unusual sets, weird angles, and other architectural oddities. The movie is a genuinely harrowing experience, perhaps all the more so because of its essential crudity. Max Schreck's vampire presents what is still perhaps the most frightening screen image imaginable (and that includes post-facelift Joan Rivers).

Safety Last (1923)

Pathe Exchange, Inc.

Directors: Fred Neymeyer and Sam Taylor; **Writers:** Hal Roach, Sam Taylor, and Tim Whelan; **Running time:** 70 minutes

Cast: Harold Lloyd (The Boy); Mildred Davis (The Girl); Bill Strother (The Pal); Noah Young (The Law)

The renewal of interest in Harold Lloyd's work is long overdue, as his influence on the silent film era was inestimable. No film illustrates this more than *Safety Last*, a simple contrivance expanded into a set piece for some of the most amazing stunts ever filmed. Lloyd is a young man who poses as a department store manager to impress his girlfriend. The plan soon goes awry, and he concocts an elaborate scheme to make his ruse appear true. The scheme mandates Lloyd act as a human fly in the most precarious—and hilarious— death-defying situations imaginable. Lloyd performed many of the most dangerous stunts himself, despite having lost two fingers previously in a movie set mishap. The film is a "must-have" for any serious movie fan.

"Play It Again, Sam"

Nosferatu was remade very efficiently in 1979 by Werner Herzog with Klaus Kinski's equally repulsive embodiment of The Count. The film was an impressive effort and highly reverent of Murnau's original. In 2000, William Dafoe earned an Oscar nomination for playing Max Schreck in *Shadow of the Vampire*, a fictionalized look at the making of *Nosferatu* that theorized Schreck was an actual vampire!

The Ten Commandments (1923)

Paramount Pictures

Director and Producer: Cecil B. DeMille; **Writer:** Jeanie MacPherson; **Running time:** 146 minutes

Cast: Theodore Roberts (Moses); Charles de Rochefort (Rameses); Estelle Taylor (Miriam); Julia Faye (wife of Pharoah); Richard Dix (John McTavish)

Few directors had more passion for filmmaking than Cecil B. DeMille. With his trademark penchant for overseeing massive productions, DeMille had an impressive talent for directing traffic but fared less well directing actors, often unintentionally bringing out the ham in them. Yet, it would be inconceivable to write about influential movies and not pay homage to DeMille. The director's silent version of *The Ten Commandments* is in many ways his most impressive achievement. Aside from the spectacle of the Biblical sequences, he added the innovative aspect of having the second half of the film revolve around a modern day sequence with two brothers caught up in a morality tale inspired by the Commandments themselves. The main event is still the parting of the Red Sea (accomplished by using heated gelatin and reversing the film!), a sequence that remains impressive today.

 "Play It Again, Sam"

DeMille remade *The Ten Commandments* in 1956 with Charlton Heston as Moses and an all-star cast. Although the film was a huge financial success, DeMille managed the Herculean task of getting some of the world's greatest actors to deliver unintentionally hilarious performances. The film should have inspired an Eleventh Commandment: "Thou Shalt Never Cast Edward G. Robinson and Vincent Price as Ancient Egyptians!"

Greed (1924)

MGM

Director: Erich Von Stroheim; **Producers:** Erich Von Stroheim and Samuel Goldwyn; **Writers:** Erich Von Stroheim and June Mathis; **Music:** James Brennan and Jack Brennan; **Running time:** 140 minutes

Cast: Zasu Pitts (Trina); Gibson Gowland (McTeague); Jean Hersholt (Marcus); Dale Fuller (Maria)

The intrigue and drama behind the scenes on *Greed* rival anything seen onscreen. Erich Von Stroheim envisioned filming a literal translation of Frank Norris's novel

McTeague and delivered a cut that ran over 8 hours. MGM bigwig Irving Thalberg cut the film to 140 minutes over the director's strenuous objections. The plot is an old standard: money not only can't buy happiness, it also can bring misery. A love triangle turns murderous when a lottery ticket provides unexpected wealth and brings out the worst in each of the principal players. The final image of a murder gone wrong in the sands of Death Valley resonates with ironic consequences.

> **Gone with the Wind**
>
> The missing reels of footage from the original cut of *Greed* are among the most sought-after rarities in film history. In 1999, a partially restored version of the film was unveiled that included stills from the missing scenes.

The Thief of Bagdad (1924)

United Artists

Director: Raoul Walsh; **Producer:** Douglas Fairbanks; **Writers:** James T. O'Donohoe and Lotta Woods; **Running time:** 155 minutes

Cast: Douglas Fairbanks (The Thief); Snitz Edwards (The Thief's Associate); Charles Belcher (The Holy Man); Julanne Johnston (The Princess)

Directed by the great Raoul Walsh, this mystical tale features Douglas Fairbanks as a loveable rogue who can only win the hand of a beautiful princess by embarking on a seemingly impossible mission to bring back legendary treasures for her father. Known for his dashing demeanor and incredible stunts, Fairbanks, who would also routinely contribute to the scripts of his films under the pseudonym Elton Thomas, came up with the story for this version of *Thief of Bagdad* and included special effects and production design that audiences had never been exposed to. It is rumored this was the first film to exceed a budget of $1 million.

> **"Play It Again, Sam"**
>
> *The Thief of Baghdad* has been remade numerous times. Among the more prominent versions: a 1940 adaptation (in Technicolor) starring Sabu, a 1961 "sword and sandals" version with Steve Reeves, and a 1978 TV movie top-lining Roddy McDowell.

Battleship Potemkin (1925)

Amkino Corporation

Director: Sergei M. Eisenstein; **Producer:** Jacob Bliokh; **Writers:** Sergei M. Eisenstein and Nina Agadzhanova-Shutko; **Music:** Edmund Meisel; **Running time:** 66 minutes

Once presented by the young Communist regime as a masterful piece of Soviet propaganda, *Battleship Potemkin* is a seminal film in European cinema. The story is based on the historical 1905 mutiny of Russian sailors against their tyrannical superiors aboard *The Potemkin*. Their victory was short-lived, however, as during their attempts to get the population of Odessa to launch a massive revolution, Cossacks arrived and laid waste to the insurgents, thus fanning the winds of war that ultimately lead to the rise of Communism in the 1917 revolution. Director Eisenstein displays his legendary ability of capturing large-scale action sequences in impressive style. His fictional massacre on the Odessa Steps is one of the truly great sequences in cinema history. The shot of the baby carriage tumbling down the long staircase has been recreated in many films, including Brian De Palma's *The Untouchables* (1987). Ironically, the film was eventually banned by Stalin over fears it might incite a riot against *his* regime. Note: Over the years, the film has been presented with various musical soundtracks. As Roger Ebert pointed out, the power of the film is directly impacted by the suitability of the score one hears while watching it.

Ben-Hur: A Tale of the Christ (1925)

MGM

Director: Fred Niblo; **Producers:** J.J. Cohn, Charles B. Dillingham, Abraham L. Erlanger, Louis B. Mayer, and Florenz Ziegfield Jr.; **Writer:** June Mathis; **Music:** William Axt; **Running time:** 143 minutes

Cast: Ramon Navarro (Ben-Hur); Francis X. Bushman (Messala); May McAvoy (Esther); Betty Bronson (Mary); Claire McDowell (Mother of Ben-Hur)

"Play It Again, Sam"

Ben Hur would be remade on an even more massive scale in 1959. William Wyler, who was one of the assistant directors on the silent version, would win the Oscar for his direction of the remake.

At $4 million, *Ben-Hur* was the most expensive film of the silent era. Surprisingly, this 1925 movie adaptation was the *second* screen version of General Lew Wallace's massive novel. In 1907, the story was condensed into a one-reel short, which is akin to watching a trailer for *War and Peace* in order to gain an appreciation of Pasternak's novel. The highlight of *any Ben-Hur*, of course, is the famed chariot race. Initially, the cast and crew flew to Italy, where the epic sequence ran into problems immediately.

Conditions were unfavorable, a stuntman was killed, and the budget began to sky-rocket. The crew relocated to Culver City where the racetrack was reconstructed with more impressive results. It remains one of the most impressive action sequences ever committed to film. Equally massive in scale was the major sea battle, shot on location in Italy. Several of the main scenes were shot in two-strip Technicolor, a true innovation for those days. For the fledgling MGM, the film insured the studio's reputation as a major player in the motion picture business.

The Big Parade (1925)

MGM

Director: King Vidor; **Producer:** Uncredited; **Writers:** Henry Behn; **Music:** William Axt and David Mendoza; **Running time:** 141 minutes

Cast: John Gilbert (James Apperson); Renee Adoree (Melisande); Hobart Bosworth (Mr. Apperson); Claire McDowell (Mrs. Apperson); Claire Adams (Justyn Reed)

Routinely touted as one of the greatest anti-war films, King Vidor's *The Big Parade* is a genuine epic. At a cost of over $300,000, the film was one of the most sweeping of the silent era. Even though the film was shot in Texas, Vidor captured the full horror of the trench warfare in France. (Some of the battle scenes were shot by George Hill after Vidor left the project.) In doing so, he not only humanized the German adversaries but also gave John Gilbert the role that cemented him as one of the first genuine superstars. What makes *The Big Parade* of historical, as well as cinematic, importance is the fact that it was shot within a few years of the end of WWI, thus providing a fascinating time capsule into how the war impacted the American people. The film became MGM's biggest grosser of that era, with revenues topping $5 million. At the Astor Theater in New York City, it played an astounding 96 weeks.

The Gold Rush (1925)

United Artists

Director, Producer, and Writer: Charles Chaplin; **Running time:** 96 minutes

Cast: Charles Chaplin (The Lone Prospector); Mack Swain (Big Jim McKay); Tom Murray (Black Larsen); Henry Bergman (Hank Curtis)

Oscar nominations (pertaining to the re-edited 1943 reissue): Sound, Musical Score (Max Terr)

Already a major star by 1925, Charles Chaplin developed *The Gold Rush* as his first starring feature film for United Artists, the new studio created by Chaplin, D.W. Griffith, and husband-and-wife superstars Douglas Fairbanks and Mary Pickford. The tale follows the adventures of Chaplin's legendary Little Tramp as he prospects for gold, fighting off wild animals and greedy competitors. As always, our hero also pursues a lover, is initially mocked and rejected, but triumphs in the end. The movie contains many classic set pieces. This film features the most famous image of Chaplin as the starving Little Tramp who prepares his boot as a hot meal for himself and his equally desperate friend. Chaplin proclaimed this to be the film he wanted to be remembered for. It's difficult to argue with his logic.

The Phantom of the Opera (1925)

Universal Pictures

Director: Rupert Julian; **Writers:** Raymond Schrock and Elliott J. Clawson; **Running time:** 93 minutes

Cast: Lon Chaney (Erik, the Phantom); Mary Philbin (Christine); Norman Kerry (Raoul); Arthur Edward Carewe (Ledox); Gibson Gowland (Simon Buquet)

A troubled production, *The Phantom of the Opera* was actually completed in 1923, but was reworked over the next two years as nervous Universal executives pandered to critics who suggested the film needed more humor to offset the macabre story of a disfigured, eccentric genius who secretly coaches an aspiring opera singer and forces her to learn to sing majestically. The relationship turns tragic when he falls in love with her and kidnaps her to prevent her from being with her fiancé. Universal shot comedic sequences with Chester Conklin, but these were (mercifully) dropped. Numerous reworkings followed before the film's premiere in 1925. Virtually everyone agreed that the raison d'etre for *Phantom* was to allow Lon Chaney to demonstrate his remarkable achievement in makeup. "The Man of a Thousand Faces" caused a sensation when he stripped away the mask of the Phantom to reveal what would become one of the most enduring images in the history of cinema.

"Play It Again, Sam"

The film has had more remakes than probably any other movie in history. The Chaney version was actually preceded by a 1916 German adaptation of the novel. Among the more notable remakes: a 1943 version with Nelson Eddy, a 1962 Hammer production (see Chapter 10 on horror films), a 1983 TV movie with Maximillian Schell, a 1989 version with Robert Englund, a 1990 TV version with Burt Lancaster, and the big budget 2004 version of Andrew Lloyd Weber's long-running stage musical.

Son of the Sheik (1926)

United Artists

Director and Producer: George Fitzmaurice; **Writers:** Francis Marion and Fred De Gresac; **Running time:** 72 minutes

Cast: Rudolph Valentino (Ahmed and the Sheik); Vilma Bankey (Yasmin); George Fawcett (Andre); Montague Love (Ghabah); Karl Dane (Ramadan)

The symbolic images found in this sequel to Valentino's *The Sheik* (1921) are so important to film lore that the movie takes on a resonance it perhaps may not otherwise deserve. The first film was a surprise hit and catapulted Valentino into stardom as an international heartthrob. *Son of the Sheik* was perhaps the first high profile film sequel. If audiences loved Valentino playing one leading role, the theory went, they'd go starry-eyed seeing him play both the original sheik and his dashing young son this time around. Virtually everyone agreed that this follow-up was a slicker production than its predecessor and possessed tongue-in-cheek humor not found in the original. The film took on a legendary status in a tragic and unexpected way: it was Valentino's last screen appearance. He died from peritonitis at age 31. Over 80,000 fans mobbed his funeral, proving that Valentino was larger-than-life even in death.

The General (1927)

United Artists

Directors: Buster Keaton and Clyde Bruckman; **Writers:** Al Boasberg and Charles Smith; **Running time:** 75 minutes

Cast: Buster Keaton (Johnny Gray); Marion Mack (Annabelle Lee); Frank Barnes (Annabelle's brother); Glen Cavender (Capt. Anderson)

A personal triumph for Buster Keaton, *The General* is an ambitious film that combines historical fact, outlandish stunts, acts of heroism, and an inventive storyline set during the Civil War. Keaton plays Johnny Gray, the engineer of the southern steam engine *The General*, who engages in a fanatical, one-man chase to recover the train when it is stolen by Union spies. The story was inspired by a real incident, though the Keaton touch adds some of the most memorable stunt work and sight gags the cinema has ever seen. With the advent of the sound era, Keaton was relegated to obscurity before being rediscovered by Hollywood in the last years of his life. A new generation has come to appreciate his classic works, of which *The General* remains the crowning achievement.

Metropolis (1927)

Universum Film A.G.

Director: Fritz Lang; **Producer:** Erich Pommer; **Writers:** Fritz Lang and Thea von Harbou; **Running time:** 117 minutes

Cast: Alfred Abel (Johan); Gustav Frohlich (Freder); Brigitte Helm (Maria); Rudolf Klein-Rogge (Rotwang)

Despite modern day filmmaking technology, no recent film threatens to surpass Fritz Lang's *Metropolis* in terms of the impact of production design and stunning visual concepts. Set in a futuristic society, the plot has a very definite Socialist bent: the great modern city of Metropolis is inhabited by two distinct classes. The industrialists live off the fat of the land, supported by the workers who literally live under the city and endure a bare-bones existence of backbreaking work. The story concerns a forbidden love between a boy from the industrialist class and an activist worker. There is subterfuge and deceit, culminating in a revolution that quickly spells disaster for all involved. Lang's eye for magnificent set pieces and effects results in some scenes of jaw-dropping magnitude. The film was greatly admired by Hitler, who "invited" Lang to head film production in the Reich. Lang chose to flee the country instead, though his wife (who cowrote the script) stayed on as an ardent supporter of National Socialism.

Gone with the Wind

Metropolis has been re-edited many times over the decades, and the original release print that ran 153 minutes seems lost forever. Various versions exist in different countries. In 1984, an 87-minute print was released with a rock soundtrack constructed by composer Giorgio Moroder.

Napoleon (1927)

MGM

Director, Producer, and Writer: Abel Gance; **Music:** Arthur Honegger; **Running time:** 235 minutes (restored version)

Cast: Albert Dieudonne (Napoleon Bonaparte); Vladimir Roudenko (Young Napoleon); Edmond Van Daele (Maximilien Robespierre); Alexandre Koubitzky (Danton); Antonin Artaud (Marat); Abel Gance (Louis Saint-Just)

French director Abel Gance was a true pioneer in filmmaking and his big-budget epic was shot in a unique filming process known as a triptych, an early precursor to today's

Imax that required shooting with three synchronized cameras. This allowed the right and left portions of the screen to present different images at times from what was being shown in the center screen. At other times, the images blended back into one. Unfortunately, *Napoleon* was released at the beginning of the sound era and few theaters showed the willingness to invest substantial sums in the equipment needed to project the film. Gance recut a sound version of the movie in 1934, and the film was re-edited into countless other versions over the years. His original cut had been presumed lost forever until British film historian Kevin Brownlow, with financial support from Francis Ford Coppola, found the footage and launched a major restoration of the film in 1980 with a triumphant new score by Coppola's father Carmine. Fortunately, Gance was still alive and was finally able to bask in the glow of a new appreciation for his lost masterpiece.

Wings (1927)

Paramount Pictures

Director: William Wellman; **Producer:** Lucien Hubbard; **Writers:** Hope Loring and Louis D. Lighton; **Music:** J.S. Zamecnik; **Running time:** 141 minutes

Cast: Clara Bow (Mary Preston); Charles "Buddy" Rogers (Jack Powell); Richard Arlen (David Armstrong); Jobyna Ralston (Sylvia Lewis); El Brendel (Herman Scwimpf); Richard Tucker (Air Commander); Gary Cooper (Cadet White)

Oscar nominations: Best Picture*, Best Effects*

Wings is the first film (and the only silent picture) to be awarded an Oscar by the newly formed Academy of Motion Picture Arts and Sciences. Beyond that, however, this WWI epic remains highly regarded for its incredible aerial battle sequences that many believe have never been equaled. These scenes take on a breathtaking resonance due to the fact that, although stunt pilots were employed for the trickiest maneuvers, the actors actually did pilot their own planes, operating cameras at the same time. The storyline concerns two friends (Charles "Buddy" Rogers and Richard Arlen) both vying for the attention of Clara Bow's Mary Preston. While the plot is mildly interesting, it is the war sequences that have cemented the status of *Wings* as a landmark film of the silent era.

The Circus (1928)

Allied Artists

Director, Producer, Writer, Composer: Charles Chaplin

Running time: 71 minutes

Cast: Charles Chaplin (The Tramp); Allan Garcia (Circus Owner and Ringmaster); Merna Kennedy (Ringmaster's Daughter); Harry Crocker (Rex); Henry Bergman (Old Clown)

Oscar nominations: Chaplin awarded honorary Oscar "For versatility and genius in acting, writing, directing and producing *The Circus.*"

Chaplin's *The Circus* earned him a special Academy Award for directing, producing, and writing this story of a tramp who joins the circus as an inept janitor only to be exploited for unintended laughs by the cruel owner. Chaplin distanced himself from *The Circus* for many years as the film reflected a troubled period in his life. The studio burned down during production and scenes showing Chaplin's harrowing stunts on a tightrope were ruined when the film stock was damaged. (The scene was filmed again, but Chaplin felt it was inferior to the original.) The great legend suffered a nervous breakdown during filming, causing completion to be delayed for months. Ultimately, it has the dubious distinction of being the only film he does not mention in his autobiography. He also kept the film out of circulation for over 40 years until he agreed to a reissue in 1969. (Chaplin also made some cosmetic changes to the film.)

The Crowd (1928)

MGM

Director and Producer: King Vidor; **Writers:** King Vidor and John V.A. Weaver; **Music:** Carl Davis; **Running time:** 104 minutes

Cast: James Murray (Johnny Sims); Eleanor Boardman (Mary); Bert Roach (Bert); Estelle Clark (Jane); Daniel G. Tomlinson (Jim)

Oscar nominations: Director and Artistic Quality of Production

More akin to the neo-realism of the European filmmaking community, King Vidor's *The Crowd* offers a rare morbid view of society far removed from the upbeat, lively fare reflected in most silent films. The story centers on an idealistic young man as he is crushed by the harsh realities of life in the modern urban metropolis. Vidor won universal acclaim for his innovative methods of illustrating the harsh, impersonal aspects of urban existence. "The crowd" is seen as a literal force dedicated to breaking down individual stamina and hope. The cinematography by Henry Sharp (much of it shot with hidden cameras) earned enthusiastic praise for his innovative style and amazing camera angles. The studio argued for upbeat changes to the movie and seven different endings were shot. Vidor managed to prevail with his version of the final cut. *The Crowd* never attained box-office success, though it stands as one of the great American film achievements.

Hollywood Confidential _____

Although James Murray gave a superb performance, his life mirrored his on-screen alter ego's tragic run of bad luck. Frustrated at not having star-making follow-up roles, he fell on hard times and became an alcoholic. His body was found in the Hudson River in 1936. Whether his death was accidental or the result of suicide has never been determined.

La Passion de Jeanne De Arc (1928)

Capitol Film Exchange

Director: Carl Theodor Dreyer; **Writers:** Joseph Delteil and Carl Theodor Dreyer; **Composer:** Ole Schmidt; **Running time:** 114 minutes

Cast: Maria Falconetti (Jeanne D'Arc); Eugene Silvain (Bishop Cauchon); Andre Berley (Jane d'Estivet); Maurice Schutz (Nicholas Loyseleur); Antonin Artaud (Jean Massieu)

Danish director Carl Dreyer's story of the life and trials of Joan of Arc, based on records of her actual trial, is regarded by many movie historians as one of the great works of the international cinema. Dreyer's inventive use of close-ups was considered to be a major breakthrough in the way films were shot. Additionally, Maria Falconetti's performance in the lead role was acclaimed by Pauline Kael as the greatest in screen history. Ironically, it would prove to be her one and only screen role. (She died in 1946.) With a new appreciation of Dreyer's work being spearheaded by filmmakers like Martin Scorsese, the director's films are more accessible to mainstream audiences than they have been in many years.

City Lights (1931)

United Artists

Director, Producer, Writer and Music: Charles Chaplin; **Running time:** 87 minutes

Cast: Charles Chaplin (The Tramp); Virginia Cherrill (Blind Girl); Florence Lee (Blind Girl's Grandmother); Harry Myers (Millionaire)

By the time *City Lights* premiered in 1931, Charles Chaplin had to use all of his considerable clout to convince studios to continue investing in silent films—but his instincts were proven right with this masterpiece. The simple story tells of the Tramp's befriending a poor blind girl who sells flowers and convincing her he is a wealthy man. Through his generosity, she finally receives the operation that restores her sight, but by then the tragedy-prone Tramp is doing a stretch in prison. In the famous final sequence, the Tramp pays a visit to her flower shop, and her gradual realization that this pathetic man is her true benefactor is one of the most touching moments in the history of cinema. *City Lights'* legacy has stood the test of time and ranks among the seminal works of the American cinema.

Modern Times (1936)

United Artists

Director, Producer, Writer, and Composer: Charles Chaplin; **Running time:** 87 minutes

Cast: Charles Chaplin (Factory Worker); Paulette Goddard (Gamine); Henry Bergman (Café owner); Stanley Sanford (Big Bill); Chester Conklin (Mechanic)

Charles Chaplin had not been seen on a theater screen for five years when *Modern Times* premiered to great acclaim in 1936. Still stubbornly resisting working in "talkies," he stood alone in his insistence upon preserving the silent film. As he did with *City Lights*, Chaplin conceded to recording a musical and sound effects track, but there would be no dialogue heard onscreen. A reactionary in terms of filmmaking techniques, he once predicted sound films would be passé by 1932! *Modern Times* is one of Chaplin's most lighthearted films. There is certainly plenty of social criticism (the film concerns the dehumanizing impact of technology), but this time he plays the story mostly for laughs. The sight gags of Chaplin haplessly trying to keep pace while testing various new gadgets in a factory define classic comedy. The film also gave Paulette Goddard, who would marry Chaplin, her first starring role. *Modern Times* deserves its legacy as the last great silent film.

Chapter 2
CRIME SAGAS

"Made it, Ma—
Top of the World!"

One of the most enduring film genres, "reel life" crime sagas, exploded in popularity during a time in which real life gangster kingpins such as Al Capone had mesmerized the nation. The vastly unpopular prohibition laws had the unforeseen consequences of turning localized street gangs into virtual armies financed by the deadly and highly competitive business of smuggling and selling illegal alcohol. It isn't surprising that this social issue, combined with the Great Depression that began in 1929, left the public eager to see such problems reflected in their screen entertainment.

Numerous studios dabbled in the gangster genre, but Warner Brothers made it an art form. The release of films such as *Little Caesar* and *The Public Enemy* not only filled box-office coffers, but also resulted in the emergence of a new generation of stars. Suddenly, the well-groomed matinee idols of the silent era were replaced by leading men who looked every bit as gritty as the characters they portrayed. James Cagney, Edward G. Robinson, and Humphrey Bogart were the most legendary beneficiaries of the nationwide obsession with crime films, but many others made a career of playing supporting roles in these highly profitable films. Most of what the studios ultimately turned out were "B" movie potboilers on limited budgets. They were as forgettable in their day as they are now. However, the gems that emerged during this era inspired the many amazing modern crime films—from *White Heat* to *The Untouchables*—that would follow. While the musical and western genres have largely been ignored by major studios in recent years, the gangster movie continues to mesmerize audiences, disproving the adage that crime doesn't pay.

Little Caesar (1930)

Warner Brothers

Director: Mervyn LeRoy; **Producers:** Hal B. Wallis and Darryl F. Zanuck (uncredited); **Writers:** Francis Edward Faragoh and Robert N. Lee; **Music:** David Mendoza (uncredited); **Running time:** 79 minutes

Cast: Edward G. Robinson (Little Caesar/Rico); Douglas Fairbanks Jr. (Joe Massara); Glenda Farrell (Olga); William Collier Jr. (Tony Passa); Sidney Blackmer (Big Boy)

Oscar nominations: Best Writing, Adaptation

The seminal film in the gangster movie genre, *Little Caesar* still packs a punch today thanks to the incredible screen presence of Edward G. Robinson. With a face curled into a perennial scowl and his "School of Hard Knocks" charisma, Robinson's Rico (known to intimates as Little Caesar) epitomized the contemporary urban gangster myth. It's been speculated that the character was based on Al Capone, but there is no hard evidence this is true. What is indisputable is that director Mervyn LeRoy broke new ground with this tale of the rise and fall of an overly ambitious hoodlum who is a bit too clever for his own good. The box-office success of *Caesar* insured a gravy train for Warner Brothers, which would become defined by its gangster films for years to come. It would also insure stardom for Robinson, a marvelous actor who would continue to grace the screen with his presence until his death in 1973.

Gone with the Wind

Rico's classic dying quote, "Mother of Mercy, is this the end of Rico?" was initially scripted to be "Mother of God, is this the end of Rico?" The change was made due to studio nervousness that the line might be seen as defamatory toward religion.

The Public Enemy (1931)

Warner Brothers

Director: William A. Wellman; **Producer:** Darryl F. Zanuck (uncredited); **Writers:** Kubec Glasmon and John Bright, Harvey Thew (adapatation); **Music:** David Mendoza (adaptation, uncredited); **Running time:** 83 minutes

Cast: James Cagney (Tom Powers); Jean Harlow (Gwen Allen); Edward Woods (Matt Doyle); Joan Blondell (Mamie); Donald Cook (Mike Powers)

Oscar nominations: Best Writing, Original Story

Just as *Little Caesar* made Edward G. Robinson a star, Warner Brothers caught lightning in a bottle a second time with the casting of James Cagney as small-time hoodlum Tom Powers, a ruthless crook who ruthlessly establishes himself as a crime kingpin only to discover the pitfalls of the life he has chosen. Interestingly, Cagney was supposed to have the second lead to star Edward Woods. However, director William A. Wellman was so impressed by Cagney's intensity that he had the actors switch roles, thus insuring a landmark performance in cinematic history. Amusingly, the scene that depicted the greatest outcry was not one of the violent interludes, but the sequence in which Cagney famously slams a grapefruit into Mae Clark's face. The movie was cited as a prime justification for the new production code that kept major films sanitized for many years to come. A side note: Jean Harlow appears as a woman of ill repute in her only film for Warner Brothers.

Scarface: The Shame of the Nation (1932)

United Artists

Director: Howard Hawks; **Producer:** Howard Hughes (uncredited); **Writer:** Ben Hecht; **Music:** Adolph Tandler and Gus Arnheim; **Running time:** 93 minutes

Cast: Paul Muni (Tony Camonti); Ann Dvorak (Cesca Camonti); Karen Morley (Poppy); Osgood Perkins (Johnny Lovo); C. Henry Gordon (Inspector Guarino); George Raft (Guino Renaldo); Boris Karloff (Gaffney)

There were great gangster films before *Scarface* but none so realistic in their depiction of violence and brutality. The title villain, brilliantly played by Paul Muni, is also devoid of any redeeming background information that helps soft-peddle his immersion in crime. The film traces this wannabe kingpin, Tony Camonti, as he systematically bumps off his boss and enemies in order to rise to the top of the gangland heap. Francois Truffaut pointed out that director Howard Hawks intentionally shot Muni as though he were a wild animal in order to capture the man's sheer brutality. The film features innovative camerawork and editing, but the story behind the movie is equally fascinating. Hawks clashed constantly with producer Howard Hughes during production, and the film was almost canceled. Its release was delayed by extensive battles over censorship, though it

Gone with the Wind

Over objections of Howard Hawks, Howard Hughes bowed to censors' demands and shot an epilogue in which Muni (seen only from behind because he was played by a double) gets tried and executed. In ensuing years, the epilogue was dropped from most prints to make it consistent with Hawks' original version.

eventually became a major moneymaker. Among its top admirers was Al Capone himself, who was rumored to have thrown Hawks a party to celebrate the movie and was said to have his own private print! Brian De Palma loosely remade *Scarface* in 1983 with Al Pacino starring.

I Was a Fugitive from a Chain Gang (1932)

Warner Brothers

Director: Mervyn LeRoy; **Producer:** Hal B. Wallis (Uncredited); **Writers:** Howard G. Green, Brown Holmes, and Sheridan Gibney (Uncredited); **Music:** Bernhard Kaun; **Running time:** 93 minutes

Cast: Paul Muni (James Allen); Glenda Farrell (Marie Woods); Helen Vinson (Helen); Noel Francis (Linda); Preston Foster (Pete)

Oscar nominations: Best Picture, Actor (Paul Muni), Sound

One of the true early American film masterpieces, *I Was a Fugitive from a Chain Gang* is a film that continues to resonate with audiences. Warner Brothers considered this project to be a major risk due to the tragic plight of its protagonist, James Allen—an impoverished WWI veteran who is forced at gunpoint to participate in a crime. He is caught and sentenced to a Georgia chain gang. He ultimately escapes and becomes an acclaimed engineer and builder only to eventually have his tortured past catch up with him. The film's exposure of the living hell suffered by inmates on chain gangs awoke a social consciousness, and the resulting outcry arguably helped bring about the end of the chain gang system in southern prisons. The movie benefits from a remarkable performance by Paul Muni as a Jean Valjean-like hero. Unique among films of the day is the realistic, haunting ending that still leaves viewers shocked. Despite studio fears that Depression-era audiences would reject a downbeat drama, *Chain Gang* became one of the top box-office hits of its time.

Hollywood Confidential

I Was a Fugitive was loosely based on the autobiography of Robert E. Burns, who served as consultant on the film, despite being wanted in Georgia at the time. Unlike the hero of the film, however, Burns found sanctuary in New Jersey until a reformist governor in Georgia convinced him to return and have his sentence commuted.

Fury (1936)

MGM

Director: Fritz Lang; **Producer:** Joseph L. Mankiewicz; **Writers:** Bartlett Cormack, Fritz Lang, and Norman Krasna (original story); **Music:** Franz Waxman; **Running time:** 90 minutes

Cast: Spencer Tracy (Joe Wilson); Sylvia Sidney (Katherine Grant); Walter Abel (District Attorney Adams); Bruce Cabot (Dawson); Edward Ellis (Sheriff Hummel); Walter Brennan ("Bugs" Meyers)

Oscar nomination: Screenplay (original story)

Fritz Lang's *Fury* resonated with the famed director's anger over the terror of mob rule and societal injustice. Lang had just left Hitler's Germany, having witnessed what lay in store for those who didn't conform to the Third Reich's ideas of social order. The film presents Spencer Tracy as Joe Wilson, a hard-working everyday guy who is mistaken for a kidnapper and presumed dead in a fire set by an angry lynch mob. He escapes, and though badly injured, plots a unique plan to insure all those responsible for his "murder" are given the death penalty themselves. This is a gripping and powerful film that very forcefully and pointedly attempted to shame small town America for tolerating the rash of lynchings that had burnished the south for many years. MGM got cold feet in the end, and watered down the finale somewhat (against Lang's wishes) in order to mitigate the guilt of the average citizens. Still, *Fury* remains a major work by one of the European cinema's great directors.

The Petrified Forest (1936)

Warner Brothers

Director: Archie L. Mayo; **Producer:** Henry Blanke; **Writers:** Charles Kenyon and Delmer Davies; **Music:** Bernhard Kaun; **Running time:** 83 minutes

Cast: Leslie Howard (Alan Squier); Bette Davis ("Gabby" Maple); Humphrey Bogart (Duke Mantee); Genevieve Tobin (Edith Chisholm); Dick Foran (Boze)

The abbreviated running time of this adaptation of Robert Sherwood's hit Broadway play proves that bigger and longer isn't necessarily better … well, at least in terms of movies. At a scant 83 minutes, the seasoned pros that brought *The Petrified Forest* to the screen make every moment meaningful. Leslie Howard is a disillusioned intellectual, who becomes embroiled in a hostage situation at a café near Arizona's petrified forest. Gangster Duke Mantee (Humphrey Bogart) and his goons are holding an eclectic group of locals captive as they try to elude police. It's a battle of brains versus brawn as Howard attempts to use his intellect to outwit Bogart and his gang. The stars of the film were to be Howard and Bette Davis, but the real buzz centered on (fourth-billed) Bogart's Dillinger-like villain, a role he initially created on Broadway opposite Howard. Although claustrophobic in atmosphere, the film boasts great dialogue and considerable suspense. Bogart recreated the role in a 1955 TV production. A mediocre big screen remake, *Escape in the Desert*, was released in 1945.

Angels with Dirty Faces (1938)

Warner Brothers

Director: Michael Curtiz; **Producer:** Samuel Bischoff (uncredited); **Writers:** Rowland Brown, John Wexley, and Warren Duff; **Music:** Max Steiner; **Running time:** 97 minutes

Cast: James Cagney (William "Rocky" Sullivan); Pat O'Brien (Fr. Jerome "Jerry" Connelly); Humphrey Bogart (James "Jim" Frazier); Ann Sheridan (Laurie); George Bancroft (Mac Keefer); Billy Halop (Soapy); Leo Gorcey (Bim); Huntz Hall (Crab)

Oscar nominations: Director, Actor (James Cagney), Screenplay

Viewed today, *Angels with Dirty Faces* may seem like a vault of cliches: the impressionable young kids idolizing a local gangster, the two boyhood friends now on opposite sides of the law, and the tough-as-nails neighborhood priest pleading with his gangster pal to surrender to police. However, the film offers a multitude of pleasures. The most enduring aspect of the movie is the Oscar-nominated performance of James Cagney as the local tough guy worshipped by the Dead End Kids. Cagney based his now famous mannerisms and swagger on a local pimp he knew from his boyhood neighborhood. The characteristics that would become so identifiable with his persona originated here. The final sequence is one for the ages as Cagney feigns terror on his way to the electric chair to dissuade his young admirers from idolizing him.

The Roaring Twenties (1939)

Warner Brothers

Director: Raoul Walsh; **Producer:** Mark Hellinger; **Writers:** Jerry Wald, Richard Macaulay, and Robert Rossen; **Music:** Heinz Roemheld and Ray Heindorf; **Running time:** 104 minutes

Cast: James Cagney (Eddie Bartlett); Pricilla Lane (Jean); Humphrey Bogart (George Halley); Gladys George (Panama Smith)

Based on producer Mark Hellinger's personal experiences as a New York reporter during the era of Prohibition, *The Roaring Twenties* was a slickly produced entry from the Warner Brothers backlot, which by now was churning out a nonstop stream of crime sagas. Cagney runs a taxi company that is a front for bootlegging and is in a power struggle with his back-stabbing former army buddy Humphrey Bogart, of late a crooked lawyer. The film was distinguished by the fact that it attempted to add social commentary by pointing out that the nation's shabby treatment of its war veterans caused many to turn to crime out of desperation. Sadly, this third—and by far the best—teaming of Cagney and Bogart would be their last.

High Sierra (1941)

Warner Brothers

Director: Raoul Walsh; **Producer:** Mark Hellinger; **Writers:** John Huston and W.R Burnett; **Music:** Adolph Deutsch; **Running time:** 100 minutes

Cast: Ida Lupino (Marie Garson); Humphrey Bogart (Roy "Mad Dog" Earle); Alan Curtis ("Babe" Kozak); Arthur Kennedy ("Red" Hattery); Joan Leslie (Velma); Henry Hull ("Doc" Banton); Henry Travers (Pa)

Although not at the top of the Warner Brothers crime movie food chain, *High Sierra* is in some ways a more important film than some of the better-remembered movies in this genre. It was on this production that Humphrey Bogart finally transformed from supporting player to full stardom. As "Mad Dog" Earle, he brings a sense of pathos and dignity to what could have been a formulaic gangster role. Earle is sprung from prison as part of a scheme to knock over a casino. When the plan goes awry, he finds himself eluding police by hiding with an eclectic group of confederates and hostages in a cabin atop the Sierras. More a character study than a shoot-em-up, *High Sierra* also marked the first time Bogart would work on a film with John Huston, who cowrote the screenplay. They would go on to collaborate on some of the most impressive films in American history.

"Play It Again, Sam"

High Sierra was remade as the western *Colorado Territory* with Joel McCrae in 1949 and as *I Died a Thousand Times* in 1955 with Jack Palance.

Double Indemnity (1944)

Paramount Pictures

Director: Billy Wilder; **Producer:** Joseph Sistrom; **Writers:** Billy Wilder and Raymond Chandler; **Music:** Miklos Rosza; **Running time:** 107 minutes

Cast: Fred MacMurray (Walter Neff); Barbara Stanwyck (Phyllis Dietrichson); Edward G. Robinson (Barton Keyes); Porter Hall (Mr. Jackson); Jean Heather (Lola Dietrichson); Tom Powers (Mr. Dietrichson)

Oscar nominations: Best Picture, Director, Actress (Barbara Stanwyck), Screenplay, Cinematography, Music, Sound

Fred MacMurray and Barbara Stanwyck weave a tangled web of lust, murder, and intrigue in this classic suspense film from Billy Wilder. *Double Indemnity* is not a "whodunit." We know precisely who done it and why. Fred MacMurray is an insurance representative who is snookered by bombshell Barbara Stanwyck into helping murder her husband to collect on his lucrative policy. The real enjoyment comes from watching Edward G. Robinson as an insurance investigator trying to painstakingly put together pieces of the puzzle. Along with *The Postman Always Rings Twice*, this stands as one of the most erotic and sensual films of its time. Both movies have startling similarities: self-consumed women with torrid sex drives lure impressionable men into committing murder on their behalf. In both cases, there is the inevitable "crime doesn't pay" finale, but getting there is all the fun. Brilliant on every level with MacMurray splendidly playing against type as a villain. James M. Cain, who wrote the source novel, also authored the classic *The Postman Always Rings Twice*.

Detour (1945)

Producer's Releasing Corporation

Director: Edgar G. Ulmer; **Producer:** Leon Fromkess; **Writer:** Martin Goldsmith; **Music:** Leo Erdody; **Running time:** 67 minutes

Cast: Tom Neal (Al Roberts); Ann Savage (Vera); Claudia Drake (Sue); Edmund MacDonald (Charles Haskell, Jr.)

Virtually ignored upon its initial release as a "poverty row" movie, *Detour* has the distinction of being the first such film to be preserved in the Library of Congress. Running a scant 67 minutes, the film is a prime example of how to tell a story economically and efficiently. The tale casts Tom Neal as a hitchhiker who becomes involved in a very tangled web of murder, deceit, and blackmail—all courtesy of a floozie played by Ann Savage. The film was shot in only six days on a shoestring budget. In recent years, it has become lionized by movie fans thanks to the spotlight shown on it by a new generation of filmmakers like Martin Scorsese.

The Killers (1946)

Universal Pictures

Director: Robert Siodmak; **Producer:** Mark Hellinger; **Writer:** Anthony Veiller; **Music:** Miklos Rosza; **Running time:** 105 minutes

Cast: Burt Lancaster ("Swede" Andersen/Pete Lund); Ava Gardner (Kitty Collins); Edmond O'Brien (Jim Collins); Albert Dekker (Big Jim Colfax); Sam Levine (Lt. Sam Lubinsky)

Oscar nominations: Director, Screenplay, Music, Editing

Burt Lancaster's breakthrough role came in this hard-boiled adaptation of an Ernest Hemingway short story. Lancaster, who got the role only because Wayne Morris was unavailable, ignites the screen as a boxer who is naively led on the path to ruin by an irresistible bad girl with ties to the mob, played with smoldering sensuality by Ava Gardner in a role that helped launch her reputation as one of the screen's legendary sex goddesses. The film is one of the top crime sagas of the 1940s cinema. It was remade in 1964 by Don Siegel (see later entry in this chapter).

The Postman Always Rings Twice (1946)

MGM

Director: Tay Garnett; **Producer:** Carey Wilson; **Writers:** Harry Ruskin and Niven Busch; **Music:** George Bassman; **Running time:** 113 minutes

Cast: Lana Turner (Cora Smith); John Garfield (Frank Chambers); Cecil Kellaway (Nick Smith); Hume Cronyn (Arthur Keats)

One of the most sensuous mainstream Hollywood films of the 1940s, *The Postman Always Rings Twice* has all the ingredients of an enduring classic: sexy leading players, a tight script, direction, and a climax that is completely unexpected. John Garfield is a drifter who chances upon a rural café run by bombshell Lana Turner and her older, buffoonish but loveable husband. Before the pancakes can get flipped on the griddle, Garfield and Turner are in a tempestuous affair that leads them to devise a method of killing Turner's hubby to collect the insurance money. As with all crime films of the era, we know the pair will get their come-uppance, but the trail to the startling conclusion is filled with red herrings and unexpected plot twists, all of it imaginatively directed by Tay Garnett. The bizarre title is explained (none-too-successfully) by Garfield at the film's conclusion. Film buffs have been debating its actual meaning since the movie's release.

"Play It Again, Sam"

The Postman Always Rings Twice had been made previously in 1939 as the French release *Le Dernier Tournant* and in 1943 by Italian director Luchino Visconti as *Ossessione*. In 1981, director Bob Rafelson's remake starred Jack Nicholson and Jessica Lang in a reasonably good, highly sexualized version. In 1998, it was remade as an acclaimed Hungarian film *Szenvedély*.

Body and Soul (1947)

United Artists

Director: Robert Rossen; **Producer:** Bob Roberts; **Writer:** Abraham Polonsky; **Music:** Hugo Friedhofer; **Running time:** 104 minutes

Cast: John Garfield (Charlie Davis); Lilli Palmer (Peg Born); Hazel Brooks (Alice); Anne Revere (Anna Davis); William Conrad (Quinn); Lloyd Goff (Roberts); Canada Lee (Ben Chaplin)

Oscar nominations: Actor (John Garfield), Screenplay, Editing*

Upon its release in 1947, *Body and Soul* stood as the most definitive look at the seamy side of the boxing industry. Although not ostensibly a crime film, gangsters play a key element in the fate of the hero, Charlie Davis, played with impressive intensity by John Garfield, one of the pioneers of the "method acting" that inspired stars like Brando and Montgomery Clift. Charlie enters the boxing arena in an attempt to move up from poverty. He succeeds only to fall victim to the temptations of fame and fortune. The stunning boxing sequences were achieved by cinematographer James Wong Howe rollerskating around the rink with a hand-held camera. Tragedy seemed to encompass many of the primary participants of this film: John Garfield died prematurely only a few years later at age 39. He, along with screenwriter Abraham Polonsky and costar Canada Lee, would all be victimized by the McCarthy era blacklisting scandals. The ensuing decades have seen several great films about the "sweet science" of boxing, all of which were at least partially inspired by *Body and Soul.* It was remade in 1981 with Leon Isaac Kennedy.

Brute Force (1947)

Universal Pictures

Director: Jules Dassin; **Producer:** Mark Hellinger; **Writer:** Richard Brooks; **Music:** Miklos Rosza; **Running time:** 98 minutes

Cast: Burt Lancaster (Joe Collins); Hume Cronyn (Capt. Munsey); Charles Bickford (Gallagher); Yvonne De Carlo (Gina); Ann Blyth (Ruth); Ella Raines (Cora)

Burt Lancaster is a convict in a battle of wits with an erudite but sadistic jailer, played as a modern Capt. Bligh with great relish by Hume Cronyn. (The role obviously inspired Patrick McGoohan's equally impressive performance as the warden in Don Siegel's 1979 film *Escape from Alcatraz.*) This is the definitive "macho" movie, directed with great flair by Jules Dassin. Richard Brooks's screenplay insures some great scenes from some wonderful supporting players including Charles Bickford, Whit Bissell, and Howard Duff in his screen debut. Kudos also to cinematographer William Daniels for his inventive use of lighting techniques that add considerably to the film's sense of dread.

A Double Life (1947)

Universal Pictures

Director: George Cukor; **Producer:** Michael Kanin; **Writers:** Ruth Gordo and Garson Kanin; **Music:** Miklos Rosza; **Running time:** 104 minutes

Cast: Ronald Colman (Anthony John); Signe Hasso (Brita); Edmond O'Brien (Bill Friend); Shelley Winters (Pat Kroll); Ray Collins (Victor Donlan); Philip Loeb (Max Lasker)

Oscar nominations: Director, Screenplay, Actor (Ronald Colman)*, Music*

Ronald Colman stars in an Oscar-winning performance as Anthony John, an acclaimed star of theater who takes on the persona of whatever role he is currently playing. Thus, he can be alternately disarming and charming as well as ill-tempered and threatening. This may read like a psychotic version of Woody Allen's *Zelig*, but in fact, Colman is quite remarkable, expressing the full gamut of human emotions. However, when he takes on the role of Shakespeare's *Othello*, his devotion to the part leads to actual murder. Shelley Winters gained kudos as one of his naive victims. The film is expertly directed by the great George Cukor.

Hollywood Confidential

The film was originally titled *The Art of Murder* and was developed for Laurence Olivier, who was ultimately unavailable to take the part of Anthony John.

Kiss of Death (1947)

20th Century Fox

Director: Henry Hathaway; **Producer:** Fred Kohlmar; **Writers:** Ben Hecht and Charles Lederer; **Music:** David Buttolph; **Running time:** 98 minutes

Cast: Victor Mature (Nick Bianco); Brian Donlevy (Louie DeAngelo); Coleen Gray (Nettie); Richard Widmark (Tommy Udo); Taylor Holmes (Earl Howser); Howard Smith (Warden); Karl Malden (Cullen)

Oscar nominations: Screenplay, Supporting Actor (Richard Widmark)

A solid, well-made crime saga that gets the distinction "classic" on the basis of Richard Widmark's Oscar-nominated performance in his screen debut. Widmark plays a lunatic

Gone with the Wind

A scene in *Kiss of Death* was originally filmed depicting Victor Mature's wife (Patricia Morrison) committing suicide after being raped by a gangster assigned to guard her. The studio insisted the scene be removed due to its controversial nature.

killer stalking one-time mob buddy Victor Mature who has ratted on the mob to gain release from prison. Widmark ignites the screen with a performance that is highlighted by the scene in which he ties frail old Mildred Dunnock to a wheelchair and sends her cascading down a staircase while laughing hysterically. The role and performance have parallels to Joe Pesci's equally impressive performance in *Goodfellas* (1990), but it is indisputable that Widmark set the standard in *Kiss of Death*. Remade in 1995 with David Caruso and Nicholas Cage.

The Big Clock (1948)

Paramount Pictures

Director: John Farrow; **Producers:** John Farrow and Richard Maibaum; **Writer:** Jonathan Latimer; **Music:** Victor Young; **Running time:** 95 minutes

Cast: Ray Milland (George Stroud); Charles Laughton (Earl Janoth); Maureen O'Sullivan (Georgette Stroud); George MacReady (Steve Hagen); Rita Johnson (Pauline York); Elsa Lanchester (Louise)

This expertly filmed thriller is highlighted by Charles Laughton's larger-than-life performance as a tyrannical publishing magnate (is there any other kind?) who murders his mistress and insinuates that one of his employees (Ray Milland) is the actual culprit. The clever twist here is that Milland is a star reporter for Laughton's crime magazine and has built his reputation on solving high profile cases. Ironically, the more light he sheds on the case, the more he implicates himself. A tightly edited production with nary a wasted frame. There's also a brief but pivotal supporting performance by Laughton's real-life wife Elsa Lanchester, who never fails to impress.

"Play It Again, Sam"

Kenneth Fearing's source novel of the same name was expertly adapted for the screen once again as the 1987 political thriller *No Way Out* starring Kevin Costner and Gene Hackman.

Key Largo (1948)

Warner Brothers

Director: John Huston; **Producer:** Jerry Wald; **Writers:** Richard Brooks and John Huston; **Music:** Max Steiner; **Running time:** 100 minutes

Cast: Humphrey Bogart (Frank McCloud); Edward G. Robinson (Johnny Rocco); Lauren Bacall (Nora Temple); Lionel Barrymore (James Temple); Claire Trevor (Gaye Dawn)

Oscar nominations: Supporting Actress* (Claire Trevor)

A topnotch entry in the Warner crime genre, *Key Largo* is based on a stage play by Maxwell Anderson, and the claustrophobic nature of the production only enhances its dramatic appeal. Humphrey Bogart plays against type as a cynical, nonheroic (at least initially) army veteran who finds himself trapped inside a tourist hotel on Florida's Key Largo as a hurricane batters the island. Adding to the suspense is the arrival of notorious gangster Edward G. Robinson and his vicious goons. The situation may be clichéd, but the interaction between Rocco and the eclectic group of hotel residents he holds captive is never less than mesmerizing. John Huston directs the flawless cast. The scene-stealers are Robinson as the brutal on-the-lam crime kingpin and Trevor, who is heartbreaking in an Oscar-winning role as his abused, humiliated mistress.

The Lady from Shanghai (1948)

Columbia Pictures

Director, Producer, and Screenplay: Orson Welles; **Music:** Heinz Roemheld; **Running time:** 87 minutes

Cast: Orson Welles (Michael O'Hara); Rita Hayworth (Elsa Bannister); Everett Sloane (Arthur Bannister); Glen Anders (Grisby); Ted DeCorsia (Sydney Broome)

Orson Welles had the misfortune to come of age creatively during the era when studios were still run by tyrannical bosses. Virtually all of his mainstream films were tampered with against his wishes, resulting in his alienation from the Hollywood establishment. This trend continued with his complex murder yarn *The Lady from Shanghai*, which pitted Welles in the offbeat role of a naive man who is snared into a bizarre sea journey with an aging millionaire and his young, sexually frustrated wife. This leads to murder and an even more bizarre trial sequence culminating in the legendary shootout amidst a funhouse hall of mirrors. The mind reels at what the film might have been had Columbia boss Harry Cohn not supervised the final cut against Welles wishes, inserting a musical number for gorgeous Rita Hayworth and cutting other sequences that added to the flavor of the film. The end result is a flawed but fascinating film from a flawed but equally fascinating artist.

White Heat (1949)

Warner Brothers

Director: Raoul Walsh; **Producer:** Louis F. Edelman; **Writers:** Virginia Kellogg (story), Ivan Goff and Ben Roberts (screenplay); **Music:** Max Steiner; **Running time:** 114 minutes

Cast: James Cagney (Arthur "Cody" Jarrett); Virginia Mayo (Verna Jarrett); Edmond O'Brien (Vic Pardo/Hank Fallon); Margaret Wycherly (Ma Jarrett); Steve Cochran (Big Ed Somers)

Oscar nomination: Best Writing (Motion Picture Story)

Probably more so than any other film, *White Heat* epitomized James Cagney as the king of the gangster film genre, even though it was his first crime film in ten years. Cagney's Cody Jarrett is a fascinating creation: a monstrous, cold-blooded killer who still manages to have an uncomfortable, Oedipal-type relationship with his domineering mother, wonderfully played by Margaret Wycherly. When Cody learns of her death while he is in prison, it results in the immortal sequence in which he destroys the entire mess hall in a fit of uncontrolled rage. The scene is only to be outdone by Cody's spectacular demise atop a flaming chemical tank. On the surface, *White Heat* is a routine caper film. However, Cagney's dynamic performance coupled with a sterling supporting cast and the steady hand of director Raoul Walsh elevates the film to the top of its genre.

The Set-Up (1949)

RKO Pictures

Director: Robert Wise; **Producer:** Richard Goldstone; **Writer:** Art Cohn; **Music:** Constantin Bakaleinikoff; **Running time:** 72 minutes

Cast: Robert Ryan (Bill "Stoker" Thompson); Audrie Totter (Julie Thompson); George Tobias (Tiny); Alan Baxter (Little Boy); Wallace Ford (Gus)

Gritty drama centering on a washed up boxer (Robert Ryan) who struggles to make a comeback in the ring—without the knowledge that his own backers are betting against him and there will be tragic consequences if he prevails. Director Robert Wise does yeoman work in capturing the unsavory underbelly of the boxing world and its inextricable link with the criminal element. The film reminds us of how underrated Robert Ryan was as an actor. Always a strong, reliable screen presence, Ryan called upon his experience as a boxing champ at Dartmouth to add realism to the fight sequences. The film plays out in real time and was shot on an expedited schedule of only 20 days! A remake of the film has been announced.

The Asphalt Jungle (1950)

MGM

Director: John Huston; **Producer:** Arthur Hornblow Jr.; **Writers:** John Huston and Ben Maddow; **Music:** Miklos Rozsa; **Running time:** 112 minutes

Cast: Sterling Hayden (Dix Handley); Louis Calhern (Alonzo D. "Lon" Emmerich); Jean Hagan (Doll Conovan); James Whitmore (Gus Minissi); Sam Jaffe (Doc Irwin Reidenschneider); John McIntire (Police Commissioner Hardy); Mark Lawrence ("Cobby" Cobb); Marilyn Monroe (Angela)

Oscar nominations: Director, Supporting Actor (Sam Jaffe), Screenplay, Cinematography

The Asphalt Jungle is an excellent adaptation of W.R. Burnett's novel about an ambitious jewel robbery orchestrated by a gang of eccentric criminals. The film helped cement John Huston's already impressive reputation as a master writer and director. Huston understood that the most appropriate actors in an urban drama such as this were not necessarily those with box-office clout. Consequently, he bypassed major stars and drew instead on the talents of an eclectic group of actors each of whom brought a unique quality to this masterful production. As with the best crime caper films, this one benefits from some surprising plot twists as well as crisp dialogue and a terrific score by Miklos Rosza. Harold Rosson's cinematography epitomizes the best elements of a true film noir classic. Marilyn Monroe makes an early career appearance here, managing to impress in her brief time on screen. The film has been loosely remade as *Cairo* (1963), as the western *The Badlanders* (1958), and as the blaxploitation film *Cool Breeze* (1972)

No Way Out (1950)

20th Century Fox

Director: Joseph L. Mankiewicz; **Producer:** Darryl F. Zanuck; **Writers:** Joseph L. Mankiewicz and Lesser Samuels; **Music:** Alfred Newman; **Running time:** 106 minutes.

Cast: Richard Widmark (Ray Biddle); Linda Darnell (Edie); Stephen McNally (Dr. Dan Wharton); Sidney Poitier (Dr. Luther Brooks); Mildred Joanne Smith (Cora Brooks)

Oscar nomination: Screenplay

A forthright look at modern urban racism, *No Way Out* is a taut, well-acted thriller about a bigoted small time crook (Widmark) who believes a black doctor (Poitier) intentionally killed his ailing brother while in police custody. Widmark escapes and concocts a scheme to lure Poitier to his death. The script dares to deal directly with racism in a way most other films had only hinted at. Widmark's Ray Biddle is an unrepentant psycho who, in the tradition of all racists, blames his own failures on scapegoats from other races. The tense film provides early career highlights for Widmark (building on his *Kiss of Death* performance) and Poitier who, at age 22, brings dignity and passion to a groundbreaking role. Keep an eye out for husband and wife Ossie Davis and Ruby Dee in early roles as Poitier's kin.

 Gone with the Wind _____

> Due to its controversial nature and the candid use of racist language, some theaters edited prints and others in the deep south refused to show the film at all. The DVD edition from 20th Century Fox has stills of a sequence, which was apparently cut from the tense conclusion, depicting Widmark humiliating Poitier in the basement of the doctor's home.

Detective Story (1951)

Paramount Pictures

Director: William Wyler; **Producer:** Sidney Kingsley; **Writers:** Philip Yordan and Robert Wyler; **Music:** No original score; **Running time:** 103 minutes

Cast: Kirk Douglas (Jim McCloud); Eleanor Parker (Mary McCloud); William Bendix (Lou Brody); Cathy O'Connell (Susan Carmichael); George MacReady (Karl Schneider)

Oscar nominations: Director, Screenplay, Actress (Eleanor Parker), Supporting Actress (Lee Grant)

Detective Story is a gritty urban police drama based on the hit Broadway play. The film is surprisingly frank in its subject matter, considering the censorship restrictions of the day. Kirk Douglas gives a towering performance as McCloud, a dedicated NYPD detective who is fanatical in his enforcement of the law. He is a complex man hiding great psychological pains that turn him into a human volcano at the slightest provocation. He is particularly enraged when he has to interrogate an erudite abortionist—a plot device that leads to a personal tragedy for McCloud. Impressive direction by William Wyler with a great supporting cast that includes Joseph Wiseman and Lee Grant, both highly compelling in their screen debuts. Shamefully, Douglas was not Oscar-nominated for this early career triumph.

The Big Heat (1953)

Columbia Pictures

Director: Fritz Lang; **Producer:** Robert Arthur; **Writer:** Sydney Boehm; **Music:** Daniele Amfitheatrof; **Running time:** 89 minutes

Cast: Glenn Ford (Dave Bannion); Gloria Grahame (Debby Marsh); Jocelyn Brando (Katie Bannion); Alexander Scourby (Mike Lagana); Lee Marvin (Vince Stone)

Pauline Kael called this film "a definitive film noir." Glenn Ford plays a police detective investigating a mob leader and finds his own life has been targeted by corrupt police brass. When his wife is murdered, he teams up with an abused mob mistress to exact vengeance. Ford, long underrated as an actor, excels in one of his most impressive roles, aided and abetted by the equally under-appreciated Gloria Grahame as the ill-treated mob moll. Lee Marvin ignites the screen with a true sense of menace as a sadistic gangster. *The Big Heat* was directed by the legendary Fritz Lang, who helmed early cinematic classics like *Metropolis* and *M*. Here, Lang proves that as late as 1953, he was still at the top of his game. Side note: Jocelyn Brando, who plays Ford's wife, is the sister of Marlon Brando.

Riot in Cell Block 11 (1954)

Allied Artists

Director: Don Siegel; **Producer:** Walter Wanger; **Writer:** Richard Collins; **Music:** Herschel Burke Gilbert; **Running time:** 80 minutes

Cast: Neville Brand (Dunn); Emile Meyer (The Warden); Frank Faylen (Haskell); Leo Gordon (Carnie)

Director Don Siegel had his first major hit with this low-budget prison drama that had an unusual inspiration. In 1951, producer Walter Wanger, whose esteemed productions included *Stagecoach* and The Marx Brothers' *Coconuts*, shot fellow producer Jennings Lang because he suspected he had bedded his wife, the actress Joan Bennett. Lang survived and went on to produce enough good films to allow us to forgive him for bringing *Earthquake* to the screen in 1974. Wanger did a brief stretch in prison, where he was appalled by the horrendous conditions. Upon his release, he teamed with Siegel to make the first realistic look at the inhumanity found in modern prisons. The story concerns convicts who riot and take hostages, demanding that the public be alerted to the need for social change in prisons. The crew received permission to shoot at Folsom Prison and used prisoners and guards as extras and technical advisors.

The film was an enormous box-office success and received strong reviews from critics who cited it as one of the top films of the genre. (A trivia note: Young Sam Peckinpah was an uncredited production assistant on the film.)

The Desperate Hours (1955)

Paramount Pictures

Director: William Wyler; **Producer:** Joseph Hayes; **Writer:** Lee Garmes; **Music:** Gail Kulik; **Running time:** 112 minutes

Cast: Humphrey Bogart (Glenn Griffin); Fredric March (Dan C. Hilliard); Arthur Kennedy (Dept. Sheriff Bard); Martha Scott (Ellie Hilliard); Dewey Martin (Hal Griffin); Gig Young (Chuck Wright)

The Desperate Hours proves that the criminal concept of a home invasion is not a new phenomenon. In this film, three escaped convicts take over the house of a white-bread family headed by Fredric March in a role originally intended for Spencer Tracy. The resulting confrontation is predictable but very tense and quite moving as March has to try to outwit the three thugs while enduring the frustration of having his own son think he is a coward. The film was a return to the crime genre for *Detective Story* director William Wyler who had concentrated on making so-called "women's pictures" such as *Mrs. Miniver* and *The Little Foxes*. Even though the film doesn't break new ground in the crime genre, it does offer viewers a chance to watch old pros Bogart and March square off against each other.

"Play It Again, Sam"

The Desperate Hours was based on a novel that was later turned into a Broadway play starring Paul Newman and Karl Malden. The film was remade in 1990 by director Michael Cimino with Mickey Rourke and Anthony Hopkins as the antagonists.

The Killing (1956)

United Artists

Director: Stanley Kubrick; **Producer:** James B. Harris; **Writers:** Stanley Kubrick and Jim Thompson; **Music:** Gerald Fried; **Running time:** 85 minutes

Cast: Sterling Hayden (Johnny Clay); Colleen Gray (Fay); Vince Edwards (Val Cannon); Jay C. Flippen (Marvin Unger)

The Killing is an early impressive crime saga from Stanley Kubrick, developed with his partner James B. Harris under their newly-formed production company. When studios refused to film author Lionel White's novel *The Snatch* about a child kidnapped for ransom, White proposed that his heist novel *The Killing* be brought to the screen instead with Kubrick directing. The plot has newly-released convict Sterling Hayden planning a foolproof caper, in this case the robbery of a racetrack. The real fun in such a clichéd plot is the execution of the caper itself, and how the participants ultimately meet their downfall. The script is clever, the performances by a cast of nonglamorous character actors are top-notch, and Kubrick's creative instincts override the film's low budget (it was shot in under a month). The film had an inglorious second-bill release, but industry players took note of Kubrick's unique style. He was soon to become a major force in the film industry. Incidentally, *The Snatch* was eventually brought to the screen in 1969 under the title *The Night of the Following Day* starring Marlon Brando.

Witness for the Prosecution (1957)

United Artists

Director: Billy Wilder; **Producer:** Arthur Hornblow Jr.; **Writers:** Billy Wilder, Henry Kurnitz, and Larry Marcus; **Music:** Matty Malneck; **Running time:** 116 minutes

Cast: Tyrone Power (Leonard Stephen Vole); Marlene Dietrich (Christine Helm Vole); Charles Laughton (Sir Wilfred Robarts); Elsa Lanchester (Miss Plimsoll); John Williams (Mr. Brogan-Moore)

Oscar nominations: Best Picture, Director, Actor (Charles Laughton), Actress (Elsa Lanchester), Editing, Sound

In *Witness for the Prosecution*, Billy Wilder expertly adapts one of Agatha Christie's most engrossing mysteries for the screen and graces it with a sterling cast. Tyrone Power plays a man accused of murdering a rich widow. When he is put on trial, the only person who can exonerate him (wife Marlene Dietrich) decides she will be a witness for the prosecution. The film boasts a larger-than-life performance by Charles Laughton as the defense attorney and an equally delightful tour-de-force by his real life wife Elsa Lanchester as his much-abused nurse/girl Friday. This was Tyrone Power's final film, as he passed away in 1958 at the age of 45. It was remade as a 1982 TV movie starring Ralph Richardson, Deborah Kerr, and Beau Bridges.

Thunder Road (1958)

United Artists

Director: Arthur Ripley; **Producer:** Robert Mitchum; **Writers:** James Atlee Phillips and Walter Wise; **Music:** Jack Marshall; **Running time:** 92 minutes

Cast: Robert Mitchum (Lucas Doolin); Gene Barry (Troy Barrett); Jacques Aubuchon (Carl Kogan); Keely Smith (Francie)

If you can picture an episode of *The Beverly Hillbillies* directed by Sam Peckinpah, you might get the gist of this crudely produced, low-budget potboiler. Yet, it's become a cult classic and a prime example of "guerilla filmmaking" put into motion by none other than Robert Mitchum, who came up with the story of a veteran who returns to the hills to run his family's moonshine business, only to become embroiled in a war with gangsters and federal agents. Despite its attraction to guys named Gomer and Goober, *Thunder Road* is very efficiently made. Shot in the area around Asheville,

 "Well, Nobody's Perfect!"

During the scene in which the feds chase Mitchum, their car changes from a 1957 Chevy to a 1957 Ford, then back again!

North Carolina, the film resonated with its intended audience much as the *Smokey and the Bandit* films would years later. Two bizarre aspects to the film: Mitchum's son James plays his *brother* and Mitchum, one of the screen's stoic men of few words, recorded a song for the soundtrack titled "Whippoorwill," which was a surprise hit. (We can only be thankful that John Wayne wasn't similarly inspired!)

Anatomy of a Murder (1959)

Columbia Pictures

Director and Producer: Otto Preminger; **Writer:** Wendell Mayes; **Music:** Duke Ellington; **Running time:** 160 minutes

Cast: James Stewart (Paul Biegler); Lee Remick (Laura Manion); Ben Gazzara (Lt. Frederick Manion); Arthur O'Connell (Parnell Emmett McCarthy); Eve Arden (Ada Rutledge); Kathryn Grant (Mary Pilant); George C. Scott (Claude Dancer)

Oscar nominations: Best Picture, Actor (James Stewart), Supporting Actor (George C. Scott), Supporting Actor (Arthur O'Connell), Screenplay, Cinematography, Editing

A riveting courtroom drama/murder mystery, Otto Preminger's *Anatomy of a Murder* was a breakthrough film due to its explicit handling of sexual passions and the crime of violent rape. Most shockingly, the lead role was played by James Stewart, the epitome of old-fashioned American values. The story has Stewart as an out-to-pasture country prosecutor who reluctantly agrees to defend a short-tempered Army lieutenant accused of murdering a man for raping his flirtatious wife. The film is best remembered for breaking the studio's ban on treating adult subject matters in a realistic way. Terms such as "rape," "sperm," "slut," and "semen" were heard for the first time on screen. Among those not impressed was James Stewart's father, who denounced the film as a "dirty picture" and urged his friends not to see it. The senior Stewart's opinions not withstanding, the film is characterized by extraordinary performances from a superb cast. Lee Remick rose to stardom as the wife of easy virtue with a seemingly insatiable sexual appetite. Duke Ellington's innovative score is a major asset.

Oceans Eleven (1960)

Warner Brothers

Director and Producer: Lewis Milestone; **Writers:** George Clayton Johnson and Jack Golden Russell; **Music:** Nelson Riddle; **Running time:** 127 minutes

Cast: Frank Sinatra (Danny Ocean); Dean Martin (Sam Harmon); Sammy Davis Jr. (Josh Howard); Peter Lawford (Jimmy Foster); Angie Dickinson (Beatrice Ocean); Richard Conte (Tony Bergdorf); Cesar Romero (Duke Santos); Joey Bishop ("Mushy" O'Connors); Akim Tamiroff (Spyros)

No film symbolizes 1960's "cool" more than *Oceans Eleven*. Although a major box-office success, it was dismissed by critics as a virtual home movie for the Rat Pack, who squeezed in a shooting schedule in between performing nightly at the Sands Hotel and Casino in Las Vegas. Although there are plenty of inside jokes that may not be meaningful to those ignorant of the Sinatra oeuvre, that's part of the fun. Much of the "script" was improvised by the Pack, who considered two takes to be an excessive waste of time. The heist plot concerns a group of WWII buddies who reunite for a preposterous scheme to rob five major Vegas casinos on New Year's Eve. The ludicrous nature of the caper is more than overshadowed by the sheer pleasure of watching these old pros trading barbs. Memorable moments include Sammy Davis Jr.'s rendition of the terrific title song and amusing cameos from Red Skelton, George Raft, and Shirley MacLaine. The "sting-in-the-tail" ending is a classic as is the final image of the gang walking past the casino marquee that bears the names of the real Rat Pack members.

 "Play It Again, Sam"

The film was cleverly remade in 2001 as a high-tech caper starring George Clooney, Brad Pitt, and an all-star cast. That, in turn, spawned the 2004 sequel *Oceans Twelve* and *Oceans Thirteen* is presently in the works. However, the Rat Pack version will probably always rank as the best.

Birdman of Alcatraz (1962)

United Artists

Director: John Frankenheimer; **Producers:** Harold Hecht (Executive Producer), Stuart Miller, and Guy Trosper; **Writer:** Guy Trosper; **Music:** Elmer Bernstein; **Running time:** 147 minutes

Cast: Burt Lancaster (Robert Stroud); Karl Malden (Harvey Shoemaker); Thelma Ritter (Elizabeth Stroud); Neville Brand (Bull Ransom); Betty Field (Stella Johnson); Telly Savalas (Feto Gomez); Edmond O'Brien (Tom Gaddis)

Oscar nominations: Actor (Burt Lancaster), Supporting Actor (Telly Savalas), Supporting Actress (Thelma Ritter), Cinematography

Birdman of Alcatraz is a sentimentalized look at famed convicted murderer Robert Stroud, who did remarkable work training birds in Levenworth (not Alcatraz, where he spent the last years of his life). In reality, however, Stroud was an unrepentant sociopath who perceived the media as useful idiots who dutifully proclaimed him as a heroic figure—despite the fact that many of his avian cures were proven to be, well, "for the birds." Thanks to Burt Lancaster's remarkable performance as Stroud, this is one of the most engrossing prison dramas ever made. Stroud gets ample support from an able supporting cast, including Thelma Ritter as his doting mother (in a scenario somewhat reminiscent of "Cody" and Ma Jarrett in *White Heat*), Karl Malden as the short-sighted warden, and Telly Savalas as a hard-bitten fellow con.

The Killers (1964)

Universal Pictures

Director and Producer: Don Siegel; **Writer:** Gene L. Coon; **Music:** John Williams; **Running time:** 93 minutes

Cast: Lee Marvin (Charlie Storm); Angie Dickinson (Sheila Farr); John Cassavetes (Johnny North); Ronald Reagan (Jack Browning); Clu Gulager (Lee)

Originally shot as a TV movie, *The Killers'* violent content precluded it from being broadcast and it was instead released theatrically. Director Don Siegel, long a master of making much ado from nothing, is the sturdy hand at the helm, and he turns this loose remake of the original 1946 film into a crackling good suspense yarn. John Cassavetes has the Burt Lancaster role from the original film, but his stock-in-trade is changed from a boxer to a racecar driver. This time, the story is seen through the eyes of the hit men, played with icy perfection by Lee Marvin and the under-rated Clu Gulager (obviously role models for Tarantino's assassins in *Pulp Fiction*). Angie

Dickinson is the two-faced sex-bomb who stirs up the trouble. The big surprise is Ronald Reagan in his final screen appearance before entering politics. Cast against type, he excels as a charismatic but brutal gangster. Not a threat to the original, this *Killers* is still well worth a look.

Bonnie and Clyde (1967)

Warner Brothers

Director: Arthur Penn; **Producer:** Warren Beatty; **Writers:** David Newman and Robert Benton, Robert Towne (uncredited); **Music:** Charles Strouse; **Running time:** 111 minutes

Cast: Warren Beatty (Clyde Barrow); Faye Dunaway (Bonnie Parker); Michael J. Pollard (C.W. Moss); Gene Hackman (Buck Barrow); Estelle Parsons (Blanche Barrow); Denver Pyle (Frank Hamer)

Oscar nominations: Supporting Actress* (Estelle Parsons), Cinematography*, Screenplay, Costume Design, Best Picture, Director, Actor (Warren Beatty), Actress (Faye Dunaway), Supporting Actor (Michael J. Pollard), Supporting Actor (Gene Hackman)

Bonnie and Clyde marked a new era of filmmaking, tearing down barriers in terms of violence and sexuality, ushering in a new wave of fashion, and glamorizing crime in a way that would have been unthinkable during the days of the Hays Code. The film was the brainchild of Warren Beatty, who hitherto had been considered to be little more than a popular leading man. Critics carped that it would unleash a tidal wave of cinematic carnage (it did), while its defenders predicted it would free filmmakers from the type of corporate chains that had stifled artistic creativity. What cannot be denied is that the film was brilliantly directed by Arthur Penn and enacted by the letter-perfect ensemble cast. The superbly edited (by Dede Allen) assassination of Bonnie and Clyde remains one of the most shocking sequences in any motion picture. Keep an eye out for Gene Wilder in his film debut as a hapless undertaker.

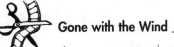 **Gone with the Wind**

A sequence was shot in which Bonnie makes a mild attempt to seduce C.W. while he is in the bathtub. The footage has not been seen, but photos survive.

In Cold Blood (1967)

Columbia Pictures

Director, Producer, and Writer: Richard Brooks; **Music:** Quincy Jones; **Running time:** 134 minutes

Cast: Robert Blake (Perry Edward Smith); Scott Wilson (Richard "Dick" Hickock); John Forsyth (Alvin Dewey); Paul Stewart (Jensen); Gerald S. O'Laughlin (Harold Nye); Jeff Corey (Mr. Hickock)

Oscar nominations: Director, Screenplay, Cinematography, Music

In Cold Blood is Richard Brooks' meticulous recreation of the infamous and senseless murder of an entire family at the hands of Perry Smith and Dick Hickcock, two tortured petty criminals. The crime was immortalized by Truman Capote, whose bestseller caused some to suspect he callously used the crime and the participants to cynically advance his own career. (The controversy is the basis of the 2005 film *Capote*.) To insure accuracy, Brooks shot on location in the small Kansas town where the Clutter family was murdered, including the house where the crime occurred. Watching the reenactment of the innocent family's step-by-step march to death is an almost unbearable experience. That one of the murderers is played by Robert Blake adds an unintended eeriness to the production that could not have been foreseen, given Blake's own sordid trial for the murder of his wife decades later. *In Cold Blood* is a major achievement in filmmaking. Remade in 1996 as a TV movie.

In the Heat of the Night (1967)

United Artists

Director: Norman Jewison; **Producer:** Walter Mirisch; **Writer:** Stirling Silliphant; **Music:** Quincy Jones; **Running time:** 109 minutes

Cast: Sidney Poitier (Virgil Tibbs); Rod Steiger (Chief Gillespie); Warren Oates (Sam Wood); Lee Grant (Leslie Colbert); Larry Gates (Eric Endicott)

Oscar nominations: Best Picture*, Actor* (Rod Steiger), Sound*, Editing*, Screenplay*, Director, Sound Effects

Norman Jewison's *In the Heat of the Night* dared to address the 800-pound gorilla that Hollywood had conveniently ignored: the heated racial situation in the American south. It may be hard for younger viewers to appreciate how groundbreaking this film was. Sidney Poitier's Philadelphia police detective Virgil Tibbs is reluctantly compelled to help a racist redneck sheriff crack a local murder case with tentacles that reach to the top of the town's high society types. Even in these more enlightened times, the film can be enjoyed as a crackling good crime yarn, embellished considerably by the skillful performances of Poitier and Rod Steiger, the latter in his Oscar-winning role. The film represented a giant leap for the image of black actors in mainstream films. When Poitier responds to a slap in the face from a rich white man by in turn slapping the white man, audiences of *all* races cheered.

"Play It Again, Sam"

The success of the film and the Virgil Tibbs character lead to two feature film sequels with Sidney Poiter reprising the role: *They Call Me MISTER Tibbs!* (1970) and *The Organization* (1971). The film also inspired the hit TV series *In the Heat of the Night,* which premiered in 1988 with Carroll O'Connor and Howard Rollins Jr. in the Steiger/Poitier roles.

Point Blank (1967)

MGM

Director: John Boorman; **Producers:** Judd Bernard and Robert Chartoff; **Writers:** Alexander Jacobs, Rafe Newhouse, and David Newhouse; **Music:** Johnny Mandel; **Running time:** 92 minutes

Cast: Lee Marvin (Walker); Angie Dickinson (Chris); Keenan Wynn (Yost); Carroll O'Connor (Brewster); Lloyd Bochner (Carter); Michael Strong (Big John Stegman); John Vernon (Mal Reese)

The testosterone levels are off the Richter Scale in this macho cult classic. Lee Marvin is cast as a career criminal bent on exacting revenge on his two-timing wife and partner who think they have successfully murdered him. *Point Blank* was not particularly successful upon its initial release, having been lost in the hype of Marvin's other 1967 blockbuster for MGM, *The Dirty Dozen.* However, in ensuing years, it became a seminal film in the actor's legacy and helped cement his reputation as one of the screen's most ruthless tough guys. Under John Boorman's breakneck direction, the film is drenched in endless fistfights, shootings, and other assorted acts of mayhem. It's crude, rude, but ultimately as good as macho movies get. Remade in 1999 as *Payback* with Mel Gibson.

The Thomas Crown Affair (1969)

United Artists

Director and Producer: Norman Jewison; **Writer:** Alan R. Trustman; **Music:** Michel LeGrand; **Running time:** 102 minutes

Cast: Steve McQueen (Thomas Crown); Faye Dunaway (Vicki Anderson); Paul Burke (Lt. Eddy Malone); Jack Weston (Erwin Weaver); Yaphett Kotto (Carl)

Oscar nominations: Best Song* (*The Windmills of Your Mind*), Score

Playing against type, Steve McQueen is an ultra-rich banker who relieves his sense of boredom by having a gang in his employ stage an audacious string of ingenious heists. Faye Dunaway is the sexy insurance investigator sent to entrap him. The fun comes from the sexually charged relationship they build even as they engage in a cat-and-mouse game designed to outwit each other. The film is filled with memorably erotic moments, including a famous prolonged kiss and a chess game with phallic overtones. Director Jewison makes good use of (then) innovative split screen techniques. The Oscar-winning song *The Windmills of Your Mind* has been recorded countless times, but the best version is still the one heard over the main titles, crooned by Noel Harrison.

"Play It Again, Sam"

The 1999 version with Pierce Brosnan and Renee Russo is one of the rare instances of a remake being as good, if not better, than the original—though it lacks the 1968 film's cynical, sting-in-the-tail ending.

The Italian Job (1969)

Paramount Pictures

Director: Peter Collinson; **Producer:** Michael Deeley; **Writer:** Troy Kennedy Martin; **Music:** Quincy Jones; **Running time:** 99 minutes

Cast: Michael Caine (Charlie Croker); Noel Coward (Mr. Bridger); Benny Hill (Prof. Simon Peach); Raf Vallone (Altabani); Tony Beckley ("Camp" Freddie); Rossano Brazzi (Roger Beckerman)

Upon its American release in 1969, *The Italian Job* made little impact with critics or the public. However, it has built an enormous cult status in England, where it has come to be regarded as one of the great British films. Michael Caine stars as a recently released con who assembles a group of eccentric thieves to enact an ingenious gold robbery in Italy that mandates using a fleet of innocuous Mini Cooper vehicles. Requires repeat viewings in order to fully appreciate the witty script and ingratiating performances, particularly by Caine and Noel Coward, whose hangdog expression and ever-present sophistication make for one of the most memorable crime bosses in screen history. The car stunts rank among the best ever seen, and the ending—a literal cliff hanger—was envisioned to set up a sequel that (happily) never materialized. A charming winner all the way.

"Play It Again, Sam"

The film inspired the 2003 remake starring charisma-challenged Mark Wahlberg in the Michael Caine role. In another burst of "creative thinking", this *Italian Job* is primarily set in Los Angeles. 'Nuff said.

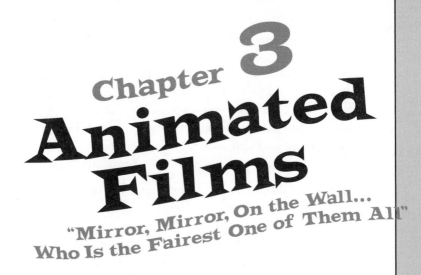

Chapter 3
Animated Films

"Mirror, Mirror, On the Wall... Who Is the Fairest One of Them All"

The practice of using animation to entertain audiences is as old as the concept of the motion picture itself. Crude animated short films were popular from the outset, but only a few names behind the creative process would resonate with the public in the early years. As far back as the late 1890's, Thomas Edison's studio was experimenting with ways of bringing animation to life. One of his protégés, J. Stuart Blackton, produced the short *Humorous Phases of Funny Faces* in 1906, which is widely considered to be the first successful animated film even though it used crude chalk drawings and cut-out figures. By 1917, pioneers like Willis O'Brien were doing innovative experiments with clay animation. O'Brien gained acclaim for his short *The Dinosaur and the Missing Link: A Prehistoric Tragedy*. Two decades later he would refine his technique and create the outstanding animation seen in *King Kong*.

By 1923, Walt Disney and his brother Roy entered the industry and combined live action with animation for a series of shorts known as *The Alice Comedies*. In 1928, the first screen appearance of Mickey Mouse in a short titled *Steamboat Willie* would fundamentally change the entire film industry. Mickey and the classic Disney characters that would follow became the first animated superstars. In 1937, Disney oversaw production of the first animated feature film, *Snow White and the Seven Dwarfs*. The film was rightly hailed as a masterpiece and set in motion the entire genre of animated feature films. Not surprisingly, it was Disney himself who would have a virtual monopoly on the most influential animated films, having attracted the top talent in the field and having refined the marketing of these films into an art itself. Other major names, such as Max Fleischer and the Looney Toons brand, would gain enormous popularity in their own right; however, these were largely confined to cartoon shorts seen prior to the main features in theaters. Disney's original films were distributed by RKO, but as his power in the industry grew he would later distribute through his own company, Buena Vista.

In preparing this book, I was a bit startled to see just how strongly Disney monopolized the animated feature film industry until recent years when computer graphics imagery (CGI) brought about a revolution in this art form. Consequently, the films covered in this section are tilted almost entirely to those produced by Disney during the glory years of the studio. The new technologies have brought us impressive hits such as *Shrek* and *Toy Story*, but most film historians would concur that we will probably never see work as impressive as that created in a smoke-filled room by hard-working animators whose tools were no more "hi tech" than pen and pencil.

Snow White and the Seven Dwarfs (1937)

RKO Radio Pictures

Directors: Perce Pearce, David Hand, Larry Morey, William Cottrell, Wilfred Jackson, Ben Sharpsteen; **Producer:** Walt Disney; **Writers:** Ted Sears & Richard Creedon, Otto Englander & Dick Rickard, Earl Hurd & Merrill De Maris, Dorothy Ann Blank & Webb Smith; **Music:** Frank Churchill, Leigh Harline, and Paul Smith; **Running time:** 83 minutes

Cast (voices): Adriana Caselotti (Snow White); Lucille La Verne (Queen); Roy Atwell (Doc); Eddie Collins (Dopey); Pinto Colvig (Sleepy/Grumpy); Billy Gilbert (Sneezy); Scotty Mattraw (Bashful); Otis Harlan (Happy); Harry Stockwell (Prince)

Oscar nominations: Score, Honorary (Walt Disney was granted a special Oscar for his achievement with this film, as well as seven miniature Oscars symbolizing the dwarfs.)

Walt Disney was already a respected name in the film business when he undertook his biggest gamble to date: to produce the first full-length animated feature film ever from an American studio. Disney had been determined to bring the legend of Snow White to the screen ever since he saw a silent film version of the tale in 1917. Virtually all that comes to mind now about the fable of Snow White is Disney's own version. This included the introduction of the Dwarf's names and other key components that are now mainstays of the story. Literally hundreds of technicians labored on the expensive production to the extent that it became known as "Disney's Folly."

However, upon release, the film became an immediate sensation, earning praise from no less than famed Russian director Sergei Eisenstein, who called it the greatest movie ever made. The superb animation, voiceover work, and production values would set the standard for all Disney animated films to follow. Along with *Pinocchio*, this is considered to be Disney's greatest film achievement.

Fantasia (1940)

RKO Radio Pictures (General release and wide roadshow engagements)

Walt Disney Productions (Limited roadshow engagements)

Directors: James Algar, Samuel Armstrong, Ford Beebee, Norm Ferguson, Jim Handley, T. Hee, Wilfred Jackson, Hamilton Luske, Bill Roberts, and Paul Satterfield; **Producer:** Walt Disney; **Writers:** Lee Blair, Elmer Plummer, Phil Dyke, Sylvia Moberly-Holland, Norman Wright, Albert Heath, Bianca Majolie, Graham Hyde, Perce Pearce, Carl Fallberg, William Martin, Leo Thiele, Robert Sterner, John Fraser McLeish, Otto Englander, Webb Smith, Erdman Penner, Joseph Sabo, Bill Peet, George Stallings, Campbell Grant, Arthur Heinemann, and Phil Duke; **Running time:** 120 minutes

Cast: Leopold Stokowski (conductor); Deems Taylor (narrator)

Oscar nominations: Honorary Oscars were given to Walt Disney and Leopold Stokowski for their work on the film.

Walt Disney's boldest film project, *Fantasia*, sets different animated sequences to classical music under the direction of famed conductor Leopold Stokowski. The end result is as bewildering as it is impressive. The animation is a triumph on every level, but audiences and critics have long debated the merits of each segment. Some drag down the pace of the narrative while others, such as the frightening *Night on Bald Mountain*, are mesmerizing in their intensity. The film is not for the small fry, even with the welcome appearance of Mickey Mouse in the famed *Sorcerer's Apprentice* segment. Disney intended to update the film annually with new segments, but its initial box-office failure precluded this from happening. Ironically, the film began to turn profitable in the late 1960s when young people adopted it as a "head trip" much as they did with Kubrick's *2001*. The checkered history of the movie includes releases of various lengths and the controversial optical editing of racially insensitive animated characters. The 60th anniversary video release is probably as close to the original 124-minute roadshow edition as we'll ever see.

Pinocchio (1940)

RKO Radio Pictures

Director: Hamilton Luske; **Producer:** Walt Disney; **Writers:** Otto Englander, Ted Sears, Webb Smith, Joseph Sabo, Erdman Penner, and Aurelius Battaglia; **Music:** Leigh Harline and Paul J. Smith; **Running time:** 88 minutes

Cast (voices): Mel Blanc (Cleo/Figaro/Gideon); Dickie Jones (Pinocchio/Alexander); Cliff Edwards (Jiminy Cricket); Christian Rub (Geppetto)

Oscar nominations: Score*, Song* (*When You Wish Upon a Star*)

Considered by many to be Walt Disney's greatest animated film, *Pinocchio* tells the famous tale of a wooden puppet who wishes he were a real boy. The outstanding animated techniques employed in *Snow White* seem even more impressive in this timeless story. The film is compelling on several levels: it's humorous, tragic, and downright suspenseful (the sequence inside the whale is one of the seminal Disney screen moments). Based on the famed novel by Carlo Collodi, Disney follows tradition and adds original characters that enhance the story. It also illustrates the underlying theme that a special friendship is one of life's most enduring treasures. Sadly, most of the great artists who did the voiceover work for these legendary characters never received screen credit or recognition until recent years when their efforts have been acknowledged in special edition documentaries for the home video market.

Dumbo (1941)

RKO Radio Pictures

Director: Ben Sharpsteen; **Producer:** Walt Disney; **Writers:** Joe Grant, Dick Huemer; **Music:** Frank Churchill and Oliver Wallace; **Running time:** 64 minutes

Cast (voices): Edward Brophy (Timothy Q. Mouse); Sterling Holloway (Mr. Stork); Herman Bing (Ringmaster); Cliff Edwards (Jim Crow)

Oscar nominations: Best Song* (*Baby Mine*), Best Score*

Long regarded as one of Walt Disney's most efficiently made films, *Dumbo* is a masterpiece on every level. The movie packs in a myriad of emotions, from sadness and tragedy to laughter and triumph, all in the course of 64 minutes, the shortest running time of any Disney feature film. The studio, RKO, was not happy with the abbreviated running time and urged Disney to either make trims and release *Dumbo* as a short or to film additional scenes to make it a longer feature film. Disney held his ground and the film is all the better for it. There isn't a wasted frame. The animation is simply stunning, and if you aren't moved to tears by Dumbo's early hardships and the incarceration of his beloved mother, you must be made of stone. The film had a modest budget (under $1 million) and was a substantial box-office and critical success.

Bambi (1942)

RKO Radio Pictures

Director: David Hand; **Producer:** Walt Disney; **Writer:** Perce Pearce; **Music:** Edward Plumb; **Songs:** Robert Sour, Helen Bliss, Frank Churchill, Henry Manners, and Larry Morey; **Running time:** 70 minutes

Cast (voices): Hardie Albright (adolescent Bambi); Stan Alexander (young Flower); Sterling Holloway (adult Flower); Peter Behn (young Thumper); Tim Davis (adult Thumper); Donnie Dunagan (young Bambi); John Sutherland (adult Bambi)

Oscar nominations: Musical Score, Best Song ("Love is a Song"), Sound

Like so many of Walt Disney's early masterpieces, *Bambi* was not an immediate success at the box-office. Years in production, the perfection-obsessed Disney doted over details of the animation, created by his fabled stable of "nine old men"—a jocular reference to the team of artists who brought his ideas to life. When the movie was released in 1942, it was immediately acclaimed as a great film, but it didn't earn a profit until its subsequent release in 1947. *Bambi* is legendary for its shocking use of tragedy within what is arguably Disney's most lovable animated film. The death of Bambi's mother at the hands of an anonymous hunter is still emotionally devastating enough to cause one to fast-forward their DVD past this brilliant but disturbing sequence. A direct-to-video sequel was released in 2006, imaginatively titled *Bambi II*.

Hollywood Confidential

It wasn't until 2005 that Donald Roan Dunagan revealed himself as the facial model and voice of young Bambi. Dunagan kept the information secret for over 60 years because he was a career U.S. Marine officer and felt the fact that he was the model for Bambi would undermine his authority in the service.

Song of the South (1946)

RKO Radio Pictures

Directors: Harvey Foster and Wilfred Jackson; **Producer:** Walt Disney; **Writers:** Bill Peet, Ralph Wright, George Stallings, Dalton Reymond, Morton Grant, and Maurice Rapf; **Music:** Daniele Amfitheatrof; **Running time:** 94 minutes

Cast (voices): Ruth Warrick (Sally); Bobby Driscoll (Johnny); James Bassett (Uncle Remus/Br're Fox); Luana Patten (Ginny)

Oscar nominations: Best Song* (*Zip-a-Dee-Doo-Dah*), Score. An honorary Oscar was given to James Bassett "For his able and heart-warming characterization of Uncle Remus, friend and story teller to the children of the world, in Walt Disney's *Song of the South*."

A major work in the Disney canon, *Song of the South* has tragically been buried by the same company as a response to self-appointed "activists" who proclaim the film as racist. Most film scholars disagree saying that the character of Uncle Remus (the good-natured, elderly black man) is simply a country guy whose idiosyncracies were a reflection of the time. This charming film features some of the Disney team's most memorable animation combined with live action, and a highlight is the Oscar-winning song *Zip-a-Dee-Doo-Dah*. Bassett himself was so impressive he was awarded a special Oscar for his work on the film. Alas, American audiences have not seen this wonderful achievement since it was withdrawn from distribution in the mid-1980s. The real question is why, if Disney really believes it is racist, the movie continues to be made available in other nations.

Cinderella (1950)

RKO Radio Pictures

Directors: Clyde Geronimi, Wilfred Jackson, and Hamilton Luske; **Producer:** Walt Disney; **Writers:** Bill Peet, Ted Sears, Homer Brighton, Ken Anderson, Erdman Penner, Winston Hibler, Harry Reeves, and Joe Rinaldi; **Music:** Mack David, Al Hoffman, Jerry Livingston, Paul J. Smith, and Oliver Wallace; **Running time:** 72 minutes

Cast (voices): Ilene Woods (Cinderella); Eleanor Audley (Lady Tremaine); Verna Felton (Fairy Godmother); William Phipps (Prince Charming); James MacDonald (Jacques/Gus Gus)

Oscar nominations: Song ("Bibbidy-Bobbidi-Boo"), Sound, Score

Cinderella was considered to be an enormous gamble for Walt Disney. During the WWII era, production cutbacks at his company relegated him to producing primarily cartoon shorts. With a budget rumored to be approximately $3 million, *Cinderella* represented a bold return to the full-length animated features Disney had concentrated on in the pre-war era. However, some of his most beloved films were not immediately successful upon initial release, and had *Cinderella* flopped, it was quite possible the fledgling Disney empire might have crumbled. Happily, the public responded overwhelmingly to the unique Disney spin on the classic fairy tale—especially to the many new characters the script introduced, some destined for screen immortality. Disney also had the foresight to pioneer ancillary merchandise and music rights from the film into major money-makers, helping to finance his ultimate dream project: the construction of Disneyland. Although a classic, as Roger Ebert points out, it also marked the beginning of a new form of Disney animation presenting main characters that are less quirky and more bland than those seen previously.

Alice in Wonderland (1951)

RKO Radio Pictures

Directors: Clyde Geronimi, Wilfred Jackson, and Hamilton Luske; **Producer:** Walt Disney;
Writers: Winston Hibler, Bill Peet, Joe Rinaldi, William Cottrell, Del Connell, Ted Sears, Erdman
Penner, Milt Banta, Dick Kelsey, Dick Huemer, Tom Oreb, and John Walbridge; **Music:** Oliver
Wallace; **Songs:** Mack David, Sammy Fain, Bob Hilliard, Al Hoffman, Jerry Livingston, Don Raye,
and Gene De Paul; **Running time:** 72 minutes

Cast (voices): Kathryn Beaumont (Alice); Ed Wynn (Mad Hatter); Richard Haydn (Caterpillar);
Sterling Holloway (Cheshire Cat); Jerry Colonna (March Hare); Verna Felton (Queen of Hearts)

Oscar nomination: Score

Inspired by two Lewis Carroll books (*Alice in Wonderland* and *Through the Looking
Glass*), this project had a very personal appeal to Walt Disney. His early work included
a number of silent short films based on the Alice stories, and he had long dreamed of
being able to fulfill his goal of producing a feature-length motion picture based on
the Carroll tales. The film was years in development and production. By the time it
was ready for release, Disney had enough clout to utilize the new medium of TV to
promote the premiere. A special titled *One Hour in Wonderland* was telecast on
December 25, 1950. The innovative marketing plan had little effect, however, as the
film was deemed a box-office failure. It was
not until the 1960s and 1970s that it became
extremely popular on the film rental market
for schools and private organizations. The
movie has not gained the cachet or reputation
of certain other Disney animated titles, but it
stands as a major achievement.

"Well, Nobody's Perfect!"

For all the time and
painstaking care put into *Alice in
Wonderland,* the title page
scene in the opening credits mis-
spells Lewis Carroll's name!

Lady and the Tramp (1955)

Buena Vista

Director: Clyde Geronimi, Wilfred Jackson, and Hamilton Luske; **Producer:** Walt Disney;
Writers: Erdman Penner, Joe Rinaldi, Ralph Wright, and Don DaGradi; **Music:** Oliver Wallace;
Songs: Peggy Lee and Sonny Burke; **Running time:** 75 minutes

Cast (voices): Peggy Lee (Darling/Si/Am/Peg); Barbara Luddy (Lady); Larry Roberts (Tramp); Bill
Thompson (Jock/Bulldog/Policeman/Dachsie/Joe)

If defined by the level of its romanticism, *Lady and the Tramp* is *An Affair to Remember*
for the Alpo set. A sweet-natured (even by Disney standards) celebration of love, the

story concerns a runaway cocker spaniel (Lady) who meets and shares adventures with Tramp, a dog from "the other side of the tracks." The movie features splendid animation (this was the first animated feature to be released in a widescreen version) and wonderful songs. The Siamese cats are classic screen villains, and the scene of Lady and Tramp sharing a spaghetti dinner ranks with the greatest romantic scenes in cinema.

One Hundred and One Dalmations (1961)

Buena Vista

Directors: Clyde Geronimi, Hamilton S. Luske, and Wolfgang Reitherman; **Producer:** Walt Disney; **Writer:** Bill Peet; **Music:** George Bruns; **Songs:** Mel Leven; **Running time:** 79 minutes

Cast (voices): Rod Taylor (Pongo); Betty Lou Gerson (Cruella De Vil/Miss Birdwell); Cate Bauer (Perdita); Ben Wright (Roger)

Although *Dalmations* can rightly be regarded as another Disney classic, the film introduced a new technology called Xerography that was designed to mitigate the skyrocketing costs of traditional animations. Consequently, with this film the look of Disney animation became, well, less animated, with an almost scratchy look to some of the drawings. This would remain in place until new technology in the 1980s allowed the animation to have a smoother look. The movie itself is not in league with the earlier triumphs, but remains wildly popular with children. Cruella De Vil is an iconic screen villainess (based on Gloria Swanson in *Sunset Boulevard?*), but has anyone thought of how gruesome her plot really is? Turning loveable puppies into fur coats makes for a bizarre Disney version of *Silence of the Lambs*. The film inspired a direct-to-video sequel, *101 Dalmations II: Patch's London Adventure*, as well as a live-action remake in 1996 with Glenn Close's acclaimed impersonation of Cruella De Vil.

The Incredible Mr. Limpet (1964)

Warner Brothers

Director: Arthur Lubin; **Producer:** John C. Rose; **Writers:** Jameson Brewer and Joe DiMona; **Music:** Frank Perkins; **Songs:** Sammy Fain and Harold Adamson; **Running time:** 102 minutes

Cast: Don Knotts (Henry Limpett); Carole Cook (Bessie Limpett); Jack Weston (George Stickel); Andrew Duggan (Harlock)

As with many of Don Knotts' kid's movies, time has been kind to the film, and it has built a cult following. Knotts plays the ultimate wimp, Henry Limpet, who is rejected from enlisting in the Navy to help fight WWII. Through a fantasy wish fulfillment, he turns into a talking fish! Against expectations, Limpet proves he isn't the Chicken of the Sea and becomes a hero by helping to sink German U Boats. It's all ridiculous, but the film is actually moving on certain levels, thanks to Knotts' ability to mix humor and pathos. Additionally, the animation is quite impressive even today.

The Jungle Book (1967)

Buena Vista

Director: Wolfgang Reitherman; **Producer:** Walt Disney; **Writers:** Larry Clemens, Ralph Wright, Ken Anderson, and Vance Gerry; **Music:** George Bruns; **Songs:** Richard M. Sherman and Terry Gilkyson; **Running time:** 78 minutes

Cast (voices): Phil Harris (Baloo); Sebastian Cabot (Bagheera); Louis Prima (King Louis); George Sanders (Shere Khan); Sterling Holloway (Kaa); Bruce Reitherman (Mowgli)

Oscar nomination: Song (*The Bare Necessities*)

Noted for being the last feature film that Walt Disney personally oversaw (it was still in production when he died in 1966), *The Jungle Book* would also be the last truly classic film to be produced by Disney studios for many years to come. A charming adaptation of Rudyard Kipling's story about the adventures of a young boy raised in the jungle by wolves, the film features memorable voiceovers from Phil Harris and Louis Prima. The song *The Bare Necessities* ranks with *Chitty Chitty Bang Bang* as one of those cutesy numbers that you can't get out of your head for days.

Gone with the Wind

Actor Frank Fontaine recorded dialogue for the part of a nearly blind rhinoceros named Rocky. However, the segment was cut before full animation could proceed.

Yellow Submarine (1968)

United Artists

Director: George Dunning; **Producer:** Al Bordax; **Writers:** Al Bordax, Jack Mendlesohn, Lee Minoff, and Erich Segal; **Music:** George Martin; **Songs:** John Lennon, Paul McCartney, and George Harrison; **Running time:** 85 minutes

Cast (voices): Paul Angels (Chief Blue Meanie/Ringo); John Clive (John); Geoff Hughes (Paul); Peter Batten (George); The Beatles (epilogue)

Gone with the Wind

An entire song, *Hey Bulldog*, was excised from American prints of *Yellow Submarine*, though it was included in the UK release. In 1999, the segment was restored for the DVD release.

Despite The Beatles aversion to moviemaking, when it was suggested they participate in an animated film based on the song *Yellow Submarine*, they agreed—despite having disapproved of the quality of a cartoon series that had aired for years on TV. The Beatles turned out to be well pleased with this film, and even consented to appearing in a quick live-action epilogue. The animation may seem unimpressive today, but this was heady stuff in the psychedelic world of 1968—and it holds up well when combined with the classic songs. The script was cowritten by future *Love Story* author Erich Segal.

A Boy Named Charlie Brown (1969)

National General Pictures

Director and Producer: Bill Melendez; **Writer:** Charles M. Schulz; **Music:** Vince Guaraldi; **Songs:** Rod McKuen and John Scott Trotter; **Running time:** 86 minutes

Cast (voices): Peter Robbins (Charlie Brown); Pamelyn Ferdin (Lucy); Glenn Gilger (Linus); Andy Pforsich (Schroeder); Sally Dryer (Patty)

Oscar nomination: Best Musical Score

Those who claim that *Seinfeld* is "about nothing" obviously haven't seen *A Boy Named Charlie Brown*. It's a loosely connected assemblage of nonevents in the life of America's favorite loser. Nominally about Charlie's preparation for a high-stakes national spelling bee, the film presents the message that when life throws children a curve ball, they are to be encouraged by Charlie's endless optimism to brush off disappointment and try again. The film successfully captures an era in time in which the main message for children was one of wholesomeness. The continuing popularity of Charlie Brown and his friends as well as the sky-high ratings of the annual Christmas TV special indicate that good taste has not entirely departed from contemporary American culture. Note: The end credits of this film allow the actors who have provided the familiar voices to be seen onscreen.

Chapter 4
Musicals

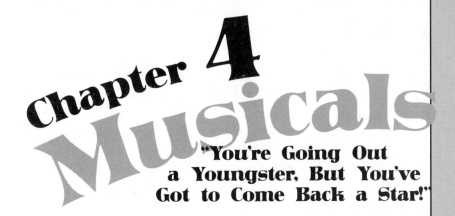

"You're Going Out a Youngster, But You've Got to Come Back a Star!"

It is ironic that the big screen musical, once arguably the most popular cinematic genre, has in recent years become the equivalent of a leisure suit. Few studios produce full-fledged musicals, and those that do attempt to reach a younger audience by concentrating on modern urban life that reflects contemporary social problems (for example, *Fame* and *Rent*). Even with these concessions to the youth market, both critical and box-office results for these films have been decidedly mixed. Between the 1930s and 1960s, big screen traditional musicals were considered to be a sure thing for major studios. Thus, hefty sums were spent to produce elaborate productions, with adaptations of popular Broadway plays particularly desirable. The great Busby Berkeley was so synonymous with the musicals he brought to the screen that his name became a box-office draw in its own right.

By the 1950s, a new generation of stars reinvigorated the format, lead by Gene Kelly, whose *Singin' in the Rain* became a seminal film in the genre. Kelly's Technicolor productions brought new luster to the screen musical and combined lively dance numbers with involving plots and characters. In the 1950's, Hollywood broke away from "backstage" musicals and turned to "book" musicals, with emphasis on the works of Rodgers and Hammerstein. Musicals remained in vogue until the latter part of the 1960s. With the advent of another generation of youthful filmmakers, audience's tastes changed. This was the era of *Easy Rider* and *Midnight Cowboy*. Suddenly, big budget productions such as *Star!*, *Hello Dolly!*, and *Paint Your Wagon* seemed positively quaint and lost large sums at the box-office. There have been a few bold attempts to revive the traditional musical format in recent years, most notably the Oscar-winner *Chicago*. However, it appears as though the era in which such films were mainstays is long since over. Fortunately, fans can revel in the first-rate releases of classic musicals on home videos, often accompanied by rare footage and fascinating documentaries. Thus, the masterpieces created by a generation of American moviemakers are assured of never being forgotten.

42ⁿᵈ *Street* (1933)

Warner Brothers

Director: Lloyd Bacon; **Producers:** Darryl F. Zanuck (uncredited); **Writers:** Rian James and James Seymour; **Running time:** 89 minutes

Cast: Warner Baxter (Julian Marsh); Bebe Daniels (Dorothy Brock); George Brent (Pat Denning); Ruby Keeler (Peggy Sawyer)

Oscar nominations: Best Picture, Sound

The cliches in *42ⁿᵈ Street* have enough mold on them to manufacture Penicillin, but in 1933, these scenarios probably looked innovative. Ruby Keeler is the stand-in who has to save the show on short notice after the leading lady is incapacitated. The real star is famed choreographer Busby Berkeley who cheerfully provides some of the most extravagant production numbers ever filmed, never letting it bother him that they may not have any relation to the central plot.

Swing Time (1936)

RKO Radio Pictures

Director: George Stevens; **Producer:** Pandro S. Berman; **Writers:** Howard Lindsay and Howard Scott; **Songs:** Jerome Kern; **Running time:** 103 minutes

Cast: Fred Astaire ("Lucky" Garnett); Ginger Rogers ("Penny" Carroll); Victor Moore ("Pop" Cardetti); Helen Broderick (Mabel)

Oscar nominations: Song* (*The Way You Look Tonight*), Dance Direction (*Bojangles of Harlem*)

The fifth teaming of Astaire and Rogers is considered by many to be their best collaborative effort. A slight comedy of manners and mixed-up love lives, *Swing Time* does have an abundance of wit. However, it's the elaborately choreographed dance numbers that have established its reputation as a classic musical. Like Hitchcock, Fred Astaire did not believe in improvisation, and painstakingly planned out key sequences in the most minute detail. Thus, the "spontaneous" dance numbers with Ginger Rogers were plotted out as elaborately as a military exercise, as witnessed in the incredible *Never Gonna Dance* number. Equally impressive is Astaire's work in the *Bojangles of Harlem* sequence. If you can overlook the now painful sight of Astaire in blackface, pay attention to the sheer beauty of his movements. The film introduced the classic song *The Way You Look Tonight*.

Top Hat (1936)

RKO Radio Pictures

Director: Mark Sandrich; **Producer:** Pandro S. Berman; **Writer:** Dwight Taylor; **Music:** Irving Berlin; **Running time:** 101 minutes

Cast: Fred Astaire (Jerry Travers); Ginger Rogers (Dale Tremont); Edward Everett Horton (Horace Hardwick); Erik Rhodes (Alberto); Eric Blore (Bates)

Oscar nominations: Best Picture, Song (*Cheek to Cheek*), Art Direction, Dance Direction

By the time Astaire and Rogers reunited for this fourth screen project, they were already a big enough force at the box-office that, for the first time, a screenplay was written precisely with them in mind. Based on the play *The Girl Who Dared*, *Top Hat* was the usual slight love story of initially unrequited love and mistaken identities, with the predictable happy ending. With a score by Irving Berlin (who would contribute to many other Astaire films), the real joy of *Top Hat* is reveling in the five major dance numbers that allow Fred and Ginger to strut their stuff. The film was released at the height of the Depression, but its showcasing of high society types only seemed to entice the public. *Top Hat* was a Thirties equivalent of a blockbuster, raking in over $3 million—an enormous sum in that era.

The Wizard of Oz (1939)

MGM

Director: Victor Young; **Producer:** Mervyn LeRoy; **Writers:** Noel Langley, Florence Ryerson, and Edgar Allan Woolf; **Music:** Harold Arlen; **Running time:** 101 minutes

Cast: Judy Garland (Dorothy Gale); Frank Morgan (Prof. Marvel/Wizard of Oz); Ray Bolger (Hunk/The Scarecrow); Bert Lahr (Zeke/The Cowardly Lion); Jack Haley (Hickory/The Tin Man); Billie Burke (Glinda); Margaret Hamilton (Miss Gulch/Wicked Witch of East and West)

Oscar nominations: Best Picture, Cinematography (color), Special Effects, Art Direction, Score*, Song* (*Over the Rainbow*)

Unless you're one of those Japanese soldiers who surfaces every now and then on a South Pacific island because he doesn't know WWII has ended, there's a good chance you're completely familiar with the basics of *The Wizard of Oz*, so we'll just relate some interesting insights you may not have been aware of. What you may not know is that the film was originally offered to W.C. Fields with the Wizard being the central character. The cantankerous actor declined to participate. Shirley Temple was the favorite to play Dorothy, but her singing skills were not strong enough. Buddy Ebsen filmed scenes as the Tin Man, but had to be replaced by Jack Haley when he suffered a severe reaction to the makeup. Prior to the film's release, MGM executives were going to delete the song *Over the Rainbow* because it slowed the pace! (It has since been voted the #1 movie song of all time by the American Film Institute.) The film has become so beloved it seems an exercise in futility to restate its many virtues. Suffice it so say, for a movie that was not initially a financial success, *Wizard* has long been established as *the* classic family film of all time—and it just gets better with each viewing.

Gone with the Wind

Cut from *The Wizard of Oz* was an elaborate scene titled *The Jitterbug*, in which the bite of this magical insect causes the victim to dance incessantly. Sadly, all of the footage of this deleted scene has long since vanished, but silent home movies of the number appear on the DVD edition.

Meet Me in St. Louis (1944)

MGM

Director: Vincente Minnelli; **Producer:** Arthur Freed; **Writers:** Irving Brecher and Fred F. Finklehoff; **Incidental Music:** George E. Stroll (uncredited); **Running time:** 113 minutes

Cast: Judy Garland (Esther Smith); Margaret O'Brien ("Tootie" Smith); Mary Astor (Anna Smith); Lucille Bremer (Rose Smith); Leon Ames (Alonzo Smith)

Oscar nominations: Screenplay, Song (*The Trolley Song*), Cinematography (color), Score

Judy Garland, under contract at MGM, was initially opposed to starring in this sentimental family tale set in St. Louis in 1903 as the inhabitants eagerly await the arrival of the World's Fair. The part required Garland to portray a teenager and, at age 21, she felt she should finally be free of the immature roles in which she had been traditionally cast. She relented when director Vincente Minnelli convinced her the film would be a highlight in her career. Garland not only was pleased with the finished production, but she must have thought well of her director, too, as she ended up marrying Minnelli. The film contains a number of show-stopping numbers, from the upbeat and merry *Trolley Song* to the beautiful

Gone with the Wind

Judy Garland sang the song *Boys and Girls Like You and Me* (originally written for *Oklahoma!*) but the sequence was dropped from the final cut.

but somber *Have Yourself a Merry Little Christmas*. Young Margaret O'Brien was so impressive as Garland's kid sister that the Academy granted her a special Oscar.

The Red Shoes (1948)

Eagle-Lion Films

Director: Michael Powell; **Producers:** Michael Powell and Emeric Pressburger; **Writers:** Michael Powell, Emeric Pressburger, and Keith Winter; **Music:** Brian Easdale; **Running time:** 133 minutes

Cast: Anton Wolbrook (Boris); Marius Goring (Julius); Moira Shearer (Victoria)

Oscar nominations: Best Picture, Score*, Art Direction-Set Decoration*(color), Editing, Screenplay

The Red Shoes is one of the most offbeat musicals ever filmed. The title refers to a ballet based on Hans Christian Andersen's morbid fairy tale about a ballerina whose shoes force her to dance to the point of death. She is saved only by having her feet hacked off! The film traces a love triangle between a beautiful ballerina and her beaus, all of whom are working together on a stage production of Andersen's tale. The bizarre, downbeat ending—along with a budget that had skyrocketed out of control—led many to believe the film would be a disaster. However, the movie built a steady following in its American showings and went on to be a major moneymaker. The 14-minute ballet is a highlight, and the film is stunningly photographed by cinematographer Jack Cardiff.

On the Town (1949)

MGM

Directors: Stanley Donen and Gene Kelly; **Producer:** Arthur Freed; **Writers:** Adolph Green and Betty Comden; **Music:** Saul Chaplin; **Running time:** 98 minutes

Cast: Gene Kelly (Gabey); Frank Sinatra (Chip); Betty Garrett (Hildy); Ann Miller (Claire); Jules Munshin (Ozzie); Vera Ellen (Ivy Smith)

Oscar nomination: Best Score*

On the Town may not have the pedigree of other famous musicals from the era, but it is certainly one of the liveliest. New York has rarely been portrayed with so much joy and exuberance. Collaborating directors Stanley Donen and Gene Kelly insisted on filming much of the movie on location—a first for a major musical. The slight story tells the adventures of three sailors and the girls they meet during a hectic 24-hour shore leave in New York. Some great tunes, with *New York, New York* (no, not the later career hit for Sinatra) standing out as an all-time great.

An American in Paris (1951)

MGM

Director: Vincente Minnelli; **Producer:** Arthur Freed; **Writer:** Alan Jay Lerner; **Music:** Saul Chaplin (Uncredited); **Running time:** 113 minutes

Cast: Gene Kelly (Jerry Mulligan); Leslie Caron (Lise Bouvier); Oscar Levant (Adam Cook); Georges Guetary (Henri); Nina Foch (Milo Roberts)

Oscar nominations: Picture*, Director, Screenplay*, Score*, Color Cinematography*, Art Direction-Set Decoration* (Color), Costume Design*, Editing

Overshadowed in recent years by the esteem granted to Gene Kelly's other MGM blockbuster, *Singin' in the Rain*, this film is still highly recommended—despite a creaky love story and sight gags that are sometimes painfully outdated. Kelly is an ex-GI working as a starving artist in Paris when he falls in love with his good friend's fiancé (Leslie Caron, replacing pregnant Cyd Charisse). The highlight is the famous 17-minute ballet sequence that cost almost $500,000 to produce. The movie helped establish MGM as *the* home of great movie musicals. Although uncredited, Kelly directed several key sequences. The film made wonderful use of classic George Gershwin songs.

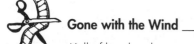

Gone with the Wind

Kelly filmed a dance number, *I've Got a Crush on You*, that was cut in the final edit of *An American in Paris*.

Singin' in the Rain (1952)

MGM

Directors: Stanley Donen and Gene Kelly; **Producers:** Arthur Freed; **Writers:** Adolph Green and Betty Comden; **Running time:** 103 minutes

Cast: Gene Kelly (Don Lockwood); Donald O'Connor (Cosmo Brown); Debbie Reynolds (Kathy Selden); Jean Hagen (Lina Lamont); Mildred Mitchell (R.F. Simpson); Cyd Charisse (Dancer)

Oscar nominations: Score, Supporting Actress (Jean Hagen)

Hoping to capitalize on the success of *An American in Paris*, MGM quickly cobbled together a reunion project for Gene Kelly and Stanley Donen. What emerged was a masterwork. Writers Adolph Green and Betty Comden discovered that MGM's early sound films featured many wonderful songs that had never gained wide exposure. Green and Comden dusted off these songs and used them as the basis of a screenplay about the trials and tribulations endured by people in the film industry when sound was introduced. The new process made plenty of new stars while destroying many established ones. The film ingeniously capitalizes on these dilemmas through some of the most engaging and exuberant musical/comedy sequences ever filmed. Kelly, ever the perfectionist, even found a way to include a wonderful extended fantasy dance number with Cyd Charisse that ranks among the best film sequences of the era. Donald O'Connor's gymnastics in the famed "Make 'Em Laugh" number are so superhuman that today's audiences would mistake them for CGI effects. Debbie Reynolds, an untested 19-year-old at the time, became a major star from her role in this film. The highlight, of course, is Kelly's unforgettable solo in the rain. The image of him hanging from a lamppost, delighted at falling in love, is one of the great images in film history. Thankfully, no one has attempted to remake the film, but as long as Mark Wahlberg is still working there is reason to worry.

Seven Brides for Seven Brothers (1954)

MGM

Director: Stanley Donen; **Producer:** Jack Cummings; **Writers:** Albert Hackett, Frances Goodrich, and Dorothy Kingsley; **Music:** Gene De Paul; **Running time:** 102 minutes

Cast: Howard Keel (Adam Pontipee); Jeff Richards (Benjamin Pontipee); Russ Tamblyn (Gideon Pontipee); Tommy Rall (Frank Pontipee); Marc Platt (Dan Pontipee); Jane Powell (Milly); Julie Newmeyer (Dorcas)

Oscar nominations: Best Picture, Score*, Cinematography (color), Screenplay, Editing

Seven guys living together in a cabin in the wilds with no women anywhere on the horizon. No, it's not the plot for *Brokeback Mountain II*, but the famed MGM musical adapted from Stephen Vincent Benet's *The Sobbin' Women* that in turn has its roots in Plutarch's *The Rape of the Sabine Women*. Got all that? There haven't been too many classic family musicals that evolve from a story with "rape" in the title, but this irresistible confection from director Stanley Donen is as imaginative as it is hokey. Seven lumberjack brothers capture a passel of unwilling brides, and the culture clash that ensues provides the basis for the laughs and extravagant musical numbers, the top of which is the famous barn-raising sequence. Howard Keel and Russ Tamblyn excel among the brothers while Julie Newmeyer got a career boost, changed her name to Julie Newmar, and went on to be the purrfect Catwoman on the *Batman* TV series. Choreography by the legendary Michael Kidd.

"Play It Again, Sam"

The 1970's TV series *Here Come the Brides* was an unofficial rip-off of the film. An official TV series premiered in 1982 but lasted only one season. The film was remade in Bollywood as the 1982 Indian film *Satte Pe Satta*.

Guys and Dolls (1955)

MGM

Director and Writer: Joseph L. Mankiewicz; **Producer:** Samuel Goldwyn; **Original Songs:** Frank Loesser; **Running time:** 150 minutes

Cast: Marlon Brando (Sky Masterson); Jean Simmons (Sarah Brown); Frank Sinatra (Nathan Detroit); Vivian Blaine (Miss Adelaide); Stubby Kaye (Nicely, Nicely)

Oscar nominations: Score, Costume Design, Cinematography (color), Art Direction-Set Decoration (color)

Often criticized as being a "near miss," *Guys and Dolls* is still a commendable adaptation of the triumphant stage hit based on the Damon Runyon story *The Idyll of Miss Sarah Brown.* Brando courageously sings his own songs and acquits himself well, though Jean Simmons was dubbed. Two new songs were written for the film *Adelaide* and *A Woman in Love*, but several others from the stage production were dropped. The simple tale revolves around two rival grifters (Brando and Sinatra) competing to corrupt prim and proper mission worker Simmons. The glorious and rousing production numbers (staged by Michael Kidd) compensate for somewhat stagnant direction.

Hollywood Confidential

The casting of *Guys and Dolls* lends itself to several "what if" scenarios. Gene Kelly was the first choice for the Sky Masterson role but MGM would not lend him out (ironically, the studio ended up distributing the film, though it didn't produce it). Similarly, Betty Grable desperately wanted to play Adelaide, but Fox boss Darryl F. Zanuck wouldn't allow it. At one point, Dean Martin and Jerry Lewis were considered for the roles of Nathan and Sky!

Oklahoma! (1955)

20th Century Fox

Director: Fred Zinnemann; **Producer:** Arthur Hornblow Jr.; **Writers:** Sonia Levien and William Ludwig; **Music:** Richard Rodgers; **Running time:** 145 minutes

Cast: Gordon MacRae (Curly McLain); Gloria Grahame (Ado Annie Carnes); Gene Nelson (Will Parker); Charlotte Greenwood (Aunt Eller Murphy); Shirley Jones (Laurey Williams); Eddie Albert (Ali Hakim)

Oscar nominations: Score*, Sound*, Editing, Cinematography (color)

At the time the most expensive musical ever produced (over $6 million), this adaptation of the Rodgers and Hammerstein 1943 Broadway smash is undoubtedly as long as it is ambitious. Still, it provides a wealth of classic tunes including the title track, *Oh, What a Beautiful Mornin'*, *The Surrey with the Fringe on Top*, and *People Will Say We're in Love*. This has to be the only cowboy film to contain an extended ballet sequence—danced by supporting actor Rod Steiger. This film was an unusual career achievement for director Fred Zinnemann, who is primarily known for his classic dramas. Interestingly, the film was shot twice—once for the Todd A-O process (an early widescreen process) and the other for general Cinemascope prints. There are subtle differences between the two versions.

The King and I (1956)

20th Century Fox

Director: Walter Lang; **Producer:** Charles Brackett; **Writer:** Ernest Lehman; **Music:** Richard Rodgers; **Running time:** 133 minutes

Cast: Deborah Kerr (Anna); Yul Brynner (King Mongkut of Siam); Rita Moreno (Tuptim); Martin Benson (Kralahome); Terry Saunders (Lady Thiang)

Oscar nominations: Best Picture, Director, Actress, Actor*, Cinematography (color), Art Direction-Set Decoration* (color), Sound*, Costume Design*, Score*

Possibly the only people not enchanted by this Rodgers and Hammerstein classic are officials of the government of Thailand (previously known as Siam) who have never officially allowed the film to be shown on the basis of the historical inaccuracies about their beloved king. As portrayed by Yul Brynner in his Oscar-winning performance, the King is a superman to his people but becomes all too human and prone to self-doubt when he meets Anna, a proper English widow who arrives to teach the King's children the ways of the western world. The Broadway production was a smash hit, and this film version was received with equal enthusiasm. Brynner gives the performance of his career as the exasperating, often tyrannical, but ultimately compassionate king and shares wonderful chemistry with Deborah Kerr, replacing the great Gertrude Lawrence who initiated the role on Broadway. (Lawrence was to star in the film version but was stricken by cancer.) It was a remake of the 1946 nonmusical *Anna and the King of Siam* which starred Irene Dunn and Rex Harrison and was remade again in 1999 with Jodie Foster as *Anna and the King*.

Jailhouse Rock (1957)

MGM

Director: Richard Thorpe; **Producer:** Pandro S. Berman; **Writers:** Ned Young and Guy Trosper; **Music:** Jeff Alexander; **Running time:** 96 minutes

Cast: Elvis Presley (Vince Everett); Judy Tyler (Peggy); Mickey Shaughnessy (Hunk); Vaughn Taylor (Mr. Shores/narrator); Jennifer Holden (Sherry); Dean Jones (Teddy Talbot)

Trying to distinguish which Elvis Presley movie is the best might seem as futile as trying to determine which episode of *The Flintstones* most resembles a Bergman film. Under the Svengali-like control of his manager Col. Parker, Elvis' potential to emote onscreen was severely suppressed. However, *Jailhouse Rock*, Elvis's third movie, is a cut above most others in that it has a reasonably engrossing plot and allows The King to perform his musical numbers in a relatively raw way; in addition, his character has some degree of emotional depth, not being the typical Mr. Nice Guy he would later play. Elvis' future movies would largely be indistinguishable "safe" studio productions that watered down his considerable screen presence. However, *Jailhouse Rock* slipped through the veil of mediocrity to rank as his most impressive screen achievement.

Hollywood Confidential

Elvis was devastated by the death of his costar Judy Tyler in an auto accident three days after filming was completed.

Gigi (1958)

MGM

Director: Vincente Minnelli; **Producer:** Arthur Freed; **Writer:** Alan Jay Lerner; **Music:** Frederick Lowe; **Running time:** 119 minutes

Cast: Leslie Caron (Gigi); Maurice Chevalier (Honore Lachaille); Louis Jourdan (Gaston Lachaille); Hermione Gingold (Madame Alvarez); Eva Gabor (Liane)

Oscar nominations: Best Picture*, Director*, Screenplay*, Score*, Song*(*Gigi*), Costume Design*, Editing*, Art Direction-Set Decoration*, Cinematography*

Lerner and Lowe's triumph won nine Oscars (though curiously none of the actors were nominated). The tale of a street waif raised to be the mistress of a wealthy man bares some resemblance to Lerner and Lowe's *My Fair Lady*, but the intoxicating score, sumptuous Parisian locales, and engaging cast make this a classic in its own right. Chevalier and Gingold performing *I Remember It Well* has timeless charm.

Caron played the part on stage, where the story was a nonmusical adaptation of the famous novel by Colette. For the musical screen version, her voice was dubbed, though demos of her test recording sessions have subsequently been released on commercial CD.

"Play It Again, Sam"
The story of Gigi was filmed twice previously as French nonmusical adaptations in 1925 and 1949.

West Side Story (1961)

United Artists

Directors: Robert Wise and Jerome Robbins; **Producer:** Robert Wise; **Writer:** Ernest Lehman; **Composer:** Leonard Bernstein; **Running time:** 152 minutes

Cast: Natalie Wood (Maria); Richard Beymer (Tony); Russ Tamblyn (Riff); Rita Moreno (Anita); George Chakiris (Bernardo); Simon Oakland (Lt. Schrank)

Oscar nominations: Best Picture*, Director*, Screenplay, Editing*, Costume Design*, Art Direction-Set Decoration (color)*, Supporting Actress (Rita Moreno)*, Sound*, Cinematorgraphy (color)*, Score*, Supporting Actor* (George Chakiris)

When *West Side Story* burst upon the screen in 1961, movie audiences had never seen a movie musical like it. The Broadway play had already become a major pop culture phenomenon. *West Side Story* side-stepped the traditions of the musical (the happy-go-lucky love story) to present a biting statement on a lost generation living in the slums of New York. Instead of Fred and Ginger tap-dancing their way through a ballroom, *West Side Story* presents a modern variation of *Romeo and Juliet* with a Puerto Rican girl (Natalie Wood) daring to fall in love with a boy who belongs to a rival Irish gang (Richard Beymer). The racial tensions that run through the story are omnipresent, even during the liveliest production numbers, some of which were elaborately staged on the streets of New York by the great Jerome Robbins. Although Robbins would share the Directing Oscar with Robert Wise, he was fired midway through production due to his perfectionist habits that were driving the film over budget. The film retains its power today and stands as one of the industry's top achievements in the musical genre.

Hollywood Confidential
Natalie Wood's songs were dubbed by Marni Nixon and Richard Beymer's vocals were dubbed by Jimmy Bryant.

The Music Man (1962)

Warner Brothers

Director and Producer: Morton Da Costa; **Writer:** Marion Hargrove; **Music:** Meredith Wilson; **Running time:** 151 minutes

Cast: Robert Preston (Harold Hill); Shirley Jones (Marian Paroo); Buddy Hackett (Marcellus); Hermione Gingold (Eulalie); Paul Ford (Mayor Shin); Pert Kelton (Mrs. Paroo); Ronny Howard (Winthrop)

Oscar nominations: Best Picture, Editing, Costume Design, Sound, Art Direction-Set Decoration (color), Score*

Robert Preston ignited Broadway in the stage version of *The Music Man* and proved wrong studio concerns that he was too old to play the lead in the film version (Frank Sinatra was under consideration for the role). Preston's Harold Hill is like a human tornado, a fast-talking, charming, confidence man who is determined to raise money for a boys marching band in turn-of-the-century River City, then abscond with the money before anyone realizes he has no knowledge of music or instruments. When he falls for the local librarian, who suspects his true nature, Hill tries to fulfill his promise by turning the dreary town into a showplace of music and dance. Lively production numbers include the classic *76 Trombones*, *Till There Was You*, and the foot-stompin' *Trouble*. Ron Howard, little more than a toddler when the film was made, was already a veteran actor!

A Hard Day's Night (1964)

United Artists

Director: Richard Lester; **Producer:** Walter Shenson; **Writer:** Alun Owun; **Songs:** John Lennon, Paul McCartney, and George Harrison; **Incidental Music:** George Martin (uncredited); **Running time:** 87 minutes

Cast: John Lennon (Himself); Paul McCartney (Himself); George Harrison (Himself); Ringo Starr (Himself); Wilfred Brambell (Grandfather)

Oscar nominations: Score, Screenplay

Many years ago, critic Rex Reed derisively referred to the script of *A Hard Day's Night* as a "nonscreenplay." Yet, that is precisely what makes this landmark movie so great. Until *A Hard Day's Night*, rock 'n' roll movies were tame, sanitized affairs designed to conform to older people's senses of morality. This unstructured look at a day in the life of The Beatles took the world by storm by proving the lads from Liverpool were not only great musicians but also had an irreverent nature that astonished critics, who began comparing them to The Marx Brothers. The Beatles get great support from the wonderful character actor Wilfred Brambell as Paul's "clean old man" of a grumpy grandfather. Richard Lester presented the most obvious example of the new wave of European filmmakers: using hand-held cameras and fast-cut editing. There is an energy and pureness to *A Hard Day's Night* that is unmatched by any other musical film of the 1960s

Mary Poppins (1964)

Buena Vista Pictures

Director: Robert Stevenson; **Producer:** Walt Disney; **Writers:** Bill Walsh and Don Da Gradi; **Music:** Richard M. Sherman and Robert B. Sherman; **Running time:** 140 minutes

Cast: Julie Andrews (Mary Poppins); Dick Van Dyke (Bert/Mr. Dawes Sr.); David Tomlinson (George W. Banks); Glynis Johns (Winifred Banks); Hermione Baddedly (Ellen)

Oscar nominations: Best Picture, Director, Actress* (Julie Andrews), Score (adaptation or treatment), Costume Design, Screenplay, Sound, Cinematography (color), Art Direction-Set Decoration (color), Editing*, Music Score (Substantially original)*, Song* (*Chim Chim Cheree)*, Visual Effects*

Walt Disney's dream project for the 1960s was this adaptation of the P.L. Travers book about a magical London nanny who mysteriously appears at a troubled household to take charge of raising a banker's two young children. Julie Andrews, who won an Oscar for her stunning screen debut in this film, often receives the lion's share of the praise at the expense of her costars. In fact, not only is leading man Dick Van Dyke an integral part of the film's appeal, but so too is the picture-perfect supporting cast. The music by the Sherman Brothers is a career highlight, with gem after gem entering popular culture as classics. The unique combination of live action and animation was a stunning effect in 1964. Poetically, Walt Disney lived to see *Mary Poppins* triumph at the 1965 Oscars (he died in 1966), where it won five awards and was nominated for eight others. So enduring is its legacy that the film inspired the recent hit London stage production that opened in 2004.

My Fair Lady (1964)

Warner Brothers

Director: George Cukor; **Producer:** Jack L. Warner; **Writer:** Alan Jay Lerner; **Music:** Frederick Loewe; **Running time:** 170 minutes

Cast: Rex Harrison (Prof. Henry Higgins); Audrey Hepburn (Eliza Doolittle); Stanley Holloway (Alfred P. Doolittle); Wilfred Hyde-White (Col. Hugh Pickering); Gladys Cooper (Mrs. Higgins)

Oscar nominations: Best Picture*, Director*, Actor (Rex Harrison)*, Art Direction-Set Decoration (color)*, Costume Design*, Sound*, Score*, Cinematography (color)*, Supporting Actress (Gladys Cooper), Screenplay, Supporting Actor (Stanley Holloway), Editing

Considered by many to be the best screen adaptation of a musical play, *My Fair Lady* is based on George Bernard Shaw's *Pygmalion*, a slight tale of an aristocratic professor who bets his friend he can turn the street urchin Eliza Doolittle into a sophisticated lady within six months. As Roger Ebert pointed out, it seems incredulous today that the same studios that currently turn out mindless slop once produced films as grand and elegant as this. Not only are stars Rex Harrison and Audrey Hepburn pure perfection, the supporting cast sparkles equally well. The timeless classic songs include *Wouldn't It Be Loverly?*, *With a Little Bit of Luck*, *The Rain in Spain*, *Get Me to the Church on Time*, *On the Street Where You Live*, and *I've Grown Accustomed to Her Face*—all in one film! Hepburn was the only major participant not nominated for an Oscar, perhaps because her songs were dubbed by Marni Nixon. An extensive renovation of the film by historians James A. Harris and James B. Katz in 1994 literally saved the film from deteriorating and brought it back to its original luster.

Robin and the Seven Hoods (1964)

Warner Brothers

Director: Gordon Douglas; **Producer:** Frank Sinatra; **Writer:** David R. Schwartz; **Music:** Nelson Riddle; **Songs:** Jimmy Van Heusen; **Running time:** 123 minutes

Cast: Frank Sinatra (Robbo); Dean Martin (Little John); Sammy Davis Jr. (Will); Bing Crosby (Allen A. Dale); Peter Falk (Guy Gisborne); Barbara Rush (Marion Stevens)

Oscar nominations: Score, Song (*My Kind of Town*)

Considered by many to be the best of the Rat Pack films, this updated version of the Robin Hood legend isn't *really* part of the Rat Pack canon (Peter Lawford and Joey Bishop are missing). This time around, everyone looks like they're really enjoying the proceedings instead of passing time between lounge appearances. Imaginatively set in Prohibition-era Chicago, Sinatra is a crook with a heart involved in a gang war with backstabber Peter Falk. Look for Sammy Davis's superb barroom shoot-'em-up dance sequence and the finale with Sinatra crooning one of his best signature songs, *My Kind of Town*. Bing Crosby makes brief but memorable appearances, especially in the delightful *Mister Booze* song sequence. Edward G. Robinson makes a funny uncredited cameo at the beginning. Why hasn't anyone transformed this into a stage musical?

The Umbrellas of Cherbourg (1964)

Landau Releasing Corporation

Director and Writer: Jacques Demy; **Producer:** Mag Bodard; **Music:** Michel LeGrand; **Running time:** 91 minutes

Cast: Catherine Deneuve (Genevieve); Nino Castelnuovo (Guy); Anne Vernon (Madame Emery); Marc Michel (Roland); Ellen Farner (Madeleine)

Oscar nominations: Best Foreign Film (France), Screenplay, Score (adaptation), Score (original), Song (*I Will Wait For You*)

This is a charming French musical with a unique twist: literally all of the dialogue is sung. Director/writer Jacques Demy also dares to present a rather poignant and downbeat story, relating the tale of a torrid love affair torn apart by dramatic circumstances. The cast is as charming as Michel LeGrand's wonderful score, with 20-year-old Catherine Deneuve radiating an almost surrealistic beauty. The songs include the now-classic *I Will Wait for You*. The master prints of the film had been in a state of alarming deterioration until a major restoration of the film was completed in 1994. In 1967, Demy reunited with Deneuve and LeGrand for a similarly-themed musical, *The Young Girls of Rochefort*, which featured an appearance by Gene Kelly.

The Sound of Music (1965)

20th Century Fox

Director and Producer: Robert Wise; **Writer:** Ernest Lehman; **Music:** Richard Rodgers; **Running time:** 174 minutes

Cast: Julie Andrews (Maria); Christopher Plummer (Capt. Von Trapp); Richard Haydn (Max); Peggy Wood (Mother Abbess); Anna Lee (Sister Margaretta); Portia Nelson (Sister Berthe); Ben Wright (Zeller)

Oscar nominations: Best Picture*, Director*, Actress (Julie Andrews), Score*, Sound*, Editing*, Cinematography (color), Costume Design, Art Direction-Set Decoration (color), Supporting Actress (Peggy Wood)

A rite of passage for many critics is to see how creatively they can dismiss *The Sound of Music*. (It was famously dismissed as *The Sound of Mucus* by one reviewer.) Yet, if the definition of a classic is defined by the legacy a film builds over time, there is no getting around the fact that the public considers this film adaptation of the hit stage play to be one of the all-time greats. The famous line, "The corn is as high as an elephant's eye," was written for *Oklahoma!* But it could easily be applied to the plot of *The Sound of Music*. The saccharine level would pose a danger to a diabetic, but the film works splendidly as entertainment and seems to only get better with each viewing. Although the songs are wonderful, most of the credit goes to Julie Andrews and Christopher Plummer (long underrated for his contribution to the success of this film). Their chemistry onscreen seems the one genuine aspect to contrast the great Ernest Lehman's often-predictable screenplay. The film does add a bit of tension with the Nazi element; the family's attempt to escape still feels suspenseful thanks to old pro Robert Wise in the director's chair. The moving rendition of *Edelweiss* will still bring a lump to your throat. The movie's legacy continues with a new generation who attend "sing-a-long" screenings in theaters around the world.

Camelot (1967)

Warner Brothers

Director: Joshua Logan; **Producer:** Jack L. Warner; **Writer:** Alan Jay Lerner; **Music:** Frederic Lowe; **Running time:** 179 minutes

Cast: Richard Harris (King Arthur); Vanessa Redgrave (Guenevere); Franco Nero (Lancelot); David Hemmings (Mordred); Laurence Naismith (Merlin); Lionel Jeffries (Pellinore)

Oscar nominations: Score*, Art Direction-Set Decoration*, Costume Design*, Sound, Cinematography

Roundly panned at the time of its release as overblown and overlong, *Camelot* was a major financial disappointment for Warner Brothers and helped expedite the erosion of big-budget musicals. Many critics complained that the production too closely resembled the stage production in that it lacked sweep, and director Logan was criticized for his obsession with close-ups. Still, *Camelot* has improved with age and remains popular with fans of traditional Hollywood musicals. The leading actors— who originally had to contend with not being Richard Burton, Julie Andrews and Robert Goulet from the stage production—now seem perfectly suitable in their roles. While a flawed film, the score is magnificent, and even a lesser musical from this era now towers over most films produced today.

Chitty Chitty Bang Bang (1968)

United Artists

Director: Ken Hughes; **Producer:** Albert R. Broccoli; **Writer:** Roald Dahl, Ken Hughes, and Richard Maibaum (additional dialogue); **Running time:** 144 minutes

Cast: Dick Van Dyke (Caractacus Potts); Sally Ann Howes (Truly Scrumptious); Lionel Jeffries (Grandpa Potts); Gert Frobe (Baron Bomburst)

Oscar nomination: Song (*Chitty Chitty Bang Bang*)

Producer Cubby Broccoli assembled much of the stock company from his James Bond films for this big-budget screen version of the only children's story ever written by Ian Fleming. A box-office disappointment in 1968, the movie has become a cult classic in ensuing years, especially in England where the car itself has achieved an iconic status. (The vehicle is now owned by former professional clown Pierre Picton.) Although overlong and occasionally suffering from a sluggish pace, *Chitty* provides some lovely melodies and the theme song is down-right contagious. The real star is production designer Ken Adam, whose ingenious sets and design of the car rival his best work in the Bond series.

"Play It Again, Sam"
One of the few movies to inspire a subsequent play. *Chitty* ran for years as a smash hit in London's West End before moving to Broadway.

Funny Girl (1968)

Columbia Pictures

Director: William Wyler; **Producer:** Ray Stark; **Writer:** Isobel Lennart; **Original Songs:** James F. Hanley, Grant Clarke, Maurice Yvain, and Billy Rose; **Running time:** 151 minutes

Cast: Barbra Streisand (Fanny Brice); Omar Sharif (Nicky Arnstein); Kay Medford (Rose Brice); Ann Francis (Georgia); Walter Pidgeon (Flo Ziegfeld)

Classic quote: "Hello, Gorgeous!"

Oscar nominations: Best Picture, Actress* (Streisand tied with Katherine Hepburn for *The Lion in Winter*), Supporting Actress (Kay Medford), Score, Cinematography, Sound, Editing, Song (*Funny Girl*)

Swimming against the tide of big budget screen musicals that flopped in the late 1960s, *Funny Girl* provided a smashing screen debut for Barbra Streisand. Loosely based on the life of Ziegfeld girl Fanny Brice, Streisand performs like a force of nature. Director William Wyler's innovative use of a helicopter to shoot Streisand's big number on a New York ferry is a classic Hollywood image.

Oliver! (1968)

Columbia Pictures

Director: Carol Reed; **Producer:** John Woolf; **Writer:** Vernon Harris; **Music:** Lionel Bart; **Running time:** 153 minutes

Cast: Ron Moody (Fagin); Shanni Wallis (Nancy); Oliver Reed (Bill Sikes); Harry Secombe (Mr. Bumble); Mark Lester (Oliver Twist); Jack Wild (Artful Dodger); Hugh Griffith (The Magistrate)

Oscar nominations: Best Picture*, Director*, Cinematography, Sound*, Art Direction-Set Decoration*, Score*, Editing, Actor (Ron Moody), Costume Design, Supporting Actor (Jack Wild), Screenplay. Special Oscar granted to Oona White for her outstanding choreography.

The last great musical of the 1960s, *Oliver!* is the screen adaptation of the smash hit stage production that debuted in London in 1960. The screen version wisely passed up "name" stars and retained several actors from the London cast, including Ron Moody, who makes for a deliciously villainous Fagin. The rich production values add to the atmosphere of one of the few musicals that has such a bittersweet and often tragic storyline. What may surprise movie fans is the revelation that angelic Mark Lester's voice was dubbed by a 20-year-old female named Kathe Green, who was paid 400 pounds for her work under the condition she keep her participation secret! The film was a major Oscar winner in 1969 but the success of *Oliver!* could not offset other high profile flops (*Paint Your Wagon, Hello Dolly!*) that all but ended the glorious era of big budget screen musicals.

"Play It Again, Sam"

Charles Dickins' novel has been transferred to the screen numerous times dating back to the silent era. Prior to *Oliver!*, the most acclaimed version was David Lean's 1948 classic *Oliver Twist* starring Alec Guiness.

CHAPTER 5
Romance
"Here's Lookin' at You, Kid."

When the first filmed kiss was shown to the public in an 1896 one-minute short titled—surprisingly—*The Kiss*, it caused a furor with critics citing that such permissiveness represented a perversion of morality. The mind reels at the reaction if these folks could only have seen the hair goo sequence in *There's Something About Mary*. In spite of the dissenting voices of the critics, *The Kiss* foresaw that the evolving motion picture technology would make romance a mainstay of the film industry. Indeed, a scant four years later, Thomas Edison would produce his own version of *The Kiss*, also lasting one minute, albeit with two new actors. This must surely count as the earliest remake.

Romance proved to be among the most durable of film genres. Westerns, musicals, and war movies have had significant peaks and valleys in terms of popularity, but there has been an unwavering and insatiable appetite on the part of moviegoers for love stories. Needless to say, this genre—like all others—evolved in ways that would have been unthinkable to the major studios decades ago. Today's emphasis on realism has brought nudity and profanity to the world of romance, not always to the betterment of the industry. It is clear that many great romantic films have suffered from being watered down by production code standards that seemed archaic even in their day. Yet, there is a timeless quality to the great romances, and their relative chasteness somehow makes them seem all the more erotic.

When Burt Lancaster and Deborah Kerr roll passionately in the surf in *From Here to Eternity*, it defies belief that the scene would have been more torrid if it were performed sans clothing. A great, well-told love story primarily needs characters we can relate to and care about, played by charismatic leading actors. For the most shining example of this, simply look at David Lean's *Brief Encounter*, the 1946 film that tells one of the most haunting love stories of all—even though the participants never consummate their romance in the physical sense.

Unlike many other genres, Hollywood can still make a good love story. For this writer's money, the most moving film romance of recent vintage was *The Bridges of Madison County*, directed, most unlikely, by Clint Eastwood. The industry has also shown signs of a refreshing maturity in accommodating more avante garde looks at romances, as evidenced by the acclaim accorded to *Brokeback Mountain*. Decades ago, the participants in a gay cowboy story would have found their careers ruined. The gamut has run full circle, and we might well expect a tidal wave of *Brokeback* rip-offs and clones to follow. Don't be surprised to see Sam Peckinpah's *Ride the High Country* be remade as *Ride the Guy Country*.

Grand Hotel (1932)

MGM

Director: Edmund Goulding; **Producer:** Irving Thalberg (uncredited); **Writer:** William A. Drake; **Running time:** 112 minutes

Cast: Greta Garbo (Gruskinsaya); John Barrymore (Baron Von Geigern); Joan Crawford (Flaemmchen); Wallace Beery (Preysing); Lionel Barrymore (Kringelein)

Oscar nominations: Best Picture*

Although this early sound film creaks with age, its significance should not be understated. This was arguably the first "all-star cast" movie ever made, chronicling the intertwined relationships of a group of people staying at a hotel in Berlin—picture *Airport* with room service. MGM mogul Irving Thalberg wanted desperately to bring the bestselling German novel and the subsequent hit stage play to the screen. Despite an avalanche of bogus studio press releases about how the stars enjoyed working together, the truth is they detested the idea, and great pains were taken to prevent clashing egos. The great Garbo was so threatened by up-and-coming Joan Crawford that the two never spoke during the entire production. Director Goulding often filmed stars separately, then used editing to make them appear as though they were in the same scene! Still, the film was a blockbuster in its day. It won the Oscar for Best Picture, though curiously received no other nominations.

Anna Karenina (1935)

MGM

Director: Clarence Brown; **Producer:** David O. Selznick; **Writers:** Clemence Dane, Salka Viertel, and S.N. Behrman; **Music:** Herbert Sothart; **Running time:** 95 minutes

Cast: Greta Garbo (Anna Karenina); Fredric March (Vronsky); Freddie Bartholomew (Sergei); Maureen O'Sullivan (Kitty); Basil Rathbone (Karenin)

This reasonably faithful adaptation of Tolstoy's classic novel was custom-made for Greta Garbo, who was at the peak of her career. Garbo's first rendition of the story in the 1927 silent film *Love* was a rare box-office failure for the great sex symbol. This MGM version, with high production values and a great cast, was far more successful. The brooding beauty plays the title character who gives up her husband and son to be with a man she is infatuated with—only to find that there may be disastrous consequences for pursuing her dreams. Those not familiar with the novel may find the ending to be a bit of a jolt. However, the film continues to resonate thanks in part to its impressive cast.

Jezebel (1938)

Warner Brothers

Director and Producer: William Wyler; **Writer:** Clements Ripley, Abem Finkel, John Huston, and Robert Buckner; **Music:** Max Steiner; **Running time:** 103 minutes

Cast: Bette Davis (Julie Marsden); Henry Fonda (Preston Dillard); George Brent (Buck Cantrell); Margaret Lindsay (Amy Bradford Dillard); Donald Crisp (Dr. Livingston)

Oscar nominations: Best Picture, Actress* (Bette Davis), Supporting Actress* (Fay Bainter), Cinematography, Score

Perhaps as compensation for Bette Davis losing the role of Scarlett O'Hara in *Gone with the Wind*, this opulent pre-Civil War romance was put on the fast track and beat *GWTW* into theaters. Davis has a field day as the strong-willed belle whose impertinent, spoiled nature wreaks havoc on her relationship with fiancé Henry Fonda. The scene in which Davis decides to spurn the tradition of a maiden wearing a white gown to a dress ball, choosing instead to appear in "scandalous" red, is a great movie moment. Davis received compensation for the loss of the O'Hara role by winning an Oscar for her performance in this film.

Dark Victory (1939)

Warner Brothers

Director: Edmund Goulding; **Producers:** Hal B. Wallis and David Lewis; **Writer:** Casey Robinson; **Music:** Max Steiner; **Running time:** 104 minutes

Cast: Bette Davis (Judith Traherne); George Brent (Dr. Frederick Steele); Humphrey Bogart (Michael O'Leary); Geraldine Fitzgerald (Ann King); Ronald Reagan (Alec Hamm)

Oscar nominations: Best Picture, Actress (Bette Davis), Score

A classic soap opera with an impressive cast from the Warner Brothers "stable" of contract players. Bette Davis is a young woman suffering from a terminal brain tumor. She begins a love affair with her doctor (George Brent) who unsuccessfully tries to hide the diagnosis from her. When she discovers the truth, it leads her to make momentous decisions in how she will spend her last days—and not all of her choices are very dignified. It was said the film sold countless boxes of Kleenex upon its release and, though somewhat dated, it still packs an emotional resonance due to Davis's strong performance. Ronald Reagan has an early supporting role.

"Play It Again, Sam"

It was remade as *Stolen Hours* (aka *Summer Flight*) with Susan Hayward in 1963 and as a well-received TV movie with Elizabeth Montgomery and Anthony Hopkins in 1976.

Gone with the Wind (1939)

MGM

Director: Victor Fleming; **Producer:** David O. Selznick; **Writer:** Sidney Howard; **Music:** Max Steiner; **Running time:** 222 minutes

Cast: Clark Gable (Rhett Butler); Vivien Leigh (Scarlett O'Hara); Leslie Howard (Ashley Wilkes); Olivia De Haviland (Melanie Wilkes); Thomas Mitchell (Gerald O'Hara); Hattie McDaniel (Mammy)

Oscar nominations: Best Picture*, Director*, Score, Sound, Actor (Clark Gable), Actress* (Vivien Leigh), Supporting Actress (Olivia De Haviland), Supporting Actress* (Hattie McDaniel), Art Direction*, Cinematography* (color), Screenplay*, Editing*, Special Effects. Two Honorary awards for technical achievements.

The granddaddy of all motion picture epics, *Gone with the Wind* had the unenviable task of living up to enormous expectations generated by the reverence held for Margaret Mitchell's only novel, which had become a cultural phenomenon. That the production company fulfilled or exceeded expectations does not mean this was an easy film to get off the ground. Volumes have been written on the pitfalls, second-guesses, and production problems that plagued the entire film. Yet, what emerged is about as splendid in movie entertainment as one could imagine. Time has done nothing to diminish its impact (although the racial stereotypes cause one to squirm today). Magnificent on every level—and next time you watch it, try to recognize how Max Steiner's sweeping and epic score contributes immeasurably to the overall greatness of the production. It's unfathomable to imagine *Gone with the Wind* without this classic score.

Hollywood Confidential

Some interesting facts about the film:

- Producer Selznick resisted demands that he take "damn" out of Rhett Butler's famous closing line. He opted to pay a $5,000 fine to keep the line intact.
- African-American Oscar-winner Hattie McDaniel opted not to attend the film's premiere in Atlanta because state law still enforced segregation in theaters.
- The film spawned a much-delayed sequel, the 1994 TV movie *Scarlett* with Timothy Dalton and Joanne Whalley-Kilmer as Rhett and Scarlet.

Wuthering Heights (1939)

United Artists

Director: William Wyler; **Producer:** Samuel Goldwyn; **Writers:** Charles MacArthur and Ben Hecht; **Music:** Alfred Newman; **Running time:** 103 minutes

Cast: Merle Oberon (Cathy); Laurence Olivier (Heathcliff); David Niven (Edgar Linton); Flora Robson (Ellen); Donald Crisp (Dr. Kenneth)

Oscar nominations: Best Picture, Actor (Laurence Olivier), Supporting Actress (Geraldine Fitzgerald), Director, Screenplay, Art Direction-Set Decoration, Cinematography* (b&w), Score

Although this prestigious adaptation of Emily Bronte's classic romance covers only the first half of the book, director William Wyler fashioned an emotionally riveting work of art. The famous tale of the trials and tribulations of a young man and woman who were raised together only to have fate intercede in their love affair has been oft filmed, but none so grandly as this. The movie made Olivier a top leading man, though he didn't prevail in his quest to have wife Vivien Leigh play Cathy. (Her "consolation prize" was getting the role of Scarlett O'Hara in *Gone with the Wind*.) The scenes on the Yorkshire moors were actually shot in Southern California! Brilliant camerawork won an Oscar for Gregg Toland. Among the best remakes is the unheralded 1970 version with Timothy Dalton as Heathcliff.

Penny Serenade (1941)

Columbia Pictures

Director and Producer: George Stevens; **Writer:** Morrie Ryskind; **Music:** W. Franke Harling; **Running time:** 119 minutes

Cast: Irene Dunne (Julie Gardiner Adams); Cary Grant (Roger Adams); Beulah Bondi (Mrs. Oliver); Edgar Buchanan (Applejack Carney)

Oscar nominations: Actor (Cary Grant)

Following their teaming in the hit comedies *The Awful Truth* and *My Favorite Wife*, Cary Grant and Irene Dunne reunited under George Stevens's direction for this sentimental and very dramatic look at a childless couple who adopt a little girl only to see their happiness turn to tragedy. Grant and Dunne convincingly portray everyday, middle-class people, and their chemistry compensates for some of the more predictable elements of the film. It's impossible not to be moved by the dramatic events that unfold under Stevens's skillful direction.

Casablanca (1942)

Warner Brothers

Director: Michael Curtiz; **Producer:** Hal B. Wallis; **Writers:** Julius Epstein, Philip G. Epstein, and Howard Koch; **Music:** Max Steiner; **Running time:** 102 minutes

Cast: Humphrey Bogart (Rick Blaine); Ingrid Bergman (Ilsa); Paul Henreid (Victor Laszlo); Claude Rains (Capt. Renault); Conrad Veidt (Major Strasser); Sydney Greenstreet (Ferrari); Peter Lorre (Ugarte)

Oscar nominations: Best Picture*, Director*, Screenplay*, Actor (Humphrey Bogart), Score, Supporting Actor (Claude Rains), Editing, Cinematography (b&w)

Certain films have a hard time living up to their reputation as a classic. *Casablanca* is not one of them. Recently, my daughter and her friends at college watched the film for the first time, and the general consensus is that it was perhaps the greatest movie ever made. To have such an emotional impact on succeeding generations, a film has to reach levels of virtual perfection—and *Casablanca* does. The film was based on an unproduced play titled *Everybody Comes to Ricks*. Although it was a prestigious production, no one envisioned its enduring legacy, even after the film won the Best Picture Oscar. Yet, over the years, *Casablanca* has gone from being a classic film to achieving a status as an integral part of international popular culture. Nothing epitomizes its impact more than the treasure-trove of classic lines of dialogue from the film that are now recited verbatim by generations of movie fans—an occurrence not repeated until *The Godfather* in 1972. Though for the record, Bogart never says "Play it again, Sam." His actual line is "Play it, Sam. Play *As Time Goes By*." Incidentally, the film spawned two short-lived TV series both titled *Casablanca* in 1955 and 1983 (with Charles McGraw and David Soul, respectively, playing the Bogart role).

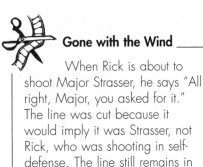

Gone with the Wind

When Rick is about to shoot Major Strasser, he says "All right, Major, you asked for it." The line was cut because it would imply it was Strasser, not Rick, who was shooting in self-defense. The line still remains in the trailer, however."

Now, Voyager (1942)

Warner Brothers

Director: Irving Rapper; **Producer:** Hal B. Wallis; **Writer:** Casey Robinson; **Music:** Max Steiner; **Running time:** 117 minutes

Cast: Bette Davis (Charlotte Vale); Paul Henreid (Jerry Durrance); Claude Rains (Dr. Jacquith); Gladys Cooper (Mrs. Vale); Bonita Granville (June Vale)

Oscar nominations: Actress (Bette Davis), Supporting Actress (Gladys Cooper), Music*

Female moviegoers went starry-eyed over this Bette Davis tearjerker. Perhaps the on-going misery of WWII gave an appreciation to this escapist fare that may have eluded it had it been released a few years earlier or later, but the film has become synonymous with the type of crowd-pleasing fare that Warner Brothers produced during this period. The story centers on Charlotte (Davis), a matronly young woman driven to near-insanity by her dominating mother (Gladys Cooper). She seeks psychiatric care only to fall in love with her married, dashing shrink (Paul Henreid). Although she knows he'll never leave his wife, in a strange twist she ends up virtually raising *his* daughter, who is suffering from severe psychiatric problems of her own. (If only Jerry Springer had been around in '42, these folks would have been a natural for an entire segment of his show.) A corny but memorable film, with Henreid's simultaneous lighting of two cigarettes a classic cinematic moment. Max Steiner's Oscar-winning score suits the mood perfectly, though Davis complained it overwhelmed her performance.

Brief Encounter (1945)

Universal Pictures

Director: David Lean; **Producer:** Noel Coward, Anthony Havelock-Allan, and Ronald Neame; **Writers:** Noel Coward, David Lean, and Anthony Havelock-Allan; **Running time:** 86 minutes

Cast: Celia Johnson (Laura Jesson); Trevor Howard (Dr. Alec Harvey); Stanley Holloway (Albert Godby); Joyce Carey (Myrtle)

Oscar nominations: Director, Actress (Celia Johnson), Screenplay

There have been glitzier love stories brought to the screen, but few with as much heart and genuine emotion as *Brief Encounter*. Based on Noel Coward's play *Still Life*, the simple, low-budget production was filmed in London in the dreary aftermath of WWII. Celia Johnson and Trevor Howard give brilliant performances as happily married professional people who meet by chance on several occasions while commuting to work. A platonic relationship gradually grows until both realize they are madly in love with each other. Yet both are torn by guilt over their feelings. The film refreshingly neither sentimentalizes nor vilifies their spouses, and the point is, you can be very much in love with one person but still fall in love with another. The film's tension derives from whether their platonic love will become physical. An emotionally shattering film superbly directed by David Lean. Remade as a TV movie in 1974, with Richard Burton and Sophia Loren who were far too glamorous to be convincing as the everyday people who fall in love.

The Heiress (1949)

Paramount Pictures

Director and Producer: William Wyler; **Writers:** Ruth Goetz and Augustus Goetz; **Music:** Aaron Copland; **Running time:** 115 minutes

Cast: Olivia de Havilland (Catherine Sloper); Montgomery Clift (Morris Townsend); Ralph Richardson (Dr. Austin Sloper); Miriam Hopkins (Livinia Penniman)

Oscar nominations: Best Picture, Director, Actress* (Olivia de Havilland), Cinematography (b&w), Supporting Actor (Ralph Richardson), Art Direction-Set Decoration* (b&w), Costume Design*, Score*

Olivia de Haviland won a second Oscar for her performance in this film adaptation of a play based on Henry James's novel. Set in pre-Civil War New York City, de Havilland is the plain-Jane daughter of tyrannical rich man Ralph Richardson, who dominates her every move trying to ward off suitors who may be fortune hunters.

Ultimately, she becomes involved with a young man (Montgomery Clift) who professes to want to marry her, but who may be harboring more sinister intentions. Unusually depressing for a major studio romance, *The Heiress* is a great film because the studio resisted any temptation to sanitize the characters, each of whom is unsympathetic in many ways. The biting tale was a multiple Oscar winner and retains its punch today, though Clift still seems a bit uneasy playing a rogue. Remade as *Washington Square* in 1997 with Ben Chaplin and Jennifer Jason Leigh.

Roman Holiday (1953)

Paramount Pictures

Director and Producer: William Wyler; **Writers:** Ian McLellan Hunter, John Dighton, and Dalton Trumbo (Trumbo uncredited); **Music:** George Auric; **Running time:** 118 minutes

Cast: Gregory Peck (Joe Bradley); Audrey Hepburn (Princess Ann); Eddie Albert (Irving Radovitch); Hartley Power (Mr. Hennessey); Harcourt Williams (Ambassador)

Oscar nominations: Best Picture, Director, Actress* (Audrey Hepburn), Editing, Cinematography (b&w), Art Direction-Set Decoration (b&w), Screenplay, Writing* (motion picture story), Supporting Actor (Eddie Albert), Costume Design*

Audrey Hepburn's star-making romantic comedy won her an Oscar in her first Hollywood film. She plays a princess who is distraught at being the center of social events and a target for the paparazzi. She flies the coop on a European tour and, while a massive manhunt takes place for her, American reporter Gregory Peck accidentally makes her acquaintance and pretends not to know her identity as he guides her on an unforgettable day around Rome. One of the most charming romances in screen history, *Roman Holiday* was a rare comedic outing for director William Wyler. Eddie Albert shines as Peck's photographer who secretly trails the couple. Remade as a forgettable 1987 TV movie with Catherine Oxenberg and Tom Conti.

Hollywood Confidential

Frank Capra was supposed to direct the film but backed out when he discovered blacklisted writer Dalton Trumbo was using Ian McLellan Hunter as his "front." Ironically, Hunter was awarded the Oscar for his script. In 1993, the Academy issued a second Oscar posthumously to Trumbo and his name has been added to the restored version of the film.

A Star Is Born (1954)

Warner Brothers

Director: George Cukor; **Producer:** Sidney Luft; **Writer:** Moss Hart; **Songs:** Harold Arlen; **Running time:** 154 minutes

Cast: Judy Garland (Esther Blodgett/Vicky Lester); James Mason (Norman Maine); Jack Carson (Matt Libby); Charles Bickford (Oliver Niles); Tom Noonan (Danny McGuire)

Oscar nominations: Actress (Judy Garland), Actor (James Mason), Song (*The Man That Got Away*), Score, Costume Design (color), Art Direction-Set Decoration (color)

Director George Cukor had filmed this American tragedy once before as *What Price Hollywood?* in 1932. In 1937, the story was shot again as *A Star is Born* with Frederic March and Janet Gaynor. Judy Garland had appeared in a radio version of the story of a talented young singer nurtured to fame and fortune by her alcoholic husband, once a great star in his own right. As her career skyrockets, his declines, leading to jealousy and emotionally devastating consequences. When MGM refused her request to finance an updated version of the film, Garland and her husband Sidney Luft formed their own production company and got Warner Brothers to back the project.

Gone with the Wind

Following the film's initial release, Warner Brothers cut 27 minutes of footage including several pivotal scenes. They were partially restored in 1981. In a cruel twist of fate, Cukor died the evening before he was about to see his restored masterpiece.

The film provides Garland with what is unquestionably her greatest performance onscreen. Even more magnificent is James Mason (in a role declined by Cary Grant), whose Norman Maine undergoes a physical and emotional decline almost unbearable to watch. Although a drama, the film contains many classic musical numbers including Garland's tremendous version of *Born in a Trunk*. The film was remade yet again in 1976 with Barbra Streisand and Kris Kristofferson. Critics snickered, but it proved to be a big box-office hit.

Summertime (1955)

United Artists

Director: David Lean; **Producer:** Ilya Lopert; **Writers:** David Lean and H.E. Bates; **Music:** Alessandro Cicognini; **Running time:** 100 minutes

Cast: Katharine Hepburn (Jane Hudson); Rossano Brazzi (Renato De Rossi); Isa Miranda (Signora Fiorini); Darren McGavin (Eddie Yeager); Mari Aldon (Phyl Yeager)

Oscar nominations: Actress (Katharine Hepburn), Director

David Lean's simple but timeless love story centers on spinster Hepburn taking her dream trip to Venice, accompanied only by her omnipresent movie camera. A chance encounter with a suave local man (Brazzi) leads to a budding romance—and some unexpected complications when she discovers he is actually married. Lean shot the entire film on location, foregoing studio shots for the actual grandeur of Venice. The location work adds immeasurably to the atmosphere of what is actually a very modest story. However, Hepburn is sensational as the vulnerable, lonely woman who first resists her romantic impulses only to succumb to them and enjoy life for the first time. Wonderful cinematography by Jack Hildyard. Released in the UK under the title *Summer Madness*.

An Affair to Remember (1957)

20th Century Fox

Director: Leo McCary; **Producers:** Leo McCary and Jerry Wald; **Writers:** Delmer Daves, Donald Ogden Stewart (uncredited), and Leo McCary; **Music:** Hugo Friedhofer; **Running time:** 119 minutes

Cast: Cary Grant (Nickie Ferrante); Deborah Kerr (Terry McKay); Richard Denning (Ken); Neva Patterson (Lois Clark); Cathleen Nesbitt (Grandmother Janjou)

Oscar nomintions: Song (An Affair to Remember), Score, Costume Design, Cinematography

This legendary weeper is a timeless favorite among soap-opera lovers, though the male of the species may well be hitting the "fast forward" button to reach the syrupy conclusion. Cary Grant and Deborah Kerr meet on a transatlantic voyage and fall passionately in love—despite the fact that they are both engaged to other people. They agree to wait six months and if they still feel passionately about each other, they will call off their weddings to marry each other. The plan is to meet at a specified date at the Empire State Building. You don't have to be Kreskin to predict that a hitch in the plan develops and leads to a devastating misunderstanding. The film relies almost entirely on the considerable charisma of its two glamorous stars, both of whom have never looked better. However, the pace ultimately drags, especially when the awful children's songs by Harry Warren are shoehorned into the production.

"Play It Again, Sam"

An Affair to Remember is a remake of *Love Affair*, a 1939 romance starring Irene Dunne and Charles Boyer. *That* film was remade in 1994 starring Warren Beatty and Annette Benning, though its generally best remembered for being Katharine Hepburn's final film. *An Affair to Remember* also figures heavily in the plot of the 1993 romance *Sleepless in Seattle*.

On the Beach (1959)

United Artists

Director and Producer: Stanley Kramer; **Writer:** John Paxton; **Music:** Ernest Gold; **Running time:** 134 minutes

Cast: Gregory Peck (Dwight Towers); Ava Gardner (Moira Davidson); Fred Astaire (Julian Osborne); Anthony Perkins (Peter Holmes); Donna Anderson (Mary Holmes)

Oscar nominations: Score, Editing

The release of Stanley Kramer's *On the Beach* at the height of the Cold War era ignited heated political debates. Liberals embraced its pacifist message while conservatives dismissed its plea for nuclear disarmament as hopelessly naive. What is certain is that this is an example of powerful, moving filmmaking. The doomsday scenario looks at the lives of Australians as they await the slow-moving radioactive winds that have wiped out all other life on earth after a nuclear war has erupted. (The specifics of which are never discussed.) Gregory Peck is the captain of a U.S. sub stranded in Melbourne, and he begins a sorrowful, desperate love affair with cynical party girl Ava Gardner. The film features haunting and powerful scenes such as the sub's eerie return to San Francisco to trace unexplained radio signals. The performances are terrific, even if the American attempts at Australian accents fall short. Fred Astaire made an impact in his first dramatic role. Ernest Gold's wonderful score, with strains of *Waltzing Matilda*, earned an Oscar nomination ... and the film's final scenes are devastating in their impact.

Some Came Running (1958)

MGM

Director: Vincente Minnelli; **Producer:** Sol C. Siegel; **Writers:** John Patrick and Arthur Sheekman; **Music:** Elmer Bernstein; **Running time:** 137 minutes

Cast: Frank Sinatra (Dave Hirsh); Dean Martin (Bama Dillert); Shirley MacLaine (Ginny); Martha Hyer (Gwen); Arthur Kennedy (Frank Hirsh)

Oscar nominations: Actress (Shirley MacLaine), Supporting Actress (Martha Hyer), Supporting Actor (Arthur Kennedy), Song (*To Love and Be Loved*), Costume Design

This long but highly-engrossing drama finds Sinatra as a famous writer who returns to his small hometown in Indiana after serving in WWII. He finds he's still the local black sheep, ostensibly welcomed by the pretentious townspeople, but secretly resented by all of them including his estranged brother (Arthur Kennedy). Much of the film centers on Sinatra juggling his love affairs with both "good girl" Martha Hyer and lovable tramp Shirley MacLaine. The tension rises and leads to a tragic conclusion. Sinatra and Martin's first on-screen team-up is impressive enough to remind one of how they would later squander their talents. Martin in particular is very amusing as the local grafter/playboy. MacLaine is wonderful as the "bad girl" desperate to find a bit of human compassion among the townspeople. Elmer Bernstein's hard-driving score is a classic.

Breakfast at Tiffanys (1961)

Paramount Pictures

Director: Blake Edwards; **Producers:** Richard Shepherd and Martin Jurow; **Writer:** George Axelrod; **Music:** Henry Mancini; **Running time:** 115 minutes

Cast: Audrey Hepburn (Holly Golightly); George Peppard (Paul "Fred" Varjak); Patricia Neal (Mrs. Failenson); Buddy Ebsen (Doc Golightly); Martin Balsam (O.J. Berman); Mickey Rooney (Mr. Yunioshi)

Oscar nominations: Actress (Audrey Hepburn), Screenplay, Art Direction-Set Decoration (Color), Score*, Song* (*Moon River*)

Truman Capote's novella is transferred to the screen with Audrey Hepburn as the madcap libertine, Holly Golightly, one of the screen's all-time great roles for a leading lady. George Peppard (playing a heterosexualized version of Capote's gay alter ego from the book) is the straight-laced writer/neighbor who falls for this liberated woman with attributes that call to mind Sally Bowles of *Cabaret* a girl with a beatnik attitude just as the counter-culture was taking hold. The film and Holly seem a bit too pretentiously cute by today's standards, but there's no denying the charm of the outstanding cast. (The sequence between Hepburn and Buddy Ebsen is especially moving.) However, the usually great Mickey Rooney doesn't gel with an over-the-top caricature of a Japanese neighbor that probably did more damage to the Japanese culture than the dropping of both atomic bombs. Henry Mancini's score is one of the all-time greats. Incidentally, Patricia Neal has long complained that her role was substantially reduced at the urging of Peppard, and she admits to carrying a grudge over the matter to this day.

Hollywood Confidential

When Paramount executives first saw the film, they agreed that one song had to go because it slowed down the pace: *Moon River*. Hepburn objected and prevailed. The film won the Best Song Oscar the following year.

Jules and Jim (1961)

Janus Films

Director: Francois Truffaut; **Producer:** Marcel Berbert; **Writers:** Francois Truffaut and Jean Gruault; **Music:** Georges Delerue; **Running time:** 105 minutes

Cast: Jeanne Moreau (Catherine); Oscar Werner (Jules); Henri Serre (Jim); Vanna Urbino (Gilberte); Bassiak (Albert)

The definitive New Wave movie from French director Francois Truffaut epitomizes the type of ground-breaking cinema originating in Europe during the post-war years through the 1960s. The simple tale concerns a ménage a trois between three young people in pre-war Paris. Jules and his best friend Jim are hopelessly smitten by Catherine, a free-spirited beautiful young woman who prides herself on defying society's idea of conventional behavior. Although she marries Jules, over the years the love affair expands to include Jim as well—though both men realize soon enough that Catherine is a high maintenance woman and that she may indeed be quite mad. The film's offbeat style may not entice everyone, but *Jules and Jim* requires multiple viewings to appreciate its unique qualities. The cinematography is innovative, the cast is glorious, and the music is enticing. The unexpected finale still sends a shock to the system.

Splendor in the Grass (1961)

Warner Brothers

Director and Producer: Elia Kazan; **Writer:** William Inge; **Music:** David Amram; **Running time:** 124 minutes

Cast: Natalie Wood (Wilma Dean "Deanie" Loomis); Warren Beatty (Bud Stamper); Pat Hingle (Ace Stamper); Audrey Christie (Mrs. Loomis); Barbara Loden (Ginny Stamper)

Oscar nominations: Actress (Natalie Wood), Screenplay*

Gone with the Wind

The sequence in which Natalie Wood storms out of a bathtub during an argument with her mother included a shot of her running down a hallway with her derriere exposed. Censorship pressure resulted in the scene being trimmed, but stills of it survive.

There had been plenty of films dealing with teenage angst prior to *Splendor in the Grass*, but none explored repressed love and sexuality as forthrightly and honestly. Natalie Wood and Warren Beatty are teen high school lovers in a small Kansas town in the 1920's. They struggle to stay together despite the constant intrusions and objections of their parents—an obstacle that eventually drives Wood's character to an insane asylum. The film refuses to provide the kind of contrived, happy ending one might expect, and its sobering storyline provides plenty of dramatic sequences for its talented young leads. Expertly directed by legendary Elia Kazan, who always excelled in bringing out the best in his actors. The film marked the screen debuts of Sandy Dennis and—of all people—Phyllis Diller.

A Man and a Woman (1966)

Allied Artists

Director and Producer: Claude Lelouch; **Writers:** Pierre Uytterhoeven and Claude Lelouch (uncredited); **Music:** Francis Lai; **Running time:** 102 minutes

Cast: Anouk Aimee (Anne Gauthier); Jean Louis Trintignant (Jean-Louis Duroc); Pierre Barouh (Pierre Gautier); Valerie Lagrange (Valerie Duroc)

Oscar nominations: Best Foreign Language Film*, Director, Screenplay*, Actress (Anouk Aimee)

One of the few foreign language films to make a considerable dent at the US box-office, French director Claude Lelouch's *A Man and a Woman* (aka *Un Homme et Une Femme*) is one of the ultimate chick-flicks of the 60s. The simple story finds a young widow trying to find love once again through a relationship with a handsome widower. As one would expect in a French romance, the new man of interest isn't named Murray and doesn't work the *fromage* counter in the local supermarket. He's a race car driver, and this allows the couple to embark on a whirlwind romance even as she questions whether she is capable of releasing herself from the attachment to her deceased husband. Visually stunning, with a great score by Francis Lai, the story is told with a minimum of dialogue. Uniquely, half the film is in black and white, the other half in color. Director Lelouch teamed the actors again in 1986 for the sequel, *A Man and a Woman: 20 Years Later* but the film was largely dismissed by critics who felt it was quite inferior to the original.

Two for the Road (1967)

20th Century Fox

Director and Producer: Stanley Donen; **Writer:** Frederic Raphael; **Music:** Henry Mancini; **Running time:** 111 minutes

Cast: Audrey Hepburn (Joanna Wallace); Albert Finney (Mark Wallace); Eleanor Bron (Cathy Manchester); William Daniels (Howard Manchester)

Oscar nomination: Screenplay

A genuinely moving look at a troubled marriage told in flashbacks as a husband and wife relive their various road trips and misadventures traveling around Europe over a period of years. What could have been a maudlin story is tempered by humor and the very engaging performances of Audrey Hepburn and the wonderful Albert Finney in a role originally envisioned for Paul Newman.

Romeo and Juliet (1968)

Paramount Pictures

Director: Franco Zeffirelli; **Producer:** Anthony Havelock-Allan; **Writers:** Franco Brusati and Masolino D'Amico; **Music:** Nino Rota; **Running time:** 138 minutes

Cast: Leonard Whiting (Romeo); Olivia Hussey (Juliet); John McEnery (Mercutio); Milo O'Shea (Friar Laurence); Pat Heywood (Nurse)

Oscar nominations: Best Picture, Director, Costume Design*, Cinematography*

Until Franco Zeffirelli gave us this dynamic vision of Shakespeare's tragic romance, the actors who played the title lovers in other versions were seemingly ready for a nursing home. Refreshingly, Zeffirelli cast actors of the appropriate age range—Olivia Hussey (15) and Leonard Whiting (17). The acclaimed Italian director provides his typical sweeping production design, emulating the actual societal conditions in which the story takes place. His version resonates with a realism previous film versions lacked. The leading actors and a terrific supporting cast overcome the common obstacle found in filming this tale: Shakespeare's dialogue has been spoofed so often that it takes extraordinary skill to insure audiences don't giggle when they hear the lines onscreen. However, the passion and sexual yearning found in this version overcame this challenge, and this adaptation of *Romeo and Juliet* still stands as the production of record.

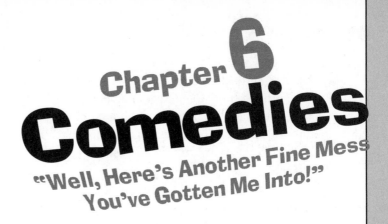

Chapter 6
Comedies
"Well, Here's Another Fine Mess You've Gotten Me Into!"

Johnny Carson used to say that comedy should never be analyzed. It's possible to debate the merits of a drama, a western, or a romance by pointing out aspects of the film that might make someone take a more appreciative viewpoint of it. However, a comedy relies on the most basic human response: it either makes you laugh or it doesn't. If a comedy doesn't strike you as funny the first time around, it's doubtful all the debate and analysis imaginable will make you find it funny the second time. Thus, when it comes to screen comedies, movie fans tend to be extremely loyal to those actors and teams whose work has particularly resonated with them. Conversely, others may be entirely dismissive of comedic actors more so than they ever would be of performers who appear in other genres. It's possible to dislike John Wayne in one film but appreciate him in another. However, in the world of comedy, fans seem to have either a visceral love of or aversion to the people who brought certain films to the screen.

I recall having some heated debates with my old friend and mentor, critic Bruce Williamson, who used to review films for *Playboy*. No matter how hard I tried to convince him that *It's a Mad, Mad, Mad, Mad World* was one of the great screen comedies, my pleas would always fall on deaf ears. Bruce would say that the film's entire premise was based on "If one car falling off a cliff is funny, then seven cars falling off a cliff must be hilarious." I realized then that Johnny Carson was indeed right—it is pointless to debate the merits of comedy, thus the films in this section are not designed to change anyone's mind. They are simply this writer's choices for the films that have always made me laugh—and with all due respect to Bruce Williamson, I've proudly included *It's a Mad, Mad, Mad, Mad World*!

The Front Page (1931)

United Artists

Director and Producer: Lewis Milestone; **Writers:** Bartlett Cormack and Ben Hecht; **Running time:** 101 minutes

Cast: Adolphe Menjou (Walter Burns); Pat O'Brien (Hildy Johnson); Mary Brian (Peggy Grant); Edward Everett Horton (Roy V. Bensinger)

Oscar nominations: Best Picture, Director, Actor (Adolphe Menjou)

A madcap farce from the early sound era whose plot revolves around a newspaper editor who tries to prevent his star reporter from going on his honeymoon so he can help him get an exclusive interview with an escaped convict (who they end up hiding in the newsroom). Holds up well despite the passage of years, and Adolphe Menjou's performance still stands as a gem.

 "Play It Again, Sam" _____

Remade several times: in 1940 as the classic *His Girl Friday*, in 1948 as a BBC TV production, in 1974 as a disappointing Billy Wilder vehicle for Jack Lemmon and Walter Matthau, and in 1988 as the woeful misfire *Switching Channels* with Burt Reynolds and Christopher Reeve.

Dinner at Eight (1933)

MGM

Director: George Cukor; **Producer:** David O. Selznick; **Writers:** Frances Marion and Herman J. Mankiewicz; **Music:** William Axt; **Running time:** 113 minutes

Cast: Marie Dressler (Carlotta Vance); John Barrymore (Larry Renault); Wallace Beery (Dan Packard); Jean Harlow (Kitty Packard); Lionel Barrymore (Oliver Jordan); Lee Tracy (Max Kane); Billie Burke (Millicent Jordan)

With *Grand Hotel* having pioneered the concept of the all-star production, MGM bought the rights to George S. Kaufman and Edna Ferber's play *Dinner at Eight* as a vehicle for an eclectic cast of popular actors. The plot concerns a dizzy socialite (Billie Burke) who is determined to keep her social status in high gear by inviting influential people to a dinner party; her focus is so consuming that she all but ignores the deteriorating health and disastrous business concerns of her husband (Lionel Barrymore). The film allows sufficient time for each individual to present his own story or dilemma. Most amusing is legendary sexpot Jean Harlow as the hateful wife of weather-beaten Wallace Beery. They are the most convincing couple in this comedic gem because they truly hated each other in real life! Remade in 1989 as a TV movie with Lauren Bacall.

Duck Soup (1933)

Paramount Pictures

Director: Leo McCary; **Producer:** Herman J. Mankiewicz; **Writers and Music:** Bert Kalmar and Harry Ruby; **Running time:** 68 minutes

Cast: Groucho Marx (Rufus T. Firefly); Harpo Marx (Pinky); Chico Marx (Chicolini); Zeppo Marx (Lt. Bob Roland); Margaret Dumont (Mrs. Gloria Teasdale)

Considered by many film historians to be the greatest Marx Brothers film, *Duck Soup* is a ludicrous, yet somehow pointedly effective, satire on war. Groucho plays the corrupt leader of Freedonia who declares war on neighboring Sylvania for his own selfish purposes. The memorable gags come at the viewer like machine gun fire. You're hardly able to react to one hilarious line or situation before another one arises. The mirror sequence is a landmark comedy setpiece, and dear old Margaret Dumont is once again the butt of old Groucho's barbs. This was the last film Zeppo would appear in with his brothers. Curiously, it was a box-office disappointment in its day; however, the Brothers relished the fact that its ridicule of dictators so offended Mussolini that he banned the film in Italy.

She Done Him Wrong (1933)

Paramount Pictures

Director: Lowell Sherman; **Producer:** William LeBaron; **Writers:** Mae West, Harvey F. Thew, and John Bright; **Music:** Ralph Rainger; **Running time:** 66 minutes

Cast: Mae West (Lady Lou); Cary Grant (Capt. Cummings); Owen Moore (Chick Clark); Gilbert Roland (Serge)

Oscar nominations: Best Picture

Cary Grant had appeared as a male lead in several films prior to *She Done Him Wrong*, but it was only after Mae West chose him as her romantic interest in this film that his career skyrocketed. West was already a major force in show business, having started her career as a child. This film was based on her controversial play *Diamond Lil* and finds West torn between two suitors: a violent gangster and a temperance advocate (played by Grant). The film is the origin of West's most famous (often transposed line) "Why don't you come up sometime and see me?". West's penchant for sex onscreen and off caused some gray hairs at the studio, but the film was completed in three weeks and helped elevate Paramount from a dire financial period. Still, the suggestiveness of the script and West's liberated view toward female sexuality helped bring in the dreaded Hays Code for censorship.

Sons of the Desert (1933)

MGM

Director: William A. Seiter; **Producer:** Hal Roach; **Writer:** Byron Morgan; **Music:** William Axt (uncredited); **Running time:** 68 minutes

Cast: Stan Laurel (Stanley); Oliver Hardy (Oliver); Charley Chase (Charley Chase); Mae Busch (Mrs. Lottie Chase Hardy); Dorothy Christie (Mrs. Betty Laurel)

Like so many other great comedic teams (for example, The Three Stooges and Abbott and Costello), Laurel and Hardy's enormous contributions to the cinema are not generally recognized through specific individual feature films. Indeed, this legendary duo did much of their most memorable work in short-films, including their Oscar-winner *The Music Box*. In researching this book, I informally polled the members of the New York City chapter of the Laurel and Hardy appreciation society, The Sons of the Desert, as to what the consensus was regarding their best feature film. Unsurprisingly, the virtually unanimous response was … *Sons of the Desert*. It's easy to see why. The basic premise lends itself to the types of inevitable disasters that would befall the loveable, inept duo. In this case, they want to attend a convention of their lodge, so Hardy feigns an illness requiring him to go on a cruise to Hawaii to recuperate. They later discover the cruise they were supposed to be on sank while they were attending the convention. The sheer joy of watching these two geniuses at work in their understated yet hilarious way makes *Sons of the Desert* required viewing.

It Happened One Night (1934)

Columbia Pictures

Director and Producer: Frank Capra; **Writer:** Robert Riskin **Running time:** 105 minutes

Cast: Clark Gable (Peter Warne); Claudette Colbert (Ellie Andrews); Walter Connolly (Alexander Andrews); Roscoe Karns (Oscar Shapely)

Oscar nominations: Best Picture*, Actor* (Clark Gable), Actress* (Claudette Colbert), Director*, Screenplay*

It's been described as "Capra-Corn," a demeaning reference to its famed director's penchant for sentimental comedies. But *It Happened One Night* stands the test of time and remains a charming, if admittedly slight, frothy romp. Claudette Colbert (in a role originally envisioned for Margaret Sullavan and Miriam Hopkins) is a runaway heiress who meets up with hardbitten, unemployed reporter Clark Gable on a long bus trip. The predictable scenario finds these two as reluctant companions who develop a romance while they traverse the backroads. Gable's appearance sans undershirt caused millions of men to follow his lead. The hitchhiking scene in which Colbert uses her leg to outperform Gable's thumb is a classic. First film to sweep the top five Oscar categories, despite being a box-office disappointment in its initial release. Remade numerous times, most notably as *You Can't Run Away From It* (1956).

A Night at the Opera (1935)

MGM

Director: Sam Wood; **Producer:** Irving Thalberg (uncredited); **Writers:** George S. Kaufman and Morrie Ryskind; **Running time:** 96 minutes

Cast: Groucho Marx (Otis B. Driftwood); Chico Marx (Fiorello); Harpo Marx (Tomasso); Kitty Carlisle (Rosa); Allen Jones (Ricardo); Margaret Dumont (Mrs. Claypool)

To many, this is the quintessential Marx Brothers movie—their first production after leaving Paramount Pictures for MGM. A madcap delight that pokes fun of stuffy opera lovers and the nouveau riche with equal aplomb. The film was constructed from highlights of the Brothers' comedy routine. Best of the lot is the classic stateroom sequence in which a virtual army attempts to squeeze into a small cabin aboard a cruise ship. As always, Groucho is the glue that holds the assorted nuts and bolts of the routines together. Fast forward through the interminable musical numbers played straight by Allen Jones and Kitty Carlisle, and you'll enjoy the experience even more. Loosely remade as the 1992 comedy *Brain Donors*.

Mr. Deeds Goes to Town (1936)

Columbia Pictures

Director and Producer: Frank Capra; **Writers:** Robert Riskind; **Running time:** 115 minutes

Cast: Gary Cooper (Longfellow Deeds); Jean Arthur ("Babe" Bennett/ Mary Dawson); George Bancroft (Mac); Lionel Stander (Cornelius Cobb); Douglas Dumbrille (John Cedar)

Oscar nominations: Best Picture, Actor (Gary Cooper), Director*, Sound, Screenplay

Another sentimental, slice-of-life comedy/drama from director Frank Capra, the All-American whose films seem to have a socialist bent in the sense that they advocate a belief in a redistribution of wealth and maintain that big businesses are suppressing the majority of citizens. In this irresistible fable, Gary Cooper is Longfellow Deeds, a Gomer Pyle-like rube who inherits a fortune and comes to the big city to see how best to give it away to the poor and downtrodden. In the course of his quest, he gets a life lesson as he's duped and manipulated by those closest to him. Naturally, the film builds to one of those Capraesque climaxes—the emotional equivalent of the common man marching on the Bastille in the name of justice. For all its predictability, it remains one of Cooper's greatest performances. Remade in 2002 as *Mister Deeds* with that modern-day embodiment of Gary Cooper, Adam Sandler. That rumbling you hear is Frank Capra rolling over in his grave.

The Awful Truth (1937)

Columbia Pictures

Director and Producer: Leo McCarey; **Writer:** Vina Delmar; **Music:** George Parrish (uncredited); **Running time:** 91 minutes

Cast: Irene Dunne (Lucy Warriner); Cary Grant (Jerry Warriner); Ralph Bellamy (Dan Leeson); Alexander D'Arcy (Armand Duvalle)

Oscar nominations: Best Picture, Director*, Actress (Irene Dunne), Screenplay, Editing, Supporting Actor (Ralph Bellamy)

A hilarious screwball comedy with Grant and Dunne as a married couple who, through a misunderstanding, agree to get a divorce when each mistakenly thinks the other is having an affair. Before the divorce is finalized, they each do all they can to sabotage their spouse's new love relationship. Grant and Dunne were such a hit together that they were reteamed in *My Favorite Wife* (1940) and *Penny Serenade* (1941). Leo McCarey won the Oscar for his direction. Filmed previously in 1925 and 1929 and remade in 1953 as *Let's Do It Again* with Jane Wyman and Ray Milland.

Bringing Up Baby (1938)

RKO Radio Pictures

Director and Producer: Howard Hawks; **Writer:** Dudley Nichols and Hagar Wilde; **Music:** Roy Webb (uncredited); **Running time:** 102 minutes

Cast: Katharine Hepburn (Susan Vance); Cary Grant (David Huxley); Charlie Ruggles (Major Horace Applegate); Walter Catlett (Constable Slocum); Barry Fitzgerald (Mr. Gogarty)

Although regarded as one of the great screen comedies, this screwball comedy was a serious box-office failure upon its initial release and temporarily tarnished the reputations of director Howard Hawks and actress Katharine Hepburn, for whom this was her first comedy. The zany story has Hepburn as an eccentric heiress tangling romantically with nerdy paleontologist Cary Grant (who bares a suspicious resemblance to Harold Lloyd). The breakneck pace involves missing dinosaur bones, a rampaging pet leopard, and other forms of general mayhem. All the major players are in top form.

Mr. Smith Goes to Washington (1939)

Columbia Pictures

Director and Producer: Frank Capra; **Writer:** Sidney Buchman; **Music:** Dimitri Tiomkin; **Running time:** 129 minutes

Cast: James Stewart (Jefferson Smith); Jean Arthur (Clarissa Saunders); Claude Rains (Sen. Paine); Edward Arnold (Jim Taylor); Guy Kibbee (Gov. Hopper); Thomas Mitchell ("Diz" Moore)

Oscar nominations: Best Picture, Director, Actor (James Stewart), Writing-Original Story*, Screenplay, Art Direction, Supporting Actor (Harry Carey), Supporting Actor (Claude Rains), Editing, Sound, Score

Yet another great film released in the legendary Golden Year of 1939, Frank Capra's *Mr. Smith Goes to Washington* wasn't always as beloved as it is today. The story of an idealistic country boy who is elected to the U.S. Senate only to find it a den of greed and corruption so infuriated real-life politicians that there were actually calls to ban the film for giving propaganda value to the Axis nations. Yet, critics and audiences responded far differently, making the film a box-office smash and the recipient of 11 Oscar nominations. Jimmy Stewart would win the Best Actor Oscar for *The Philadelphia Story*, but by all counts, *this* is arguably the performance of his career. His classic filibuster scene is often cited by both parties as an illustration of the sacredness of this procedure, even while some politicians seek to eliminate it. Given the number of scandals caused by corrupt lobbyists and politicians in recent years, *Mr. Smith* should be required viewing for all elected officials.

Ninotchka (1939)

MGM

Director and Producer: Ernst Lubitsch; **Writers:** Charles Brackett, Billy Wilder, and Walter Reisch; **Music:** Werner R. Heyman; **Running time:** 110 minutes

Cast: Greta Garbo (Ninotchka); Melvyn Douglas (Count Leon d'Algout); Ina Claire (Grand Duchess Swana); Bela Lugosi (Commissar Razinin); Sig Rumann (Michael Iranoff)

Oscar nominations: Best Picture, Actress (Greta Garbo), Writing-original story, Writing-screenplay

Garbo's twenty-sixth movie is her first comedy. The dour beauty fought with MGM to do this project, though studio executives remained skeptical that audiences would buy her in a lighthearted romp. *Ninotchka* is a convoluted comedy with Garbo as a committed Communist functionary sent to Paris to reign in some diplomats who were themselves sent there to raise funds by selling imperial jewels to finance the bankrupt nation. The most amusing scenes find Garbo reluctant to admit her blossoming feelings for dashing count Melvyn Douglas—and his initially unsuccessful attempts to get her to laugh. The movie remained unnamed until production was completed. Among the rejected titles: *We Want to Be Alone*, which was thought to be too obvious a play on Garbo's much mimicked line "I want to be alone." The film earned her a final Oscar nomination, but this was the year of *Gone with the Wind* and she lost to Vivian Leigh. Garbo would make one more film and then quietly retire to a reclusive life. Remade as the 1957 Fred Astaire musical *Silk Stockings* and as a 1960 TV production with Maria Schell.

The Bank Dick (1940)

Universal Pictures

Director: Edward F. Cline; **Writer:** Mahatma Kane Jeeves (aka W.C Fields); **Music:** Charles Previn; **Running time:** 72 minutes

Cast: W.C. Fields (Egbert Souse); Cora Witherspoon (Agatha Souse); Una Merkel (Myrtle Souse)

This is the best W.C. Fields feature film, with a script written by the great comedian himself. He plays a henpecked family man working as an inept bank guard who becomes embroiled in a madcap scheme to help his son-in-law hide the fact that he's lost substantial sums of the bank's money through a bad investment. Most of the fun derives from Fields's elaborate attempts to distract bank auditor Franklin Pangborn. Future Stooge Shemp Howard has a role as Fields's favorite bartender. Hilarious all the way. This was Fields's last starring role. Fragile health aggravated by his penchant for drinking relegated him to cameo appearances in subsequent films until his death in 1946.

The Great Dictator (1940)

United Artists

Director, Producer, and Writer: Charles Chaplin; **Music:** Meredith Wilson; **Running time:** 124 minutes

Cast: Charles Chaplin (Adenoid Hynkel/Jewish barber); Paulette Goddard (Hannah); Jack Oakie (Benzini Napoloni); Reginald Gardner (Commander Schultz); Henry Daniell (Garbitsch); Billy Gilbert (Herring)

Oscar nominations: Best Picture, Actor (Charles Chaplin), Supporting Actor (Jack Oakie), Score, Screenplay

Probably no one was happier than Charles Chaplin that the Axis powers suffered defeat in WWII. Had they not, Hitler would have created a special place for him on the basis of this scathing satire that mocks Der Fuhrer and his allies, most notably Mussolini. Chaplin's perceptions proved to be chillingly accurate considering he began the project in 1937. By the time *The Great Dictator* was released in 1940, America was not yet in the War, but by this point, Hitler's threat was beginning to resonate even within the isolationist movement. Chaplin plays a Jewish barber who is mistaken for a tyrannical dictator and plays up the charade, actually taking charge of the country. This was Chaplin's first feature film with full sound. In addition to his great performance, there is memorable support from Jack Oakie, hilarious as a Mussolini clone. Inspired lunacy all the way.

His Girl Friday (1940)

Columbia Pictures

Director and Producer: Howard Hawks; **Writer:** Charles Lederer; **Running time:** 92 minutes

Cast: Cary Grant (Walter Burns); Rosalind Russell (Hildy Johnson); Ralph Bellamy (Bruce Baldwin); Gene Lockhart ("Pinky" Hartwell); Porter Hall (Murphy)

This whirling dervish of a comedy moves at the speed of sound, thanks to director Howard Hawks' innovative vision of remaking the classic comedy *The Front Page*. The main elements of the plot are still there, only they have been refined and improved. Cary Grant gives a hilarious performance as a self-centered newsman determined to keep his star-reporter ex-wife on staff to help get the scoop on an escaped murderer—and to also prevent her marriage to square Ralph Bellamy. The nonstop action is truly a remarkable feat of moviemaking as actors never stop to take a breath, shouting out overlapping dialogue so fast it becomes almost indiscernible. Rosalind Russell is also at her best as the street-wise gal reporter who gives as good as she takes in the wisecrack department. A classic American comedy.

The Philadelphia Story (1940)

MGM

Director: George Cukor; **Producer:** Joseph L. Mankiewicz; **Writer:** David Ogden Stewart; **Music:** Franz Waxman; **Running time:** 112 minutes

Cast: Cary Grant (C.K. Dexter Haven); Katharine Hepburn (Tracy Lord); James Stewart (MaCaulay Connor); Ruth Hussey (Elizabeth); John Howard (George Kittredge); Roland Young (Uncle Willie)

Oscar nominations: Best Picture, Director, Actress (Katharine Hepburn), Actor* (James Stewart), Supporting Actress (Ruth Hussey), Screenplay*

A dated but stylish comedy of manners and marriage based on the hit Broadway play that also starred Katharine Hepburn, for whom the show was expressly written. Hepburn wisely deferred her salary for the film version in return for a percentage of the profits. The movie proved to be a blockbuster justifying her decision and in the process rendering moot her reputation as "box-office poison." Although parts of the story seem creaky and overly verbose today, there is no denying the charm of the three leads in their historic teaming. Stewart was given the Best Actor Oscar, though even he admitted it was a make-good gesture for having denied him the award the previous year for his more impressive performance in *Mr. Smith Goes to Washington.*

"Play It Again, Sam"

Remade as the 1956 musical *High Society* with Bing Crosby, Frank Sinatra, and Grace Kelly and in 1959 as a TV special with Gig Young and Mary Astor.

Meet John Doe (1941)

Warner Brothers

Director and Producer: Frank Capra; **Writer:** Robert Riskin; **Music:** Dimitri Tiomkin; **Running time:** 122 minutes

Cast: Gary Cooper (John Doe/Willoughby); Barbara Stanwyck (Ann Mitchell); Edward Arnold (D.B. Norton); Walter Brennan (The Colonel); James Gleason (Henry Connell)

Oscar nominations: Screenplay

Frank Capra's sentimental (some say *overly* sentimental) comedy-drama is about an opportunistic female reporter (Barbara Stanwyck) who creates a bogus "everyman" named John Doe who writes newspaper columns designed to speak for the common person. When Doe becomes a national hero, she has to produce a person to embody him. She bribes street bum Gary Cooper to pose as Doe. As the national adulation for him grows, "Doe" feels guilty but is increasingly manipulated by Stanwyck and her politically ambitious boss (Edward Arnold). Doe turns the tables in a calculated and highly publicized suicide bid designed to expose the scam to the public. Cooper is perfectly cast as the slow-witted but ultimately innovative honest man who, in the great Capra tradition, manages to overcome the forces of corporate greed and corruption. Capra was forced to make the ending more saccharine than even he preferred, but the film still packs an emotional wallop.

Sullivan's Travels (1941)

Paramount Pictures

Director and Writer: Preston Sturges; **Producer:** Paul Jones; **Music:** Charles Bradshaw and Leon Shuken; **Running time:** 90 minutes

Cast: Joel McCrae (John Lloyd Sullivan); Veronica Lake (The Girl); Robert Warwick (Mr. LeBrand); William Demarest (Mr. Jones); Franklin Panghorn (Mr. Casalsis)

The wonderful films of Preston Sturges are often ignored in discussions of classic cinema. Arguably his most enduring film is *Sullivan's Travels*, a moving comedy/drama about a pampered Hollywood director who decides to make a film about the downtrodden of society. He researches the subject by setting off with only a dime in his pocket. His adventures and misadventures lead to some unexpected consequences, including being jailed for his own murder! Joel McCrae, an actor whose work is also often undervalued, gives a charming performance as the Hollywood hack who learns to identify with the regular folk through a disastrous string of incidents. Veronica Lake (who was six months pregnant at the time, infuriating Sturges) is a wanna-be actress who accompanies McCrae on his journey. The somewhat overly complicated plot is more than offset by the uplifting spirit of the film.

The Road to Morocco (1942)

Paramount Pictures

Director: David Butler; **Producer:** Paul Jones; **Writers:** Frank Butler and Don Hartman; **Songs:** James Van Heusen; **Running time:** 82 minutes

Cast: Bing Crosby (Jeff Peters); Bob Hope ("Turkey" Jackson); Dorothy Lamour (Princess Shalmar); Anthony Quinn (Mullay Kasim)

Oscar nominations: Screenplay, Sound

As hard as it is to believe, in days gone by, America's greatest threat to the Arab states was the cornball jokes of Hope and Crosby. In this *Road* opus, they are shipwrecked and washed up in the desert, sold into slavery, and must outrun and outfox every clichéd Arab imaginable. There is nothing exceptional about the plot or direction. However, there *is* a certain guilty pleasure in reveling in the unpretentious one-liners and expert timing of one of Hollywood's most legendary comedy teams. Perhaps because their timing was so good, many film historians and critics have been slow to recognize the comedic gifts of Hope and Crosby. The title song is a particularly pleasing tune.

To Be or Not to Be (1942)

United Artists

Director and Producer: Ernst Lubitsch; **Writer:** Edwin Justus Mayer; **Music:** Werner R. Heymann; **Running time:** 99 minutes

Cast: Carole Lombard (Maria Tura); Jack Benny (Joseph Tura); Robert Stack (Sobinski); Felix Bressart (Greenberg); Lionel Atwill (Rawitch)

I once asked the famous British actor Christopher Lee, a man known for playing villains and deadly serious urbane characters, what film made *him* laugh most. Without hesitation, he responded, "Ernst Lubitsch's *To Be or Not to Be*," which he described as a "perfect" screen comedy. It's hard to argue with the esteemed Mr. Lee—the film is a true classic. The cast is populated by actors who are at the peak of their careers. They include Jack Benny and Carole Lombard, the leading players in a company of hammy Polish Shakespearian actors who find themselves out of work when the Nazis invade. They find a patriotic use for their costumes and acting abilities, however, when they become embroiled in a complicated plot to prevent a double agent from delivering vital information to the Nazi brass. Lubitsch was heavily criticized for making light of an ongoing holocaust, but as a German refugee he made the successful argument that spoofing the Nazis was an act of patriotism. Sadly, Lombard (who was married to Clark Gable) died shortly after production was concluded. She was on a war bond junket when her plane crashed. Mel Brooks's 1983 remake comes close to equaling the hilarity of the original.

Life with Father (1947)

Warner Brothers

Director: Michael Curtiz; **Producer:** Robert Buckner; **Writer:** David Ogden Stewart; **Music:** Max Steiner; **Running time:** 118 minutes

Cast: William Powell (Clarence Day); Irene Dunne (Vinnie Day); Elizabeth Taylor (Mary Skinner); Edmund Gwenn (Rev. Dr. Lloyd); Zasu Pitts (Cousin Cora)

 "Well, Nobody's Perfect!"

Although set in 1883, Father gripes about the incumbent Mayor of New York City, Hugh Grant (not *that* Hugh Grant). However, Grant did not become Mayor of the city until 1889.

Oscar nominations: Actor (William Powell), Cinematography (color), Art Direction-Set Decoration (color), Score

A dated but delightful film version of the smash hit play based on Clarence Day Jr.'s autobiography about growing up under the ironclad rule of his stern but loving father. Predictable shenangians revolve around the large family trying to cope with Father's stern rules and regulations. However,

William Powell's wonderful lead performance earned him a well-deserved Oscar nomination, and the film remains recommended family fun.

Miracle on 34th Street (1947)

20th Century Fox

Director and Writer: George Seaton; **Producer:** William Perlberg; **Writers:** Valentine Davies and George Seaton; **Music:** Cyril Mockridge **Running time:** 96 minutes

Cast: Maureen O'Hara (Doris Walker); John Payne (Fred Gailey); Edmund Gwenn (Kris Kringle); Gene Lockhart (Judge Harper); Natalie Wood (Susan Walker)

Oscar nominations: Best Picture, Supporting Actor* (Edmund Gwenn), Screenplay*, Original Story*

For many, this is the ultimate celluloid celebration of Christmas. Natalie Wood is a precocious little girl whose well-meaning mother (Maureen O'Hara) has raised her not to believe in Santa Claus. When their lives intersect with Edmund Gwenn as Macy's hired Santa, Wood begins to suspect he may be the real deal. The story involves a jealous fellow employee of Gwenn's framing him for a vicious assault, leading to a trial in which Gwenn threatens to be deemed insane. The twist in the tale, which virtually everyone knows by now, results in the children of the world exonerating the loveable old man. Although the studio didn't think much of the film (they released it in summer to dump it quickly), it became a box-office smash and ran in theaters through the holiday season. Gwenn's immortal performance earned him a well-deserved Oscar. The film's legacy is such that Macy's still decorates its windows during the Christmas season with displays based on the story.

"Play It Again, Sam"

The film was remade several times: as TV movies in 1955 (with Thomas Mitchell), in 1959 (with Ed Wynn) and 1974 (with Sebastian Cabot.) A big screen 1994 remake with Richard Attenborough was severely under-rated by critics.

Mr. Blandings Builds His Dream House (1948)

RKO Radio Pictures

Director: H.C. Potter; **Producers and Writers:** Melvin Frank and Norman Panama; **Music:** Leigh Harline; **Running time:** 94 minutes

Cast: Cary Grant (Jim Blandings); Myrna Loy (Muriel Blandings); Melvyn Douglas (Bill Cole); Reginald Denny (Henry Simms); Sharyn Moffett (Joan Blandings)

A comedy that relies more on a steady string of guffaws rather than belly laughs, the plot finds Grant and Loy as a couple who try to fulfill their fantasy of building a dream house in the country—only to find a great many unexpected pitfalls. Consistently amusing with Grant in top form as a harried ad executive who discovers his dream home is more like a nightmare, all the while having to deal with a hellish commute. Melvyn Douglas shines as his sarcastic and sardonic best friend. Loosely remade as the amusing 1986 Tom Hanks comedy *The Money Pit*. As of this writing, an official big screen remake is promised (threatened?) starring everyone's favorite casting choice for a film inspired by Cary Grant—the immortal Ice Cube!

Adam's Rib (1949)

MGM

Director: George Cukor; **Producer:** Lawrence Weingarten; **Writers:** Ruth Gordon and Garson Kanin; **Music:** Miklos Rosza; **Running time:** 101 minutes

Cast: Spencer Tracy (Adam Bonner); Katharine Hepburn (Amanda Bonner); Judy Holliday (Doris Attinger); Tom Ewell (Warren Attinger); David Wayne (Kip Lurie)

Oscar nominations: Screenplay

In this film, Tracy and Hepburn are at their pinnacle under the steady hand of director George Cukor and armed with witticisms from the hilarious script by Ruth Gordon and Garson Kanin. The plot involves husband and wife lawyers on opposite sides of an attempted murder case that has overtones of women's rights. The courtroom shenanigans spill over into their home lives with amusing consequences. Priceless fun all the way. Judy Holliday excels in a star-making role and David Wayne steals the show as an opportunistic neighbor who wastes no time in putting the moves on Hepburn when he sees her marriage in turmoil. Inspired a short-lived TV series in 1973.

Kind Hearts and Coronets (1949)

Eagle-Lion Films

Director: Robert Hamer; **Producer:** Michael Balcon; **Writers:** Robert Hamer and John Dighton; **Music:** Ernest Irving (uncredited); **Running time:** 106 minutes

Cast: Dennis Price (Duke Louis Mazzini); Valerie Hobson (Edith); Joan Greenwood (Sibella); Alec Guiness (8 different roles)

A brilliant British comedy about a ruthlessly ambitious aristocrat who is so intent on gaining a title that he systematically murders each of the individuals in the chain of succession. An unusually macabre subject matter for its time, but impeccably enacted, particularly by Alec Guiness, who plays each of the ill-fated family members. His tour-de-force performance elevated him from supporting player to full-fledged leading man.

Born Yesterday (1950)

Columbia Pictures

Director: George Cukor; **Producer:** S. Sylvan Simon; **Writer:** Albert Mannheimer; **Music:** Frederick Hollander; **Running time:** 103 minutes

Cast: Judy Holliday (Billie Dawn); Broderick Crawford (Harry Brock); William Holden (Paul Verrall); Howard St. John (Jim Devery)

Oscar nominations: Best Picture, Actress* (Judy Holliday), Director, Costume Design (b&w), Screenplay

Although Judy Holliday triumphed in the stage version of *Born Yesterday* on Broadway, Hollywood wasn't impressed. It was only after the studio failed to sign other actresses for the lead role (Jean Arthur among them) that they relented and gave the part to Holliday, who went on to win an Oscar. Holliday plays the dumb mistress of a tycoon (Broderick Crawford) who comes to Washington to lobby congressmen. He enlists the aid of William Holden to teach her a crash course in manners and common sense, but as she improves her education, she realizes how she's been used by Crawford and begins to extract revenge in amusing ways. A good cast is virtually wiped off the screen by Holliday's infectious charm. The part relegated her to dumb blonde roles in future films, though, ironically, she had an I.Q. of 172. Melanie Griffith starred in the flop 1993 remake.

Father of the Bride (1950)

MGM

Director: Vincente Minnelli; **Producer:** Pandro S. Berman; **Writers:** Frances Goodrich and Albert Hackett; **Music:** Adolph Deutsch; **Running time:** 92 minutes

Cast: Spencer Tracy (Stanley T. Banks); Joan Bennett (Ellie Banks); Elizabeth Taylor (Kay Banks); Don Taylor (Buckley Dunstan); Billie Burke (Doris Dunstan); Leo G. Carroll (Mr. Massoula)

Oscar nominations: Best Picture, Screenplay, Actor (Spencer Tracy)

A slight but highly enjoyable comedy with Tracy in an Oscar-nominated performance as the exasperated father of bride-to-be Elizabeth Taylor. Tracy does expert work with his slow but steady descent into virtual madness brought on by the day-to-day problems and expenses associated with the wedding. The success of the film resulted in a 1951 sequel *Father's Little Dividend*, a 1961 TV series, and a well-made 1991 remake with Steve Martin.

Harvey (1950)

Universal Pictures

Director: Henry Koster; **Producer:** John Beck; **Writers:** Mary Chase and Oscar Brodney; **Music:** Frank Skinner; **Running time:** 104 minutes

Cast: James Stewart (Elwood P. Dowd); Josephine Hull (Veta Louise Simmons); Peggy Dow (Miss Kelly); Charles Drake (Dr. Sanderson); Cecil Kellaway (Dr. Chumley)

Oscar nominations: Actor (James Stewart), Supporting Actress* (Josephine Hull)

No role has been as synonymous with James Stewart as that of loveable drunk Elwood P. Dowd, an amiable fellow who travels everywhere with his best friend—a 6-foot-tall invisible rabbit named Harvey. Dowd seems oblivious to the fact that no one else can see Harvey and continues to introduce him to new acquaintances and carry on in-depth conversations with him. Naturally, well-meaning friends and family try to have Elwood "cured" in a scenario that brings to mind the more serene *One Flew Over the Cuckoo's Nest*. In this case, however, it is the affable Dowd who converts his caregivers. It's one of the gentlest films imaginable, and Stewart's love for the role is quite apparent. The last scene is also a true crowd pleaser. Stewart remade the film for TV in 1972, and Harry Anderson starred in yet another TV remake in 1998.

The Lavender Hill Mob (1951)

Universal Pictures

Director: Charles Crichton; **Producer:** Michael Balcon; **Writer:** T.E.B. Clarke; **Music:** Georges Auric; **Running time:** 81 minutes

Cast: Alec Guiness (Henry Holland); Stanley Holloway (Alfred); Sidney James (Lackery); Alfie Bass (Shorty); Marjorie Fielding (Mrs. Chalk)

Oscar nominations: Actor (Alec Guiness), Screenplay*

Alec Guiness in an early starring role as a meek British bank clerk who masterminds a plan to steal gold bullion from his employers and melt it into innocuous souvenirs of the Eiffel Tower. Witty dialogue, excellent pacing, and another amazing performance by Guiness, who was truly the cinema's "Man of a Thousand Faces." He was able to portray men from every background and walk of life. This film is one of his early screen highlights. Look for a brief appearance by a young unknown actress named Audrey Hepburn.

The Quiet Man (1952)

Republic Pictures

Director: John Ford; **Producers:** Merian C. Cooper, John Ford, G.B. Forbes, and L.T. Russo; **Writer:** Frank S. Nugent; **Music:** Victor Young; **Running time:** 129 minutes

Cast: John Wayne (Sean Thornton); Maureen O'Hara (Mary Kate Danaher); Barry Fitzgerald (Flynn); Ward Bond (Father Lonergan); Victor McLaglen ("Red" Will Danaher)

Oscar nominations: Best Picture, Director*, Screenplay, Supporting Actor (Victor McLaglen), Art Direction-Set Decoration (color), Sound, Cinematography* (color)

John Ford's homage to his ancestral Ireland is perhaps a wee bit too cute, but the cast is winning and the cinematography is glorious. John Wayne, playing Ford's thinly-disguised alter-ego, is an ex-boxer with a painful past who visits a small Irish village only to encounter more eccentrics than can be found in the 42nd Street subway station. As he attempts to romance gorgeous Maureen O'Hara (has the screen ever seen a more ravishing natural beauty?), he must deal with her violent, overly-possessive brother, played by Victor McLaglen. A highlight of the film is the classic, knock-down brawl between McLaglen and Wayne that extends over hill and dale and right into the local pub. Ford won an Oscar for his direction. His estranged brother Francis acts in the film (as he did in other Ford productions), though the two continued their long-running feud and never spoke while on location!

The Ladykillers (1955)

Continental Distributing

Director: Alexander Mackendrick; **Producer:** Michael Balcon (uncredited); **Writer:** William Rose; **Music:** Tristram Cary; **Running time:** 97 minutes

Cast: Alec Guiness (Prof. Marcus); Cecil Parker (Claude); Herbert Lom (Louis); Peter Sellers (Harry); Katie Johnson (Mrs. Wilberforce)

Oscar nominations: Screenplay

Alec Guiness didn't star in every great British screen comedy of the 1950s, but it sometimes seems that way. This is one of the last of the famed Ealing Studios British comedies. Guiness is the head of a motley group of small-time crooks who rent rooms in an old woman's boarding house as they plan an elaborate bank robbery. Although the scheme goes well, they are endangered by the bothersome, if innocent, habits of their eccentric landlady—and plan to bump her off with hilariously disastrous results. Another major accomplishment for the incomparable Guiness, this time assisted by first-rate second bananas Peter Sellers and Herbert Lom. Remade in 2004 with Tom Hanks.

Mister Roberts (1955)

Warner Brothers

Directors: John Ford and Mervyn LeRoy; **Writers:** Joshua Logan and Frank S. Nugent; **Music:** Franz Waxman; **Running time:** 123 minutes

Cast: Henry Fonda (Doug Roberts); James Cagney (Capt. Morton); William Powell (Doc); Jack Lemmon (Ensign Pulver); Ward Bond (Dowdy)

Oscar nominations: Best Picture, Supporting Actor* (Jack Lemmon), Sound

Henry Fonda won a Tony Award for his performance as Mister Roberts in the long-running smash hit Broadway production. When the film version came about, his old mentor John Ford was in the director's seat. However, the crusty Ford allegedly clashed with Fonda over his interpretation of the role and left the film. Mervyn LeRoy took over mid-way, though the film plays seamlessly. The rollicking comedy traces the misadventures of the frustrated crew of the *U.S.S. Reluctant*, a dumpy Navy cargo ship in WWII. Fonda's Roberts wants to transfer to a fighting ship, but the tyrannical captain (James Cagney) keeps him aboard for spite. A great cast seen at their best. This is the role that still defines Henry Fonda's screen persona. Jack Lemmon won an Oscar as the bumbling, would-be tough guy Ensign Pulver, and William Powell is wonderfully cynical in his final film appearance. Cagney should have been nominated for playing one of the least sympathetic characters in his long career. The last sequence manages to combine pathos with a great upbeat endnote.

"Play It Again, Sam"

A lightweight sequel, *Ensign Pulver* starring Robert Walker Jr. was released in 1964. Roger Smith starred in the 1965 TV series that lasted one season.

The Seven Year Itch (1955)

20th Century Fox

Director: Billy Wilder; **Producers:** Billy Wilder and Charles K. Feldman; **Writers:** Billy Wilder and George Axelrod; **Music:** Alfred Newman; **Running time:** 105 minutes

Cast: Marilyn Monroe (The Girl); Tom Ewell (Richard Sherman); Evelyn Keyes (Helen Sherman); Sonny Tufts (Tom MacKenzie); Robert Strauss (Mr. Kruhulik)

A Broadway hit, *The Seven Year Itch* was brought to the screen with a beefed up role for red-hot Marilyn Monroe as the beautiful object of desire of married man Tom Ewell (who starred in the play). The entire quaint plot centers on Ewell trying to control his libido in the presence of his sensuous neighbor. In real life, Monroe's personal demons—including her rocky marriage to Joe DiMaggio—wreaked havoc on the production, and her distractions caused the film to go over-budget, though it was quite profitable in the long run. The film is primarily remembered for the iconic image of Monroe standing above a subway vent with her dress rising up from the air blast. Censors forced a good deal of the suggestiveness to be removed from the script, and several scenes were trimmed to tone down sexual innuendos.

Desk Set (1957)

20th Century Fox

Director: Walter Lang; **Producer:** Henry Ephron; **Writers:** Phoebe and Henry Ephron; **Music:** Cyril J. Mockridge; **Running time:** 103 minutes

Cast: Spencer Tracy (Richard Sumner); Katharine Hepburn (Bunny Watson); Gig Young (Mike Cutler); Joan Blondell (Peg); Dina Merrill (Sylvia Blair)

Based on a 1955 play by William Marchant, this represented the eighth screen pairing of Tracy and Hepburn. Although not one of their top offerings, *Desk Set* is consistently amusing because it keeps in the pair's well-established formula of having them in a battle of wits that ends in romance. Tracy is an efficiency expert sent to a company to see if Hepburn and her research department can be replaced by technology. The first color film featuring America's top screen couple.

The Horse's Mouth (1958)

United Artists

Director: Ronald Neame; **Producers:** Ronald Neame and John Bryan; **Writer:** Alec Guiness; **Music:** Kenneth V. Jones; **Running time:** 97 minutes

Cast: Alec Guiness (Gully Jimison); Kay Walsh (Miss D. Coker); Renee Houston (Sara); Mike Morgan (Nosey)

Oscar nominations: Screenplay

Alec Guiness shines as a modern Don Quixote, the eccentric artist Gully Jamison, in this adaptation of the book by Joyce Carey (one of a trilogy about the character). Gully is an *artiste* who chooses to live a fairly impoverished life rather than sell out to commercialism. In his search for the perfect wall upon which to create his next masterpiece, he discovers the appropriate site is in the home of a local rich man who is away from the premises. Gully and his fellow artists move in and take over the home for their varied artistic projects, and the predictable mayhem ensues. Guiness is priceless in one of his most inspired roles. He also wrote the screenplay, earning an Oscar nomination for his efforts.

Pillow Talk (1959)

Universal Pictures

Director: Michael Gordon; **Producers:** Ross Hunter and Martin Melcher; **Writers:** Stanley Shapiro and Maurice Richlin; **Music:** Frank De Vol; **Running time:** 103 minutes

Cast: Rock Hudson (Brad Allen); Doris Day (Jan Morrow); Tony Randall (Jonathan Forbes); Thelma Ritter (Alma); Nick Adams (Tony Walters)

Oscar nominations: Actress (Doris Day), Supporting Actress (Thelma Ritter), Screenplay*, Score, Art Direction-Set Decoration (color)

The premise of this comedy is dated enough to make *Love's Labor Lost* look like a biting contemporary satire. Younger viewers will have to understand the concept of telephone party lines that had several different households sharing the same line. Doris Day is the sexy urban chick who resents obnoxious playboy Hudson who keeps tying up the phone by calling his stable of willing bedmates. As they've never met, Hudson wants to add Day as a notch on the bedpost by posing as a hopelessly naive and gentlemanly southerner. The corny scenario still provides plenty of laughs thanks to the chemistry of Day and Hudson plus the priceless contribution of Tony Randall. The trio would reunite on two more films, *Lover Come Back* and the best of the lot, *Send Me No Flowers*.

Some Like It Hot (1959)

United Artists

Director and Producer: Billy Wilder; **Writers:** Billy Wilder and I.A.L. Diamond; **Music:** Adolph Deutsch; **Running time:** 120 minutes

Cast: Marilyn Monroe (Sugar); Tony Curtis (Joe/Josephine); Jack Lemmon (Jerry/Daphne); George Raft (Spats); Pat O'Brien (Mulligan); Joe E. Brown (Osgood Fielding III)

Oscar nominations: Director, Screenplay, Actor (Jack Lemmon), Cinematography (b&w), Art Direction-Set Decoration (b&w), Costume Design*

The premise of this story has been exploited so many times over the decades it's jarring to realize there was a time when the idea of guys dressing like girls to avoid their pursuers was actually an innovative concept. (The film is based on an obscure German movie titled *Fanfares of Love*.) Curtis and Lemmon are luckless musicians who are marked for death by gangster George Raft after accidentally witnessing the St. Valentine's Day Massacre. To avoid detection, they pose as members of a traveling women's band. Curtis and Lemmon's expert performances in and out of drag elevate this Billy Wilder comedy to the level of art. Marilyn Monroe has one of her most popular roles as a dumb blonde who doesn't realize her roommates are hot-blooded males, and Curtis's out-of-drag seduction attempt using the voice of Cary Grant is classic cinema. Although Wilder reported this to be one of his happiest directing experiences, it was in spite of Monroe's behavior, which was erratic and frustrating for the cast and crew. However, Monroe has never looked more glamorous than when she delivers several show-stopping musical numbers. *Some Like It Hot* was voted #1 in the American Film Institute's listing of the greatest American screen comedies.

The League of Gentlemen (1960)

Rank Film Distributors

Director: Basil Dearden; **Producer:** Michael Relph; **Writer:** Bryan Forbes; **Music:** Philip Green; **Running time:** 116 minutes

Cast: Jack Hawkins (Hyde); Nigel Patrick (Race); Roger Livesey (Mycroft); Richard Attenborough (Lexy); Bryan Forbes (Porthill)

There used to be a distinct difference between American and British crime movies, and this charming comedy is a prime example of the contrasting styles. American crime films generally dwelled on violent, vulgar gangsters, while the U.K. film industry usually had the criminals presented as well-mannered, dapper men who use their minds instead of guns as their weapons of choice. This film exemplifies the typical British crime saga from this era, though admittedly it's a very funny one. Jack Hawkins, in arguably his best performance, is a disgruntled ex-Army colonel who gathers together a group of equally distraught ex-servicemen to plan an audacious bank heist. The plot itself defies belief but the charming manner in which it is carried out is the entire show. A remarkable cast of some of Britain's best actors, including an early performance by Richard Attenborough. Future director Bryan Forbes, who plays Foothill, also wrote the script. Don't confuse this with Sean Connery's sci-fi flick *The League of Extraordinary Gentlemen!*

One, Two, Three (1961)

United Artists

Director and Producer: Billy Wilder; **Writers:** Billy Wilder and I.A.L. Diamond; **Music:** Andre Previn; **Running time:** 115 minutes

Cast: James Cagney (C.R. MacNamara); Horst Bucholz (Otto); Pamela Tiffin (Scarlett); Arlene Francis (Phyllis); Howard St. John (Hazeltine); Hanns Lothar (Schlemmer)

Oscar nominations: Cinematography (b&w)

Billy Wilder's Cold War comedy runs at such a rapid clip one can only compare it to Howard Hawks' *His Girl Friday* in terms of the frantic pace. The laugh-a-minute plot involves James Cagney as the head of Coca Cola's West Berlin headquarters who simultaneously has to cope with a failing marriage, Soviet industrial spies, and the unenviable task of safeguarding his boss's sex-crazed teenage daughter, who ends up taking up with a committed Communist. Uninformed younger viewers may be puzzled by the politics and clever inside jokes about old gangster movies, but for anyone who grew up in this era, this is an inventive and hilarious comedy. Cagney gives a truly remarkable performance, rattling off one-liners and extended dialogues that will make your head spin. Alas, the production was not a pleasant one to film. The Soviets began construction of the Berlin Wall during the shoot and, on a personal level, Cagney detested working with up-and-coming German star Horst Bucholz, whom he regarded as a self-centered scene-stealer. This would be Cagney's last film until he returned to the screen in *Ragtime* 20 years later.

Lolita (1962)

MGM

Director: Stanley Kubrick; **Producer:** James B. Harris; **Writer:** Vladimir Nabokov; **Music:** Nelson Riddle; **Running time:** 152 minutes

Cast: James Mason (Humbert Humbert); Shelly Winters (Charlotte Haze); Sue Lyon (Lolita); Peter Sellers (Quilty); Diane Decker (Jean Farlow); Jerry Stovin (John Farlow); Lois Maxwell (Nurse Mary Lore)

Oscar nominations: Screenplay

An eccentric middle-aged man is driven to ruin because of his obsession with a teenager. We're not talking about the transcripts of the Michael Jackson trial, but Stanley Kubrick's long and imperfect but admirable adaptation of Vladimir Nabokov's scandalous novel *Lolita*. James Mason is superb as the uptight Humbert Humbert whose passion for young Lolita leads him to marry her obnoxious, sex-starved mother

(Shelly Winters in one of her most memorable roles). Kubrick hired Nabokov to author the screenplay but ended up rewriting most of it himself, though Nabokov ended up earning the film's sole Oscar nomination. In answer to the famous tagline "How Did They Ever Make a Movie of *Lolita?*" the truth is, they really didn't. Censorship restrictions at the time mandated that Kubrick raise the age of the title character from 12 to 15 years old and feature nothing more overtly sexual than a pedicure in this "forbidden" relationship. However, anyone with an ounce of imagination can fill in the blanks. Sue Lyon is suitably tempting as the target of Mason's affections, and Peter Sellers gives a memorable performance as Quilty, another pedophile whose competition with Humbert leads to disaster. It was remade very effectively in 1997 with Jeremy Irons and Dominique Swain. This newer version concentrated more on the dramatic aspects of the story.

It's a Mad, Mad, Mad, Mad World (1963)

United Artists

Director and Producer: Stanley Kramer; **Writers:** William Rose and Tania Rose; **Music:** Ernest Gold; **Running time:** 161 minutes

Cast: Spencer Tracy (Culpepper); Milton Berle (Russell Finch); Sid Caesar (Melville Crump); Buddy Hackett (Benjy Benjamin); Ethel Merman (Mrs. Marcus); Mickey Rooney ("Dingy" Bell); Dick Shawn (Sylvester); Phil Silvers (Otto Meyer); Terry-Thomas (Hawthorne); Jonathan Winters (Lennie Pike)

Oscar nominations: Sound, Cinematography, Editing, Song (*It's a Mad, Mad, Mad, Mad World*), Score, Effects*

With all the talk about a big dubya in this film, one might think it's a biography of George W. Bush. However, it refers to dying crook Jimmy Durante's pronouncement that a stolen fortune lies beneath a big "W" somewhere in a California park. This sets a group of total strangers on a madcap race to California to solve the puzzle and claim the fortune. Critics have always turned their noses up at Stanley Kramer's big-budget, slapstick extravaganza, but you'd be hard-pressed to find a movie fan that doesn't consider it one of the funniest films of all time. More classic comedy scenes are in this one movie than can be found in a dozen feature films. My personal favorite: Jonathan Winter's one-man demolition of a gas

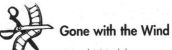 **Gone with the Wind**

Mad World was cut substantially from its original roadshow release. Although a good deal of footage has been restored, it is still not complete. The best reference for the movie is Paul and George Ann Scrabo's terrific documentary released on MGM's laser disc and VHS editions from the 1990s.

station. Countless stars make cameo appearances, including Jerry Lewis, Jack Benny, and Buster Keaton.

Lilies of the Field (1963)

United Artists

Director and Producer: Ralph Nelson; **Writer:** James Poe; **Music:** Jerry Goldsmith; **Running time:** 94 minutes

Cast: Sidney Poitier (Homer Smith); Lilia Skala (Mother Superior Maria); Lisa Mann (Sister Gertrude); Isa Crino (Sister Agnes); Francesca Jarvis (Sister Albertine); Pamela Branch (Sister Elizabeth); Stanley Adams (Juan)

Oscar nominations: Best Picture, Actor* (Sidney Poitier), Cinematography (b&w), Supporting Actress (Lilia Skala), Screenplay

The "feel good" movie of 1963 was also a ground breaker on a social level: Sidney Poitier became the first black man to win an Oscar for his wonderful performance as a drifter who is conned into building a chapel in the desert for an order of German nuns. Incredibly, this film was shot in only a couple of weeks. It's moving and touching without ever being overly-sentimental, and Poitier's nemesis is played by Lilia Skala as a tough-as-nails mother superior. The script doesn't water down the characters as it progresses and, refreshingly, Poitier's race is never even brought up. The film inspired a 1979 TV movie, *Christmas Lilies of the Field* with Billy Dee Williams playing Poiter's character.

Hollywood Confidential

The part of the construction company owner who gives Poitier a job is played by director/producer Ralph Nelson, who refused to take screen credit for his performance.

The Nutty Professor (1963)

Paramount Pictures

Director: Jerry Lewis; **Producer:** Ernest D. Glucksman; **Writers:** Jerry Lewis and Bill Richmond; **Music:** Walter Scharf; **Running time:** 107 minutes

Cast: Jerry Lewis (Julius Kelp/Buddy Love); Stella Stevens (Stella Purdy); Del Moore (Hamius Warfield); Kathleen Freeman (Millie Lemmon); Howard Morris (Elmer Kelp)

With the Dean Martin and Jerry Lewis team splitting up half a century ago, it's often overlooked just how enormously popular their act was. With the exception of Beatlemania, nothing approached the fanaticism the public had for the duo. Yet, the series of films they starred in have not aged well. Lewis, with his borderline psychotic man-child act, seems almost creepy. His usual character isn't just a nerd, he seems mentally impaired, making the obligatory romantic scenes look almost perverted. After the Martin and Lewis split, Jerry Lewis made some impressive comedies, generally under the direction of Frank Tashlin. With *The Nutty Professor*, however, he directed himself and cowrote the script. A contemporary spoof of Jeykll and Hyde, Lewis does some amazing emoting, leaving one to think all those Frenchmen are right about his cinematic talents. His monstrous transformation was a stunner at the time: he does not turn into an ogre, but rather a handsome, conceited playboy (Lewis has long denied the character was based on Dean Martin). The film makes a poignant observation that in modern society, cruelty and selfishness are often rewarded while kindness and compassion are deemed weaknesses. The movie inspired the successful Eddie Murphy remake, though it bore little resemblance to the original 1963 classic.

Tom Jones (1963)

United Artists

Director and Producer: Tony Richardson; **Writer:** John Osborne; **Music:** John Addison; **Running time:** 128 minutes

Cast: Albert Finney (Tom Jones); Susannah York (Sophie); Hugh Griffith (Squire Western); Edith Evans (Miss Western); Joan Greenwood (Lady Bellaston); Diane Cilento (Molly Seagrim)

Oscar nominations: Best Picture*, Director*, Score*, Screenplay*, Actor (Albert Finney), Supporting Actor (Hugh Griffith), Art Direction-Set Decoration (color), Supporting Actress (Joyce Redman), Supporting Actress (Diane Cilento), Supporting Actress (Edith Evans)

Director Tony Richardson and screenwriter John Osborne seemed an unlikely team to adapt Henry Fielding's 1749 romp to the screen. The men were known for collaborating on highly dramatic films such as *Look Back in Anger* and *The Entertainer*. Yet their bawdy film version of *Tom Jones* won universal acclaim as well as the Oscar for Best Picture. Albert Finney gives a very charismatic performance as the sex-mad young man who dallies with every willing lady in England—often with disastrous results. *Tom Jones* is delightful, madcap fun with convincing period costumes and atmosphere. Finney's erotic banquet with Joyce Redman remains one of the most sexually-charged sequences in cinematic history—even though the passion is all conveyed through the devouring of food!

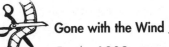 **Gone with the Wind**

For the 1989 reissue, Tony Richardson cut seven minutes of footage, most of them trims rather than entire scenes.

The Americanization of Emily (1964)

MGM

Director: Arthur Hiller; **Producer:** Martin Ransohoff; **Writer:** Paddy Chayefsky; **Music:** Johnny Mandel; **Running time:** 115 minutes

Cast: James Garner (Charles Madison); Julie Andrews (Emily Barham); Melvyn Douglas (Admiral Jessup); James Coburn ("Bus" Cummings); Joyce Grenfell (Mrs. Barham)

Oscar nominations: Cinematography (b&w), Art Direction-Set Decoration (b&w)

One of the most cynical comedies of the 1960s, courtesy of the great Paddy Chayefsky's biting script. James Garner is cast against type as a cowardly aide to an aging admiral who concocts a mad plan to get good publicity for the Navy by having a sailor be the first fatality on Omaha Beach during the D-Day invasion. Garner is the self-centered schmuck who finds himself reluctantly chosen for the task, thus interrupting his love affair with Julie Andrews, also playing against type as a woman who has one-night stands with seemingly doomed servicemen. Garner and Andrews generate considerable sparks and the script refreshingly does not have Garner redeem himself in any tangible way. Witty dialogue and wonderful supporting performances from James Coburn and Melvyn Douglas.

Marriage Italian-Style (1964)

Embassy Pictures

Director: Vittorio De Sica; **Producer:** Carlo Ponti; **Writers:** Renato Castellani, Tonino Guerra, Leo Benvenuti, and Piero De Bernardi; **Music:** Armando Travajoli; **Running time:** 102 minutes

Cast: Sophia Loren (Filumena); Marcello Mastroianni (Domenico); Aldo Puglisi (Alfredo); Tecla Scarano (Rosalia)

Oscar nominations: Best Foreign Film, Actress (Sophia Loren)

An acclaimed comedy based on the play *Filumena*. Loren plays the long-time mistress of successful businessman Mastroianni, and she employs a number of inventive, if not dishonest, methods to finally lure him to the alter and make an "honest woman" of herself. Loren and Mastroianni, great friends in real life, previously teamed for director De Sica in *Yesterday, Today and Tomorrow*. This clever and witty 1964 romantic romp helped establish them as one of the most popular screen couples.

Dr. Strangelove or: How I Learned to Stop Worrying and Love the Bomb (1964)

Columbia Pictures

Director and Producer: Stanley Kubrick; **Writers:** Stanley Kubrick, Terry Southern, and Peter George; **Music:** Laurie Johnson; **Running time:** 93 minutes

Cast: Peter Sellers (Madrake/Pres. Muffley/Dr. Strangelove); George C. Scott (General "Buck" Turgidson); Sterling Hayden (General Jack D. Ripper); Keenan Wynn (Col. "Bat" Guano); Slim Pickins (Major T. J. "King" Kong)

Oscar nominations: Best Picture, Director, Screenplay, Actor (Peter Sellers)

Perhaps the most perfectly realized comedy of the 1960s, *Dr. Strangelove* was originally envisioned by Stanley Kubrick as a dramatic look at the Cold War (it's loosely based on the novel *Red Alert)*. Kubrick later felt it was more effective to satirize the nuclear situation. The plot involves a mad U.S. general (Sterling Hayden, superb) who launches an unauthorized atomic bomb raid on Moscow as a way of compensating for his impotence. The most remarkable performance in a film brimming with remarkable performances is Peter Sellers, who plays three major roles with equal skill. George C. Scott is outstanding as a hawkish general, though after seeing the first cut of the film, Scott felt he came across poorly. The supporting cast includes James Earl Jones in his first film role and Slim Pickens, whose famous phallic ride atop a falling atom bomb is one of the most enduring cinematic images ever. Ken Adam's set of the War Room is a triumph. A comic masterpiece that gets better with every viewing.

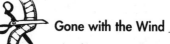

Gone with the Wind

The film originally ended with an elaborate pie fight inside the War Room. However, the expensive scene did not play well as the characters lost all identity amidst the muck. The scene was cut and the only print resides in The British Film Institute in London.

The Pink Panther (1964)

United Artists

Director: Blake Edwards; **Producer:** Martin Jurow; **Writers:** Maurice Richlin and Blake Edwards; **Music:** Henry Mancini; **Running time:** 113 minutes

Cast: David Niven (Sir Charles Lytton); Peter Sellers (Inspector Jacques Clouseau); Robert Wagner (George Lytton); Capucine (Simone); Claudia Cardinale (Princess Dala)

Oscar nominations: Score

Fans familiar only with the later entries in the *Panther* series may find this initial entry to be relatively slow-moving compared to the slapstick-laden farces that followed. However, the Inspector Clouseau character was never intended to inspire an entire series of films, and the sheer sophistication of this film has never been equaled in the sequels (with the exception of *A Shot in the Dark*, which had actually been completed prior to this film). With a cast that approaches cinematic royalty, the film evokes a bygone era in which screen heroes were seemingly always dressed in tuxedos and gowns and had a clever witticism or seductive line for every occasion. Peter Sellers's Clouseau was not yet the over-the-top character he would morph into and is therefore more believable and enjoyable. Henry Mancini's famous musical theme is an integral part of cinematic history.

 "Play It Again, Sam"

The film inspired the wildly successful Blake Edwards/Peter Sellers collaborations that followed in the series: *A Shot in the Dark, Return of the Pink Panther, The Pink Panther Strikes Again,* and *Revenge of the Pink Panther.* A compilation tribute (ripoff?) to Sellers, *Trail of the Pink Panther,* was released after the actor's death. Three *Panther* films were made without Sellers: *Inspector Clouseau* with Alan Arkin, the dreadful *Curse of the Pink Panther* with Ted Wass as Clouseau's nephew, and *Son of the Pink Panther* with Roberto Benigni. In 2006, Steve Martin starred in a weak remake of the original film. The Panther cartoon character became a successful star in his own right, inspiring a long running series of shorts.

A Shot in the Dark (1964)

United Artists

Director and Producer: Blake Edwards; **Writers:** Blake Edwards and William Peter Blatty; **Music:** Henry Mancini; **Running time:** 102 minutes

Cast: Peter Sellers (Inspector Jacques Clouseau); Elke Sommer (Maria); George Sanders (Benjamin Ballon); Herbert Lom (Dreyfus); Tracy Reed (Dominique); Graham Starke (Lajoy); Burt Kwouk (Cato)

The second film in *The Pink Panther* canon is arguably the best of the series. With the focus predominantly on Sellers's immortal Clouseau, the script allows the introduction of two mainstay characters central to future films: his long suffering boss Dreyfuss (wonderfully played by Herbert Lom) and his loyal and equally inept servant Cato (Burt Kwok) who keeps Clouseau in shape by attacking him at unlikely moments. Best scene: Sellers and Elke Sommers misadventures in a nudist colony.

Hollywood Confidential _____

A Shot in the Dark was based on a stage play, and the character of Clouseau was written into the story to make it a vehicle for Sellers. The movie was made before *The Pink Panther* but sat on a shelf until the studio responded to the overwhelming popularity of the Clouseau character in that film. Thus, this "sequel" was able to be released only a few months after *Panther*. The fact that it's a prequel also explains the lack of any reference to *The Pink Panther*.

Alfie (1966)

Paramount Pictures

Director and Producer: Lewis Gilbert; **Writer:** Bill Naughton; **Music:** Sonny Rollins; **Running time:** 114 minutes

Cast: Michael Caine (Alfie); Shelly Winters (Ruby); Millicent Martin (Siddie); Julia Foster (Gilda); Jane Asher (Annie); Shirley Anne Field (Carla); Vivien Merchant (Lily)

Oscar nominations: Best Picture, Director, Actor (Michael Caine), Supporting Actress (Vivien Merchant), Song (*Alfie*)

As the "mod movement" emerged in England, *Alfie* became the definitive representation of the younger generation's casual attitude toward sexuality. Based on a radio play turned theatrical play turned novel, the film version presents Michael Caine's Alfie as a streetwise, self-absorbed bloke who lives only to seduce and abandon as many women as he can. He makes sure he's there at bedtime, but beats a hasty retreat in the morning. Alfie gets a life lesson, however, when a casual lover becomes pregnant with shattering consequences. The sequence with Denholm Elliott as the disinterested abortionist is sobering and unforgettable. The gimmick of having Alfie address the audience directly seems clichéd today, but was innovative in its day. Caine's performance is a towering achievement. Spawned a low-budget 1975 sequel, *Alfie, Darling* (sans Caine) and a tepid, politically correct 2004 remake with Jude Law.

The Fortune Cookie (1966)

United Artists

Director and Producer: Billy Wilder; **Writers:** I.A.L. Diamond and Billy Wilder; **Music:** Andre Previn; **Running time:** 125 minutes

Cast: Jack Lemmon (Henry Hinkle); Walter Matthau (Willie Gingrich); Ron Rich ("Boom Boom" Jackson); Judi West (Sandy Hinkle); Cliff Osmond (Purky)

Oscar nominations: Supporting Actor* (Walter Matthau), Screenplay, Art Direction-Set Decoration (b&w), Cinematography (b&w)

This film features the first teaming of Jack Lemmon and Walter Matthau, and it's a gem. Lemmon is a sports cameraman accidentally injured on the field during a televised football game. Although not seriously injured, he is browbeaten by his shyster lawyer/brother-in-law Matthau into feigning serious injury in order to collect an insurance payment. The plan goes awry when investigators suspect a fraud, leading Lemmon to have to extensively act like he's an invalid. Although long for a comedy, director Wilder keeps the pace fast and even builds a considerable level of suspense. The final scenes of Lemmon's emancipation are classic.

Hollywood Confidential

Walter Matthau suffered a heart attack during production, delaying shooting for weeks. He ultimately won an Oscar for his portrayal of one of the screen's great con men.

The Ghost and Mr. Chicken (1966)

Universal Pictures

Director: Alan Rafkin; **Producer:** Edward J. Montagne; **Writers:** Jim Fritzell and Everett Greenbaum; **Music:** Vic Mizzy; **Running time:** 90 minutes

Cast: Don Knotts (Luther Heggs); Joan Staley (Alma); Liam Redmond (Kelsey); Dick Sargent (George Beckett); Skip Homier (Ollie)

No, this isn't a misprint. *The Ghost and Mr. Chicken* is indeed a great comedy film, albeit one with modest production values. Knotts, a genuine comic genius, is at his peak as a nervous cub reporter who tries to build a reputation by spending a night in an allegedly haunted house. There's a reason why the film has built an enthusiastic and enduring cult following: it's very funny. Vic Mizzy's distinctive music led to a CD soundtrack release almost 40 years later. *Chicken* was a box-office smash, as were several other follow up vehicles Knotts did for Universal.

Hollywood Confidential

Knotts had only recently left his Emmy-winning role as Barney Fife on *The Andy Griffith Show* when Universal mogul Lew Wasserman signed him to a multi-picture deal. Knotts enlisted the writers and many cast members from the *Griffith* show to work on *Ghost and Mr. Chicken* (which was shot under the title *Running Scared*). The script was actually cowritten by Andy Griffith, who declined to take screen credit.

The Knack ... and How to Get It (1966)

United Artists

Director: Richard Lester; **Producer:** Oscar Lewenstein; **Writer:** Charles Wood; **Music:** John Barry; **Running time:** 85 minutes

Cast: Rita Tushingham (Nancy Jones); Ray Brooks (Tolen); Michael Crawford (Colin); Donal Donnelly (Tom)

Another hip British comedy from director Richard Lester, who was riding high from his two Beatles hits *A Hard Day's Night* and *Help!* Although tame by today's standards, the story was considered edgy in 1966. A shy young man wants to emulate his roommate, who has the knack of bedding any woman he sets his eyes on. Conflict comes when he finally meets a dream girl only to have his pal attempt to seduce her. A good snapshot of London at the peak of the "mod" movement. John Barry's music is perfectly suited to the film and its era.

The Russians Are Coming! The Russians Are Coming! (1965)

United Artists

Director and Producer: Norman Jewison; **Writer:** William Rose; **Music:** Johnny Mandel; **Running time:** 126 minutes

Cast: Carl Reiner (Walt Whittaker); Alan Arkin (Rozanov); Eva Marie-Saint (Elspeth Whittaker); Brian Keith (Chief Mattocks); Jonathan Winters (Norman Jones); Paul Ford (Hawkins); Theodore Bikel (Russian Captain); John Philip Law (Alexei)

Oscar nominations: Best Picture, Actor (Alan Arkin), Screenplay, Editing

Hilarious Cold War-era comedy about a Soviet sub that accidentally beaches on a sandbank near a tiny New England town and the panic the incident causes among the local eccentrics. Well drawn characters brought to life by a wonderful cast of supporting actors, with Paul Ford a standout as the hawkish would-be militia commander, and Brian Keith is great as the slow-to-burn local police chief. Alan Arkin plays a star-making role as the sub's Executive Officer forced to "blend" with the local population. The film is thoroughly amusing despite the lengthy running time. Johnny Mandel's imaginative blending of American and Russian patriotic themes is an inspiration.

The Graduate (1967)

Embassy Pictures

Director: Mike Nichols; **Producer:** Lawrence Turman; **Writers:** Calder Willingham and Buck Henry; **Music:** Dave Grusin; **Songs:** Paul Simon; **Running time:** 105 minutes

Cast: Anne Bancroft (Mrs. Robinson); Dustin Hoffman (Benjamin Braddock); Katharine Ross (Elaine Robinson); William Daniels (Mr. Braddock); Murray Hamilton (Mr. Robinson)

Oscar nominations: Best Picture, Director*, Actor (Dustin Hoffman), Actress (Anne Bancroft), Cinematography, Screenplay, Supporting Actress (Katharine Ross)

The seminal youth-oriented comedy of the late 1960s, *The Graduate*, arrived without much fanfare-or bankable stars but immediately became a cultural phenomenon. Dustin Hoffman is a college graduate torn between the advice of the older generation and a desire to follow his instincts. He ends up courting beautiful rich girl Katharine Ross while simultaneously bedding her mother, the sexy ice queen Mrs. Robinson (given screen immortality by Anne Bancroft). The film retains its wit and sarcastic bite, though in retrospect it is curiously devoid of references to the main issues obsessing young people in this period (such as Vietnam, protest movements, and political debate). Hoffman was a virtual unknown who jumped to superstardom with this film. Simon and Garfunkel's songs are used to great effect. The poorly received 2005 film *Rumor Has It* was based on characters from this movie.

Hollywood Confidential

Robert Redford, Warren Beatty, Charles Grodin, and beach movie star Aron Kincaid were also considered for the role of Benjamin Braddock.

The Odd Couple (1968)

Paramount Pictures

Director: Gene Saks; **Producer:** Howard W. Koch; **Writer:** Neil Simon; **Music:** Neal Hefti; **Running time:** 105 minutes

Cast: Jack Lemmon (Felix Unger); Walter Matthau (Oscar Madison); John Fielder (Vinnie); Herbert Edelman (Murray); David Sheiner (Roy); Larry Haines (Speed); Monica Evans (Cecily Pigeon); Carole Shelly (Gwendolyn Pigeon)

Oscar nominations: Screenplay, Editing

The Odd Couple has become such an integral part of modern American comedy that it seems pointless to rehash its premise. Suffice it to say, Neil Simon's comedy started as a Broadway smash starring Walter Matthau and Art Carney, who was passed over for the film version in favor of Jack Lemmon (probably in an attempt to replicate the success of the Lemmon/Matthau hit *The Fortune Cookie*). With all respect to the great

Carney, the decision was a sound one. Lemmon and Matthau's "reel life" friendship extended to real life, and their chemistry shines through in every witty scene. The movie also benefits from a good cast of supporting actors, and Neal Hefti's catchy theme is a classic.

"Play It Again, Sam"

While everyone remembers the long-running TV series with Tony Randall and Jack Klugman that premiered in 1970, few recall a short-lived follow up series from 1982 starring Ron Glass and Demond Wilson. Neil Simon wrote a 1998 big screen sequel for Lemmon and Matthau, but sadly, *The Odd Couple II* seemed tired and unworthy of the talents involved. Matthew Broderick and Nathan Lane starred in a hit 2005 Broadway revival.

The Producers (1968)

Avco Embassy Pictures

Director and Writer: Mel Brooks; **Producer:** Sidney Glazier; **Music:** John Morris; **Running time:** 88 minutes

Cast: Zero Mostel (Max Bialystock); Gene Wilder (Leo Bloom); Kenneth Mars (Franz Liebkin); Estelle Winwood (Old Lady); Renee Taylor (Eva Braun); Christopher Hewitt (Roger De Bris); Lee Meredith (Ula); Dick Shawn (Lorenzo St. DuBois)

Oscar nominations: Screenplay*, Supporting Actor (Gene Wilder)

Mel Brooks's first feature film is his most accomplished work, though, ironically, he doesn't appear in the movie. The now-famous scenario finds Zero Mostel as a failed theatrical producer and Gene Wilder as his timid accountant who hatch a bizarre plot to make a fortune from investors by opening a Broadway play guaranteed to fail. Brooks cynicism doesn't pause for a second: every group and individual is a target, and the premise for the play *Springtime for Hitler* was even more tasteless in 1968 than it is today. (The onscreen production number with dancing Nazis is brilliant.) Mostel's tendency to ham it up is perfectly suitable here, and his performance is a delight, as is Wilder in his star-making role. Every supporting character is terrific, with Mars and Shawn particularly memorable. This time around, appreciate how good Brooks's songs are when heard in conjunction with John Morris's music.

"Play It Again, Sam"

Remade as a surprisingly flat 2005 film version of the smash Broadway musical production starring Nathan Lane and Matthew Broderick.

Bob & Carol & Ted & Alice (1969)

Columbia Pictures

Director: Paul Mazursky; **Producer:** Larry Tucker; **Writers:** Paul Mazursky and Larry Tucker; **Music:** Quincy Jones; **Running time:** 105 minutes

Cast: Natalie Wood (Carol); Robert Culp (Bob); Elliott Gould (Ted); Dyan Cannon (Alice); Horst Ebersberg (Horst)

Oscar nominations: Supporting Actress (Dyan Cannon), Supporting Actor (Elliott Gould), Screenplay, Cinematography

Although somewhat quaint by today's standards, this was considered to be *the* hip comedy of the year. Natalie Wood and Robert Culp are a pretentious, wealthy, and bored Southern California couple desperate to put some zing in their love life by indulging in trendy sexual experimentation. They talk a lot about it with their potential swap mates, Elliott Gould and Dyan Cannon, leading to some very funny scenes and a "will-they-or-won't-they?" finale that many found unsatisfying. Still, the film holds up well as a time capsule view of sexuality in the Age of Aquarius. Gould and Cannon catapulted to stardom and earned Oscar nominations. Culp, one the most engaging leading men of the era, has long been criminally ignored by Hollywood in subsequent feature films. Spawned a forgotten TV series in 1973 that featured Jodie Foster in one of her first roles.

Take the Money and Run (1969)

Cinerama Releasing

Director: Woody Allen; **Producer:** Charles H. Joffe; **Writers:** Woody Allen and Mickey Rose; **Music:** Marvin Hamlisch; **Running time:** 85 minutes

Cast: Woody Allen (Virgil Starkwell); Janet Margolin (Louise); Marcel Hillaire (Fritz); Jacqueline Hyde (Miss Blair)

Gone with the Wind

Allen originally shot a finale in which Virgil is killed in a *Bonnie and Clyde*-type massacre. The consensus was that it didn't work, so he wrote and shot a more subdued ending for the film.

After working as a supporting actor on the overblown and out-of-control 1967 budget-buster *Casino Royale*, comedy writer and standup comic Woody Allen decided he could make funnier movies in a far more efficient and economic manner. Though he initially wanted Jerry Lewis to direct him in his first starring role, Allen ended up taking on the task himself. *Take the Money and Run* is a hilarious mockumentary that spoofs those old Quinn Martin Productions crime shows right down to the ominous narrator. The film recounts the misadventures of would-be master criminal Virgil Starkwell. At times the jokes misfire, but a second later another one works very well. The most inspired scene is Virgil's experiences in prison, including an escape attempt—using a gun made of soap—that goes awry when it begins to rain. The film has aged well and obviously inspired the machine-gun like jokes in films made by the Zucker brothers such as *Airplane* and *The Naked Gun*.

Chapter 7

Dramas

"I Coulda Had Class... I Coulda Been a Contender!"

Of all the films considered for this book, dramas outnumbered all other genres by a long shot. Drama is a sweeping category that is often difficult to encapsulate in the way one can discuss the great westerns, horror films, or musicals. The very nature of a dramatic film mandates that the story can take place in any time period and extend to characters that are from different ethnic and economic backgrounds. If there is one common denominator, however, it is that the main characters generally face a crisis, either of conscience or one that is imposed upon them by their relationship with family or lovers.

The films presented in this section are perhaps the most eclectic in terms of storylines and the personal dilemmas facing the protagonists. From the relatively benign "crisis" facing Al Jolson in *The Jazz Singer* (his father wants him to be a cantor but he would prefer to be an entertainer) to the mentally tortured Blanche DuBois of *A Streetcar Named Desire* to the psychological sexual sadism practiced by George and Martha in *Who's Afraid of Virginia Woolf?*, the dramatic film has been the most durable of all screen genres. More so than any other type of movie, the drama has had an impact on societal norms and human rights. From the plight of the impoverished Oakies of *The Grapes of Wrath* to Sidney Poitier's defiant declaration, "They call me *Mister* Tibbs!" in *In the Heat of the Night*, the dramatic film has raised social consciousness in a way no other genre could. It's fair to say that one film that connects with mainstream audiences can be a more useful instrument for social change than the campaign rhetoric of a dozen politicians.

Hollywood has come under fire in recent years because of actors and filmmakers championing causes that are often out of step with mainstream values. Yet, as George Clooney adroitly pointed out when accepting his Oscar in 2006, the film community has often been in the forefront of advocating social changes that are now accepted as the norm but were wildly unpopular in their day. Hopefully, that is a tradition that will carry on with the next generations of filmmakers.

The Jazz Singer (1927)

Warner Brothers

Director: Alan Crosland; **Writer:** Alfred A. Cohn; **Music:** Louis Silvers; **Running time:** 88 minutes

Cast: Al Jolson (Jakie Rabinowitz); Mary McAvoy (Mary Dale); Warner Oland (Cantor Rabinowitz); Eugenie Besserer (Sara)

Oscar nominations: Screenplay, Honorary Award for use of sound

Widely credited with being the first sound movie, the accolade is somewhat misleading. Other films had experimented with synchronized sound prior to this. However, *The Jazz Singer* was the first full-length feature film to have a soundtrack that included dialogue (though only the musical numbers and some select conversations were recorded for sound). The story centers on a rebellious young Jewish man who would rather be a cabaret singer than follow his family's tradition of having all males become Cantors. Eddie Cantor and George Jessel (who played the role on stage) turned the screen version down, leaving Al Jolson to gain movie immortality. The film was a huge financial hit, though ironically Sam Warner, one of the founders of the studio and the creative force behind the film, died at age 40 one day before the movie's premiere.

"Play It Again, Sam"

Remade in 1952 with Danny Thomas and in 1980 with Neil Diamond and Laurence Olivier. Though widely panned, the latter version spawned a blockbuster soundtrack album.

The Informer (1935)

RKO Radio Pictures

Director and Producer: John Ford; **Writer:** Dudley Nichols; **Music:** Max Steiner; **Running time:** 91 minutes

Cast: Victor McLaglen (Gypo Nolan); Heather Angel (Mary McPhillip); Preston Foster (Dan Gallagher); Margaret Grahame (Katie Madden); Wallace Ford (Frankie McPhillip)

Oscar nominations: Best Picture, Actor* (Victor McLaglen), Director*, Score*, Screenplay*, Editing

Victor McLaglen, the gentle giant who rose to fame in the films of John Ford, won an Oscar for this early career highlight. McLaglen plays a poor Irishman who sells out the whereabouts of his best friend, an IRA man wanted by the British. He receives a twenty pound reward but realizes all too soon it came at the cost of his self-respect and maybe even his life. Incredibly, Dudley Nichols wrote the script in six days and Ford shot the film in less than three weeks. This is a multi-Oscar winner that still resonates today. Made originally in 1929 and remade in 1968 as the Blaxploitation film *Uptight!*

Goodbye, Mr. Chips (1939)

MGM

Director: Sam Wood; **Producer:** Victor Saville; **Writers:** R.C. Sherriff, Claudine West, and Eric Maschwitz; **Music:** Richard Addinsell; **Running time:** 114 minutes

Cast: Robert Donat (Mr. Chipping); Greer Garson (Katharine Chipping); Terry Kilburn (John Colley/Peter Colley); John Mills (Young Peter Colley); Paul Von Hernreid (Staefel)

Oscar nominations: Best Picture, Actor* (Robert Donat), Editing, Actress (Greer Garson), Screenplay, Sound, Director

A touching tale following the life and career of a beloved British schoolmaster from his days as a nervous young teacher to his status as the school's elder statesman. Throughout his entire life, his first devotion is to his students. The film has many moving moments, particularly in the final scenes. Robert Donat's performance was impressive enough to win the Best Actor Oscar over the presumed "shoo-in" Clark Gable for *Gone with the Wind*.

 "Play It Again, Sam"

The film was remade as a big-budget 1969 musical. Although a commercial failure, the movie did feature a very fine performance by Peter O'Toole who was also Oscar-nominated.

The Hunchback of Notre Dame (1939)

RKO Radio Pictures

Director: William Dieterle; **Producer:** Pandro S. Berman; **Writers:** Sonya Levien and Bruno Frank; **Music:** Alfred Newman; **Running time:** 116 minutes

Cast: Charles Laughton (Quasimodo); Cedric Hardwicke (Frollo); Thomas Mitchell (Clopin); Maureen O'Hara (Esmeralda); Edmond O'Brien (Gringoire)

Oscar nominations: Sound, Score

An impressive remake of the 1923 Lon Chaney silent film. Charles Laughton is superb as the pitiable hunchback, Quasimodo—the unlikely hero who comes to the aid of beautiful damsel Maureen O'Hara. Laughton's legendary makeup was kept a secret until the film premiered, and it had quite an effect on startled audiences. The process of applying the makeup took almost three hours a day. Remade numerous times, most notably in 1956 with Anthony Quinn and in 1996 as a Disney animated feature.

The Grapes of Wrath (1940)

20th Century Fox

Director: John Ford; **Producer:** Darryl F. Zanuck; **Writer:** Nunnally Johnson; **Music:** Alfred Newman (uncredited); **Running time:** 128 minutes

Cast: Henry Fonda (Tom Joad); Jane Darwell (Ma Joad); John Carradine (Casy); Charley Grapewin (Granda Joad); Dorris Bowden (Rose-of-Sharon Rivers)

Oscar nominations: Best Picture, Director*, Supporting Actress* (Jane Darwell), Actor (Henry Fonda), Sound, Screenplay, Editing

In 1940, the year John Ford brought John Steinbeck's classic novel of the Great Depression to the screen, the economic crisis that had afflicted America was still raw enough to resonate with the population. Thus, *The Grapes of Wrath* touched a nerve with a public that was being squeezed between the two great catastrophies of the 20th century: the depression and the rise of the Axis powers in Europe and Asia. Unlike many films that lose their resonance over time, however, this movie still maintains a very powerful punch. The story of the Joads, a hard-working Oklahoma farm family who lose everything, is a timeless story that continues to resonate. Henry Fonda gives the performance of his career as Tom Joad, earning praise from Steinbeck himself who said Fonda was convincing enough to make him "believe my own words." John Ford was awarded the Oscar for his direction. Remade as a TV movie with Gary Sinise in 1991.

Citizen Kane (1941)

RKO Radio Pictures

Director and Producer: Orson Welles; **Writers:** Herman J. Mankiewicz and Orson Welles; **Music:** Bernard Hermann; **Running time:** 119 minutes

Cast: Orson Welles (Charles Foster Kane); Joseph Cotton (Jedediah Leland); Dorothy Comingore (Susan Alexander Kane); Agnes Moorehead (Mary Kane); Ruth Warrick (Emily Kane); Ray Collins (James Gettys); Everett Sloane (Mr. Bernstein)

Oscar nominations: Best Picture, Director, Screenplay*, Editing, Cinematography (b&w), Score, Art Direction-Set Decoration (b&w), Sound, Actor (Orson Welles)

Those who are seeing *Citizen Kane* for the first time may well wonder what all the fuss is about. The film has been universally acclaimed as the greatest motion picture of all time, thus making it virtually impossible to live up to the expectations of "newbies" to the *Kane* mystique. Yet, *Kane* has always been an *experience* as opposed to a mere movie and has traditionally required repeated viewings in order to fully appreciate its influence and greatness. Boy Wonder Orson Welles was a mere 25 years old when he created this masterwork that chronicles the rise and fall of a publishing titan (an overt reference to Welles's nemesis William Randoph Hearst). The techniques seen in the film, primarily the groundbreaking cinematography by Greg Toland and Robert Wise's exciting editing style have influenced films ever since. Equally impressive is the supporting cast, many of whom worked as members of Welles's famed Mercury Players on radio presentations of classic stories. No film can be described as being pure perfection, but in every aspect, *Citizen Kane* comes as close as one could possibly hope. Sadly, the maverick Welles, a true artiste more comfortable with the experimental films of Europe than Hollywood schlock, quickly ran afoul of the major studio bosses. Although he made a few important films in the post-*Kane* period, most were diminished by short-sighted executives who undermined his work. However, *Citizen Kane* will always stand as one of the landmark American cinematic works of art. Its power is so great it probably remains the one classic movie no one will ever try to remake.

Hollywood Confidential

Publishing magnate William Randolph Hearst was so outraged over this thinly disguised depiction of his private scandals that he banned his newspaper empire from advertising the film. Nervous industry executives actually tried to buy the negative from RKO and destroy it rather than offend Hearst.

How Green Was My Valley (1941)

20th Century Fox

Director: John Ford; **Producer:** Darryl F. Zanuck; **Writer:** Philip Dunne; **Music:** Alfred Newman; **Running time:** 118 minutes

Cast: Walter Pidgeon (Mr. Gruffydd); Maureen O'Hara (Angaharad); Anna Lee (Bronwyd); Donald Crisp (Gwilym Morgan, Sr.); Roddy McDowall (Huw Morgan)

Oscar nominations: Best Picture*, Cinematography* (b&w), Supporting Actor* (Donald Crisp), Art Direction-Set Decoration* (b&w), Director*, Supporting Actress (Sara Allgood), Editing, Screenplay, Score, Sound

John Ford's classic was an adapatation of Richard Llewellyn's novel about the ups-and-downs of a large Welsh mining family at the turn of the century. The happy brood faces internal strife and ostracism from their friends when the family patriarch refuses to join the newly formed union. The film was nominated for ten Oscars, winning in several key categories. The convincing Welsh town was actually built in California! The film still resonates with audiences in a tragic way due to high profile industry disasters in recent years that cost the lives of many miners. Remade as a British TV production in 1975 with Stanley Baker.

The Magnificent Ambersons (1942)

RKO Radio Pictures

Director, Producer, and Writer: Orson Welles; **Music:** Bernard Hermann and Roy Webb (uncredited); **Running time:** 88 minutes

Cast: Joseph Cotton (Eugene); Dolores Costello (Isabel); Anne Baxter (Lucy); Tim Holt (George); Agnes Moorehead (Fanny)

Oscar nominations: Best Picture, Supporting Actress (Agnes Moorehead), Cinematography (b&w), Art Direction-Set Decoration (b&w)

Although nominated for Best Picture, Orson Welles's much-anticipated follow up to his masterpiece *Citizen Kane* is one of Hollywood's great tragedies—both onscreen and off. Welles adapted Booth Tarkington's novel about the fall of a once aristocratic family at the turn of the century into a major film release for RKO. When an audience preview went negatively, the studio ordered Welles's *Kane* editor Robert Wise to drastically cut the film. (Welles would never forgive Wise for assisting in butchering his film.) Freddie Fleck was hired to shoot a (relatively) upbeat ending without Welles's approval. The running time, even with the new epilogue, was reduced to a mere 88 minutes. The final indignity came when the movie was released as a double feature with a lightweight entry in the *Mexican Spitfire* comedy series. What remains is still a superior piece of work, though Welles all but disowned it. *Ambersons* features superb performances, particularly by Tim Holt, who was heretofore known for playing All-American good guy types. The missing footage from *Ambersons* has been sought by archivists for decades, but it appears to have been destroyed. Only stills of the missing scenes remain.

Mrs. Miniver (1942)

MGM

Director: William Wyler; **Producer:** Sidney Franklin; **Writers:** Arthur Wimperis, George Froeschel, James Hilton, and Claudine West; **Music:** Herbert Stothart; **Running time:** 134 minutes

Cast: Greer Garson (Kay Miniver); Walter Pidgeon (Clem Miniver); Teresa Wright (Carol); Dame May Whitty (Lady Beldon); Reginald Owen (Foley); Henry Wilcoxon (Vicar)

Oscar nominations: Best Picture*, Screenplay*, Actress* (Greer Garson), Cinematography* (b&w), Supporting Actress* (Teresa Wright), Director*, Editing, Sound, Supporting Actor (Henry Travers), Supporting Actress (Dame May Whitty), Special Effects, Actor (Walter Pidgeon)

Although the United States had entered WWII by the time this film was released, it had been shot when the nation was still technically neutral. It was designed as an homage to the British people, then holding out alone against Hitler's forces. The screenplay is pure schmaltz by today's standards, but the story about how the war affected the lives of a typical British family touched a nerve in its day. No less than Winston Churchill pronounced it vital to the war effort, and Goebbels himself had grudging admiration for its propaganda value. The final inspirational speech by the Vicar was rewritten the night before shooting and was considered so effective it was reproduced in leaflets dropped over Germany! A box office blockbuster, the feature spawned a dud sequel, *The Miniver Story*, in 1950 and a 1960 TV production starring Maureen O'Hara.

Hollywood Confidential

Greer Garson's Oscar acceptance speech is still the longest in history: a staggering 5½ minutes!

The Pride of the Yankees (1942)

RKO Radio Pictures

Director: Sam Wood; **Producer:** Samuel Goldwyn; **Writer:** Damon Runyon; **Music:** Leigh Harline; **Running time:** 128 minutes

Cast: Gary Cooper (Lou Gehrig); Teresa Wright (Eleanor Twistle); Walter Brennan (Sam Blake); Dan Duryea (Hank Hanneman); Babe Ruth (Himself)

Oscar nominations: Best Picture, Editing*, Actor (Gary Cooper), Art Direction-Interior Decoration (b&w), Screenplay, Writing-Original Story, Score, Cinematography (b&w), Sound, Actress (Teresa Wright), Special effects

A moving story of the life of New York Yankees legend Lou Gehrig, who played in 2,130 consecutive games without an absence. The beloved baseball star had dramatically and heroically battled ALS (later named "Lou Gehrig's Disease") until his death in 1941 at age 37. His famous final speech at Yankee Stadium is still guaranteed to bring a tear to your eye thanks to Gary Cooper's earnest performance. The audience at the time could especially relate to the film because it was released only a year after Gehrig's death. Babe Ruth and other famed players appear as themselves. There is a lack of actual baseball footage in the film because, try as he might, Cooper never got the hang of the game.

Yankee Doodle Dandy (1942)

Warner Brothers

Director: Michael Curtiz; **Producers:** Hal B. Wallis and Jack Warner; **Writer:** Edmund Joseph; **Songs:** George M. Cohan; **Running time:** 126 minutes

Cast: James Cagney (George M. Cohan); Joan Leslie (Mary Cohan); Walter Huston (Jerry Cohan); Richard Whorf (Sam Harris); Irene Manning (Fay Templeton); Rosemary DeCamp (Nellie Cohan); Jeanne Cagney (Josie Cohan)

Oscar nominations: Best Picture, Director, Actor* (James Cagney), Score*, Sound*, Editing, Screenplay, Supporting Actor (Walter Huston)

The life of prolific, super-patriotic songwriter George M. Cohan gets the full Hollywood treatment in this production that won James Cagney an Oscar for Best Actor. Cohan, whose remarkable life is distorted and sanitized in this glossy, big budget production, is depicted from boyhood through middle age, as he continues to perform musical acts with his mother, father, and sister (played by Cagney's real-life sister Jeanne). Despite the factual liberties, the movie is a rousing affair all the way, as classic songs like *Over There* and *You're a Grand Old Flag* are presented as major productions. Cagney is terrific, bringing a humanity and fallibility to the role of Cohan (who wanted Cagney to play him onscreen). The film also provides many touching sequences between Cohen and his father, wonderfully played by Walter Huston. Tragically, Cohan died only months after the film premiered.

 "Well, Nobody's Perfect!"
The film makes a key error in the climactic finale. Cohan was not awarded the Congressional Medal of Honor—that is reserved for military achievements. He was, in fact, given the Congressional Gold Medal for civilian recognition.

The Life and Death of Colonel Blimp (1943)

United Artists

Directors, Producers, and Writers: Michael Powell and Emeric Pressburger; **Music:** Allan Gray; **Running time:** 163 minutes

Cast: Roger Livesey (Clive Candy); Deborah Kerr (Edith/Johnny/Barbara); Anton Walbrook (Theo); Roland Culver (Betteridge); James McKechnie (Spud Wilson)

A film that is as unique as its title, this British Technicolor production was produced in the midst of WWII and follows two former adversaries—a British military officer and his German counterpart—who become friends only to have their love lives intersect and their relationship continue through the dark days of the present conflict. The film's cast, largely unknown to American audiences, is nonetheless incredibly talented. The intriguing story ultimately centers on the old German ex-warrior trying to explain to his doddering old British friend that the honorable methods of warfare have given way to a new form of barbarism. Deborah Kerr plays three different roles and is equally impressive in each. Winston Churchill was so outraged that the film humanized a German military man that he successfully prevented the film from being exported to the United States until after the war.

The Lost Weekend (1945)

Paramount Pictures

Director: Billy Wilder; **Producer:** Charles Brackett; **Writers:** Charles Brackett and Billy Wilder; **Music:** Miklos Rosza; **Running time:** 101 minutes

Cast: Ray Milland (Don Birnem); Jane Wyman (Helen St. James); Phillip Terry (Wick Birnem); Howard Da Silva (Nat); Doris Dowling (Gloria); Frank Faylin ("Bim" Nolan)

Oscar nominations: Best Picture*, Actor* (Ray Milland), Screenplay*, Director*, Score, Cinematography (b&w), Editing

To call this masterful film "sobering" would be an unpardonable pun. In the era prior to the Lifetime TV network, it was actually *unusual* for major films to deal with social problems such as alcoholism. Billy Wilder's *The Lost Weekend* was considered a major gamble, especially for Ray Milland. The popular star of light comedies portrays an alcoholic writer driven to madness by his quest for a drink. Milland actually went through part of Bellevue's rehab process, and its sheer horror convinced Wilder to replicate the experience by shooting the actual sequence at the famed hospital. (Bellevue regretted giving permission given the black eye the institute received in the film.) The movie was a major Oscar winner and Milland took home the prize. Alcoholics pestered Milland for rehab advice for the rest of his life!

The Best Years of Our Lives (1946)

RKO Radio Pictures

Director: William Wyler; **Producer:** Samuel Goldwyn; **Writer:** Robert E. Sherwood; **Music:** Hugo Friedhofer; **Running time:** 172 minutes

Cast: Myrna Loy (Milly Stephenson); Fredric March (Al Stephenson); Dana Andrews (Fred Derry); Teresa Wright (Peggy); Virginia Mayo (Marie); Harold Russell (Homer Parrish)

Oscar nominations: Best Picture*, Director*, Score*, Editing*, Actor* (Fredric March), Supporting Actor* (Harold Russell), Screenplay*, Sound

Amidst the euphoria over the end of WWII, producer Samuel Goldwyn had read an article in *Life* about the psychological problems G.I.'s were having after returning home. He commissioned a major film about the dilemma against conventional wisdom that said audiences only wanted upbeat films in the post-war environment. *The Best Years of Our Lives* swept the Oscars and became a major hit. Perhaps because it was filmed as servicemen were being repatriated, the film has a feeling of immediacy and authenticity that probably could not have been achieved years later. The picture is a long one, but engrossing throughout, and you can't fail to be moved by the wonderful sequence in which Fredric March surprises his wife by returning home unexpectedly. Filled with unforgettable scenes and vignettes, the movie was a rarity amidst the post-war penchant for over-stuffed patriotic epics. Remade as a 1975 TV movie called *Returning Home*.

Hollywood Confidential

Harold Russell, who plays the sympathetic sailor who lost both hands in the war, was in fact a real-life serviceman who suffered that exact fate. He used hooks for his hands and made remarkable progress in being self-sufficient. In addition to winning a Supporting Actor Oscar, the Academy also granted him an honorary award for inspiring fellow servicemen. Russell retired from acting for decades, but made a few screen appearances in the 1980s.

Great Expectations (1947)

Universal Pictures

Director: David Lean; **Producer:** Ronald Neame; **Writers:** David Lean, Ronald Neame, Anthony Havelock-Allen, Cecil McGivern, and Kay Walsh; **Music:** Walter Goehr; **Running time:** 118 minutes

Cast: John Mills (Pip); Anthony Wager (Pip as a boy); Valerie Hobson (Estella); Jean Simmons (Estella as a girl); Bernard Miles (Joe Gargery); Francis L. Sullivan (Mr. Jaggers); Finlay Currie (Magwitch); Martita Hunt (Miss Fabersham); Alec Guiness (Herbert Pocket)

Oscar nominations: Best Picture, Screenplay, Art Direction-Set Decoration* (b&w), Cinematography* (b&w), Director

The ultimate screen adaptation of Dickens's oft-filmed tale of the adventures of Pip, an impoverished young lad who, through the generosity of a mysterious benefactor, is able to live a gentleman's life. The fascinating tale follows Pip through manhood and introduces a series of surprising plot twists and intriguing characters as he doggedly pursues the beautiful girl he has been obsessed with since boyhood. Stunning cinematography by Guy Green and marvelous performances by a cast of outstanding thespians. John Mills is perfect as Pip, and Alec Guiness had an early major screen role as his friend and London roommate.

"Play It Again, Sam"

This was the third screen version of *Great Expectations* following versions released in 1917 and 1934. A version set in contemporary New York was released in 1998 starring Ethan Hawke and Gwyneth Paltrow. Numerous TV versions have also been produced.

Hamlet (1948)

Universal Pictures

Director, Writer, and Producer: Laurence Olivier; **Music:** William Walton; **Running time:** 155 minutes

Cast: Laurence Olivier (Hamlet); Eileen Herlie (Gertrude); Basil Sydney (Claudius); Norman Wooland (Horatio); Felix Aylmer (Polonius)

Oscar nominations: Best Picture*, Actor* (Laurence Olivier), Costume Design* (b&w), Art Direction-Set Decoration* (b&w), Director, Supporting Actress (Jean Simmons), Score

Laurence Olivier's triumphant screen version of Shakespeare's masterpiece was the first non-American film to win Best Picture. Olivier also won the Best Actor and Director awards. Yet, if the film has a major fault, it is that it is too streamlined. Basically, Olivier produced a masterful Cliff Notes version of the story, leaving out scenes and characters such as Rosencrantz and Guildenstern. This was probably due to the fact that the film had already racked up a budget of over $2 million, which was very sizable for its day. Nevertheless, Olivier's performance is peerless and remains the definitive screen Hamlet. As an interesting note, this was the first film in which Christopher Lee and Peter Cushing appeared together (though Lee is an uncredited extra). While set decoration isn't the hottest category for film buffs, this movie really has a stunning set that allows the action to flow in very creative ways. Remade countless times, with Mel Gibson's 1990 production a surprisingly effective endeavor.

Oliver Twist (1948)

Eagle-Lion Films

Director: David Lean; **Producer:** Ronald Neame; **Writers:** David Lean and Stanley Haynes; **Music:** Arnold Bax; **Running time:** 105 minutes

Cast: Alec Guiness (Fagin); Robert Newton (Bill Sikes); Kay Walsh (Nancy); Francis L. Sullivan (Mr. Bumble); John Howard Davies (Oliver Twist); Anthony Newley (Artful Dodger)

Following the acclaim accorded *Great Expectations*, David Lean gave Alec Guiness (who was only a supporting player in that film) a major starring role as Fagin in this spirited adaptation of Dickens's masterpiece. However, the film turned out to be steeped in controversy. While no one denied Guiness played the sly Fagin with great skill, U.S. censors complained that his portrayal was blatantly anti-Semitic. It would take three years before the film could be shown in the United States, and then only after some offending scenes were edited to tone down Fagin's Jewish characteristics. John Howard Davies, who played Oliver, would become a major producer and director of classic British TV shows including *Benny Hill* and *Monty Python's Flying Circus*. Remade many times, most effectively as the Oscar-winning 1968 musical *Oliver!*

The Bicycle Thief (1949)

Arthur Mayer & Joseph Burstyn Inc.

Director: Vittorio De Sica; **Producer:** Giuseppe Amato; **Writer:** Cesare Zavattini; **Music:** Alessandro Cicognini; **Running time:** 93 minutes

Cast: Lamberto Maggiorani (Antonio Ricci); Enzo Staiola (Bruno); Lianella Carell (Maria); Gino Saltamerenda (Baiocco)

Oscar nominations: Screenplay, Won special award for Best Foreign Film of 1949.

Vittorio De Sica's masterpiece of neo-realism is so spellbinding the viewer may come to think they are watching a documentary. This is a simple tale of a hard working family man who finds his world destroyed when the bicycle he relies upon to get to work is stolen. He becomes desperate to find and recover the bike to avoid losing his livelihood. The film is far more complex in execution than it is in description as De Sica explores the inner demons we all possess. De Sica used amateur actors to insure audiences were not distracted by the personas and mannerisms of well-known stars. *The Bicycle Thief* exemplifies the dynamic qualities of the post-WWII Italian cinema. These achievements are all the more impressive when one considers that the films were made on miniscule budgets in a country that had only recently been ravaged by destructive battles and bombings.

All the King's Men (1949)

Columbia Pictures

Director, Producer, and Writer: Robert Rossen; **Running time:** 109 minutes

Cast: Broderick Crawford (Willie Stark); John Ireland (Jack Burden); Joanne Dru (Anne Stanton); Mercedes McCambridge (Sadie Burke)

Oscar nominations: Best Picture*, Director, Actor* (Broderick Crawford), Supporting Actress * (Mercedes McCambridge), Editing, Screenplay, Supporting Actor (John Ireland)

Broderick Crawford won a well-deserved Oscar in this biting political drama obviously inspired by the life and death of infamous Louisiana political boss Huey Long. Crawford's Willie Stark starts out as a crude but honest man who runs for office so the public can have an alternative to the corrupt hacks who dominate the state's political machine. By the time he achieves his dream, he is hopelessly corrupted by the very system he opposed. His brutal and repressive tactics lead to a tragic conclusion. It was brilliantly directed by triple-threat director, producer, and writer Robert Rossen. Remade as a 1958 TV production. Sean Penn starred in a theatrical remake in 2005.

Champion (1949)

United Artists

Director: Mark Robson; **Producer:** Stanley Kramer; **Writer:** Carl Foreman; **Running time:** 99 minutes

Cast: Kirk Douglas ("Midge" Kelly); Marilyn Maxwell (Grace Diamond); Arthur Kennedy (Connie Kelly); Paul Stewart (Tommy Haley)

Oscar nominations: Editing*, Actor (Kirk Douglas), Supporting Actor (Arthur Kennedy), Screenplay, Art Direction-Set Decoration (b&w), Score

The granddaddy of boxing movies, *Champion* was one of the first films to show the brutal sport in all its ugliness. Kirk Douglas gives the performance of his career as a young man who rises to the top in the world of boxing—only to find himself isolated and psychologically destroyed by the moral compromises he has made. The fight scenes are brutal, the supporting cast is terrific, and Mark Robson's direction is top-notch. The final poignant view of Douglas is an almost primal image of human suffering.

Rashomon (1950)

RKO Radio Pictures

Director: Akira Kurosawa; **Producer:** Minoru Jingo; **Writers:** Akira Kurowsawa and Shinobu Hashimoto; **Running time:** 88 minutes

Cast: Toshiro Mifune (Tajomaru); Machiko Kyo (Masako); Masayuki Mori (Takehiro); Takashire Shimura (Woodcutter); Minoru Chiaki (Priest)

Oscar nominations: Art Direction-Set Decoration (b&w), Honorary Award for Outstanding Foreign Language Film

"Play It Again, Sam"

Rashomon was remade as a 1960 TV production directed by Sidney Lumet and as the 1964 western *The Outrage* starring Paul Newman. A 1991 remake titled *Iron Maze* was set in modern times and starred Bridget Fonda.

Akira Kurosawa's powerful drama of rape and murder has been acclaimed as a masterpiece since its release in 1950. The intriguing storyline concerns a woman who is violently raped and the murder of her nobleman husband. Told in flashback by one of the participants in the trial of the bandit involved in the crime, we learn that each of the four people involved in the incident has a substantially different version of the murder. Kurosawa's film presents us with the dilemma that we can never be completely sure we are being told the truth. Kurosawa's success with this film helped reignite the Japanese cinema in the aftermath of WWII.

Sunset Boulevard (1950)

Paramount Pictures

Director: Billy Wilder; **Producer:** Charles Brackett; **Writers:** Charles Brackett, Billy Wilder, and D.M. Marshman Jr.; **Music:** Franz Waxman; **Running time:** 110 minutes

Cast: William Holden (Joe Gillis); Gloria Swanson (Norma Desmond); Erich Von Stroheim (Max Von Mayerling); Nancy Olson (Betty)

Oscar nominations: Best Picture, Director, Actor (William Holden), Actress (Gloria Swanson), Art Direction-Set Decoration* (b&w), Screenplay*, Score*, Supporting Actress (Nancy Olson), Editing, Cinematography, Supporting Actor (Erich Von Stroheim)

Billy Wilder's sordid classic about a delusional, aging silent film queen, Norma Desmond, and her frustrated young gigolo who doesn't have the self-respect to leave the pampered life she's afforded him. Silent screen star Gloria Swanson made a real-life comeback with this film, paralleling the one Norma Desmond dreams about. Although only 50 years old at the time, Swanson was made to appear much older. Her striking appearance and peerless delivery of classic lines are the factors most responsible for *Sunset Boulevard*'s status as a true cinematic masterpiece. William Holden gives the best performance of his career as the boy toy whose disgust for Norma is only exceeded by the disgust he has for himself. Great German silent director Erich Von Stroheim gives a wonderful supporting performance as Norma's long-suffering butler. This film inspired the Andrew Lloyd Weber stage musical that is also being made as a feature film.

Gone with the Wind

Sunset Boulevard originally included a prologue in the morgue, where the body of Holden's Joe Gillis rises from the dead and relates in flashback how he was murdered. When the scene elicited snickers from preview audiences, Wilder cut it and replaced it with the famous opening scene of Holden's corpse floating in the swimming pool.

A Place in the Sun (1951)

Paramount Pictures

Director and Producer: George Stevens; **Writers:** Michael Wilson and Harry Brown; **Music:** Franz Waxman; **Running time:** 122 minutes

Cast: Montgomery Clift (George Eastman); Elizabeth Taylor (Angela Vickers); Shelly Winters (Alice Tripp); Anne Revere (Hannah Eastman); Keefe Brasselle (Earl Eastman); Raymond Burr (D.A. Marlowe)

Oscar nominations: Best Picture, Director*, Actor (Montgomery Clift), Supporting Actress (Shelly Winters), Score*, Cinematography* (b&w), Editing*, Costume Design*, Screenplay*

George Stevens's big budget adaptation of Theordore Dreiser's acclaimed novel *An American Tragedy* caused quite a stir in its day. The dramatic tale (previously made under the book's title in 1931 and based on a real-life case) is about an ambitious young man (Clift) from the other side of the tracks who falls madly in love with a rich young girl (Taylor) and seems destined to marry into a rich and opulent lifestyle. However, when his frumpy ex-girlfriend (Winters) announces he must marry *her* because she is pregnant, his life becomes a nightmare that culminates with him standing trial for her murder (a crime he didn't commit). The film is a soap opera, but an engrossing one made by some of the best talent of the era. Taylor was only 17 when she was signed for the role. She formed a deep friendship with Clift, whose personal woes almost rivaled those afflicting his character in this film. Winters gained an Oscar nomination for a great performance, but she would henceforth be cast in similar parts as frumpy victims.

A Streetcar Named Desire (1951)

Warner Brothers

Director: Elia Kazan; **Producer:** Charles K. Feldman; **Writer:** Tennessee Williams; **Music:** Alex North; **Running time:** 122 minutes

Cast: Vivien Leigh (Blanche DuBois); Marlon Brando (Stanley Kowalski); Kim Hunter (Stella Kowalski); Karl Malden (Mitch)

Oscar nominations: Best Picture, Actor (Marlon Brando), Supporting Actress* (Kim Hunter), Actress* (Vivien Leigh), Art Direction-Set Decoration* (b&w), Sound, Director, Score, Cinematography (b&w), Screenplay, Supporting Actor* (Karl Malden), Costume Design

Following his phenomenal Broadway run in *Streetcar*, Marlon Brando starred in the highly anticipated big screen version. His stage costar Jessica Tandy was replaced by Vivien Leigh, who was deemed a bigger box-office draw. The studio wisely had

Tennessee Williams write the screenplay based upon his own play, though the production code forced many changes that watered down this saga of the sexually-charged marriage of Stella Kowalski (Kim Hunter) to her brutish husband Stanley (Marlon Brando). The situation becomes more complex with the arrival of Stella's sister Blanche, an aging southern belle whose habit of putting on airs leads to dramatic consequences. Although the movie was filmed in a confined setting, it dramatically conveys the sweltering heat and atmosphere of New Orleans, thanks to impressive production design and Alex North's flavorful score. Brilliant acting on all levels, and Brando's performance is perhaps the most influential in screen history, ushering in the era of the realistic antihero sans the "redeeming qualities" generally attached to such characters. Remade as TV movies in 1984 and 1995.

Gone with the Wind

Prior to release, the Production Code censors forced the removal of key scenes and dialogue that greatly altered the intentions and backgrounds of the characters. The original cut was finally restored in 1993 for video release.

The Bad and the Beautiful (1952)

MGM

Director: Vincente Minnelli; **Producer:** John Houseman; **Writer:** Charles Schnee; **Music:** David Raksin; **Running time:** 118 minutes

Cast: Lana Turner (Georgia Lorrison); Kirk Douglas (Jonathan Shields); Walter Pidgeon (Harry Pebbel); Dick Powell (James Lee Bartlow); Barry Sullivan (Fred Amiel); Gloria Graham (Rosemary Bartlow); Gilbert Roland ("Goucho" Ribera); Leo G. Carroll (Henry Whitfield)

Oscar nominations: Actor (Kirk Douglas), Cinematography (b&w)*, Screenplay*, Costume Design (b&w)*, Supporting Actress* (Gloria Graham), Art Direction-Set Decoration (b&w)*

A well-made exposé about the rise of a Hollywood heel (Kirk Douglas) who achieves fame and fortune as a director—albeit with the loss of his humanity as the price he pays for success. The tale is told in flashbacks by several of his "victims." Douglas deserved his Oscar nomination, and it is truly ironic that this icon of the American cinema never won the award in competition, though he was granted a lifetime achievement Oscar.

Hollywood Confidential

The film was originally titled *Tribute to a Badman* but the change was made to accommodate a reference to luscious Lana Turner. The *Badman* title was resurrected by MGM and used for a 1956 western.

Limelight (1952)

United Artists

Director, Producer, and Writer: Charles Chaplin; **Music:** Charles Chaplin, Ray Rasch, and Larry Russell; **Running time:** 137 minutes

Cast: Charles Chaplin (Calvero); Claire Bloom (Terry); Nigel Bruce (Postant); Buster Keaton (Calvero's partner); Sydney Chaplin (Neville); Norman Lloyd (Bodalink)

Oscar nominations: Score*

Although criticized by some as a self-love festival for Chaplin, *Limelight* still ranks as a late career highlight for the king of comedy. It's a sentimental tale of an aging Vaudeville clown past his prime who finds renewed meaning in life after he rescues a young ballerina from suicide. There are many touching moments, and the film features an historic, albeit brief, comedy act teaming Chaplin with Buster Keaton. *Limelight* won an Oscar for Best Score 20 years after its initial release because the film hadn't been shown in Los Angeles until that time! This was due to a truncated initial release caused by the hysteria of the McCarthy era wherein Chaplin was accused of having Communist sympathies. Outraged, he went into self-imposed exile in Switzerland and did not return for many years. Hollywood made amends by awarding Chaplin a lifetime achievement award in 1972. Chaplin appeared at the Oscars ceremony that year to accept the award in one of the most emotional evenings in Academy history.

Moulin Rouge (1952)

United Artists

Director and Producer: John Huston; **Writers:** John Huston and Anthony Veiller; **Music:** Georges Auric; **Running time:** 119 minutes

Cast: Jose Ferrer (Henri de Toulouse-Lautrec/The Comte); Zsa Zsa Gabor (Jane Avril); Suzanne Flon (Myriamme); Claude Nollier (Countess); Colette Marchand (Marie)

Oscar nominations: Best Picture, Director, Actor (Jose Ferrer), Art Direction-Set Decoration* (color), Costume Design* (color), Editing, Supporting Actress (Colette Marchand)

John Huston's dramatic look at the pained life of Toulouse-Lautrec features a remarkable performance by Jose Ferrer as the famed artist afflicted with a disorder that stunted his growth. Ferrer managed the feat of appearing to be short by working with Huston to design clever camera angles, makeup, and set devices along with a painful procedure to have his legs bound behind him so he could walk on his knees. The story itself is a painful one and Ferrer evokes much sympathy as the genius so desperate for love he willingly becomes a pawn for a cruel woman. Superior production design replicates the Paris of Lautrec's era. Georges Auric's score is achingly beautiful. Not related in any meaningful way to the Nicole Kidman *Moulin Rouge* of recent years.

The Wild One (1953)

Columbia Pictures

Director: Laslo Benedek; **Producer:** Stanley Kramer; **Writer:** John Paxton; **Music:** Leith Stevens; **Running time:** 79 minutes

Cast: Marlon Brando (Johnny); Mary Murphy (Kathie); Robert Keith (Sheriff Bleeker); Lee Marvin (Chino); Jay C. Flippen (Sheriff Singer)

The Wild One may not be a great film in many respects, but its social impact was significant. Loosely based on a 1947 incident in which the town of Hollister, California was inundated by motorcycle gangs, the film plays up the hooliganism of the bikers for dramatic effect. Brando's brooding, misunderstood gang leader became an iconic image to teenagers and helped launch an international interest in real-life biker gangs such as the Hell's Angels. The most memorable line of dialogue in the film occurs when Brando is asked "What are you rebelling against, Johnny?" and he responds, "Whaddya got?" thus expressing the angst of millions of young people eager to break the social confinements of the 1950s. They would do so in the next decade, and *The Wild One* would go on to inspire an entire genre of films based on biker gangs. By the time *The Wild Angels* was released in 1966, the violence and sex depicted onscreen would make *The Wild One* look like a Disney production. Incidentally, *The Wild One* was considered such a bad influence on young people, it was banned from England until 1968.

The Caine Mutiny (1954)

Columbia Pictures

Director: Edward Dmytryk; **Producer:** Stanley Kramer; **Writers:** Stanley Roberts and Michael Blankfort; **Music:** Max Steiner; **Running time:** 124 minutes

Cast: Humphrey Bogart (Lt. Cmdr. Queeg); Van Johnson (Steve Maryk); Jose Ferrer (Barney Greenwald); Fred MacMurray (Tom Keefer); Robert Francis (Willis Keith); May Wynn (May Wynn); Tom Tully (DeVreiss)

Oscar nominations: Best Picture, Actor (Humphrey Bogart), Sound, Editing, Screenplay, Score, Supporting Actor (Tom Tully)

The Caine Mutiny is based on Herman Wouk's best-selling novel about a mutiny that occurs after the apparent mental breakdown of a Naval captain during a typhoon. The gripping tale provided Humphrey Bogart with his last Oscar nomination, and he's magnificent as the paranoid Queeg, making him alternately despicable yet sympathetic. Fred MacMurray is outstanding as the officer who incites the mutiny only to turn yellow at the court martial proceedings. The best scene is the finale, in which defense attorney Jose Ferrer gives a stunning soliloquy in support of Queeg–the man he has just destroyed on the witness stand. The only weak link is newcomer Robert Francis who has a "gee whiz" persona not in line with his hard-broiled costars. *The Caine Mutiny* was remade as a 1988 TV movie directed by Robert Altman and starring the late Brad Davis, miscast as Queeg.

La Strada (1954)

Trans Lux

Director: Federico Fellini; **Producers:** Dino De Laurentiis and Carlo Ponti; **Writers:** Federico Fellini, Ennio Flajano, and Tullio Penelli; **Music:** Nino Rota; **Running time:** 115 minutes

Cast: Anthony Quinn (Zampano); Giulietta Masina (Gelsomnia); Richard Basehart (The Fool); Aldo Silvani (Mr. Giraffe)

Oscar nominations: Best Foreign Language Film*, Screenplay

For those who only associate Fellini with avante-garde films and bizarre setpieces, the "normalcy" of *La Strada* may come as a revelation. Many argue it is the master director's finest film. A simple tale of life on the road with a brutish circus strongman (a magnificent Anthony Quinn) and his slow-witted but likeable female companion (Fellini's wife Giulietta Masina). As with most Fellini films, tragedy is introduced in very unusual and innovative ways. The haunting story is greatly enhanced by the acclaimed performance of Giulietta, Fellini's real-life wife, who was compared to a female Chaplin for her extraordinary acting skills that combined comedy and pathos. The film features an impressive supporting performance by Richard Basehart as a tightrope walker who unwittingly incites the tragic finale.

On the Waterfront (1954)

Columbia Pictures

Director: Elia Kazan; **Producer:** Sam Spiegel; **Writer:** Budd Schulberg; **Music:** Leonard Bernstein; **Running time:** 108 minutes

Cast: Marlon Brando (Terry Malloy); Karl Malden (Father Barry); Lee J. Cobb (Johnny Friendly); Rod Steiger (Charley Malloy); Eva Marie Saint (Edie)

Oscar nominations: Best Picture*, Screenplay*, Actor* (Marlon Brando), Art Direction-Set Decoration* (b&w), Cinematography* (b&w), Director*, Editing*, Supporting Actress * (Eva Marie Saint), Score, Supporting Actor (Lee J. Cobb), Supporting Actor (Karl Malden), Supporting Actor (Rod Steiger)

The big Oscar winner of 1954 was based on a series of 1948 newspaper crime exposés that shed light on corrupt union practices on the New York waterfront (though the film was shot on location in Hoboken, New Jersey). Budd Schulberg's masterful script made Columbia brass nervous about financing a film that might alienate their own trade unions. Frank Sinatra desperately wanted the role of ex-boxer Terry Malloy, of late a stooge for waterfront crime bosses. However, Marlon Brando was awarded the part and won an Oscar for his brilliant performance as a man torn between loyalty and morality. Many see his character as an alter-ego for director Elia Kazan, who named names during the McCarthy hearings. Politics aside, this is brilliant cinema.

Hollywood Confidential

Although the famed taxi cab sequence between Brando and Rod Steiger is considered a masterpiece of acting, Brando enraged his costar by refusing to stay on the set while Steiger shot his close-ups, thus making it difficult for the actor to maintain the proper mood. Steiger held a grudge for decades, and the actor only forgave Brando when he encountered him in a restaurant in the 1990s and chatted with him.

The Blackboard Jungle (1955)

MGM

Director and Writer: Richard Brooks; **Producer:** Pandro S. Berman; **Music:** Charles Wolcott; **Running time:** 101 minutes

Cast: Glenn Ford (Richard Dadier); Anne Francis (Anne Dadier); Louis Calhern (Jim Murdock); Margaret Hayes (Lois); Richard Kiley (Joshua Edwards); Vic Morrow (Artie West); Sidney Poitier (Gregory W. Miller)

Oscar nominations: Screenplay, Art Direction-Set Decoration (b&w), Cinematography (b&w), Editing

This is a hard-hitting urban drama about the trials of a well-meaning New York City teacher (Glenn Ford) assigned to a rathole of a high school where hoodlums and sadists terrorize fellow students as well as faculty. The film hit a nerve at the time with its unusually brutal depiction of the social conditions of big city schools. The movie is like a modern *High Noon* with steely Ford as the one teacher willing to take on the thugs. Young Vic Morrow and Sidney Poitier are standouts as the chief delinquents. This was the first movie to feature rock 'n' roll music, and it propelled Billy Haley and the Comets' *Rock Around the Clock* to the top of the charts.

East of Eden (1955)

Warner Brothers

Director and Producer: Elia Kazan; **Writer:** Paul Osborn; **Music:** Leonard Rosenmann; **Running time:** 115 minutes

Cast: Julie Harris (Abra); James Dean (Cal Trask); Raymond Massey (Adam Trask); Burl Ives (Sam); Richard Davalos (Aron Trask); Jo Van Fleet (Kate)

Oscar nominations: Director, Actor (James Dean), Supporting Actress* (Jo Van Fleet), Screenplay

A riveting adaptation of John Steinbeck's novel that in turn was inspired by the biblical tale of Cain and Abel. James Dean's breakout film made him an unexpected teenage idol. His death after the film's release not only earned him the first posthumous Oscar nomination in history but also ensured his status as a legendary antihero. Dean plays a troubled youth in competition with his brother for the love of his stern father. Paul Newman had screentested for the role of Dean's brother, but Richard Davalos landed the part. Remade as a TV mini-series in 1981. Ron Howard has announced plans for a big screen remake.

The Man with the Golden Arm (1955)

United Artists

Director and Producer: Otto Preminger; **Writers:** Walter Newman and Lewis Meltzer; **Music:** Elmer Bernstein; **Running time:** 119 minutes

Cast: Frank Sinatra (Frankie Machine); Eleanor Parker (Zosch); Kim Novak (Molly); Arnold Stang (Sparrow); Darren McGavin (Louie)

Oscar nominations: Actor (Frank Sinatra), Score, Art Direction-Set Decoration (b&w)

This look at the unsuccessful attempts of a drug addict to stay off junk while building a career as a drummer was considered so shocking in 1955 that the Motion Picture Association of America (MPAA) refused to grant it their seal of approval. The film's acclaim made the MPAA loosen its restrictions on subject matter the following year. Frank Sinatra is riveting in an Oscar-nominated performance, and the supporting cast is outstanding. The film features groundbreaking titles by Saul Bass and a classic score by Elmer Bernstein. (See Hart Sharp's special edition DVD for an in-depth discussion by the late composer over the impact this score had on his career.)

Marty (1955)

United Artists

Director: Delbert Mann; **Producer:** Harold Hecht; **Writer:** Paddy Chayefsky; **Music:** Roy Webb; **Running time:** 91 minutes

Cast: Ernest Borgnine (Marty Piletti); Betsy Blair (Clara); Esther Minciotti (Mrs. Piletti); Augusta Ciolli (Aunt Catherine); Joe Mantell (Angie)

Oscar nominations: Best Picture*, Actor* (Ernest Borgnine), Director*, Screenplay*, Supporting Actress (Betsy Blair), Supporting Actor (Joe Mantell), Art Direction-Set Decoration (b&w), Cinematography (b&w)

This low-budget film shocked the film industry when it won several major Academy Awards including Best Picture. Based on a 1953 TV production that starred Rod Steiger, *Marty* is the simple story of a New York butcher who is popular with friends but a zero in terms of meeting girls. When he finally gets the attention of a girl and falls in love, he has to contend with objections from his dominating mother and his friends, who denounce her for superficial reasons (she's a "plain jane"). The film was rumored to be envisioned as a tax write-off for Burt Lancaster and Harold Hecht's production company, but when it generated good buzz, they sank more money into the marketing campaign than they spent on the film itself. Borgnine's warm and winning performance gained him the Best Actor Oscar. The film is moving without being overly sentimental. The supporting cast includes future TV director and actor Jerry Paris; and Frank Sutton, who would star as Sgt. Carter on *Gomer Pyle*. The success of *Marty* proved to studios that modestly budgeted films could produce bonanza profits at the box-office.

Rebel Without a Cause (1955)

Warner Brothers

Director: Nicholas Ray; **Producer:** David Weisbart; **Writer:** Stewart Stern; **Music:** Leonard Rosenman; **Running time:** 111 minutes

Cast: James Dean (Jim Stark); Natalie Wood (Judy); Sal Mineo (Plato); Jim Backus (Frank Stark); Ann Doran (Carol Stark)

Oscar nominations: Supporting Actor (Sal Mineo), Supporting Actress (Natalie Wood), Screenplay

Nicholas Ray's ode to teenaged angst came on the heels of Brando's success in *The Wild One* which had paved the way for a string of largely unremarkable films about juvenile delinquency. *Rebel Without a Cause* was the best of the lot, showing a good deal of sensitivity about the "lost generation" of the 1950s. James Dean is the new kid in town taking on violent gang members while finding comfort with fellow outcasts Natalie Wood and Sal Mineo. The film was partially shot in black and white, but remarkably the studio decided to stop production and reshoot in color. A fine supporting cast includes Dennis Hopper, Edward Platt, and Jim Backus, who is especially memorable as Dean's henpecked, emasculated father. Tragically, the three lead actors all met untimely deaths: Dean died in a car crash, Mineo was stabbed to death, and Wood drowned under mysterious circumstances, all adding additional gravitas to the luckless souls they play in *Rebel Without a Cause*.

Anastasia (1956)

20th Century Fox

Director: Anatole Litvak; **Producer:** Buddy Adler; **Writer:** Arthur Laurents; **Music:** Alfred Newman; **Running time:** 105 minutes

Cast: Ingrid Bergman (Anna/Anastasia); Yul Brynner (Sergei Bounin); Helen Hayes (Dowager Empress Feodorovna); Akim Tamiroff (Boris Chernov)

Oscar nominations: Actress* (Ingrid Bergman), Score

A mesmerizing story about a con man (Yul Brynner) who concocts an outlandish plot to pass off a beautiful amnesiac (Ingrid Bergman) as Anastasia, the daughter of Czar Nicholas who was long-rumored to have survived the execution squad that murdered the other members of her family. The suspenseful story has a neat twist: the woman becomes so convincing that Brynner begins to suspect she may really be Anastasia—even as he begins to fall in love with her. Bergman won an Oscar for her performance in the film that ended her isolation from Hollywood for having had a child out of wedlock with director Roberto Rossellini. Inspired the 1997 animated remake.

Giant (1956)

Warner Brothers

Director: George Stevens; **Producers:** George Stevens and Henry Ginsberg; **Writers:** Fred Guiol and Ivan Moffat; **Music:** Dimitri Tiomkin; **Running time:** 201 minutes

Cast: Elizabeth Taylor (Leslie Benedict); Rock Hudson (Bick Benedict); James Dean (Jett Rink); Carroll Baker (Luz); Jane Withers (Vashti Snythe); Chill Wills (Uncle Bawley); Mercedes McCambridge (Luz Benedict); Dennis Hopper (Jordy Benedict); Sal Mineo (Angel)

Oscar nominations: Best Picture, Director*, Screenplay, Editing, Actor (Rock Hudson), Art Direction-Set Decoration (color), Costume Design (color), Supporting Actress (Mercedes McCambridge), Supporting Actor (James Dean), Score

Based on Edna Ferber's sprawling novel of the same name, this appropriately titled soap opera covers decades in the lives of a Texas ranching family. George Stevens won an Oscar for his direction of this big-budget production that was a box-office blockbuster. Rock Hudson and Liz Taylor are the young couple whose marriage faces increasing challenges—not the least of which is her spurned would-be lover James Dean, in his second posthumous Oscar nominated-performance. Dean's Jett Rink is the most compelling character in the film—a brooding loser who is all but destroyed by – the unexpected wealth his discovery of oil brings him. The cinematography is stunning and, although the sweeping epic is a long sit, the larger-than-life cast makes it highly watchable.

Lust for Life (1956)

MGM

Director: Vincente Minnelli; **Producer:** John Houseman; **Writer:** Norman Corwin; **Music:** Miklos Rosza; **Running time:** 122 minutes

Cast: Kirk Douglas (Vincent Van Gogh); Anthony Quinn (Paul Gauguin); James Donald (Theo Van Gogh); Pamela Brown (Christine); Everett Sloane (Dr. Gachet)

Oscar nominations: Actor (Kirk Douglas), Supporting Actor* (Anthony Quinn), Screenplay, Art Direction-Set Decoration (color)

It took producer John Houseman almost a decade to bring Irving Stone's bestselling semi-fictional biography of Van Gogh to the screen. The temperamental artist is brought to life by Kirk Douglas, in a glorious, fiery performance. The production design should get equal billing, as actual European locales used in Van Gogh's paintings were used for filming. Anthony Quinn won a Supporting Actor Oscar for his brief appearance as Gauguin, Van Gogh's competitor and friend.

A Face in the Crowd (1957)

Warner Brothers

Director and Producer: Elia Kazan; **Writer:** Budd Schulberg; **Music:** Tom Glazer; **Running time:** 125 minutes

Cast: Andy Griffith ("Lonesome" Rhodes); Patricia Neal (Marcia Jeffries); Anthony Franciosa (Joey); Walter Matthau (Mel Miller); Lee Remick (Betty Lou)

Andy Griffith makes an astonishing screen debut in this Elia Kazan film that has been unjustly overlooked for decades. Griffith tears up the screen as a charismatic but inherently evil country singer named Lonesome Rhodes, who is idolized by the very masses he disdains in private. Patricia Neal and Lee Remick (in her film debut) are among the women used, abused, and discarded by Rhodes. The film builds to a shattering conclusion, with Rhodes getting his comeuppance in a very unexpected way. Griffith has been such an icon of light comedy for so many years it's easy to forget what a powerful dramatic actor he can be. *A Face in the Crowd* is a triumph in his long career.

Nights of Cabiria (1957)

Lopert Pictures Corp.

Director: Federico Fellini; **Producer:** Dino De Laurentiis; **Writers:** Pier Paolo Pasolini and Federico Fellini; **Music:** Nino Rota; **Running time:** 110 minutes

Cast: Giulietta Masini (Cabiria); Francois Perier (Oscar); Amedeo Nazzari (Alberto); Aldo Silvani (Hypnotist)

Oscar nominations: Best Foreign Language Film*

Years after their triumphant collaboration on *La Strada*, Fellini and his wife Giuletta Masini reunited for another classic film. *Cabiria* follows the days in the life of a sweet, gentle streetwalker who experiences an endless series of heartbreaks, yet never loses her optimism or indulges in self-pity. Once again, the waifish Giuletta proves why she was considered to be one of Italy's finest actresses. The movie was awarded the Oscar for Best Foreign Language Film and served as the basis for the musical *Sweet Charity*.

The Seventh Seal (1957)

Janus Films

Director and Writer: Ingmar Bergman; **Producer:** Allan Ekelund; **Music:** Erik Nordgren; **Running time:** 92 minutes

Cast: Max Von Sydow (Antonius Block); Gunnar Bjornstrand (Jons); Nils Poppe (Jof); Bibbi Andersen (Mia); Bengt Ekerot (Death)

Writer and Ingmar Bergman scholar Raymond Benson refers to the master filmmaker as "the best director whose films you've probably never seen." *The Seventh Seal* is a prime example of Benson's point. Although relatively few American moviegoers have viewed this masterwork, its images of a knight playing chess with the shrouded figure of Death are iconic. The film concerns a disillusioned knight who has returned from the Crusades unable to believe in God any longer, having witnessed so many cruelties. When Death appears to claim him, the knight challenges him to a chess match with his life as the prize. What unfolds is a series of grim but captivating sequences as

Death interrupts the game in order to spread more calamities on the world without ever answering the knight's almost desperate inquiries about the existence of God. Unforgettable images and a fine performance by future Bergman "stock company" member Max Von Sydow in his first collaboration with the director. Like most Bergman films, *The Seventh Seal* is a major achievement, though by the time this grim sojourn ends, you might be tempted to watch *The Three Stooges in Orbit*.

The Sweet Smell of Success (1957)

United Artists

Director: Alexander Mackendrick; **Producer:** James Hill; **Writers:** Clifford Odets and Ernest Lehman; **Music:** Elmer Bernstein; **Running time:** 96 minutes

Cast: Burt Lancaster (J.J. Hunsecker); Tony Curtis (Sidney Falco); Susan Harrison (Susan Hunsecker); Martin Milner (Steve Dallas)

A searing look at the sleazy world of entertainment publicity, *The Sweet Smell of Success* features remarkable performances by Burt Lancaster as the sinister Broadway columnist (based on Walter Winchell) who delights in destroying his enemy's careers and Tony Curtis as the publicist desperate to curry favor with him. Lancaster is completely compelling, hiding a volcano of rage beneath his quiet exterior. He also has a barely-concealed incestuous interest in his younger sister and destroys any man who shows an interest in her. Curtis, long underrated as an actor, gives his finest performance in a role that earned him a British Academy Award nomination. Great music by Elmer Bernstein, and James Wong Howe's black and white cinematography is glorious. Sadly, the film was a commercial failure in its day. It inspired the short-lived Broadway musical of the same name.

12 Angry Men (1957)

United Artists

Director: Sidney Lumet; **Producers:** Henry Fonda and Reginald Rose; **Writer:** Reginald Rose; **Music:** Kenyon Hopkins; **Running time:** 96 minutes

Cast: Henry Fonda (Davis/Juror #8); Martin Balsam (Juror #1); John Fielder (Juror #2); Lee J. Cobb (Juror #3); E.G. Marshall (Juror #4); Jack Klugman (Juror #5); Ed Begley (Juror #10)

Oscar nominations: Best Picture, Director, Screenplay

Sidney Lumet made his feature film directorial debut with this engrossing adaptation of a Studio One 1954 TV drama about twelve jurors serving on a murder case. Eleven vote for a quick conviction but one holdout painstakingly tries to convince them that the suspect may indeed be innocent, despite overwhelming evidence against him. Lumet rehearsed his cast for two weeks then confined them in an actual jury room where virtually the entire film was shot. The claustrophobic setting combined with the combustible personalities of a dynamic, all male cast make for riveting drama. Henry Fonda excels as the holdout juror (he also produced the film). Remade as a 1997 TV movie with Jack Lemmon and George C. Scott and recently revived on Broadway.

Wild Strawberries (1957)

Janus Films

Director and Writer: Ingmar Bergman; **Producer:** Allan Ekelund; **Music:** Erik Nordgren; **Running time:** 91 minutes

Cast: Victor Sjorstrom (Prof. Isak Borg); Bibi Andersson (Sara); Ingrid Thulin (Marianne Borg); Gunnar Bjornstrand (Evald Borg)

Oscar nominations: Screenplay

Ingrid Bergman's first commercial success in America is a hypnotic odyssey about a revered professor who is traveling on an extended automobile journey to pick up a prestigious award. He is joined by his daughter-in-law with whom he has a prickly relationship. Enroute, the professor indulges in a series of surrealistic flashbacks that make him reevaluate key moments in his life and their significance to the man he is today. Typical of a Bergman film, this is depressing material, but it's also thought-provoking and engrossing thanks largely to the central performance of Victor Sjorstrom, who brings empathy to a man who has spent his life as a cold and insulated person.

The Defiant Ones (1958)

United Artists

Director and Producer: Stanley Kramer; **Writers:** Harold Jacob Smith and Nathan E. Douglas (aka Nedrick Young); **Running time:** 97 minutes

Cast: Sidney Poitier (Noah Cullen); Tony Curtis ("Joker" Jackson); Theodore Bikel (Sheriff Muller); Charles McGraw (Capt. Gibbons); Lon Chaney Jr. (Big Sam)

Oscar nominations: Best Picture, Director, Actor (Sidney Poitier), Actor (Tony Curtis), Supporting Actress (Cara Williams), Supporting Actor (Theodore Bikel), Cinematography* (b&w), Screenplay*, Editing

The concept of two convicts who hate each other but are chained together had mold on it even in 1958. However, Stanley Kramer's effective look at the insanity of racism was a provocative "message picture" in its day, thanks to the performances of Tony

Curtis and Sidney Poitier. The tale is never less than engrossing even though we know these two enemies will grudgingly grow to respect each other. The final chase scene is packed with suspense. Note that no music is heard in the film except for in the natural context of songs heard on a radio. The script was cowritten by blacklisted writer Nedrick Young using the pseudonym Nathan E. Douglas.

The Diary of Anne Frank (1959)

20th Century Fox

Director and Producer: George Stevens; **Writers:** Frances Goodrich and Albert Hackett; **Music:** Alfred Newman; **Running time:** 180 minutes

Cast: Millie Perkins (Anne Frank); Joseph Schildkraut (Otto Frank); Shelly Winters (Mrs. Van Daan); Richard Beymer (Peter); Ed Wynn (Mr. Dussell)

Oscar nominations: Best Picture, Director, Cinematography* (b&w), Art Direction-Set Decoration* (b&w), Supporting Actress* (Shelly Winters), Supporting Actor (Ed Wynn), Score, Costume Design (b&w)

A reverent adaptation of the stage play based on the century's most famous—and tragic—diarist. Director George Stevens knew well the horrors of the Holocaust, having been among the first to film the atrocities in concentration camps during their liberation. Although the film is long, it is never tedious, and Stevens does a remarkable job of compensating for the necessarily claustrophobic set by inspiring his cast to deliver painfully honest performances. Winters won an Oscar, and Schildkraut is magnificent in presenting Otto Frank with understated dignity. The one weak link is Millie Perkins, who is too sugary to convey the pathos of Anne Frank, though she tries mightily. The film is completely engrossing right up to its inevitable and heartbreaking conclusion. Remade numerous times as TV productions.

The 400 Blows (1959)

Zenith International Films

Director and Producer: Francois Truffaut; **Writers:** Francois Truffaut and Marcel Moussy; **Music:** Jean Constantin; **Running time:** 99 minutes

Cast: Jean-Pierre Leaud (Antoine Doinel); Claire Maurier (Gilberte Doinel); Albert Remy (Julien Doinel); Guy DeColmbe (French teacher); Georges Flament (Mr. Bigey)

Oscar nominations: Screenplay

Francois Truffaut's 1959 film is the most prominent example of the "New Wave" cinema created by young French directors in the late 1950s through the 1960s. This accomplished achievement is Truffaut's debut as director, graduating from being a well-regarded film critic. Somewhat autobiographical, the story follows a 12-year-old boy as he tries to cope with the pressures of living in a modern metropolis as well as finding a way to relate to his self-centered mother and father. He begins to drift into petty crimes as his parents take sterner measures to bring him into line. The simplistic nature of the story is precisely what makes it compelling—along with an astonishing performance by Jean-Pierre Leaud, who would star in many other films for Truffaut. Using innovative camera angles and editing techniques, Truffaut paints a portrait of lost youth as a byproduct of distracted parental priorities. The film provides no simple solutions, and its ambiguous ending (a minor triumph for the young lad) features a freeze frame effect that has been widely imitated but never equaled in its impact.

The Apartment (1960)

United Artists

Director and Producer: Billy Wilder; **Writers:** Billy Wilder and I.A.L. Diamond; **Music:** Adolph Deutsch; **Running time:** 125 minutes

Cast: Jack Lemmon (C.C. Baxter); Shirley MacLaine (Fran Kubelik); Fred MacMurray (Sheldrake); Ray Walston (Joe Dobisch); Jack Kruschen (Dr. Dreyfuss)

Oscar nominations: Best Picture*, Director*, Editing*, Art Direction-Set Decoration (b&w)*, Screenplay*, Sound, Supporting Actor (Jack Kruschen), Cinematography (b&w), Actor (Jack Lemmon), Actress (Shirley MacLaine)

Billy Wilder's triumphant multiple Oscar-winner is a heartfelt drama about an up-and-coming young executive played by Jack Lemmon who willingly pays the price of success by lending his apartment to his bosses so they can "entertain" their mistresses. He encounters a dilemma when he falls in love with his immediate superior's mistress and begins to question whether giving up a successful career path is worth a strong backbone. Both moving and funny, the film showcases great performances from Jack Lemmon, Shirley MacLaine (as the loveable floozy of his dreams), and Fred MacMurray, who is wonderful in his all-out sinister mode. (A pity so many people only remember his work on TV sitcoms and light Disney films.) The last black-and-white film to win Best Picture until *Schindler's List*. The film was the basis for the Broadway musical *Promises, Promises*.

Elmer Gantry (1960)

United Artists

Director and Writer: Richard Brooks; **Producer:** Bernard Smith; **Music:** Andre Previn; **Running time:** 146 minutes

Cast: Burt Lancaster (Elmer Gantry); Jean Simmons (Sister Sharon Falconer); Arthur Kennedy (Jim Lefferts); Dean Jagger (William Morgan); Shirley Jones (Lulu Baines)

Oscar nominations: Best Picture, Actor* (Burt Lancaster), Screenplay*, Supporting Actress* (Shirley Jones), Score

Burt Lancaster tears up the screen in his Oscar-winning performance as Elmer Gantry, a con man-turned-evangelist who mesmerizes his flocks even as he fleeces them to pay for his life of hidden lust and avarice. Lancaster's theatrics may have seemed outlandish in 1960, but it's clear that today's TV evangelists have used this movie as a training film, seducing emotionally vulnerable suckers with fire-and-brimstone speeches and phony "cures." The film was considered to be sexually provocative at the time and, although no ratings system was yet in place, the studio made it clear the movie should be avoided by anyone under age 16. Leisurely paced but never boring thanks to Lancaster's dynamic portrayal.

The Entertainer (1960)

Continental Distributing Company

Director: Tony Richardson; **Producer:** Harry Saltzman; **Writers:** John Osborne and Nigel Kneale; **Music:** John Addison; **Running time:** 96 minutes

Cast: Laurence Olivier (Archie Rice); Brenda De Banzie (Phoebe Rice); Roger Livesey (Billy Rice); Joan Plowright (Jean Rice); Alan Bates (Frank Rice); Daniel Massey (Graham); Albert Finney (Mark Rice)

Oscar nominations: Best Actor (Laurence Olivier)

A prime example of the British "kitchen sink" dramas produced in the post-war era through the mid 1960s. Laurence Olivier, who created the role of Archie Rice in the stage production, stars in this film adaptation. Rice is an aging Vaudeville entertainer who refuses to accept the fact that his era and career are over. A monstrous man, Archie uses and abuses everyone in his life including his long-suffering family. Olivier is brilliant in a role that, surprisingly, is said to be much like himself in real life. The sterling supporting cast includes Alan Bates, Albert Finney, and Joan Plowright, who Olivier would marry the next year. *The Entertainer* is depressing as all hell, but riveting as drama. Producer Harry Saltzman would go on to make the 007 films. Remade as a TV movie with Jack Lemmon in 1975.

Inherit the Wind (1960)

United Artists

Director and Producer: Stanley Kramer; **Writers:** Nedrick Young (aka Nathan E. Douglas) and Harold Jacob Smith; **Music:** Ernest Gold; **Running time:** 128 minutes.

Cast: Spencer Tracy (Henry Drummond); Fredric March (Matthew Harrison Brady); Gene Kelly (E.K. Hornbeck); Dick York (Bertram Cates); Donna Anderson (Rachel Brown)

Oscar nominations: Screenplay, Actor (Spencer Tracy), Cinematography (b&w), Editing

This is a highly engrossing adaptation of the classic stage play based on the famous Scopes Monkey Trial of the 1920s in which a teacher was arrested and prosecuted by religious zealots for teaching Darwin's theory of evolution. The real fireworks come from cinematic giants Spencer Tracy and Fredric March squaring off in one of the screen's best courtroom battles. Gene Kelly is very effective in a dramatic role as a cynical reporter. (Robert Vaughn was originally considered for this part.) Crackling good dialogue and witty repartee from Tracy and March. Should be required viewing for school boards who are bringing back the "controversy" about the theory of evolution in recent years. Remade as TV movies in 1965, 1988, and 1999.

La Dolce Vita (1960)

Astor Pictures Corp.

Director: Federico Fellini; **Producers:** Giuseppe Amato and Angelo Rizzoli; **Writers:** Federico Fellini, Ennio Flaiano, Tullio Pinelli, and Brunello Rondi; **Music:** Nino Rota; **Running time:** 174 minutes

Cast: Marcello Mastroianni (Marcello); Anita Ekberg (Sylvia); Anouk Aimee (Maddalena); Yvonne Furneaux (Emma)

Oscar nominations: Director, Screenplay, Art Direction-Set Decoration (b&w), Costume Design* (b&w)

Fellini's leisurely-paced look at the life of a gossip column writer set in contemporary Rome presents a fascinating time capsule of the city life circa 1960. Marcello Mastroianni is perfectly cast as the disillusioned writer, ashamed of the shallowness of his profession but too weak to remove himself from the nightly temptations it offers: booze, willing women, and exotic fun. The movie is one of Fellini's more linear stories, though there are plenty of scenes that will have you scratching your head about their meaning. That's part of the fun of a Fellini film, however. The exact meaning may have only been known by him, but you can relish the fascinating action as stand-alone sequences if you can't determine how they fit into the overall story.

Mastroianni is the coolest of screen personas without the pretentiousness of today's stars who try desperately to emulate his charisma. The movie is credited with entering the term "paparazzi" into popular culture. It derives from the name of a photographer in the film.

Saturday Night and Sunday Morning (1960)

Continental Distributing

Director: Karel Reisz; **Producer:** Tony Richardson; **Writer:** Allan Sillitoe; **Music:** John Dankworth; **Running time:** 89 minutes

Cast: Albert Finney (Arthur Seaton); Shirley Anne Field (Doreen); Rachel Roberts (Brenda); Hylda Baker (Aunt Ada); Norman Rossington (Bert)

One of the best of the so-called "angry young man" movies that emanated from England in the late 1950s through mid 1960s. In his first starring role, Albert Finney is a charismatic young man who seems destined to follow his parents' and grandparents' footsteps by following a mundane, working-class lifestyle. Employed as a lathe operator in a Midlands factory, Finney's Arthur Seaton lives for the weekend, when he puts his meager wages to good use by drinking and womanizing to excess. However, when he opts to have an affair with a coworker's wife, he finds himself facing decisions he never expected to have to make. Writer Allan Sillitoe based the grim but interesting storyline on his own experiences working in a factory and used the film as a plea for the younger generation of Brits to break the bonds that restricted them to predictable and unfulfilling lives.

Two Women (1960)

Embassy Pictures Corporation

Director: Vittorio De Sica; **Producer:** Carlo Ponti; **Writers:** Vittorio De Sica and Cesare Zavattini; **Music:** Armando Trovajoli; **Running time:** 100 minutes

Cast: Sophia Loren (Cesira); Jean-Paul Belmondo (Michele); Eleonora Brown (Rosetta); Raf Vallone (Giovanni); Carlo Ninchi (Michele's Father)

Oscar nominations: Actress* (Sophia Loren)

Vittorio De Sica originally wanted Anna Magnani to star in this film along with Sophia Loren as her daughter. Magnani didn't want to be seen as old enough to play the emerging sex siren's mom, so the film was re-envisioned with Loren in the role of the mother. This is a tale of survival in war torn Italy with Loren and her teenage daughter on the run to avoid Allied bombing raids and trying to seek sanctuary in a dangerous landscape. When they endure a brutal gang rape at the hands of Moroccan soldiers, their lives are forever altered. Loren was the first actress from a foreign language film to receive the Best Actress Oscar. The movie proved that she had far more depth as an actress than most American studios were willing to believe, though her best roles would continue to be in Italian films.

The Virgin Spring (1960)

Janus Films

Director: Ingmar Bergman; **Producers:** Ingmar Bergman and Allan Ekelund; **Writer:** Ulla Isacsson; **Music:** Erik Nordgren; **Running time:** 89 minutes

Cast: Max Von Sydow (Tore); Birgitta Valberg (Mareta); Gunnel Lindblom (Ingeri); Birgitta Pettersson (Karin)

Oscar nominations: Best Foreign Language Film*, Best Costume Design (b&w)

Ingmar Bergman's film brings to life an ancient Swedish legend about a young virgin who is brutally raped by three vagabonds and the terrible revenge her father takes upon them. As with most Bergman films, there is plenty of symbolism and vivid imagery along with an intense performance from the director's "stock company" player Max Von Sydow. The winner of the Oscar for Best Foreign Language Film, the movie inspired the 1972 Wes Craven gorefest *Last House on the Left*.

Judgment at Nuremberg (1961)

United Artists

Director and Producer: Stanley Kramer; **Writer:** Abby Mann; **Music:** Ernest Gold; **Running time:** 186 minutes

Cast: Spencer Tracy (Dan Haywood); Burt Lancaster (Ernst Janning); Richard Widmark (Ted Lawson); Marlene Dietrich (Mrs. Bertholt); Judy Garland (Irene Hoffman Wallner); Montgomery Clift (Rudolph Petersen); Maximilian Schell (Hans Rolfe)

Oscar nominations: Best Picture, Actor (Spencer Tracy), Actor* (Maximilian Schell), Screenplay*, Editing*, Director, Cinematography (b&w), Costume Design (b&w), Supporting Actor (Montgomery Clift), Supporting Actress (Judy Garland), Art Direction-Set Decoration (b&w)

One critic cynically described this film as "An all-star concentration camp drama, with special guest-victim appearances." This is only partly accurate. Director Stanley Kramer specialized in message movies but also knew that to get the widest audience, he needed star power. Unlike George Stevens's *The Greatest Story Ever Told*, wherein stars pop up unexpectedly for a few seconds at a time like a Biblical version of *Laugh-In*, the legends starring in *Judgment at Nuremberg* are used very effectively; and for

Montgomery Clift and Judy Garland, this would be their last acclaimed screen appearances. This sober retelling of the trial of Nazi war criminals was a big budget affair shot on location in Germany. Maximilian Schell won an Oscar as the native German with the dubious task of defending some of history's worst criminals. Burt Lancaster (in a role Laurence Olivier considered playing), in an older and subdued role, is very effective as the educated, aristocratic man who was lured under Hitler's spell—a metaphor for the German population. The film had its premiere in Berlin along with one of the biggest press junkets in history. Germans were offended that their recent past was being dissected on the big screen, but the film received nearly universal critical praise and became a major hit and Oscar contender.

The Hustler (1961)

20th Century Fox

Director and Producer: Robert Rossen; **Writers:** Robert Rossen and Sydney Carroll; **Music:** Kenyon Hopkins; **Running time:** 134 minutes

Cast: Paul Newman (Eddie Felson); Jackie Gleason (Minnesota Fats); Piper Laurie (Sarah); George C. Scott (Burt Gordon); Myron McCormick (Charlie Burns); Murray Hamilton (Findley)

Oscar nominations: Best Picture, Art Direction-Set Decoration* (b&w), Cinematography*, Supporting Actor (Jackie Gleason), Actress (Piper Laurie), Actor (Paul Newman), Director, Screenplay, Supporting Actor (George C. Scott)

It takes considerable skill to make a personalized game such as billiards appear riveting on a movie theater screen, but director Robert Rossen pulled off the near-impossible with this classic look at the ups and downs of a pool hustler. Paul Newman scores in another dynamic performance as Fast Eddie Felson, a cheap pool hustler who works his way into the big leagues as he travels with equally unscrupulous manager George C. Scott. Along the way he encounters and uses vulnerable Piper Laurie—with tragic results. Jackie Gleason is unforgettable as Minnesota Fats. Although only onscreen a short time, he received an Oscar nomination. The art direction and cinematography are so penetratingly real, you can practically smell the cigarettes and stale booze. Newman and Gleason made most of the pool shots themselves under the direction of champion Willie Mosconi. Newman won an Oscar for the 1986 sequel *The Color of Money*.

The Misfits (1961)

United Artists

Director: John Huston; **Producer:** Frank E. Taylor; **Writer:** Arthur Miller; **Music:** Alex North; **Running time:** 124 minutes

Cast: Clark Gable (Gay Langland); Marilyn Monroe (Roslyn Taber); Montgomery Clift (Perce Howland); Thelma Ritter (Isabelle); Eli Wallach (Guido)

The only thing more somber than Arthur Miller's screenplay about depressed, disillusioned people is the story behind the film. The plot casts Gable and Monroe in a contemporary tale of the West that centers on aging cowboys who herd wild horses and sell them to be butchered. The thinly-disguised parallel is that the hopeless plight of the horses mirrors that of their captors. Miller wrote the script as a vehicle for Monroe, who was desperate to show she could emote dramatically. She's good, but still the weakest link among the other old pros in the cast. The notorious publicity surrounding the film revolved around Monroe's unreliable work habits and temper tantrums, coupled with Gable's death shortly after the film was finished. Monroe would commit suicide within a year of its release. Still, it's an impressive film that admittedly has more resonance because of its tragic background story. The scenes of rounding up the horses are particularly well staged, even though Gable's insistence on doing many of his own stunts probably contributed to his death.

A Raisin in the Sun (1961)

Columbia Pictures

Director: Daniel Petrie; **Producers:** Philip Rose and David Susskind; **Writer:** Lorraine Hansberry; **Music:** Laurence Rosenthal; **Running time:** 128 minutes

Cast: Sidney Poitier (Walter Lee Younger); Claudia McNeil (Lena Younger); Ruby Dee (Ruth Younger); Diana Sands (Beneatha Younger); Ivan Dixon (Asagai); John Fielder (Mark Linder)

This breakthrough drama examines the lives of a poor black family who inherit $10,000 and the ensuing disagreements over what they should do with the money. The mother (Claudia McNeil) wants to elevate their status by buying a decent home, while hot-headed, know-it-all son Sidney Poitier wants to risk it on a scheme to buy a liquor store. Heartwrenching at times, humorous at others, the screenplay was written by Lorraine Hansberry, one of the first black playwrights to have their work presented on Broadway. Most of the cast members from the stage production reprised their roles in this powerful film. With superb dialogue and performances, the film was especially significant because it was the first mainstream Hollywood film to present the modern urban black experience from the viewpoint of blacks themselves. Remade as a 1989 TV movie with Danny Glover.

A Taste of Honey (1961)

Continental Distributing

Director and Producer: Tony Richardson; **Writers:** Shelagh Delaney and Tony Richardson; **Music:** John Addison; **Running time:** 100 minutes

Cast: Rita Tushingham (Jo); Dora Bryan (Helen); Robert Stephens (Peter); Murray Melvin (Geoffrey); Paul Danquah (Jimmy)

Yet another classic British "kitchen sink" drama from director/producer Tony Richardson, this one based on an acclaimed stage play. The story centers on Jo, a down-and-out young woman from the wrong side of the tracks who is kicked out of her home by her self-centered mother. After a onenight stand with a black sailor, she finds herself pregnant. She becomes the roommate of a sensitive gay man who dotes on her as they prepare for the arrival of the baby. All seems blissful until Jo's mother's own problems prove to have a devastating impact on her life once again. Richardson passed up an offer of American financing if he signed Audrey Hepburn as the lead, choosing Rita Tushingham instead. In her screen debut, Tushingham gives a dynamic performance as a sympathetic lost soul and she gets able support from Murray Melvin as the other half of the "odd couple" that sets up house together. A riveting drama from a creatively rich period for the British film industry.

Through a Glass Darkly (1961)

Janus Films

Director and Writer: Ingmar Bergman; **Producer:** Allan Ekelund; **Music:** Erik Nordgren (uncredited); **Running time:** 89 minutes

Cast: Harriet Andersson (Karin); Gunnar Bjornstrand (David); Max Von Sydow (Martin); Lars Passgard (Minus)

Oscar nominations: Best Foreign Language Film*, Screenplay

Bergman's grim but interesting character study centers on a young woman recently released from a mental institution who recuperates in a small island cottage with her husband, father, and younger brother. Fears that she may not be cured are well-founded as her normalcy begins a rapid decline back into madness. Her condition leads to introspection from the men in her life and also results in a life-altering incident with her brother. Superlative performances, particularly by Harriet Andersson as the woman who is panicked at the prospect of not being able to achieve normalcy.

Viridiana (1961)

Kingsley-International Pictures

Director: Luis Bunuel; **Producer:** Gustavo Alatriste; **Writers:** Luis Bunuel and Julio Alejandro; **Music:** Gustavo Pittaluga; **Running time:** 90 minutes

Cast: Silvia Pinal (Viridiana); Francisco Rabal (Jorge); Fernando Rey (Don Jamie); Jose Calvo (Beggar); Margarita Lozano (Ramona)

Spain encouraged acclaimed director Luis Bunuel to return to his native country after an absence of 25 years to make a new film. At age 60, the old boy could still provoke controversy. *Viridiana* generated as much scandal as it did acclaim. The story follows a virginal young woman about to take her vows to become a nun. However, before entering the convent, she is sent to visit her kindly uncle who has been her benefactor. At his estate, a series of dramatic events unfold, including her discovery that he has an unhealthy obsession with her because she bares a striking resemblance to his late wife. This development leads to sexual abuse, suicide, and a new lifestyle for Viridiana as she abandons any hopes of becoming a nun after she fears she has been defiled by her uncle. Bunuel's intense film is filled with allegories and symbolism, much of it critical of Spain's obedient servitude to the Catholic church. Although the movie won the Golden Palm at Cannes, it was banned in several nations including Italy and Bunuel's native Spain. It remains a major work by an undisputed master director.

Whistle Down the Wind (1961)

Pathe-American Film Company

Director: Bryan Forbes; **Producer:** Richard Attenborough; **Writers:** Keith Waterhouse and Willis Hall; **Music:** Malcolm Arnold; **Running time:** 99 minutes

Cast: Hayley Mills (Kathy Bostock); Bernard Lee (Mr. Bostock); Alan Bates (The Man); Norman Bird (Eddie); Elsie Wagstaff (Auntie Dorothy)

Although little known in the United States, this fine film has been a cult favorite in England for years. Producer, actor, and writer Bryan Forbes made an impressive directorial debut with this modest tale of a murder suspect who hides in a family's barn and convinces a group of children he is actually Jesus Christ. The story does not play as absurdly as it reads nor is there the type of heavy-handed symbolism you might expect. Fourteen-year-old Hayley Mills gives a very credible performance in this screen adaptation of a novel written by her mother Mary Hayley Bell. Alan Bates is a standout as the mysterious escaped convict, and the great character actor Bernard Lee ("M" in the 007 films) turns in another fine performance. Malcolm Arnold's score is suitably moody. Inspired the unsuccessful Andrew Lloyd Weber stage musical.

Days of Wine and Roses (1962)

Warner Brothers

Director: Blake Edwards; **Producer:** Martin Manulis; **Writer:** J.P. Miller; **Music:** Henry Mancini; **Running time:** 117 minutes

Cast: Jack Lemmon (Joe Clay); Lee Remick (Kirsten); Charles Bickford (Ellis Arnesen); Jack Klugman (Jim Hungerford)

Oscar nominations: Actor (Jack Lemmon), Actress (Lee Remick), Costume Design (b&w), Art Direction-Set Decoration (b&w), Song* (*Days of Wine and Roses*)

This shattering look at the effects of alcoholism on a likeable young couple has lost none of its impact over the years. The story was first shown as an episode of *Playhouse 90* with Cliff Robertson in the starring role. The feature film was an important one for Jack Lemmon, heretofore known only for his skills in comedies. He and Lee Remick (certainly one of cinemas great natural beauties) are brilliant as they demonstrate a clean cut couple's slow descent into agony and madness. Good support from Charles Bickford as Remick's heartbroken father and Jack Klugman as an AA member trying to salvage Lemmon. Henry Mancini's memorable title song became a popular standard.

The Loneliness of the Long Distance Runner (1962)

Continental Releasing Company

Director and Producer: Tony Richardson; **Writer:** Alan Sillitoe; **Music:** John Addison; **Running time:** 104 minutes

Cast: Tom Courtenay (Colin Smith); Michael Redgrave (The Governor); Avis Bunnage (Mrs. Smith); Peter Madden (Mr. Smith); Alec McCowan (Brown); Joe Robinson (Roach)

This somber but acclaimed British film from influential director Tony Richardson features the impressive screen debut of Tom Courtenay as an angry young man sent to a reform school after he robs a bakery. An expert runner, he is chosen to represent the school in a key long-distance race. Much of the story is told through flashbacks as the young man practices incessantly for the big race. The finale finds him enacting a startling gesture of defiance. It's impressive on all counts. Look for future James Bond villain Joe Robinson (*Diamonds Are Forever*) in an early screen role.

The Miracle Worker (1962)

United Artists

Director: Arthur Penn; **Producer:** Fred Coe; **Writer:** William Gibson; **Music:** Laurence Rosenthal; **Running time:** 106 minutes

Cast: Anne Bancroft (Annie Sullivan); Patty Duke (Helen Keller); Victor Jory (Arthur Keller); Inga Swenson (Kate Keller); Andrew Prine (James Keller)

Oscar nominations: Director, Actress* (Anne Bancroft), Supporting Actress* (Patty Duke), Screenplay, Costume Design (b&w)

Anne Bancroft and Patty Duke both won well-deserved Oscars for their magnificent on-screen recreations of the roles they played in the Broadway version of this story of Helen Keller's remarkable achievements in overcoming her challenges from being both blind and deaf. It's a harrowing film, often too emotionally intense to watch, but Sullivan's hard-fought triumph in getting through to the young girl is a scene of magnificent inspiration. Remade as TV movies in 1979 and 2000. The former starred Patty Duke in the Annie Sullivan role.

Requiem for a Heavyweight (1962)

Columbia Pictures

Director: Ralph Nelson; **Producer:** David Susskind; **Writer:** Rod Serling; **Music:** Laurence Rosenthal; **Running time:** 95 minutes

Cast: Anthony Quinn ("Mountain" Rivera); Jackie Gleason (Maish Rennick); Mickey Rooney (Army); Julie Harris (Grace Miller); Stan Adams (Perelli)

Gone with the Wind

Consumer Alert! The final injustice has been done to poor "Mountain" Rivera: Sony's DVD edition has caused a firestorm of criticism for inexplicably using an edited print that eliminates over seven minutes of key footage that had been inserted into the film years ago for its television broadcasts. In the ensuing years, this extended edition had become the definitive version of the film.

Rod Serling adapted his own TV production for the big screen for this unrelentingly grim look at the underbelly of the boxing world. (Has anyone ever filmed an *upbeat* look at the boxing world?) Anthony Quinn is magnificent as a slow-witted but kind-hearted boxer used and manipulated by his manager played by Jackie Gleason in an outstanding performance. Mickey Rooney also shines as Quinn's one true friend, and Julie Harris provides the only glimmer of class as a social worker who becomes smitten by Quinn. This is a gut-wrenching drama that leads to a sad conclusion, but it's riveting throughout.

To Kill a Mockingbird (1962)

Universal

Director: Robert Mulligan; **Producer:** Alan J. Pakula; **Writer:** Horton Foote; **Music:** Elmer Bernstein; **Running time:** 129 minutes

Cast: Gregory Peck (Atticus Finch); Mary Badham ("Scout"); Phillip Alford ("Jem"); Robert Duvall ("Boo" Radley); John Megna (Dill); Brock Peters (Tom Robinson)

Oscar nominations: Best Picture, Art Direction-Set Decoration* (b&w), Actor* (Gregory Peck), Screenplay*, Supporting Actress (Mary Badham), Score, Director, Cinematography (b&w)

This adaptation of Harper Lee's semi-autobiographical novel is one of the great American films. The beautifully told memoir of a woman looking back on her childhood in a poor southern town centers on her memories of a time when she and her brother witnessed their father's defense of a black man falsely accused of raping a white woman. The young children witness the horrors of racism while trying to maintain the innocence of their youth. Gregory Peck's magnificent Oscar-winning performance as the noble Atticus Finch is such an enduring part of cinema history that his character was recently voted the #1 film hero in the American Film Institute poll. Expertly directed by Robert Mulligan with an achingly beautiful score by Elmer Bernstein. The character of Dill is based on Harper Lee's childhood friend, Truman Capote.

Hud (1963)

Paramount Pictures

Director: Martin Ritt; **Producers:** Martin Ritt and Irving Ravetch; **Writers:** Irving Ravetch and Harriet Frank Jr.; **Music:** Elmer Bernstein; **Running time:** 112 minutes

Cast: Paul Newman (Hud Bannon); Melvyn Douglas (Homer Bannon); Patricia Neal (Alma); Brandon De Wilde (Lonnie Bannon)

Oscar nominations: Supporting Actor* (Melvyn Douglas), Actress* (Patricia Neal), Cinematography* (b&w), Actor (Paul Newman), Art Direction-Set Decoration, Screenplay, Director

A raw and realistic contemporary western with Paul Newman in one of the signature performances of his career—and the most unsympathetic character he has ever played. Hud Bannon is a womanizing, self-centered manipulator who is itching to get his hands on his aging father's cattle empire. In the course of his efforts, he both charms and alienates the tough-as-nails housekeeper (Patricia Neal) and his kid brother (Brandon De Wilde) who idolizes him. Superbly directed by Martin Ritt with an ensemble cast that is letter-perfect. Melvyn Douglas is wonderful as the fading but proud elderly rancher cursed with having a son waiting like a vulture for his departure. Patricia Neal is equally memorable as the one woman who can resist Hud's charms. James Wong Howe's black and white cinematography makes the Texas landscape as bleak as Hud's soul. One of the top dramatic films of the 1960s.

The Night of the Iguana (1963)

MGM

Director: John Huston; **Producers:** Ray Stark and John Huston; **Writers:** Anthony Veiller and John Huston; **Music:** Benjamin Frankel; **Running time:** 125 minutes

Cast: Richard Burton (Shannon); Ava Gardner (Maxine); Deborah Kerr (Hannah); Sue Lyon (Charlotte); Grayson Hall (Judith Fellowes)

Oscar nominations: Costume Design* (b&w), Cinematography (b&w), Art Direction-Set Decoration (b&w), Supporting Actress (Grayson Hall)

Huston's gripping screen adaptation of Tennessee William's tale follows a drunken, de-frocked minister involved with three different women as he leads a tour bus of women through Mexico. Gardner is the hoity-toity bad girl, Kerr is the virginal spinster, and Lyon is the sex-crazed teenager. All are terrific, but it's Richard Burton's cynical, world-weary reverend that truly entrances viewers. The Mexican town of Puerto Vallarta was virtually unknown in 1963. Burton and wife Liz Taylor knew their presence on location would make it the new hot spot, and they shrewdly bought up a good deal of land that soon skyrocketed in value.

This Sporting Life (1963)

Continental Distributing

Director: Lindsay Anderson; **Producer:** Karl Reisz; **Writer:** David Storey; **Music:** Roberto Gerhard; **Running time:** 134 minutes

Cast: Richard Harris (Frank Machin); Rachel Roberts (Mrs. Hammond); Alan Badel (Weaver); William Hartnell (Johnson)

Oscar nominations: Actor (Richard Harris), Actress (Rachel Roberts)

Richard Harris's star-making role elevated him to the ranks of Britain's most durable leading men. He plays a young coal miner determined to break free of his lower class lifestyle by becoming a champion rugby player. Along the way, his sheer determination proves to be an asset on the field, but a character flaw in his personal relationships. *This Sporting Life* is considered to be one of the finest dramatic films produced in England during the 1960s. Excellent performances and thrilling rugby scenes that bring home the brutality of the sport. Look for Edward Fox and Glenda Jackson as unbilled extras.

Becket (1964)

Paramount Pictures

Director: Peter Glenville; **Producer:** Hal B. Wallis; **Writer:** Edward Anhalt; **Music:** Laurence Rosenthal; **Running time:** 148 minutes

Cast: Richard Burton (Thomas Becket); Peter O'Toole (King Henry II); John Gielgud (King Louis VII); Donald Wolfit (Gilbert Folliot); Martita Hunt (Empress Matilda)

Oscar nominations: Best Picture, Cinematography (color), Score, Actor (Richard Burton), Actor (Peter O'Toole), Director, Supporting Actor (John Gielgud), Costume Design (color), Sound, Editing, Art Direction-Set Decoration (color), Screenplay*

This is a magnificent screen adaptation of Jean Anouilh's stage play about a bit of sub-terfuge on the part of King Henry II that ended up shaking the throne of England to the core. In order to gain more control over the church, Henry slyly appoints his best friend and fellow secularist carouser Thomas Becket as Archbishop of Canterbury. The move outrages the church, but instead of being Henry's loyal puppet, Becket gains respect by adopting church doctrine—a move that puts him in direct conflict with Henry. The Oscar-winning screenplay centers on the innocent friendship of the two men and how its dramatic destruction leads to a decision of unspeakable horror on the part of Henry. A glorious, intelligent production that never stoops to inserting superfluous action sequences to "open up" the story. This is a talky film, but the dia-logue is enthralling and it is delivered with passion by Burton and O'Toole, both giv-ing brilliant performances. O'Toole would play the same king four years later in *The Lion in Winter.*

The Hill (1965)

MGM

Director: Sidney Lumet; **Producer:** Kenneth Hyman; **Writer:** Ray Rigby; **Running time:** 123 minutes

Cast: Sean Connery (Joe Roberts); Harry Andrews (Wilson); Ian Bannen (Harris); Alfred Lynch (Stevens); Ossie Davis (Jacko King); Roy Kinnear (Bartlett); Ian Hendry (Williams); Michael Redgrave (Medical Officer)

One of the most under-rated films of the 1960's, Sidney Lumet's *The Hill* is a triumph of cinematic neo-realism and ensemble acting. Set in a British military prison in the

African desert, the plot pits a group of hard-bitten prisoners against a brutal guard who delights in torturing them both psychologically and physically. Although set in WWII, this is not a war film—all the principals are in the British army. The film was especially important to Sean Connery who was trying desperately to gain credibility outside of the James Bond role. He succeeds brilliantly as a tough-nut, non-conformist. Every member of the outstanding cast gets plenty of opportunity to shine, and Harry Andrews is particularly riveting as the commandant who doesn't realize his power is being undermined by his sadistic sergeant (Ian Hendry). The piercing black and white photography will make you sweat along with the prisoners as they trudge the damnable "hill," which they are required to run in the blistering heat. The film's final sequence is haunting and unforgettable. The best of the numerous films on which Connery and Lumet would collaborate.

The Pawnbroker (1964)

American International Pictures

Director: Sidney Lumet; **Producers:** Ely A. Landau, Philip Langer, Roger Lewis, and Herbert R. Steinmann; **Music:** Quincy Jones; **Running time:** 116 minutes

Cast: Rod Steiger (Sol Nazerman); Geraldine Fitzgerald (Marilyn Birchfield); Brock Peters (Rodriguez); Jamie Sanchez (Jesus)

Oscar nominations: Best Actor (Rod Steiger)

Watching Sidney Lumet's dark and dramatic tale of a Holocaust survivor plagued by guilt and depression is like watching a horrendous auto accident: you feel like an intruder observing someone else's pain, but it's too riveting to look away. Rod Steiger gives the greatest performance of his career as a cynical, introverted concentration camp survivor who eeks out a barebones existence as a pawnbroker in decaying Harlem. He shuts out all attempts of friendship and spurns anyone who might show him love. The film shocked audiences with its hints of Nazi atrocities glimpsed in flashback. It was the first film to win a Production Code Seal of Approval despite showing partial female nudity. Great atmospheric location shots and an interesting supporting cast with Brock Peters a standout as an effete but brutal Harlem crimelord. This is Morgan Freeman's first film as an unbilled extra.

Who's Afraid of Virginia Woolf (1966)

Warner Brothers

Director: Mike Nichols; **Producer and Writer:** Ernest Lehman; **Music:** Alex North; **Running time:** 131 minutes

Cast: Elizabeth Taylor (Martha); Richard Burton (George); George Segal (Nick); Sandy Dennis (Honey)

Oscar nominations: Best Picture, Actress* (Elizabeth Taylor), Actor (Richard Burton), Supporting Actor (George Segal), Supporting Actress* (Sandy Dennis), Director, Costume Design* (b&w), Art Direction-Set Decoration* (b&w), Cinematography* (b&w), Score, Editing, Sound, Screenplay

Edward Albee's 1962 play was a sensation on Broadway, but many movie fans groaned when it was announced that Elizabeth Taylor and Richard Burton would play the leading roles in the film version. The Hollywood "It" couple had been criticized for turning their films into empty vanity productions. Liz and Dick shocked everyone, however, by frumping themselves up and delivering the finest performances of their careers. (Taylor won the Oscar). Had it not been for Burton and Taylor's presence, the film probably would have been relegated to the art house circuit instead of becoming a major box-office success. The bizarre story focuses on a young couple who are invited for drinks at the home of a henpecked professor and his vulgar, sexually aggressive wife. In the course of the evening, all manner of psychological games reveal shocking secrets about each person. Ernest Lehman produced and adapted the play to the screen and Mike Nichols, primarily known as a comedy writer and performer, does excellent work in his directorial debut. Outstanding score by Alex North and cinematography by Haskell Wexler. The film broke barriers in the use of explicit language.

Belle De Jour (1967)

Allied Artists

Director: Luis Bunuel; **Producers:** Henri Baum, Raymond Hakim, and Robert Hakim; **Writers:** Luis Bunuel and Jean-Claude Carriere; **Running time:** 101 minutes

Cast: Catherine Deneuve (Severine); Jean Sorel (Pierre); Michel Piccoli (Henri Husson); Genevieve Page (Madame Anais)

The great director Luis Bunuel's most commercial film, *Belle De Jour*, is one of the most erotic movies of the 1960s, though it's largely devoid of nudity. Catherine Deneuve is a beautiful, sheltered new bride in a lucrative but boring marriage. When she hears about a local brothel that employs housewives to ply their skills in secret, she makes the ominous decision to fulfill her own fantasies by becoming a prostitute. The film is a quasi-fantasy, and it is often debatable whether these scenarios are actually happening to Deneuve's character or are merely being imagined by her. In the most famous sequence, a client shows her a small box and begs her to use the object inside in their sex play, which she adamantly refuses to do. Moviegoers have long debated what was inside the box, but Bunuel (refreshingly) never spilled the beans. Deneuve is simply ravishing, certainly one of the most gorgeous faces to emerge in 1960s cinema.

Cool Hand Luke (1967)

Warner Brothers

Director: Stuart Rosenberg; **Producer:** Gordon Carroll; **Writers:** Donn Pierce and Frank R. Pierson; **Music:** Lalo Schifrin; **Running time:** 126 minutes

Cast: Paul Newman (Luke Jackson); George Kennedy (Dragline); J.D. Cannon (Society Red); Lou Antonio (Koko); Robert Drivas (Loudmouth Steve); Strother Martin (Captain)

Oscar nominations: Actor (Paul Newman), Supporting Actor* (George Kennedy), Screenplay, Score

There's nothing strikingly original about this look at a nonconformist sentenced to a southern chain gang for a petty crime. However, Paul Newman turns the wisecracking rebel Luke Jackson into one of the screen's most memorable characters, and he gets top support from a fine cast of character actors, including George Kennedy in an Oscar-winning role and the great Strother Martin as the sadistic chain gang captain. Best scene is the egg-eating contest. Lalo Schifrin's score contributes mightily.

To Sir, with Love (1967)

Columbia Pictures

Director, Producer, and Writer: James Clavell; **Music:** Ron Grainer; **Running time:** 105 minutes

Cast: Sidney Poitier (Mark Thackery); Christian Roberts (Denham); Judy Geeson (Pamela); Suzy Kendall (Gillian); Lulu ("Babs")

A decade after making Glenn Ford's life miserable in the classroom in *The Blackboard Jungle*, Sidney Poitier got a taste of his own medicine in *To Sir, with Love*. Poitier plays a charismatic school teacher in London at the height of the youthful "mod" movement. He is assigned to a high school where discipline has completely broken down and delinquents are the real power brokers. Poitier's innovative methods of asserting power while still respecting students make for some wonderful sequences. The film is a near-perfect blend of comedy and drama, with a dash of pathos tossed in. The title song sung by Lulu was a major hit in 1967.

"Play It Again, Sam"

The film inspired a TV movie in 1974 and a 1996 TV sequel, *To Sir, with Love II* directed by Peter Bogdanovich with Sidney Poitier, Lulu, and Judy Geeson reprising their roles.

Charly (1968)

Cinerama Releasing Corp.

Director and Producer: Ralph Nelson; **Writer:** Sterling Silliphant; **Music:** Ravi Shankar; **Running time:** 103 minutes

Cast: Cliff Robertson (Charly Gordon); Claire Bloom (Alice Kinnian); Lila Skala (Dr. Anna Strauss)

Oscar nominations: Best Actor* (Cliff Robertson)

Nowadays, the surest way for an actor to get an Academy Award is to portray a character who is physically or mentally handicapped. Back in 1968, however, it was considered a suicidal career move. Yet Cliff Robertson went against the grain and brought the story *Flowers for Algernon* to the big screen, portraying a retarded man who undergoes a medical experiment that turns him into a genius. It's a mixed blessing, however, because although he finds love, he also now sees how many of his "friends" had been mocking and exploiting him. There is also a dramatic side effect to the "cure" that leads to a devastating conclusion. Robertson is simply superb and earned his Best Actor Oscar, even though he didn't even campaign for the award. A moving and touching film that still packs an emotional wallop. Remade as a TV movie in 2000 with Matthew Modine.

Hollywood Confidential

Cliff Robertson had starred in the original TV productions of *The Days of Wine and Roses* and *The Hustler* only to see the big screen versions go to Jack Lemmon and Paul Newman, respectively. When he played the part of Charly Gordon on TV, Robertson avoided a third disappointment and bought the feature film rights himself—though it took him a decade to cobble together financing for the production. He is currently at work on a long-planned sequel.

Faces (1968)

Continental Distributing Company

Director and Writer: John Cassavetes; **Producers:** John Cassavetes and Maurice McEndree; **Music:** Jack Ackerman; **Running time:** 130 minutes

Cast: John Marley (Richard Forst); Gena Rowlands (Jeannie Rapp); Lynn Carlin (Maria Frost); Seymour Cassel (Chet)

Oscar nominations: Supporting Actor (Seymour Cassel), Supporting Actress (Lynn Carlin), Screenplay

Although a consummate actor, John Cassavetes was primarily devoted to directing and screenwriting. He used his income as an actor to finance bold, experimental films that were of such limited commercial appeal major studios would not back them. More often than not, he would run out of money and have to put a production on hiatus until more funds could be found. Consequently, he emerged as one of the most important and respected independent filmmakers. *Faces*, which details the disintegration of a middle-aged, upper middle-class couple's marriage, was one of Cassavetes' most acclaimed works. Filmed in black and white, it's as close to an American version of a Bergman film as we're ever likely to see. This is not a "feel-good" movie, and watching it can be a difficult emotional experience. However, Cassavetes was a bold American filmmaker, and his work is appreciated more now than when it was originally released. *Faces* is a major work by a major talent who was absolutely devoted to the cinema.

The Lion in Winter (1968)

Embassy Pictures Corp.

Director: Anthony Harvey; **Producer:** Martin Poll; **Writer:** James Goldman; **Music:** John Barry; **Running time:** 134 minutes

Cast: Peter O'Toole (Henry II); Katharine Hepburn (Eleanor of Acquitaine); Anthony Hopkins (Richard); John Castle (Geoffrey); Nigel Terry (John); Timothy Dalton (King Philip)

Oscar nominations: Best Picture, Actor (Peter O'Toole), Actress* (Katharine Hepburn, shared with Barbra Streisand for *Funny Girl*), Score*, Screenplay*, Costume Design, Director

James Goldman's adaptation of his play is a virtual celebration of the English language. Peter O'Toole is magnificent as the bellicose Henry II (whom he played previously in *Becket)* and his never-ending battles with his strong-willed wife Eleanor (Oscar-winner Katharine Hepburn) and useless sons (Anthony Hopkins and Timothy Dalton in their screen debuts). In less capable hands, the constant bickering could have resembled a Medieval version of *The Honeymooners*, but Anthony Harvey's steady direction of this superb cast makes this a riveting film experience. John Barry's innovative score won the Oscar. Remade as a TV movie in 2003 with Patrick Stewart and Glenn Close.

Hollywood Confidential

Katharine Hepburn's blasé attitude about Hollywood and the Oscars was no act. She refused to attend the Oscar ceremonies in 1969 where she won Best Actress for this film. The director Anthony Harvey accepted her Oscar and delivered it to her home, which Hepburn was then renovating and painting herself. She put the wrapped parcel in the cupboard. Harvey once told me that years later he visited her home and went into the cupboard where he found Oscar still resting unopened in the original wrapping paper!

The Swimmer (1968)

Columbia Pictures

Director: Frank Perry; **Producers:** Roger Lewis and Frank Perry; **Writer:** Eleanor Perry; **Music:** Marvin Hamlisch; **Running time:** 95 minutes

Cast: Burt Lancaster (Ned Merrill); Janet Landgard (Julie Ann Hooper); Janice Rule (Shirley); Marge Champion (Peggy)

A strange but fascinating allegorical film based on John Cheever's short story with Burt Lancaster (in superhuman physical condition) as a depressed and lost middle-aged businessman who one day inexplicably decides to "swim" home by way of a trail through his neighbors' pools. The people he interacts with on this bizarre odyssey include former lovers and pretentious nouveau riche—all leading to a shocking revelation about his character and the superficiality of modern suburban lifestyles. The film was largely misunderstood by both critics and audiences and faded quickly at the box office. Yet, amidst the pretentiousness, Lancaster gives one of his finest performances, and throughout the film you wonder where it is leading you. The final scene of Lancaster standing desperately in the rain, pounding on the door of his vacant home is an image that is both haunting and unforgettable.

Medium Cool (1969)

Paramount Pictures

Director and Writer: Haskell Wexler; **Producers:** Haskell Wexler, Tully Friedman, and Jerrold Wexler; **Music:** Mike Bloomfield; **Running time:** 110 minutes

Cast: Robert Forster (John Cassellis); Verna Bloom (Eileen Horton); Peter Bonerz (Gus); Mariana Hill (Ruth)

Acclaimed cinematographer Haskell Wexler directed this raw, innovative counter-culture statement shot in semi-documentary style. The film follows TV reporter John Cassellis as he shoots hard-to-get footage of disasters, accidents, and other unseemly incidents that his network salivates for. Cassellis faces a moral dilemma when he learns his bosses are providing the footage to the FBI to track down dissidents. Made at the height of the Vietnam protest movement, the film became rather scandalous because of actual riot footage Wexler shot at the disastrous 1968 Democratic convention in Chicago. It gives the film a sense of immediacy and danger that wouldn't have resonated as much if Wexler hadn't shot in the cinema verite style. The film was slapped with a dreaded "X" rating, preventing its core youth audience from seeing it in theaters. In recent years, copyright problems relating to the film's music have resulted in the substitution of some rock songs on the video release versions.

Midnight Cowboy (1969)

United Artists

Director: John Schlesinger; **Producer:** Jerome Hellman; **Screenplay:** Waldo Salt; **Music:** John Barry and Harry Nilsson; **Running time:** 113 minutes

Cast: Dustin Hoffman (Ratso Rizzo); Jon Voight (Joe Buck); Sylvia Miles (Cass); John McGiver (Mr. O'Daniel); Brenda Vaccaro (Shirley)

Oscar nominations: Best Picture*, Director*, Actor (Dustin Hoffman), Actor (Jon Voight), Screenplay*, Editing, Supporting Actress (Sylvia Miles)

Back in 1969 when the film industry was still mature enough to make and market a quality X-rated film, *Midnight Cowboy* rode high as the year's big Oscar-winner. The story centers on Joe Buck, a good-looking, dim-witted Texas hick who comes to New York City with delusions of getting rich by being a male gigolo. Instead, he is imme-diately crushed and stomped down by the dregs of Gotham society and only survives by forming a friendship with Ratso Rizzo, a repulsive, impoverished grifter. Viewing the film in the context of New York's recent renaissance, the urban environment depicted here seems as realistic as Oz, but it certainly reflected the New York of the late 1960s. Both Hoffman and Voight (in his first major role) are unforgettable, as is the innovative music combining the great Harry Nilsson song *Everybody's Talkin'* with atmospheric incidental tracks by John Barry. The film's most amusing scene features the great character actor John McGiver as a perverted religious fanatic whom Joe Buck mistakenly thinks runs a male whorehouse. Never watch this film on broadcast TV! It is inevitably cut to shreds even in today's "enlightened" times.

Easy Rider (1969)

Columbia Pictures

Director: Dennis Hopper; **Producer:** Peter Fonda; **Writers:** Dennis Hopper, Peter Fonda, and Terry Southern; **Running time:** 94 minutes

Cast: Peter Fonda (Wyatt); Dennis Hopper (Billy); Jack Nicholson (George Hanson); Antonio Mendoza (Jesus); Robert Walker (Jack)

Oscar nominations: Supporting Actor (Jack Nicholson), Screenplay

Rude, crude, and rambling, *Easy Rider* can only be viewed as a period piece today. Unlike many important films of bygone eras, this one hasn't aged well. However, the film provides many unforgettable moments. Peter Fonda and Dennis Hopper are two hippie drug dealers enroute to New Orleans for Mardi Gras. The simplistic tale is hardly "fair and balanced." Virtually every mainstream person they encounter is either a total square or a bigoted redneck. By contrast, every hippie is presented as a deep thinker, even as they are seen distorting their brains with drugs. The film comes alive with the brief but memorable sequences featuring Jack Nicholson (in a role turned down by Rip Torn) as a goofy establishment lawyer with a penchant for self-destructive vices. His scenes are both hilarious and moving. The film's shattering conclusion is still jarring and makes sitting through the mumble jumble worthwhile. The success of this low-budget film revolutionized the film making business and hastened the end of the era of power resting in the hands of a few studio moguls. *Easy Rider* was one of the first films to use popular rock songs in place of original music.

Chapter 8
Sci-Fi & Fantasy
"They're Here Already. You're Next! You're Next!"

Perhaps I'm a relic of the past, but in reviewing many of the films designated as science fiction and fantasy, I realized just how anemic most films of this type have become in recent years. There are exceptions, to be sure. Films such as *E.T.* and *The Lord of the Rings* will no doubt be among the most durable classics of this genre. However, they were made by filmmakers who had an enthusiastic vision and a boundless determination to bring these stories to the screen. Many of the modern sci-fi and fantasy movies are simply excuses to show off special effects technology. What these filmmakers fail to realize is that any film needs an emotional core, not just head-spinning visuals. Thus, it's rather enlightening to review the great sci-fi and fantasy films because one comes to the realization that even the most simplistic of these tales generally strove to relate a message or cautionary tale about the human condition. The best listened to the old adage "leave the messages to Western Union" and were somewhat subtle in the life lessons they tried to convey. However, if you dig beneath the surface of the majority of the films in this chapter, you will see a depth that may not be immediately recognizable upon an initial viewing.

The great sci-fi and fantasy films have given us some of the most immortal screen moments of all time: Jimmy Stewart recognizing the value of his life in the finale of *It's a Wonderful Life*, Kevin McCarthy's frantic attempt to warn humanity about the *Invasion of the Bodysnatchers*, the tragic Grant

Williams's self-realization that even the smallest creature has an importance in the universe in *The Incredible Shrinking Man*, and Edward Arnold debating Old Scratch, Walter Huston, for one man's soul in *The Devil and Daniel Webster*. We live in an age in which there is little wonderment left in the movies. They still entertain us, but ask yourself when was the last time you saw a film that actually took you in a direction that was completely unexpected. If you're looking for a stellar example, just watch the original *Planet of the Apes* and compare its devastating final scene with the muddled climax of the recent remake. Perhaps the greatest fantasy is that the new generation of filmmakers will cease playing with CGI effects and emulate the great movies that inspired them to enter the business.

The Invisible Man (1933)

Universal Pictures

Director: James Whale; **Producer:** Carl Laemmle, Jr.; **Writers:** R.C. Sheriff and Philip Wylie; **Music:** Heinz Roemheld (uncredited); **Running time:** 71 minutes

Cast: Claude Rains (Jack Griffin/The Invisible One); Gloria Stuart (Flora); William Harrigan (Arthur Kemp); Henry Travers (Dr. Cranley)

A vintage classic from the Universal Monsters golden period, expertly directed by the great James Whale. Claude Rains makes an unforgettable screen debut as a British scientist who finds a way to become invisible—with the slight caveat that it also turns him into a murderer who terrorizes a quaint British village. Rains's performance is all the more impressive when one considers he has to primarily use his vocal skills to emote, as he is invisible throughout a good part of the film. While the production is a bit creaky with age, the effects are still highly impressive.

"Play It Again, Sam"

The success of *The Invisible Man* led Universal to create a number of belated official spin-offs of varying quality. They are: *The Invisible Man Returns* (1940), *The Invisible Woman* (1940), *Invisible Agent* (1942), and *The Invisible Man's Revenge* (1944). Tellingly, Claude Rains did not appear in any of them. David McCallum starred in an updated TV version in the 1970s.

King Kong (1933)

RKO Radio Pictures

Directors: Merian C. Cooper and Ernest B. Schoedsack; **Writers:** James Creelman and Ruth Rose; **Music:** Max Steiner; **Running time:** 100 minutes

Cast: Fay Wray (Ann Darrow); Robert Armstrong (Carl Denham); Bruce Cabot (Jack Driscoll); Frank Reicher (Capt. Englehorn); Sam Hardy (Charles Weston)

Merian C. Cooper's landmark 1933 production of King Kong was a groundbreaking cinematic experience in terms of its ability to weave Willis O'Brien's startling special effects with an emotionally moving story. The "Eighth Wonder of the World" was, in fact, an 18-inch puppet. The dinosaurs that Kong battles with were actually envisioned by O'Brien for an aborted monster film titled *Creation*. He incorporated this technology into the sequences in which Kong battles other exotic beasts. Surprisingly, Kong never completely overshadows the human elements of the story, and the lead characters are all well developed. Fay Wray shot to stardom in a role rumored to have been turned down by Jean Harlow. Until her death in 2004, Wray enjoyed an iconic status in Hollywood based mostly upon her appearance as Kong's love interest. The film reflects a period when the concept of a towering beast could still resonate with audiences as the worst possible kind of horror. In the post-World War II era, however, it's safe to say the movie would not have had the same initial impact. After the real-life horrors of Hitler, Nazism, and the atomic bomb, the prospect of an enraged ape would have seemed almost quaint. Yet, virtually every aspect of *King Kong* is still revered by film historians. The American Film Institute has voted it as #43 on the list of the 100 greatest films of all time. Max Steiner's triumphant music was an inspiration for a generation of film composers.

"Play It Again, Sam"

The success of *King Kong* inspired two high-profile remakes. The first, released in 1976, starred a shaggy Jeff Bridges, looking only slightly less hairy than the ape himself. The film suffered from poor special effects and pretentious attempts to contemporize the story with quips about women's lib and sexual innuendos. Far more successful was the 2005 remake by Peter Jackson, who brought a reverence and passion to the film that had inspired him to become a director.

Babes in Toyland (1934)

MGM

Directors: Gus Mines and Charles Rogers; **Producer:** Hal Roach (uncredited); **Writers:** Nick Grinde and Frank Butler; **Running time:** 77 minutes

Cast: Stan Laurel (Stannie Dum); Oliver Hardy (Ollie Dee); Charlotte Henry (Little Bo Peep); Felix Knight (Tom-Tom Piper); Henry Kleinbach (Silas Barnaby)

This charming children's film gained popularity over the years by being broadcast on TV. The clever fairy tale setting finds Laurel and Hardy battling the evil Silas Barnaby and his bogeymen henchmen in the duo's quest to prevent them from wreaking havoc on the beloved characters who inhabit Toyland. This is not a traditional Laurel and Hardy film. The boys are, in fact, supporting players, with ample screen time given to a romance between Tom-Tom Piper and Little Bo Peep (scenes that have all the blazing excitement of Harpo's interminable musical numbers in the Marx Brothers films). However, the finale is a classic, with an army of full-sized wooden soldiers coming to the rescue. The film has since been retitled *March of the Wooden Soldiers.* There have been numerous remakes but none so beloved.

Lost Horizon (1937)

Columbia Pictures

Director and Producer: Frank Capra; **Writer:** Robert Riskin; **Music:** Dimitri Tiomkin; **Running time:** 134 minutes

Cast: Ronald Colman (Robert Conway); Jane Wyatt (Sondra); Edward Everett Horton (Lovett); John Howard (George Conway); Thomas Mitchell (Henry Barnard); Margo (Maria); Isabel Jewel (Gloria Stone); H.B. Warner (Chang); Sam Jaffe (High Lama)

Oscar nominations: Best Picture, Editing*, Art Direction*, Score, Assistant Director, Sound, Supporting Actor (H.B. Warner)

Until *Lost Horizon*, Columbia Pictures was regarded as not being quite up to par with the other major studios. After investing $2 million in Frank Capra's adaptation of this James Hilton novel, Columbia gained parity with the other studios in terms of industry respect and willingness to gamble on high profile productions. The famous fantasy involves Ronald Colman as a British diplomat who, along with a group of eclectic fellow passengers, finds his plane has crash-landed in a remote Tibetan area near the paradise of Shangri-La. Warmly greeted, the local populace entrances the group with tales that their secret city is a true paradise, where there is no war or crime and life expectancy reaches hundreds of years old. People being people, however, disaster strikes when some of the group decide to escape back to civilization. The film is a rousing success on every level, with stunning sets and cinematography—and some of the most haunting images in film history. Remade in 1973 as a legendarily awful musical.

Gone with the Wind

Lost Horizon was severely cut after its first preview. Among the scenes sacrificed were an extended prologue in which Colman recounts his adventures before escaping back to Shangri-La. A painstaking restoration began in 1973 and was completed by Robert Gitt for the 1998 DVD, though some sequences had to be recreated with still photos. The film was reissued during WWII under the title *The Lost Horizon of Shangri-La* and was amended to include some anti-Japanese propaganda.

The Devil and Daniel Webster (1941)

RKO Radio Pictures

Director and Producer: William Dieterle; **Writers:** Dan Totheroh and Stephen Vincent Benet; **Music:** Bernard Hermann; **Running time:** 107 minutes.

Cast: Walter Huston (Mr. Scratch); Edward Arnold (Daniel Webster); James Craig (Jabez Stone); Jane Darwell (Ma Stone); Simone Simon (Belle); Ann Shirley (Mary Stone)

Oscar nominations: Actor (Walter Huston), Score*

One of the least-seen classics of the 1940s, *The Devil and Daniel Webster* is basically a European Expressionist film masquerading as a major American studio release. Based on Stephen Vincent Benet's 1937 short story, the tale relates the story of legendary orator Daniel Webster's debate with the Devil for possession of a poor farmer's soul. This is an offbeat film in every respect. The camerawork is superb and Bernard Hermann's Oscar-winning score is truly a magnificent achievement. The cast also excels: James Craig is perfect as the frantic, self-pitying Stone; Edward Arnold (who took the role over on a day's notice when Thomas

Gone with the Wind

The film was originally titled *All That Money Can Buy*. Because it was a box-office failure, the title was changed several times from *Mr. Scratch* to *Daniel and the Devil* then finally to *The Devil and Daniel Webster*. Significant footage was cut for subsequent releases, though in recent years the restored version has been released on Criterion's DVD edition.

Mitchell was injured) is wonderfully blustery and larger-than-life as Webster; and Simone Simon is unforgettable as the mysterious and intoxicating beauty who lures victims to a dance of death. The scene-stealer is Walter Huston, who portrays the Devil not as a man of sinister menace, but appropriately enough as a charismatic and avuncular old salt who hides his evil intentions while he seduces victims to sell their soul. Remade in 2001 with Alec Baldwin and Anthony Hopkins but never completed due to funding problems.

Here Comes Mr. Jordan (1941)

Columbia Pictures

Director: Alexander Hall; **Producer:** Everett Riskin; **Writers:** Sidney Buchman and Seton I. Miller; **Music:** Frederick Hollander; **Running time:** 94 minutes

Cast: Robert Montgomery (Pendleton/Farnsworth/Murdoch); Evelyn Keyes (Betty Logan); Claude Rains (Mr. Jordan); Rita Johnson (Julia); Edward Everett Horton (Messenger 7013)

Oscar nominations: Best Picture, Screenplay*, Original Story*, Director, Actor (Robert Montgomery), Supporting Actor (James Gleason), Cinematography (b&w)

A charming, well-acted fantasy with Robert Montgomery as a prize fighter on the verge of winning the championship. He's involved in an airline accident and mistakenly taken to heaven before his time by an inept angel. To rectify the problem and to give him a chance to win the boxing title, he's put back on earth in another man's body—without realizing his new alter ego has been marked for murder by his scheming wife. The film features a good cast of character actors with Claude Rains in his delightfully entertaining mode as a charismatic celestial schemer who orchestrates the convoluted goings-on. *Mr. Jordan* inspired a tepid 1947 sequel (without Rains) titled *Down to Earth* and an acclaimed 1978 remake, *Heaven Can Wait*, starring Warren Beatty.

It's a Wonderful Life (1946)

RKO Radio Pictures

Director and Producer: Frank Capra; **Writers:** Frances Goodrich, Albert Hackett, and Frank Capra; **Music:** Dimitri Tiomkin; **Running time:** 130 minutes

Cast: James Stewart (George Bailey); Donna Reed (Mary Bailey); Lionel Barrymore (Mr. Potter); Thomas Mitchell (Uncle Billy); Henry Travers (Clarence); Beulah Bondi (Ma Bailey)

Oscar nominations: Best Picture, Director, Actor (James Stewart), Sound, Editing

Made in the immediate aftermath of WWII, Frank Capra's *It's a Wonderful Life* was a "feel good" film that took the long way around the barn before reaching it's emotionally uplifting conclusion—too long, as it turned out, to please audiences that were used to Capra's pre-war movies known for their snappy dialogue and light comedic aspects. The sobering tale tells the story of George Bailey, a small town young man with dreams of traveling and achieving great success. Through a series of unforeseen personal misfortunes, he is prevented from following his dreams—and ends up facing financial disaster, betrayal, and other catastrophes. He contemplates suicide until a guardian angel shows him what life would be like for his loved ones if he follows through on his intentions. The post-war audience was in the mood for joviality, and despite being a critical success, *Life* was a huge flop at the box-office, severely disappointing Capra who felt he had made a masterpiece. It was only after the film fell out of copyright for years and was broadcast endlessly on TV as cheap filler programming that it built a widespread following. The film is perfect in virtually every respect, with special praise to James Stewart for the most nuanced performance of his career. Remade as a 1977 TV movie with Marlo Thomas titled *It Happened One Christmas.*

A Christmas Carol (1951)

United Artists

Director and Producer: Brian Desmond-Hurst; **Writer:** Noel Langley; **Music:** Richard Addinsell; **Running time:** 86 minutes

Cast: Alistair Sim (Ebeneezer Scrooge); Kathleen Harrison (Mrs. Dilber); Mervyn Johns (Bob Crachit); Hermione Baddeley (Mrs. Crachit); Michael Hordern (Jacob Marley); James Gleason (Max Corkle)

Few of the participants in this modestly-budgeted adaptation of Dickens's classic story could have imagined that many years later the film would be more beloved than ever. There had been numerous film versions of the story prior to this and countless others since, but it is Alistair Sim's "spirited" interpretation of Scrooge that has set the standard. His priceless delivery of "Humbug!" is but one of the enjoyable elements of this classic that will doubtless be entertaining future generations of children of all ages. The only other production that has a durable quality is George C. Scott's Emmy-nominated performance in the 1984 TV production.

The Day the Earth Stood Still (1951)

20th Century Fox

Director: Robert Wise; **Producer:** Julian Blaustein; **Writer:** Edmund H. North; **Music:** Bernard Hermann; **Running time:** 92 minutes

Cast: Michael Rennie (Klaatu); Patricia Neal (Helen Benson); Hugh Marlowe (Tom Stevens); Sam Jaffe (Prof. Barnhardt); Billy Gray (Bobby)

An over-rated but still impressive sci-fi story with Michael Rennie memorable as Klaatu, a representative from a federation of other planets sent to earth to warn mankind that their experiments with atomic weapons are threatening the safety of other civilizations. Fine performances, with Patricia Neal keeping a straight face even when being carried about by the giant robot Gort. The household sequences bare the absurdities of films from the 50s (everyone dresses in suits and ties, even when relaxing at home). The effects are cleverly staged, and Robert Wise's direction insures the action never reaches absurd proportions. (Though it strains credibility that the alien spaceship would be left in the middle of an open field in the center of Washington D.C. protected by only two inept National Guardsmen!) The film suffers from a naive pacifist message that mankind should destroy its nuclear weapons. Sounds good in theory, but it looks like Stalin didn't get Klaatu's memo. Bernard Hermann's score is impressively innovative.

"Well, Nobody's Perfect!"

The robot Gort is supposed to be made out of metallic substance, but when actor Lock Martin walked, the costume wrinkled at his knees. This always disturbed producer Julius Blaustein but no "cure" could be thought of for the blooper.

The Thing (aka *The Thing From Another World*) (1951)

RKO Radio Pictures

Director: Christian Nyby; **Producer:** Howard Hawks; **Writers:** John W. Campbell Jr. and Charles Lederer; **Music:** Dimitri Tiomkin; **Running time:** 87 minutes

Cast: Kenneth Tobey (Capt. Patrick Hendry); Margaret Sheridan (Nikki); Robert Cornthwaite (Dr. Carrington); Douglas Spencer (Scotty); James Arness (The Thing)

A group of Air Force investigators uncovers the remains of a spaceship in the Arctic—and in the process discover a frozen alien who, upon thawing out, becomes a murderous menace, stalking the group and killing them one-by-one. Intelligently scripted with a minimum of special effects (the Thing itself is generally only glimpsed in the shadows, adding to the sense of menace). The movie was supposedly directed by Christian Nyby, but conventional wisdom has it that producer Howard Hawks did most of the heavy lifting, though he allowed Nyby to take screen credit. James Arness, soon to be famous as Matt Dillon in *Gunsmoke*, plays the alien. The 1982 remake by John Carpenter starring Kurt Russell is even more riveting.

Godzilla (Japanese title: Gojira) (1954)

Toho Film

Director: Ishiro Honda; **Producer:** Tomoyuki Tanaka; **Writers:** Takeo Murata and Ishiro Honda; **Music:** Akira Ifukube; **Running time:** 98 minutes

Cast: Akira Takarada (Ogata); Momoko Kochi (Emiko); Akihito Hirata (Daisuke); Taskashi Shimura (Kyohei)

Don't be fooled, this is not your father's *Godzilla*. After a generation was weaned on an Americanized version of the Japanese sci-fi classic, the superior original film was finally made available in the United States in 2004. Although the premise of the giant sea monster spawned from nuclear testing was treated by critics as one step beneath an Ed Wood production, since the time of its release, old Godzilla has achieved international respect. Released in Japan under the title *Gojira*, the innovative, low-budget film from Toho studios was a sensation at the box-office. When it was imported to America, however, the film was severely cut and extra scenes with Raymond Burr were added. That version was released as *Godzilla, King of the Monsters*. The original version is superior, restoring key sequences cut the first time around. The effects are quite ingenious, despite the low budget. Godzilla was actually actor Haru Nakajima, who had the unenviable task of wearing a monster suit that weighed 200 pounds! The movie inspired countless spin-offs and sequels, including the immortal *Godzilla vs. the Smog Monster*. Despite their wide variance in quality, virtually all of the sequels were superior to the overblown, witless 1998 American remake starring Matthew Broderick.

20,000 Leagues Under the Sea (1954)

Buena Vista Pictures

Director: Richard Fleischer; **Producer:** Walt Disney; **Writer:** Earl Felton; **Music:** Paul Smith; **Running time:** 127 minutes

Cast: Kirk Douglas (Ned Land); James Mason (Capt. Nemo); Paul Lukas (Prof. Arronax); Peter Lorre (Conseil)

Oscar nominations: Special Effects*, Art Direction-Set Decoration* (color), Editing

An excellent film adaptation of Jules Verne's classic nautical adventure. Kirk Douglas, Peter Lorre, and Paul Lukas are the hapless shipwrecked trio sunk and rescued by James Mason's Capt. Nemo, an ingenious pacifist who plans to use violence to bring an end to war. Go figure. Nemo is sinking ships with his futuristic submarine, *The Nautilus*, which is widely mistaken for a sea serpent. The film was the very first non-animated feature film produced by Walt Disney for his own studio. An ambitious project costing over $5 million, Disney spared no expense on special effects—and the battle with the giant squid still stands as one of the cinema's great action setpieces. The film features excellent performances, with Mason particularly effective as the mad but charismatic Nemo. Kirk Douglas sings the catchy tune *Whale of a Tale*. The film was directed by Richard Fleischer, son of legendary animator Max Fleischer, who was ironically Walt Disney's most formidable competitor.

Forbidden Planet (1956)

MGM

Director: Fred McLeod Wilcox; **Producer:** Nicholas Nayfack; **Writer:** Cyril Hume; **Music:** Louis Barron and Bebe Barron; **Running time:** 98 minutes

Cast: Walter Pidgeon (Dr. Morbius); Anne Francis (Altaira); Leslie Nielsen (John J. Adams); Warren Stevens ("Doc" Ostrow); Jack Kelly (Jerry Farman)

Oscar nominations: Special Effects

Much-beloved by science fiction fans, *Forbidden Planet* creaks with age, but if viewed in the context of the time in which it was produced, it remains quite impressive. An expedition of astronauts are sent to a distant planet to find out why a previous expedition has not been heard from. On the planet, they find the reclusive professor Morbius (Walter Pidgeon) living with his beautiful daughter Altaira (Anne Francis) and an amazing robot named Robby who has a distinct personality and human traits. It soon becomes apparent, however, that Morbius's story about the fate of the previous settlers is something less than the truth. Very loosely based on Shakespeare's *The Tempest*, *Forbidden Planet* is an intelligent sci-fi entry, even if the performances are sometimes over-the-top. (Has anyone been able to take Leslie Nielsen's dramatic roles seriously after his brilliant self-spoofing in *The Naked Gun* films?)

Hollywood Confidential

Robert Kinoshita, who built the cult "hero" Robby the Robot, also created the robot on the *Lost in Space* TV series, but despite the similarities, they are not supposed to be one-and-the-same.

The Incredible Shrinking Man (1957)

Universal Pictures

Director: Jack Arnold; **Producer:** Albert Zugsmith; **Writer:** Richard Matheson; **Running time:** 81 minutes

Cast: Grant Williams (Scott Carey); Randy Stuart (Louise Carey); April Kent (Clarice); Paul Langton (Charles Carey)

In a classic episode of *Seinfeld*, George Costanza is humiliated when he steps out of a cold swimming pool and his girlfriend witnesses the extent of his "shrinkage." Well, Costanza's problem is nothing compared to the case of shrinkage suffered by Grant Williams in this sci-fi classic. After being exposed to a radioactive cloud (apparently the cause of every ailment suffered in the 1950s from athlete's foot to Dutch Elm Disease), Williams's entire body begins to shrink in size. By the time he ends up living in a dollhouse, he's battling "giant" spiders and cats just to stay alive. Despite the ludicrous premise, this is one of the top science fiction films of the decade thanks to an intelligent, thought-provoking script by Richard Matheson and "play-it-straight" direction from Jack Arnold. The special effects shots are ingenious and hold up well today. Inspired the Lily Tomlin comedy *The Incredible Shrinking Woman*. A (presumably satiric) remake has been announced starring Keenen Ivory Wayans.

Invasion of the Bodysnatchers (1956)

Allied Artists

Director: Don Siegel; **Producer:** Walter Wanger; **Writer:** Daniel Mainwaring; **Music:** Carmen Dragon; **Running time:** 80 minutes

Cast: Kevin McCarthy (Miles Bennell); Dana Wynter (Becky); Larry Gates (Danny); King Donovan (Jack); Carolyn Jones ("Teddy")

Without question one of the greatest science fiction films of all time, Don Siegel's masterpiece of low-budget moviemaking has survived being branded with one of the most misleading titles in the history of cinema. Instead of the blood-and-guts monster movie the title implies, this is one of the most intelligent films the genre has ever produced. A small California town is quietly invaded by aliens who clone people's bodies while they sleep. The twist here is that these intruders look and sound just like their victim—except they are devoid of any human emotion or feeling. (Think interplanetary versions of Enron executives.) Kevin McCarthy is excellent as the everyman hero who tries to alert the disbelieving populace even as his few allies inevitably succumb to the desire to sleep. The film, which was made at the height of the Cold War, has been theorized as either a jab at Communists or right wing McCarthyites—though Siegel dismissed both points of view and said there was nothing political in his intentions. Siegel, a master at economical filmmaking, rose to the top of his craft with this film—and its legacy has been an enduring one. Note: the epilogue with Whit Bissel and Richard Deacon was added by the studio over Siegel's objections because it was felt the original finale—McCarthy's futile attempts to convince drivers of the menace—was too downbeat.

"Play It Again, Sam"

The 1978 version by director Philip Kaufman is a rarity: a remake that rivals the original in terms of quality and entertainment value. Donald Sutherland and Leonard Nimoy starred with a creative cameo by Kevin McCarthy. Another quasi-remake, *Bodysnatchers*, directed by Abel Ferrara, was released in 1993.

The Blob (1958)

Paramount Pictures

Director: Irvin S. Yeaworth, Jr.; **Producer:** Jack H. Harris; **Writers:** Kate Philips and Theodore Simonson; **Music:** Ralph Carmichael; **Running time:** 82 minutes

Cast: Steve McQueen (Steve Andrews); Aneta Corsaut (Jane Martin); Earl Rowe (Lt. Dave); Olin Howlin (Old Man); Steven Chase (Dr. Hallen)

A camp classic, *The Blob* is arguably the best of the low-budget horror/sci-fi films aimed at teenagers in the 1950s. It afforded Steve McQueen (billed here as "Steven McQueen") his first starring role, and the film's unexpected gross of $4 million led to him getting the lead role in the TV western *Wanted: Dead or Alive*. The film is as hokey as the title implies. A gigantic blob of slow moving, seemingly unstoppable jelly menaces a small town, and only a stalwart group of teenagers may be able to save the populace. (As with most films in which the menace moves at a snail's pace, one wonders why the potential victims don't simply move briskly aside.) The dialogue is filled with knee-slappers, and the cast overacts appropriately, but *The Blob* is well-made fun that has proved to have a more enduring legacy than many large budget films of this

"Well, Nobody's Perfect!"

In the scene in which the teenagers pour into the street from the movie theater that the blob is menacing, many of the "terrified" kids are laughing and smiling broadly, proving tempestuous blobs of jelly don't instill terror the way they once did.

type. The film spawned a 1972 sequel *Beware! The Blob*, a 1988 remake, and yet another remake that is promised (or threatened) for release in 2006. Note: female lead Aneta Corsaut would go on to star as Helen Crump in *The Andy Griffith Show*. Burt Bacarach wrote the title song.

The Fly (1958)

20th Century Fox

Director and Producer: Kurt Neumann; **Writer:** James Clavell; **Music:** Paul Sawtell; **Running time:** 94 minutes

Cast: David Hedison, billed as Al Hedison (Andre Delabmbre); Vincent Price (Francoise Delambre); Patricia Owens (Helene); Herbert Marshall (Inspector Charas)

The original "fly by night" movie was based on a short story from *Playboy* magazine. This cheesy but fun sci-fi flick presents David Hedison (then known as "Al Hedison") as a scientist whose experiment with matter transference goes awry when a common housefly enters the transfer zone. Hedison emerges as a man with a fly's head while the equally distraught insect ends up with Hedison's noggin. (Hey, at least he got a guy with good looks!) Producer/director Kurt Neumann didn't get to savor the success of the franchise. Sadly, he died shortly after the premiere. An unconfirmed urban legend has it that the original ads for the film contained unintended sexual innuendos such as "The Fly Opens Wednesday!" Although Vincent Price reported the cast and crew kept giggling on the set during the making of this film, we'll refrain from making any corny jokes about the premise, such as "Why didn't they call in the SWAT team?" The movie spawned two inept sequels: *Return of the Fly* (1959) and *Curse of the Fly* (1965). David Cronenberg made the gory 1986 remake with Jeff Goldblum.

Journey to the Center of the Earth (1959)

20th Century Fox

Director: Henry Levin; **Producer:** Charles Brackett; **Writers:** Charles Brackett and Walter Reisch; **Music:** Bernard Hermann; **Running time:** 132 minutes

Cast: James Mason (Prof. Lindenbrook); Pat Boone (Alec McEwen); Arlene Dahl (Carla); Diane Baker (Jenny); Thayer David (Count Saknussem); Peter Ronson (Hans)

Oscar nominations: Art Direction-Set Decoration (color), Special Effects, Sound

An entertaining, if liberal, adaptation of Jules Verne's classic novel with James Mason leading an eclectic group of adventurers on a journey to … well, you know where.

The land down under proves to be far from hospitable with any number of unpleasantness to overcome, not the least of which is miscast teen idol Pat Boone (as a Scotsman!) crooning love songs in a sci-fi epic. Nonetheless, the effects are excellent for their day and the story grips you—thanks mostly to the great skill of James Mason who is well-cast as the expedition's leader. Remade several times as TV movies. Disney has a forthcoming big screen remake slated for 2007.

The Time Machine (1960)

MGM

Director and Producer: George Pal; **Writer:** David Duncan; **Music:** Russell Garcia; **Running time:** 103 minutes

Cast: Rod Taylor (George); Alan Young (James Philby/David Filby); Yvette Mimieux (Weena); Sebastian Cabot (Dr. Hillyer); Whit Bissell (Walter Kemp)

Oscar nominations: Special Effects*

Imaginative adaptation of H.G. Wells's classic story about a Victorian age scientist who invents a machine that transports him through time. He lands hundreds of thousands of years in the future and discovers a race of pacifist humans menaced by hordes of ferocious man-beasts. The film is strongest in its early stages when scientist Rod Taylor tries to convince his disbelieving colleagues of his achievement. The time machine itself is one of the cinema's great props, and the sequence in which Taylor watches the centuries fly by as he observes the progress from the window of his home is a fascinating segment. The script loses much of its punch once Taylor arrives in the future, where he is smitten by a pretty blonde (Yvette Mimieux) named … Weena (no comment).

"Play It Again, Sam"

Remade as a 1978 TV movie and as a weak 2002 feature film directed by Simon Wells, great-grandson of H.G. Wells.

Village of the Damned (1960)

MGM

Director: Wolf Rilla; **Producer:** Ronald Kinnoch; **Writers:** Wolf Rilla and George Barclay; **Music:** Ron Goodwin; **Running time:** 77 minutes

Cast: George Sanders (Gordon Zellaby); Barbara Shelley (Anthea Zellaby); Martin Stevens (David Zellaby); Michael Gwynn (Major Bernard)

An understated but intelligent British sci-fi film set in a small village where everyone inexplicably falls asleep for hours simultaneously. Months later, it's discovered that all women of child-bearing age are pregnant. They give birth to children with identical shocking blonde hair and penetrating eyes. The children possess amazing intelligence but are completely emotionless. As they start to grow, it becomes clear they are not of this world—and their intentions are anything but benign. Atmospheric and chilling, with fine performances by George Sanders, Barbara Steele, and especially young Martin Stevens as the eeriest of the eerie children. A sequel, *Children of the Damned*, was released in 1963. A 1995 remake starred Christopher Reeve.

The Day the Earth Caught Fire (1961)

Universal International Pictures

Director and Producer: Val Guest; **Writers:** Val Guest and Wolf Mankiewicz; **Music:** Stanley Black; **Running time:** 98 minutes

Cast: Janet Munro (Jeannie Craig); Leo McKern (Bill Maguire); Edward Judd (Peter Stenning); Michael Goodlife ("Jacko")

Despite the hokey sci-fi title, this is an unusually intelligent film made during the height of Cold War fears about the nuclear arms race leading to an ecological disaster. The premise here is that all the atomic testing has knocked earth off its axis and hurtled it toward the sun. Gradually, the planet begins to dry up, leading to panic as people realize that ultimately they will all be incinerated. (The upside? Those fees for overdue books at the library probably won't have to be repaid.) Director Val Guest works wonders with a limited budget, using creative matte paintings to illustrate major British landmarks devastated by the crisis. One of the best films of this genre.

Mysterious Island (1961)

Columbia Pictures

Director: Cy Endfield; **Producer:** Charles H. Schneer; **Writers:** John Prebble, Daniel Ullman, and Crane Wilbur; **Music:** Bernard Hermann; **Special Effects:** Ray Harryhausen; **Running time:** 101 minutes

Cast: Michael Craig (Capt. Cyrus Harding); Joan Greenwood (Mary); Michael Callen (Herbert Brown); Gary Merrill (Gideon Splitt); Herbert Lom (Captain Nemo)

Jules Vernes's sequel to *20,000 Leagues Under the Sea* is brought to the screen with great skill and the incomparable special effects work of Ray Harryhausen. The story concerns a group of Civil War POW's who escape prison camp by way of a hot air balloon and end up on a remote, unchartered island. Two stranded women end up along for the ride, but the birds and the bees on this island are not of the sexual kind: they are literally gigantic beasts that menace the group, along with (no kidding) a bloodthirsty chicken! The film's highlight is the appearance of Herbert Lom as the famed Captain Nemo. A captivating and thoroughly entertaining tale.

The Wonderful World of the Brothers Grimm (1962)

MGM

Directors: Henry Levin and George Pal (Fairy tale scenes); **Producer:** George Pal; **Music:** Leigh Harline; **Running time:** 135 minutes

Cast: Laurence Harvey (Wilhelm Grimm/The Cobbler); Karl Boehm (Jacob Grimm); Claire Bloom (Dorothea); Walter Slezak (Stossel); Russ Tamblyn (The Woodsman/Tom Thumb); Yvette Mimieux (The Princess); Terry-Thomas (Ludwig); Buddy Hackett (Hans)

Oscar nominations: Costume Design* (color), Art Direction-Set Decoration (color), Score, Cinematography (color)

Largely overlooked by contemporary audiences due to limited availability on TV and home video, *Brothers Grimm* was a high-profile production in its day—the first non-documentary film released in the three camera process of Cinerama, which required a special projection system and a massive curved screen. (An early forerunner of today's IMAX technology.) The film explains how the Grimm brothers (allegedly) were inspired to write their classic fairy tales. The film presents several different enactments of their individual stories, including some charming sequences with puppets. The effects may be crude by today's standards, but in a way they add to the dated look of the movie and enhance its sense of innocence. A wonderful musical score and some impressive European locations add immensely to the overall quality of the production.

Federico Fellini's 8½ (1963)

Embassy Pictures Corporation

Director: Federico Fellini; **Producer:** Angelo Rizzoli; **Writers:** Federico Fellini, Ennio Flaiano, Tullio Pinelli, and Brunello Rondi; **Music:** Nino Rota; **Running time:** 138 minutes

Cast: Marcello Mastroianni (Guido); Claudia Cardinale (Claudia); Anouk Aimee (Louisa); Sandra Milo (Sandra); Barbara Steele (Gloria)

Oscar nominations: Best Foreign Language Film*, Costume Design* (b&w), Director, Screenplay, Art Direction-Set Decoration (b&w)

Fellini's reputation for utilizing bizarre, surrealistic imagery became well-established with this comical, semi-autobiographical film that finds Marcello Mastroianni as

Guido, a world famous director in a panic because he has lost his creative desire to continue work on his latest movie, a science fiction epic. Devoid of any inspiration, he comes under constant pressure from studio hacks, adoring fans, and ever-present paparazzi. In his angst, he begins to have delusional fantasies that represent his inner fears, memories, and desires. Some are allegorical in nature (he floats like a balloon over an oppressive traffic jam). Others are more basic: he envisions every woman in his life as part of his personal harem. (A sequence that, if included in a film today, would require speed bumps in theaters to slow the stampede of feminists running out the doors.) What does it all mean? Film scholars have been debating that issue since the movie was released, but it's safe to say only Fellini knew for sure. What is not in dispute is its fascinating premise and execution, including outstanding cinematography and a great score by Nino Rota. (The title of the film refers to the number of movies Fellini had made up until that point, including a feature he co-directed.)

Jason and the Argonauts (1963)

Columbia Pictures

Director: Don Chaffey; **Producer:** Charles H. Schneer; **Writers:** Beverly Cross and Jan Reed; **Music:** Bernard Hermann; **Special Effects:** Ray Harryhausen; **Running time:** 104 minutes

Cast: Todd Armstrong (Jason); Nancy Kovack (Medea); Gary Raymond (Acastus); Laurence Naismith (Argos); Honor Blackman (Hera)

Ray Harryhausen's remarkable special effects are the primary asset of this retelling of the legend of *Jason and the Golden Fleece*. Benefiting from some above-average production values, the exciting adventure has a good deal of atmosphere and several memorable action sequences, the most enduring being the battle between Jason and his Argonauts and an army of skeletons. Nothing in the present era of CGI can come close to matching these ingenious effects. Todd Armstrong in the lead role fills the physical requirements well enough, but as a thespian he makes Steve Reeves look like Olivier. (His voice was dubbed by Tim Turner.) One can only imagine how much the film might have benefited from Kirk Douglas in the starring role. Music by Bernard Hermann, with Honor Blackman as Hera immediately prior to her sensational success as Pussy Galore in *Goldfinger*. Remade as a TV movie in 2000.

First Men in the Moon (1964)

Columbia Pictures

Director: Nathan Juran; **Producer:** Charles H. Schneer; **Writer:** Nigel Kneale and Jan Read; **Music:** Laurie Johnson; **Special Visual Effects:** Ray Harryhausen; **Running time:** 103 minutes

Cast: Edward Judd (Arnold Bedford); Martha Hyer (Kate); Lionel Jeffries (Cavor)

Special effects genius Ray Harryhausen is the real star of this adaptation of H.G. Wells's novel about a group of Victorian adventurers who manage to successfully launch a flight to the moon—only to find it inhabited by a menacing race of beings. The story has been ingeniously updated to include the (then) on-going space race to the moon. The inspired opening scene finds what is believed to be the first men on the moon discovering evidence that people had actually been there previously. Well-acted by an engaging cast including the always enjoyable Lionel Jeffries.

Hollywood Confidential

Actress Martha Hyer had married legendary producer Hal B. Wallis and wrote the screenplay for the 1975 John Wayne film *Rooster Cogburn* under the nom-de-plume "Martin Julien."

Fantastic Voyage (1966)

20th Century Fox

Director: Richard Fleischer; **Producer:** Saul David; **Writers:** Harry Kleiner and David Duncan; **Music:** Leonard Rosenman; **Running time:** 100 minutes

Cast: Stephen Boyd (Grant); Raquel Welch (Cora); Edmond O'Brien (General Carter); Donald Pleasence (Dr. Michaels); Arthur O'Connell (Col. Reid); William Redfield (Owens); Arthur Kennedy (Duval)

Oscar nominations: Visual Effects*, Art Direction-Set Decoration* (color), Editing, Cinematography (color), Sound Effects

A sci-fi classic with an ingenious premise. A diplomat suffering from a potentially lethal blood clot possesses invaluable military secrets involving the process for miniaturizing human beings. A team of scientists are shrunken down to microscopic size and inserted into his body. They have one hour to repair the blood clot before the body's natural defenses turn against them. The film won kudos for its (then) state-of-the-art special effects, many of which hold up well today. This was actually Raquel Welch's first leading role, not *One Million Years B.C.*, which was released months later. Inspired a Saturday morning cartoon spin-off.

Fahrenheit 451 (1966)

Universal Pictures

Director: Francois Truffaut; **Producer:** Lewis M. Allen; **Writers:** Francois Truffaut, Jean-Louis Richard, David Rudkin, and Helen Scott; **Music:** Bernard Hermann; **Running time:** 112 minutes

Cast: Oskar Werner (Guy Montag); Julie Christie (Clarisse/Linda Montag); Cyril Cusack (The Captain); Anon Diffring (Anton)

Francois Truffaut's only English language film is a loose adaptation of Ray Bradbury's classic story about an oppressive futuristic society where books are illegal. The irony in this society is that firemen are used to *cause* infernos as they raid homes to burn books that intellectuals have stashed away. The story was obviously inspired by the Nazi book-burning events in the early days of the Third Reich. *Fahrenheit 451* is the story of Montag, a career fireman who becomes inspired to undertake the subversive act of reading the books he destroys—thus placing his life in danger. The film is not without flaws: it's executed as coldly and dispassionately as the character of Montag himself. Also, for a society obsessed with stamping out reading, one wonders how everyone became so well-spoken and literate. Still, it's a thought-provoking premise with many memorable sequences, such as the firetrucks racing to destroy the homes of people whose only crime was to expand their intellectual horizons. Director Frank Darabont is preparing a major remake.

Seconds (1966)

Paramount Pictures

Director: John Frankenheimer; **Producers:** John Frankenheimer and Edward Lewis; **Writer:** John Lewis Carlino; **Music:** Jerry Goldsmith; **Running time:** 100 minutes

Cast: Rock Hudson (Tony Wilson); Salome Jens (Nora); John Randolph (Arthur Hamilton); Will Geer (Old Man); Jeff Corey (Mr. Ruby)

Oscar nominations: Cinematography (b&w)

One of the most under-rated films of the 1960s, John Frankenheimer's *Seconds* was a box-office and critical bomb upon its initial release and was ignored by audiences who were not used to seeing Rock Hudson in anything but lightweight movies. Ironically, Hudson gives the performance of his career as a once-burned out executive who is approached by a mysterious organization that can feign a person's death and make them reborn in a completely new body. Our protagonist, played first by John Randolph, makes the momentous decision to leave behind his friends and family and embark on a new life as an artist. The good news is that his new body is that of Rock

Hudson, but in a *Twilight Zone*-like twist, he learns that his newfound happiness may come at a terrible price. The stature of the film has grown over time and is now considered one of Frankenheimer's most intriguing efforts. James Wong Howe's stunning cinematography earned an Oscar nomination. The main titles sequence gives a foretaste of the chilling tale about to unfold through its disturbing imagery.

The Love Bug (1968)

Buena Vista Pictures

Director: Robert Stevenson; **Producer:** Bill Walsh; **Writers:** Bill Walsh and Don DaGradi; **Music:** George Bruns; **Running time:** 107 minutes

Cast: Dean Jones (Jim Douglas); Michele Lee (Carole Bennett); David Tomlinson (Peter Thorndyke); Buddy Hackett (Tennessee Steinmetz); Joe Flynn (Havershaw); Benson Fong (Mr. Wu)

"Play It Again, Sam"

The unexpected and enduring success of *The Love Bug* lead to a series of sequels: *Herbie Rides Again, Herbie Goes to Monte Carlo, Herbie Goes Bananas*, and the 2005 film *Herbie: Fully Loaded*. Dean Jones also starred in a 1982 *Love Bug* TV series.

What started as a nondescript, routine Disney family comedy has since morphed into a virtual cottage industry as international enthusiasm for Herbie. The magical 1963 Volkswagen Beetle has spawned fan clubs, collectibles, and a loyal following that spans generations. Disney regular Dean Jones plays a down-and-out race car driver who finds that the old VW he has purchased not only has a mind of its own, but also impressive self-survival instincts that help thwart villains. The special effects are convincing enough to make you forget this bucket of bolts really isn't a living, breathing character.

Planet of the Apes (1968)

20th Century Fox

Director: Franklin J. Schaffner; **Producer:** Arthur P. Jacobs; **Writers:** Michael Wilson and Rod Serling; **Makeup:** John Chambers; **Music:** Jerry Goldsmith; **Running time:** 112 minutes

Cast: Charlton Heston (Taylor); Maurice Evans (Dr. Zaius); Roddy McDowell (Cornelius); Kim Hunter (Zira); Linda Harrison (Nova)

Oscar nominations: Score, Costume Design, Honorary Award given to John Chambers for his makeup designs.

An outstanding achievement in science fiction filmmaking, *Planet of the Apes* is based on the novel *Monkey Planet* by Pierre Boulle, author of *The Bridge Over the River*

Kwai. In the book, a trio of astronauts crash lands on a strange planet ruled by civilized apes presiding over technological achievements that dwarf those on Earth. To keep the film's budget under control, however, the decision was made to have the apes live in a rather primitive society compared to that which the astronauts have left. The movie is consistently thrilling and thought-provoking, with intriguing issues such as man's place in the universe addressed in an intelligent manner. John Chambers's amazing makeup effects remain among the best ever seen on film. The movie benefits from a brilliant cast with Maurice Evans particularly impressive as Dr. Zaius, the ape statesman who hides a shocking secret. (Edward G. Robinson was originally cast for this role, but the grueling daily makeup ritual was too tiring for him.) Equally impressive is Charlton Heston as one of the least-admirable characters he's ever played. Heston is perfectly cast and gives one of the best performances of his career. Jerry Goldsmith's score is as chilling as it is innovative. The ending still packs a wallop even if you've already seen it a hundred times.

"Play It Again, Sam" _____

Planet of the Apes inspired several sequels of diminishing quality: *Beneath the Planet of the Apes, Escape from the Planet of the Apes, Conquest of the Planet of the Apes,* and *Battle for the Planet of the Apes.* A 1974 TV series followed, and in 2001, Tim Burton directed a pointless and boring remake starring—yes, there's that name again—Mark Wahlberg, king of the pointless remakes.

2001: A Space Odyssey (1968)

MGM

Director and Producer: Stanley Kubrick; **Writers:** Stanley Kubrick and Arthur C. Clarke; **Running time:** 141 minutes

Cast: Keir Dullea (Dave Bowman); Gary Lockwood (Frank Poole); William Sylvester (Dr. Floyd); Daniel Richter (Moon Watcher); Douglas Rain (voice: Hal 9000)

Oscar nominations: Special Effects*, Director, Screenplay, Art Direction-Set Decoration

One of the most original works in cinema history, *2001* is a film so complex and thought-provoking that you know you're in trouble when it starts to make complete sense to you. The film is broken into distinct segments. The stunning opening scene shows apes in the pre-human era discovering a strange stone monolith that appears from nowhere and instigates an emotional response in the animals. The scene then switches to the year 2001 (as the film was made in 1968, it's amusing to see Kubrick's vision of the space age we are now living in). A similar monolith has been discovered on the moon, and a spacecraft manned by Frank Poole and Dave Bowman is sent to investigate. This middle segment of the film is the most memorable—and the most straight forward. The ship's computer, HAL 9000, possesses human intellect and vocal ability. After a malfunction, HAL begins to work against the astronauts in a life-or-death battle of wits. The final segment finds Bowman encountering a life-altering head trip experience that is impossible to describe, but which is stunning to experience. What Kubrick and cowriter Arthur C. Clark meant to convey is open to interpretation, but that's the most fascinating aspect to *2001:* it can mean a thousand different things to a thousand different people. The special effects are still more impressive than anything seen in the CGI age, and Kubrick's use of classic music instead of an original musical score is pure inspiration (though Kubrick had commissioned Alex North to write a score that was never used). An ambitious but ultimately unsatisfying sequel, *2010*, was released in 1984.

Hollywood Confidential

In 2001, I interviewed Roger Caras, a longtime friend of Stanley Kubrick and a former consultant on *2001*, for inclusion on a documentary I wrote for Sony titled *Inside Dr. Strangelove*. Caras said that in 1964 Kubrick invited him to lunch at Trader Vic's in New York City and described the early premise of *2001*, which originally involved man's first meetings with aliens. Kubrick made some crude sketches of the aliens on a cocktail-napkin. To my amazement, Caras produced the item from his files, saying he kept it because Kubrick was a genius and all his ideas should be preserved. Caras also shot extensive interviews with international scientists that were to be used in the film, but this segment was ultimately dropped. It was also Caras who put Kubrick in touch with his old friend Arthur C. Clark and proposed him as a collaborator.

Chapter 9

THRILLERS

"We All Go a Little Mad Sometimes."

Alfred Hitchcock once encapsulated the secret of making a successful thriller. He described a scene in which we watch a villain sneak into a house and plant a bomb with a timer set for 15 minutes under a coffee table. A group of people enter the room and sit down at the table and begin to talk of inconsequential things while the camera cuts back to the time bomb ticking ever closer to exploding. The audience becomes increasingly tense and, as the precious seconds tick by, they are practically screaming for the people to realize there is a bomb under the coffee table! Hitchcock explained that this method insures that the audience is "hooked" for an extended period of time (though he cautioned there must be a logical method found for *not* having the bomb explode, lest the audience feel cheated). Another director might simply have had people sit at the table and the bomb explode unexpectedly. The audience would be startled for a few seconds, but Hitchcock delighted in torturing his audience, who were always willing masochists when it came to his films.

It's probably no surprise that Hitchcock dominates this chapter. He may not have invented the cinematic thriller, but he certainly set the high water mark to which other filmmakers had to aspire. If Hitchcock had given us nothing but *Psycho*, he still would have insured that generations of people never quite felt safe in their own showers. Yet, many other notable films by a number of directors succeed in putting audiences on the edge of their seats. It is my hope that you may be inspired to view some of the more esoteric examples of the thriller genre: Peter Lorre's immortal performance as the child killer in *M*, Robert Mitchum's outstanding performance in Charles Laughton's criminally neglected *The Night of the Hunter*. And also find startling examples of the "new wave" of filmmakers who came of age in the 1960s: Michelangelo Antonioni's *Blow Up* and Peter Bogdanovich's *Targets*. If you expand your horizons, you will find some rich rewards—as well as many unforgettable moments—among these films.

M (1931)

Foremco Pictures Corp.

Director: Fritz Lang; **Producer:** Seymour Nebenzal (uncredited); **Writers:** Thea Von Harbou and Fritz Lang; **Running time:** 99 minutes

Cast: Peter Lorre (Hans Beckert); Ellen Widman (Frau Beckmann); Inge Landgut (Elsie); Otto Wernicke (Insp. Lohmann)

German director Fritz Lang's first sound film also marks the screen debut of Peter Lorre, unforgettable as a psychologically tortured child molester/murderer who terrorizes Berlin. When the authorities fail to catch the culprit, the city's criminal underworld joins forces to do the job. Lang never actually depicts a murder onscreen, but the symbols and atmosphere leading up to each crime are terrifying. (The murderer always whistles his trademark song from *Peer Gynt* prior to enacting a crime.) A masterful thriller that makes full use of groundbreaking lighting techniques to maximize the sense of horror. A lukewarm English language remake was released in 1951.

Hollywood Confidential

Adolf Hitler was a very enthusiastic fan of both Lang and Lorre. The Nazi party "suggested" that Lang begin to make propaganda films. Both he and Lorre, seeing the writing on the wall for the future of Germany, fled their native countries and established successful careers in England, though Lorre would forever be typecast as a creepy character. The Nazis ended up using footage of Lorre out of context in the notorious antiSemitic propaganda "documentary" *The Eternal Jew*.

Rebecca (1940)

United Artists

Director: Alfred Hitchcock; **Producer:** David O. Selznick; **Writers:** Robert E. Sherwood and Joan Harrison; **Music:** Franz Waxman; **Running time:** 130 minutes

Cast: Laurence Olivier (Maximillian de Winter); Joan Fontaine (Mrs. de Winter); George Sanders (Jack Favell); Judith Anderson (Mrs. Danvers); Nigel Bruce (Major Lacey)

Oscar nominations: Best Picture*, Director, Cinematography* (b&w), Special Effects, Actress (Joan Fontaine), Actor (Laurence Olivier), Editing, Supporting Actress (Judith Anderson), Screenplay, Score, Art Direction (b&w)

Alfred Hitchcock's first American film after becoming a movie icon in Great Britain was an unpleasant experience for the famed director. He immediately locked horns with mogul producer David O. Selznick over virtually every aspect of this expensive production. Yet, what emerged was Hitchcock's only film to win the Best Picture Oscar, and the one aspect of the movie he and Selznick agreed on—that Joan Fontaine was a weak choice for the lead—turned out to be happily mistaken as Fontaine scored an Oscar nomination and great praise. The romantic gothic suspense film finds Fontaine marrying a brooding widower (Laurence Olivier), whose wife Rebecca drowned in a mysterious accident. After settling in at his mansion, she finds that everyone she meets seems to have a strange obsession with the late Rebecca, and she begins to wonder if she isn't exerting a power from beyond the grave. Judith Anderson is unforgettable as the sinister housekeeper, and a supporting cast of old pros contribute to making this a classic thriller.

Shadow of a Doubt (1943)

Universal Pictures

Director: Alfred Hitchcock; **Producer:** Jack H. Skirball; **Writers:** Thornton Wilder, Sally Benson, and Alma Reville; **Music:** Dimitri Tiomkin; **Running time:** 108 minutes

Cast: Joseph Cotton (Uncle Charlie); Teresa Wright (Charlie); MacDonald Carey (Jack Graham); Henry Travers (Joseph Newton); Hume Cronyn (Herbie Hawkins)

Oscar nominations: Original Story

Ever the cynic, only Alfred Hitchcock could have looked at a quaint, small American town and seen the face of horror. Hitchcock hired *Our Town* writer Thornton Wilder to develop this story of a charismatic serial killer who graces a charming town with his presence in the guise of loveable Uncle Charlie (Joseph Cotton), a man so beloved that his adoring niece Charlie (Teresa Wright) has been named after him. During his visit, however, Charlie begins to suspect there is a darker side to her popular uncle—one that hides a sinister hatred for women. Unlike many of his thrillers, Hitchcock is in no hurry to present dramatic or frightening setpieces. They unfold in a leisurely manner here, making us reluctant to believe good old Uncle Charlie could be anything but the charming man-of-the-world his clueless family thinks he is and leading to a tension-filled climax. Cotton is superb as one of the screen's most notorious villains. This film was Hitchcock's favorite among his own work. Remade as a TV movie in 1991.

Gaslight (1944)

MGM

Director: George Cukor; **Producer:** Arthur Hornblow Jr.; **Writers:** John Van Druten, Walter Reisch, and John L. Balderston; **Music:** Bronislau Kaper; **Running time:** 114 minutes

Cast: Charles Boyer (Gregory Anton); Ingrid Bergman (Paula Anton); Joseph Cotton (Brian Cameron); Dame May Whitty (Miss Bessie Thwaites); Angela Lansbury (Nancy Oliver)

Oscar nominations: Best Picture, Actress* (Ingrid Bergman), Art Direction-Set Decoration* (b&w), Screenplay, Actor (Charles Boyer), Supporting Actress (Angela Lansbury), Cinematography (b&w)

George Cukor, a director known for light-hearted fare, helmed this sensational thriller set in Victorian London. Ingrid Bergman won an Oscar for her sensational performance as a new bride who returns to her family home where she had discovered the body of her aunt years ago. Soon, a series of unexplained incidents leads her to suspect she may be suffering from an inherited mental disorder and that she is slowly going mad. Charles Boyer is equally impressive as Bergman's new husband—who may or may not be sincere in his sympathy for her plight. Angela Lansbury made her film debut here, scoring an Oscar nomination at the tender age of 17. The movie was filmed previously as *Angel Street* in 1940.

And Then There Were None (1945)

20th Century Fox

Director: Rene Clair; **Producers:** Rene Clair and Harry M. Popkin; **Writer:** Dudley Nichols; **Music:** M. Castelnuovo-Tedesco; **Running time:** 97 minutes

Cast: Barry Fitzgerald (Quincannon); Walter Huston (Armstrong); Louis Hayward (Morley/Lombard); Roland Young (Det. Blore)

Agatha Christie's classic suspense story transferred to the screen with considerable skill. Ten people are invited by a mysterious host to join him for a weekend on an exotic island. Once there, they find he is not present, and a phonograph recording tells them they are all to be killed for injustices they have committed. The fun, of course, is comparing wits with the victims in their mad scramble to find out who the murderer is—perhaps he is one of their own group? Numerous remakes have been made under the title *Ten Little Indians*, most notably in 1965 and 1974. The original British title of Christie's story was *Ten Little Niggers* and, for obvious reasons, it was deemed too insensitive to use in the United States.

Sorry, Wrong Number (1948)

Paramount Pictures

Director: Anatole Litvak; **Producers:** Anatole Litvak and Hal B. Wallis; **Writer:** Lucille Fletcher; **Music:** Franz Waxman; **Running time:** 89 minutes

Cast: Barbara Stanwyck (Leone Stevenson); Burt Lancaster (Henry Stevenson); Ann Richards (Sally Lord); Wendell Corey (Dr. Alexander)

Oscar nominations: Actress (Barbara Stanwyck)

Lucille Fletcher wrote the screenplay for this big screen adaptation of her 1943 radio play that had been a nationwide sensation. Barbara Stanwyck is an invalid confined to her bed and all alone when she overhears a telephone conversation of two men planning someone's murder. Her desperate attempts to try to identify the potential victim in time to prevent the crime lead to a complex story told in flashback involving her husband (Burt Lancaster) and his business dealings with organized crime figures. It's a long way to the suspense-filled conclusion, but the story is engrossing throughout—aided by top performances by Stanwyck as the spoiled, hypochondriac socialite and Burt Lancaster as her hunky husband who tires of being her boy toy. Remade in 1989 as a TV movie with Loni Anderson!

D.O.A. (1950)

United Artists

Director: Rudolph Mate; **Producer:** Leo C. Popkin; **Writers:** Russell Rouse and Clarence Green; **Music:** Dimitri Tiomkin; **Running time:** 83 minutes

Cast: Edmond O'Brien (Frank Bigelow); Pamela Britton (Paula); Luther Adler (Majak); Beverly Campbell (Miss Foster)

Released as a nondescript "B" movie, this expertly directed thriller has a fascinating premise. Edmond O'Brien is a groom-to-be who decides to unwind from pre-wedding jitters with a stay in San Francisco. While there, he discovers someone has inexplicably slipped him a slow-working poison that is certain to kill him within a matter of days. O'Brien then goes on a relentless manhunt to try to solve the mystery of who might want him dead. Great location photography and a stirring performance by O'Brien. Remade in 1969 (as *Color Me Dead*) and under the original title in 1988 starring Dennis Quaid.

Strangers on a Train (1951)

Warner Brothers

Director and Producer: Alfred Hitchcock; **Writers:** Raymond Chandler and Czenzi Ormonde; **Music:** Dimitri Tiomkin; **Running time:** 101 minutes

Cast: Farley Granger (Guy Haines); Robert Walker (Bruno Anthony); Ruth Roman (Ann Morton); Leo G. Carroll (Sen. Morton); Patricia Hitchcock (Barbara Morton)

Raymond Chandler was hired by Alfred Hitchcock to write the screenplay for this superb thriller, but the two men instantly despised each other and the script was largely rewritten by Czenzi Ormonde. Despite the difficulties, this is one of Hitch's best. Tennis pro Farley Granger jokes theoretically with stranger Robert Walker about each man agreeing to murder a bothersome person in the other man's life to avoid making themselves the object of suspicion. Granger learns too late that his new "friend" has taken him literally—and now expects Granger to keep his end of the bargain. Robert Walker (who died shortly after the film was completed) emerges as one of the screen's great villains. The climax on the merry-go-round is the most complex scene Hitchcock ever filmed. A stunning achievement in all respects. A big screen remake is planned.

Gone with the Wind

The American and British versions have several differences, with certain scenes added and deleted from each. Both versions appear on the DVD release.

Dial M for Murder (1954)

Warner Brothers

Director and Producer: Alfred Hitchcock; **Writer:** Frederick Knott; **Music:** Dimitri Tiomkin; **Running time:** 105 minutes

Cast: Ray Milland (Tony Wendice); Grace Kelly (Margot Wendice); Robert Cummings (Mark Halliday); John Williams (Insp. Hubbard); Anthony Dawson (Charles Swan)

Writer Frederick Knott wrote the screenplay for Alfred Hitchcock's adaptation of his popular play. Ray Milland plays an aristocratic man of wealth who learns wife Grace

Kelly once had an affair with a friend of his (Robert Cummings). He hires an assassin to murder her, but when the plan goes awry, he devises a method to frame his wife for murder. This is an old-fashioned, drawing-room suspense with upper crust people matching wits with each other as detective John Williams tries to unravel the case. The murder scene is a classic, though this was a strange property for Hitchcock to film in 3D, which was all the rage for a brief period in the 1950s. However the gimmick was short-lived as audiences felt it was cumbersome and distracting to watch and entire film while wearing the special glasses required to enjoy the effects. After some limited engagements, it was released to general audiences in a standard "flat" format. Remade numerous times as TV movies and as the 1998 Michael Douglas-Gwyneth Paltrow vehicle *A Perfect Murder*.

Rear Window (1954)

Paramount Pictures

Director and Producer: Alfred Hitchcock; **Writer:** John Michael Hayes; **Music:** Franz Waxman; **Running time:** 112 minutes

Cast: James Stewart (L.B. Jeffries); Grace Kelly (Lisa); Wendell Corey (Tom Doyle); Thelma Ritter (Stella); Raymond Burr (Lars Thorwald)

Oscar nominations: Director, Screenplay, Cinematography (color), Sound

Along with *Lifeboat*, *Rear Window* is one of Alfred Hitchcock's most innovative films because it forced him to make a suspense picture within the confines of a claustrophobic environment. Here, James Stewart is a sports photographer who is recuperating from a leg injury and confined to a wheelchair. He spends the day obsessively spying out his back window on the occupants of the building facing his. He gets to "know" each neighbor without ever meeting them and becomes convinced one man has murdered his wife. The scenario is played out ingeniously, with all the music appearing naturally as part of the on-going action on screen. The massive apartment complex was the largest set ever built indoors on the Paramount lot. The script has a good dose of humor courtesy of Grace Kelly and Thelma Ritter as the long-suffering women in Stewart's life, but the finale builds to a crescendo of suspense. The film underwent a major restoration by Robert Harris and James C. Katz in 1998, the same year it was remade as a TV movie with Christopher Reeve.

Diabolique (1955)

United Motion Pictures Organization

Director and Producer: H.G. Clouzot; **Writers:** H.G. Clouzot, Rene Masson, Frederic Grendel, and Jerome Geronimi; **Music:** Georges Van Parys; **Running time:** 116 minutes

Cast: Simone Signoret (Nicole); Vera Clouzot (Christina); Paul Meurisse (Michele Delasalle); Charles Vanel (Fichet)

Clever suspense thriller set in a decrepit French boy's school, which is run by an abusive skinflint headmaster whose wife and mistress concoct an audacious plan to drown him and make it appear to be an accident. Things go awry when the women begin to witness chilling evidence that the man they've killed may not be dead at all. Director Henri-Georges Clouzot milks the tension until the final, improbable conclusion. The bathtub scene is a seminal sequence in suspense cinema. Simone Signoret and Vera Clouzot (real life wife of the director) put on splendid performances. Charles Vanel is charming as the ragtag detective who appears to be the inspiration for Peter Falk's Columbo. Alfred Hitchcock narrowly missed getting the screen rights to the novel *Celle Qui n'était Plus* on which the story was based. However, the authors of the novel were eager to have Hitchcock adapt their work and so wrote the story that became the basis for *Vertigo* for the legendary director. Sharon Stone starred in the pointless 1996 remake.

Night of the Hunter (1955)

MGM

Director: Charles Laughton; **Producer:** Paul Gregory; **Writer:** James Agee; **Music:** Walter Schumann; **Running time:** 93 minutes

Cast: Robert Mitchum (Harry Powell); Shelly Winters (Willa); Lilian Gish (Rachel Cooper); Billy Chapin (John Harper); Sally Jane Bruce (Pearl Harper)

The only film ever directed by Charles Laughton is reminiscent of the old German Expressionist movies of the 1930s. Almost surrealistic in style, the story concerns two young children trying to flee their murderous stepfather, a crazed preacher played with maximum skill by Robert Mitchum in one of the great performances of his career. The film contains many great sequences and lines of dialogue, but the best asset is the eerie camerawork by Stanley Cortez that adds immeasurably to the frightening atmosphere. A box-office flop in its day, the film is now regarded as a masterpiece of suspense. Remade as a TV movie with Richard Chamberlin.

Touch of Evil (1958)

Universal Pictures

Director and Writer: Orson Welles; **Producer:** Albert Zugsmith; **Music:** Henry Mancini; **Running time:** 95 minutes

Cast: Charlton Heston (Ramon "Mike" Vargas); Orson Welles (Capt. Quinlan); Janet Leigh (Susie Vargas); Joseph Calleia (Sgt. Mendez); Akim Tamiroff (Joe Grandy)

Orson Welles had long been considered persona non grata by Hollywood studios when Universal agreed to hire him as director and actor to induce Charlton Heston to star in *Touch of Evil*. The lurid murder caper set at a sleazy Mexican border town turned out to be one of Welles's greatest achievements, but as usual, he fell out with his employer when Universal instituted cuts and additional scenes filmed by director Sam Keller. Welles virtually disowned the film—until it won the International Prize at the Brussel's World's Fair. A revised cut was issued in 1975, but it was only in 1998 when Heston discovered Welles's notes about his preference for how the film should be cut that a major new restoration was undertaken. The film features a marvelous supporting cast with cameos by Marlene Dietrich, Zsa Zsa Gabor, Joseph Cotton, Mercedes McCambridge, and a memorable performance (rumored to be the inspiration for Norman Bates) by Dennis Weaver as a sexually disturbed hotel clerk. The film's long establishing shot, achieved without any cuts, was acclaimed by critics and was discussed in Robert Altman's *The Player*.

Vertigo (1958)

Paramount Pictures

Director and Producer: Alfred Hitchcock; **Writers:** Alec Coppel and Samuel Taylor; **Music:** Bernard Hermann; **Running time:** 128 minutes

Cast: James Stewart ("Scotty" Ferguson); Kim Novak (Madeline/Judy); Barbara Bel Geddes (Midge); Tom Helmore (Gavin Elster)

Oscar nominations: Sound, Art Direction-Set Decoration (color)

Hitchcock's most complex film is regarded by many as his most ambitious work, although it only received a lukewarm reception when it was first released. James Stewart is a private detective whose paralyzing fear of heights ultimately figures into a routine assignment of following a man's wife (Kim Novak) that unexpectedly turns into sexual obsession and murder. Stewart becomes entranced by the woman he follows and is soon fixated by her. When she commits suicide, he is devastated—until he believes she has been reincarnated to be his lover. Stewart plays the most complicated role of his career, and he morphs from his all-American persona into a man driven to the edge of insanity by his obsession with a woman he fears he can never have. Novak is the epitome of the Hitchcockian icy blonde in a role Vera Miles had to turn down when she became pregnant. The film is noted for its groundbreaking camera techniques to simulate the sensation of vertigo. The movie underwent a well-received restoration in 1996 by Robert Harris and James C. Katz.

Peeping Tom (1960)

Astor Pictures Corp.

Director and Producer: Michael Powell; **Writer:** Leo Marks; **Music:** Brian Easdale; **Running time:** 101 minutes

Cast: Carl Boehm (Mark Lewis); Moira Shearer (Vivian); Anna Massey (Helen); Maxine Audley (Mrs. Stephens)

When this film was released in 1960, the outcry of criticism was substantial enough to derail the illustrious career of director Michael Powell. However, in recent years the movie has gained a great deal of respect among film scholars who have championed Powell's achievement. Carl Boehm plays a disturbed young man who had been psychologically abused as a boy by his quack scientist father who experimented on him to see his reaction to pain. As a man, Boehm's character, Mark Lewis, is a photographer who lures young women to his studio and films their expressions as he murders them. The gruesome theme doesn't detract from the expert execution of the story.

Psycho (1960)

Paramount

Director and Producer: Alfred Hitchcock; **Writer:** Joseph Stefano; **Music:** Bernard Hermann; **Running time:** 109 minutes

Cast: Anthony Perkins (Norman Bates); Janet Leigh (Marion Crane); Vera Miles (Lila Crane); John Gavin (Sam Loomis); Martin Balsam (Arbogast)

Oscar nominations: Director, Supporting Actress (Janet Leigh)

In the same year that Michael Powell's career was ruined for releasing the sexually-oriented murder film *Peeping Tom*, Alfred Hitchcock found his greatest success with an equally disturbing film about the same subject matter. Paramount was so convinced that *Psycho* would bomb, they gave Hitchcock a limited budget. The wily director financed much of the film himself in return for a large percentage of the profits, which would earn him millions. The film's murder sequences are so famous and terrifying, people often forget there are only two such scenes in the entire movie. The shower murder was a textbook example of brilliant film editing, and the production design of the old house where eccentric Norman Bates and his mother live is enough to give anyone nightmares. It's inconceivable that Anthony Perkins did not get an Oscar nomination for his legendary performance, though Janet Leigh did for her limited but pivotal role. Hitch's decision to kill off the leading lady early threw audiences for a loop. Vera Miles, John Gavin, and Martin Balsam contributed fine supporting roles. Try to imagine the film without Bernard Hermann's masterful and terrifying score! *Psycho* inspired three TV movie sequels and a spinoff called *Bates Motel*—all unworthy of being linked to the original. Director Gus Van Sant made the pointless "color by numbers" 1998 remake.

Cape Fear (1962)

Universal Pictures

Director: J. Lee Thompson; **Producer:** Sy Bartlett; **Writer:** James R. Webb; **Music:** Bernard Hermann; **Running time:** 105 minutes

Cast: Gregory Peck (Sam Bowden); Robert Mitchum (Max Cady); Polly Bergen (Peggy Bowden); Lori Martin (Nancy); Martin Balsam (Dutton); Telly Savalas (Sievers)

A terrifying story of revenge with Gregory Peck as a defense attorney who finds he and his family have been targeted by a sadistic ex-con played with sinister expertise by Robert Mitchum. The suspense is played to the hilt under J. Lee Thompson's assured direction, as Peck and Mitchum match wits before coming fist to fist in the gut-wrenching climax aboard an isolated houseboat. The sexual menace was very daring for its day, and Mitchum's Max Cady remains one of the screen's most enduring villains.

"Play It Again, Sam"

Remade with reverence in 1991 by Martin Scorsese with Robert DeNiro and Nick Nolte. Gregory Peck, Robert Mitchum, and Martin Balsam, who all appeared in the original, made cameo appearances. Scorsese wisely retained Bernard Hermann's chilling original score.

Knife in the Water (1962)

Kanawha

Director: Roman Polanski; **Prodcer:** Stanislaw Zylewicz; **Writers:** Jakub Goldberg, Roman Polanski, and Jerzy Skolimowski; **Music:** Krzysztof T. Komeda; **Running time:** 94 minutes

Cast: Leon Niemczuk (Andrzej); Jolanta Umecka (Krystyna); Zygmunt Malanowicz (Boy)

Oscar nominations: Best Foreign Language Film

Roman Polanski's first major feature film is also the first Polish movie to be nominated for a Best Foreign Language picture Oscar. A moody, atmospheric psychological thriller about a couple who ask a young hitchhiker to join them on a short boating excursion. Tension soon builds between the husband and boy, and this leads to an altercation with a surprising outcome. Polanski, who was an accomplished actor, wanted to play the part of the boy but was vetoed by the studio for not being attractive enough. Polanski did get a revenge of sorts, as he dubbed the young man's voice in the final cut. Remade as *Kaaterskill Falls* (2001) and *Dead in the Water* (2002).

The Manchurian Candidate (1962)

MGM

Director: John Frankenheimer; **Producers:** George Axelrod and John Frankenheimer; **Writer:** George Axelrod; **Music:** David Amram; **Running time:** 126 minutes

Cast: Frank Sinatra (Bennett Marco); Laurence Harvey (Raymond Shaw); Janet Leigh (Eugenie); Angela Lansbury (Mrs. Iselin); Henry Silva (Chunjin); James Gregory (Sen. John Iselin)

Oscar nominations: Supporting Actress (Angela Lansbury), Editing

One of the most controversial films of the Cold War period, *The Manchurian Candidate* is an innovative and highly stylized thriller that catapulted John Frankenheimer to the top ranks of American film directors. The plot concerns an American soldier (Laurence Harvey) who is captured by Communists during the Korean War and brainwashed. He is released back into society where he unknowingly awaits a secret signal that will force him to make a political assassination that will insure the U.S. elects a secret Red sympathizer as President. Superb performances, especially by the oddly-cast, overly erudite Laurence Harvey and Angela Lansbury as his Lady MacBeth-like mother (she was only three years older than

"Well, Nobody's Perfect!"

A theater marquee in the background shows the 1961 film *Pirates of Tortuga*, though *The Manchurian Candidate* is set years before *Pirates* was made.

Harvey in real life!). When Frank Sinatra got the rights to the film in the 1970s, it was withdrawn from circulation until he reissued it in 1988, but the rumor is not true that it was pulled out of release following the assassination of JFK. Remade with Denzel Washington in 2004.

What Ever Happened to Baby Jane? (1962)

Warner Brothers

Director and Producer: Robert Aldrich; **Writer:** Lukas Heller; **Music:** Frank De Vol; **Running time:** 134 minutes

Cast: Bette Davis (Baby Jane Hudson); Joan Crawford (Blanche Hudson); Victor Buono (Edwin Flagg); Wesley Addy (Marty McDonald)

Oscar nominations: Actress (Joan Crawford), Supporting Actor (Victor Buono), Costume Design* (b&w), Cinematography (b&w), Sound

When it was suggested to studio mogul Jack Warner to pair fading superstars Bette Davis and Joan Crawford he allegedly replied, "I wouldn't give a plugged nickel for either of those two old broads." However, under Robert Aldrich's direction, the "two old broads" revitalized their careers with this gothic suspense yarn that finds them cast as sisters who were both once major stars in the silent era. After Davis's Baby Jane caused an accident that left her more successful sister Blanche (Crawford) in a wheelchair, she has been reluctantly caring for her in their old house. As Jane descends into madness, Blanche is her prisoner and subject to psychological tortures. The two legendary stars give remarkable performances with Davis brilliant as the raving mad Jane. Although critics applauded the on-screen chemistry between Davis and Crawford, their real-life feud is the stuff of Hollywood legend as they despised each other off-camera. Supporting actor Victor Buono made a memorable screen debut.

The Birds (1963)

Universal Pictures

Director and Producer: Alfred Hitchcock; **Writer:** Evan Hunter **Running time:** 119 minutes

Cast: Rod Taylor (Mitch); "Tippi" Hedren (Melanie); Jessica Tandy (Lydia); Suzanne Pleshette (Annie); Veronica Cartwright (Cathy)

Oscar nominations: Special Effects

Alfred Hitchcock's *The Birds* (based on a short story by Daphne Du Maurier) was so unlike anything the legendary director had attempted previously that it caused a media sensation in 1963. The tale of a small northern California coastal town that is inexplicably attacked and rendered helpless by massive flocks of birds is slow to get off the ground. Hitchcock takes his time introducing the main characters and establishing the relationships. However, once the incidents start, they pick up momentum and suspense. Hitchcock used electronic sounds instead of a musical score to great effect. This was the first starring role for Tippi Hedren, a Hitchcock discovery. The final scene of the film is chilling due to Hitchcock's refusal to provide a logical explanation for the events. Screenplay by Evan Hunter, better known as author "Ed McBain."

Charade (1963)

Universal Pictures

Director and Producer: Stanley Donen; **Writer:** Peter Stone; **Music:** Henry Mancini; **Running time:** 113 minutes

Cast: Cary Grant (Peter Joshua); Audrey Hepburn (Reggie Lampert); Walter Matthau (Bartholomew); James Coburn (Tex); George Kennedy (Herman); Ned Glass (Gideon)

Oscar nominations: Song (*Charade*)

The best Hitchcock movie not directed by Hitchcock, *Charade* is a classy, witty, and letter-perfect example of the type of sophisticated entertainment the film industry used to produce regularly but which is sadly lacking today. Cary Grant is a man of mystery who tries to help widow Audrey Hepburn discover which of her late husband's possessions is worth a fortune—before a trio of his old friends can solve the mystery and kill her in the process. Wonderful location scenes in Paris, a great cast of legendary character actors, and Henry Mancini's score (arguably his best) make this a comedy/suspense classic. Remade in 2002 as *The Truth About Charlie* starring … you guessed it, Mark Wahlberg.

Fail Safe (1964)

Columbia Pictures

Director: Sidney Lumet; **Producer:** Max E. Youngstein; **Writer:** Walter Bernstein; **Running time:** 112 minutes

Cast: Dan O'Herlihy (Gen. Black); Walter Matthau (Prof. Groeteschele); Henry Fonda (The President); Frank Overton (Gen. Bogan); Fritz Weaver (Col. Cascio)

Sidney Lumet's brilliant Cold War thriller represents minimalist filmmaking at its most effective. The premise has a squadron of U.S. jets accidentally sent on a mission to destroy Moscow—and the frantic efforts to recall them before the Soviets retaliate. Largely confined to enclosed areas, the movie's sense of claustrophobia heightens the tension, as does the intense black and white cinematography and the lack of musical score. The latter half of the film, with Henry Fonda wonderfully authoritative as the U.S. President, is packed with nail-biting suspense right up until the shocking conclusion. Remade by George Clooney as a live TV production in 2000.

Hollywood Confidential

Stanley Kubrick was so concerned that the similar plot line of *Fail Safe* would undermine his satire *Dr. Strangelove,* that he had Columbia buy the distribution rights to the Lumet film and keep it on a shelf until after his movie was released. The result was that *Fail Safe* was a critical success but box-office failure, as audiences only had the stomach for one film about a nuclear holocaust.

Seven Days in May (1964)

Paramount Pictures

Director: John Frankenheimer; **Producer:** Edward Lewis; **Writer:** Rod Serling; **Music:** Jerry Goldsmith; **Running time:** 118 minutes

Cast: Burt Lancaster (General James Mattoon Scott); Kirk Douglas ("Jiggs" Casey); Fredric March (Pres. Jordan Lyman); Ava Gardner (Ellie); Edmond O'Brien (Sen. Ray Clark); Martin Balsam (Paul Girard); Andrew Duggan (Col. Henderson)

Oscar nominations: Supporting Actor (Edmond O'Brien), Cinematography (b&w)

Rod Serling adapted this novel for the screen and fashioned one of the great political thrillers. Filmed at the height of the Cold War and fears of Armageddon, the story pre-supposes that a pacifist President (Fredric March) signs a nuclear disarmament treaty with Soviets—an act vastly unpopular with both the military and the public who suspect the Communists will not keep their end of the deal. Burt Lancaster is a charismatic General who devises a complex plan for a military takeover. Kirk Douglas is his aid who sympathizes with him, but feels it's his duty to prevent the takeover. Brilliantly acted and directed, the highlight is the verbal showdown between Lancaster and March, which demonstrates why both men were acting legends. Refreshingly, the screenplay presents both viewpoints intelligently . The issues the film raises about the limits of Constitutional power in the hands of well-meaning Presidents remain as timely today as in 1964. The film presents John Houseman's role as an Admiral embroiled in the plot, which was his first on-screen acting appearance. Remade as the 1994 TV movie *The Enemy Within.*

Repulsion (1965)

Royal International Films

Director: Roman Polanski; **Producer:** Gene Gutowski; **Writers:** Roman Polanksi and Gerard Brach; **Music:** Chico Hamilton; **Running time:** 104 minutes

Cast: Catherine Deneuve (Carole Ledux); Ian Hendry (Michael); John Fraser (Colin); Yvonne Furneaux (Helene); Patrick Wymark (Landlord)

Roman Polanski's shocking urban thriller finds Catherine Deneueve as a beautiful but mentally disturbed young woman who visits her sister in London. Left alone in the apartment for days, her mental condition deteriorates as her love/hate feelings about sex drive her to madness and murder. The movie pushed the envelope in terms of its violence and depiction of sexuality (it was the first British film to allow the sounds of a woman having an orgasm). An excellent and intriguing performance by Deneuve playing against type as a woman who is repulsed by sex.

Blow-Up (1966)

MGM/Premiere Sound Films

Director: Michelangelo Antonioni; **Producer:** Carlo Ponti; **Writers:** Michelangelo Antonioni, Tonnio Guerra, and Edward Bond; **Music:** Herbie Hancock; **Running time:** 111 minutes

Cast: Vanessa Redgrave (Jane); David Hemmings (Thomas); Sarah Miles (Patricia); Jane Birkin (The Blonde)

Oscar nominations: Director, Screenplay

Michelangelo Antonioni's stylish thriller was designated for the art house circuit but proved to be a mainstream box-office hit when controversies about the film received extensive press coverage. The intriguing story, set amidst the "mod" scene of London, finds David Hemmings as a hip fashion photographer who believes he may have accidentally taken shots of a murder in progress. The plot often plays second-fiddle to the extensive scenes of promiscuous sex and partying, but the main question—can we believe what we see?—is poignantly illustrated by the haunting final image of the film. To avoid Production Code censorship of the groundbreaking use of nudity, MGM released the movie through a dummy corporation called Premiere Sound Films.

Targets (1968)

Paramount Pictures

Director and Producer: Peter Bogdanovich; **Writers:** Peter Bogdanovich and Polly Platt;
Running time: 90 minutes

Cast: Tim O'Kelly (Bobby Thompson); Boris Karloff (Byron Orlok); Arthur Petersen (Ed
Loughlin); Monty Landis (Marshall Smith); Peter Bogdanovich (Sammy Michaels)

Peter Bogdanovich's directorial debut is a bold, original thriller loosely based on a
real incident involving a Texas gunman who randomly picked off victims from atop
a tower. Tim O'Kelly is the amiable, all-American young man who one day decides
to go on a homicidal spree. The film inventively interweaves his actions with Boris
Karloff as Byron Orlok, a once-revered horror film icon who has fallen on hard times
and is reduced to making personal appearances at drive-in theaters. The two men's
paths cross at a drive-in during a tension-filled climax. Bogdanovich provided Karloff
with the last great role of his career at a time when the industry had largely ignored
him. Bogdanovich has a supporting role as a movie director. Note: the horror film
clips of Karloff seen in the movie are from Roger Corman's *The Terror* (1963).

CHAPTER 10
HORROR
"IT'S ALIVE! IT'S ALIVE!"

Human beings are unique creatures in the sense that there is no other species that will go to great lengths to insure they are terrified. However, we Masters of the Universe spend exorbitant sums to engage in activities that bring us sheer terror: extreme sports, theme park rides, and planning elaborate weddings. A natural byproduct of this obsession with self-flagellation is the public's fixation on horror films. From the earliest moments of cinematic history, audiences have been determined to reward those films and filmmakers who have caused them to lose countless hours of sleep.

At the risk of sounding like a broken record, I must point out that like so many other genres covered in this book, the horror film has suffered greatly in recent years. Whereas filmmakers of bygone eras used the power of imagination to frighten audiences, most of today's horror films should be more aptly titled *horrible* films. The emphasis on blood and guts may get a twinge of revulsion from audiences, but compare that to our reactions to the great horror films of the past. The first sight of Bela Lugosi (and for that matter Christopher Lee) as Dracula still makes an indelible and frightening impression—before he even utters a word. Compare Robert Wise's terrifying version of *The Haunting*, in which all of the events are merely *suggested*, to the anemic recent special effects-laden remake, and you will have all the evidence you need that the greatest achievements in this genre are mostly in the distant past. I say "mostly" because there are occasional gems. For my money, the film that has come closest to capturing the essence of the great horror films is *The Blair Witch*

Project. Unfortunately, that begat *Book of Shadows: Blair Witch 2*, which generated the truly horrific scene of patrons slapping down hard-earned money for admission!

When you indulge in the great horror films, you are seeing works of art, though they may not have been regarded as such in their day. No one today comes remotely close to Karloff, Lugosi, and Chaney in terms of instilling mass fear in audiences. Sit back and watch these masters at work—and by all means, leave the light on!

Dracula (1931)

Universal Pictures

Director: Tod Browning; **Producers:** Tod Browning and Carl Laemmele Jr.; **Writer:** Garrett Fort; **Running time:** 75 minutes

Cast: Bela Lugosi (Count Dracula); Helen Chandler (Mina Seward); David Manners (John Harker); Dwight Frye (Renfield); Edward Von Sloan (Van Helsing)

Director Tod Browning's landmark film helped establish Universal as the premiere studio for the horror genre. This is actually an adaptation of the hit 1920s stage production, which was authorized by Bram Stoker's estate. The centerpiece, of course, is Bela Lugosi's immortal interpretation of the Count—all the more remarkable because he spoke little English and had to speak his lines phonetically. Effectively devoid of music, the film does creak with age, and it too often resembles the stage production in that the sets are quite claustrophobic. Lugosi's Dracula is not the most frightening—for that we must visit Max Schreck and Klaus Kinski in both versions of *Nosferatu* and Christopher Lee in *Horror of Dracula*. However, there is no denying Lugosi's status as one of the most enduring icons of the cinema. (Tragically he would die impoverished and addicted to drugs in 1955.) Curiously, a Spanish language version was shot simultaneously on the same sets using different actors.

Gone with the Wind

The original theatrical release ended with an epilogue in which cast member Edward Van Sloan warned the audience that vampires did indeed exist. Sadly, this was cut and has never been restored.

Frankenstein (1931)

Universal Pictures

Director: James Whale; **Producer:** Carl Laemmle Jr.; **Writers:** John L. Balderston, Garrett Fort, and Francis Edward Faragoh; **Music:** Bernhaud Kaun (uncredited); **Makeup:** Jack Pierce; **Running time:** 71 minutes

Cast: Colin Clive (Henry Frankenstein); Mae Clarke (Elizabeth); John Boles (Victor Moritz); Boris Karloff (The Monster); Edward Van Sloan (Dr. Waldman)

Released shortly after their blockbuster *Drac-ula*, this Universal Pictures adaptation of Mary Shelly's novel takes a good deal of artistic license, especially in the physical look of the monster. It's safe to say that it's impossible to now think of this character without envisioning the ingenious makeup design created by Jack Pierce and Boris Karloff. (The process of getting into full makeup and costume took hours and often subjected Karloff to excruciating pain.) Moreso than *Dracula*, this Universal classic has withstood the passage of time and in many ways improves with age. So convinc-ing was Karloff's performance that ever since people have erroneously refered to the monster as Frankenstein himself. It also spawned a cottage industry of sequels and remakes that continue to this day.

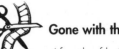

Gone with the Wind

After the film's initial release, a key sequence was cut showing the monster unintentionally drowning a little girl. Ironically, the abbreviated scene implied a much worse fate for the child. A prologue was also cut in which Edward Van Sloan warned audience members to leave the theater if they were weak of heart. The scenes have since been restored.

Dr. Jekyll and Mr. Hyde (1932)

Paramount Pictures

Director and Producer: Rouben Mamoulian; **Writers:** Samuel Hoffenstein and Percy Heath; **Running time:** 98 minutes

Cast: Fredric March (Dr. Jekyll/Mr. Hyde); Miriam Hopkins (Ivy); Rose Hobart (Muriel); Holmes Herbert (Dr. Lanyon)

Oscar nominations: Actor* (Fredric March, tied with Wallace Beery for *The Champ*), Cinematography, Writing

Perhaps the best version of Robert Louis Stevenson's oft-filmed tale. Fredric March won an Oscar for his remarkable performance as a British gentleman whose experiments lead to his dual personality as a monstrous killer. Director Rouben Mamouolian and cinematographer Karl Struss never fully revealed how they accomplished the transformation scenes, but they are still remarkable today. When MGM remade the film in 1941 with Spencer Tracy, they acquired the rights to this version as well and shelved it for decades.

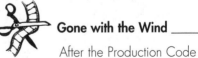

Gone with the Wind

After the Production Code was established, the film was shorn of about 15 minutes of footage, including a brief nude scene with Miriam Hopkins. The original cut was not restored until recent years.

Freaks (1932)

MGM

Director and Producer: Tod Browning; **Writers:** Willis Goldbeck, Leon Gordon, and Edgar Allan Woolf; **Running time:** 64 minutes

Cast: Wallace Ford (Phroso); Leila Hyams (Venus); Olga Baclanova (Cleopatra); Henry Victor (Hercules)

This MGM production had a history as tortured as the real-life freaks depicted onscreen. MGM had hired Tod Browning to direct a horror film to emulate those being made at Universal. Browning's story concept centered on a group of circus freaks who exert a horrific revenge on a cruel "normal" woman and her despicable lover. Both the studio and public were horrified by the film due to its disturbing depiction of real-life people suffering from such severe physical deformaties. Thus, the movie was a major financial bomb. For decades it was banned outright in the U.K. Ironically, the movie takes a sympathetic stand toward the freaks even as it exploits them. They are treated with dignity and they are clearly the heroes of the piece. The movie remains a disturbing but fascinating experience with an ending that is unforgettable.

Gone with the Wind

After its release, the studio trimmed key sequences in which the villainous strongman is castrated during an attempted rape and reemerges later singing Soprano as part of the freak show.

The Mummy (1933)

Universal Pictures

Director: Karl Freund; **Producer:** Carl Laemmle Jr.; **Writer:** John Balderston; **Music:** James Dietrich (uncredited); **Makeup:** Jack Pierce; **Running time:** 73 minutes

Cast: Boris Karloff (Im-ho-tep/Ardath Bey); Zita Johann (Helen/Princess Anckesen-Amon); David Manners (Frank Whemple); Arthur Byron (Sir Joseph Whemple); Edward Van Sloan (Dr. Miller)

When *Frankenstein* was released in 1931, Boris Karloff's name was buried in fourth place in the credits. With the release of his second major horror film for Universal, his appeal was so broad his name now rose above the title. Karloff himself, not the film, was now the attraction. *The Mummy* is one of his most inspired films, benefiting from a truly eerie atmosphere and outstanding cinematography (possibly because director Karl Freund was primarily known as a cinematographer). Karloff is the titular character, brought back to life with the discovery of his tomb. He haunts present day Cairo stalking his ancient love, who has also been reincarnated. Karloff's makeup (again by the great Jack Pierce) is another triumph.

"Play It Again, Sam"

The Mummy inspired four sequels, none starring Karloff. In 1959, Hammer Films produced a remake with Peter Cushing and Christopher Lee that was largely original in concept and very well done. In 1999, Universal made the big budget remake starring Brendan Frasier that begat the 2001 sequel *The Mummy Returns*. The raison d'etre for both seemed to be to justify the theme park ride at Universal Studios.

Bride of Frankenstein (1935)

Universal Pictures

Director: James Whale; **Producer:** Carl Laemmele Jr.; **Writers:** William Hurlbut and John Balderston; **Music:** Franz Waxman; **Running time:** 75 minutes

Cast: Boris Karloff (The Monster); Colin Clive (Dr. Frankenstein); Valerie Hobson (Elizabeth Frankenstein); Elsa Lanchester (The Bride/Mary Shelly); Ernest Thesiger (Dr. Pretorious)

Oscar nominations: Sound

A true rarity: a sequel that is regarded by many as superior to the original. Director James Whale added liberal doses of overt humor to the mix this time. Thus, *Bride of Frankenstein* can either be regarded as a comedy with elements of horror or a horror film with elements of comedy. Karloff reprises his legendary role as the unluckiest man-made monster in history, his every act of kindness met with derision and violence. Even his "bride" (Elsa Lanchester, unforgettable in her breakthrough role) finds him hideous—and she's no looker herself! It includes remarkable sets, atmospheric cinematography, and a dynamic musical score by Franz Waxman. Curiously, Karloff never cared for the film, as he objected to having The Monster speak.

Gone with the Wind

After completion of *The Bride of Frankenstein*, the studio cut several key scenes, totaling 12 minutes, that have never been recovered.

Cat People (1942)

RKO Radio Pictures

Director: Jacques Tourneur; **Producer:** Val Lewton; **Writer:** Dewitt Bodeen; **Music:** Roy Webb; **Running time:** 73 minutes

Cast: Simone Simon (Irena); Kent Smith (Oliver Reed); Tom Conway (Dr. Judd); Jane Randolph (Alice)

The first film produced by Val Lewton was a major box-office hit and inspired him to make similarly-themed horror movies in the years to come. However, *Cat People* is director Jacques Tourneur's triumph of style over content—he insisted on making the film in a modern urban setting and utilizing the amazing skills of cinematographer Nicholas Musuraca, who created an eerie world defined by menacing shadows. The plot finds kittenish virgin Simone Simon reluctant to consummate her marriage to frustrated Kent Smith because she is convinced she suffers from a curse that causes any sexual arousal to turn her into a killer panther. The script wisely leaves doubt as to whether this is true or whether Simone is mentally ill. The film's many eerie and unforgettable images provide far more scares than if we saw the manifestation of Simone's fears, as was the case with Paul Schrader's 1982 remake that relied on overt special effects as opposed to ambiguities. *Cat People* inspired the 1944 sequel *The Curse of the Cat People*.

Dead of Night (1945)

Universal Pictures

Directors: Cavalcanti, Basil Dearden, Charles Chricton, and Robert Hamer; **Producer:** Michael Balcon; **Writers:** John Baines, Angus MacPahil, and T.E.B. Clarke; **Music:** Georges Auric; **Running time:** 102 minutes

Cast: Michael Redgrave (Maxwell Frere); Mervyn Johns (Walter Craig); Roland Culver (Elliott Foley); Sally Ann Howes (Sally O'Hara)

Gone with the Wind

When initially released in the United States, Universal Pictures cut two entire segments, thus rendering the conclusion of the film to be confusing and partly inexplicable. Happily, the footage has been restored in recent years.

Dead of Night is a sophisticated British production about a group of strangers invited to the home of a man who informs them they have each appeared in his recurring nightmares. The episodic script presents each of the character's stories before leading to an eerie conclusion that ties up the loose ends. The highlight is undoubtedly Michael Redgrave's appearance as a ventriloquist who becomes possessed by his dummy. (Seemingly the inspiration for *Magic*.)

House of Wax (1953)

Warner Brothers

Director: Andre de Toth; **Producer:** Bryan Foy; **Writer:** Crane Wilbur; **Music:** David Buttolph; **Running time:** 90 minutes

Cast: Vincent Price (Prof. Jarrod); Frank Lovejoy (Tom Brennan); Phyllis Kirk (Sue Allen); Carolyn Jones (Cathy Gray)

This box-office blockbuster established Vincent Price as one of the kings of the horror film genre. He gives an excellent performance as an ingenious sculptor of wax statues who suffers horrible disfigurement when a doublecrossing business partner burns down his wax museum. Price is driven mad and begins to murder both his enemies and innocent victims, then displaying them as waxen figures to an unknowing public. Warner Brothers tried to imply that this was the first 3D film, but in fact *Bwana Devil* preceded it by a year. The 3D gimmick proved so popular that some theaters showed the film around the clock. Intelligently written with wonderful effects. Look for Charles Bronson (billed as Charles Buchinsky) playing Price's creepy assistant named Igor (no kidding!). Remade in 2005 starring another intellectually vacant waxen figure named Paris Hilton.

The Abominable Snowman of the Himilayas (1957)

20th Century Fox

Director: Val Guest; **Producer:** Aubrey Baring; **Writer:** Nigel Kneale; **Running time:** 85 minutes

Cast: Peter Cushing (John Rollason); Forrest Tucker (Tom Friend); Maureen Connell (Helen); Richard Watts (Peter Fox)

This is an intelligently written and directed adventure film based on screenwriter Nigel Kneale's British TV production *The Creature* (1957). The plot involves a scientist who leads an expedition in search of the legendary Yeti. Director Val Guest understands the impact of not showing the creatures until the very end, thus building the tension. The film benefits from excellent performances, particularly from the always impressive Peter Cushing and Forrest Tucker as a hardheaded Yank. Despite the limited budget, the film grows progressively eerie as the group nears its quarry—and the ending is both thought-provoking and moving. A little-discussed gem from the famed Hammer Studios.

Horror of Dracula (1958)

Universal Pictures

Director: Terence Fisher; **Producer:** Anthony Hinds; **Writer:** Jimmy Sangster; **Music:** James Bernard; **Running time:** 82 minutes

Cast: Peter Cushing (Van Helsing); Christopher Lee (Count Dracula); Michael Gough (Arthur Holmwood); Melissa Stribling (Mina); Carol Marsh (Lucy)

Peter Cushing and Christopher Lee had costarred in Hammer Studios' *The Curse of Frankenstein* with good results. The studio brought them together again for what is possibly the best Hammer production of all. Released as simply *Dracula* in the U.K., this version of the Bram Stoker tale plays it straight with Lee's interpretation of the Count both charismatic and terrifying. So strong is his screen presence that you barely realize how infrequently he appears in the film. Cushing makes a wonderfully vibrant Ven Helsing, and his final confrontation with Dracula is terrifically exciting and well staged. This film displays a hallmark of the Hammer films: rich production design and impressive cinematography that belie their relatively low budgets. The film's liberal violence and sexuality helped make it a box-office smash, though critics were largely immune to its merits until many years later.

House on Haunted Hill (1959)

Allied Artists

Director and Producer: William Castle; **Writer:** Robb White; **Music:** Von Dexter; **Running time:** 75 minutes

Cast: Vincent Price (Frederick Loren); Carolyn Craig (Nora Manning); Richard Long (Lance Schroeder); Elisha Cook (Watson Pritchard)

A masterpiece of camp from schlockmaster producer/director William Castle. Subtlety was never Castle's strong point—both his films and marketing were exercises in how to go "over the top" in a big way. Vincent Price seems to be having the time of his life hamming it up as a millionaire who invites a group of strangers to a "haunted house" party at his mansion. There is a reward of $10,000 for anyone who spends the entire night. Even in 1959, the prospect of making ten grand would seem a slim reward once the hangings, floating skeletons, and acid baths start materializing. Castle released the tongue-in-cheek film with a gimmick called Emergo, in which a skeleton would fly over the audience on a wire at precisely the same time it appeared on screen. The grosses were as huge as the laughs. Stay away from the 1999 remake—sans Price it isn't worth the effort.

The Innocents (1961)

20th Century Fox

Director and Producer: Jack Clayton; **Writers:** Truman Capote and William Archibald; **Music:** Georges Auric; **Running time:** 100 minutes

Cast: Deborah Kerr (Miss Giddens); Peter Wyngarde (Peter Quint); Megs Jenkins (Mrs. Grose); Michael Redgrave (The Uncle); Martin Stephens (Miles); Pamela Franklin (Flora)

One of the best screen chillers of all time, *The Innocents* is Jack Clayton's brilliant film version of Henry James's Victorian ghost story *The Turn of the Screw*. Deborah Kerr gives an Oscar-caliber performance as a spinster governess who is placed in charge of two precocious children at a remote British mansion. She soon suspects the children are being haunted by the apparitions of a perverted groundskeeper who died under mysterious circumstances. The genius of the story (coscripted by Truman Capote) is that one is never sure whether the ghostly happenings are real or whether they are in the mind of the governess. The tension builds to a spellbinding and terrifying conclusion. The stunning black and white cinematorgraphy is by Freddie Francis. The film inspired a 1974 TV movie and director Michael Winner's under-rated 1972 prequel, *The Nightcomers* with Marlon Brando.

The Haunting (1963)

MGM

Director and Producer: Robert Wise; **Writer:** Nelson Gidding; **Music:** Humphrey Searle; **Running time:** 112 minutes

Cast: Julie Harris (Eleanor Lance); Claire Bloom (Theo); Richard Johnson (Markway); Russ Tamblyn (Luke); Lois Maxwell (Grace)

For this author's money, Robert Wise's adaptation of Shirley Jackson's *The Haunting of Hill House* might well be the most terrifying movie ever made. Richard Johnson leads a small group to a supposedly haunted mansion to conduct experiments to see if the supernatural does exist. It's an eclectic bunch consisting of a psychologically tortured spinster, a lesbian with ESP powers, and a hip young cynic. The house itself should receive equal billing, as it's the main character—a sinister looking place that is a masterpiece of production design. Wise correctly refuses to show special effects or spell out easy answers, knowing the audience's imagination will concoct horrors far worse than he could show. Outstanding performances by all. Disregard the overblown, big budget 1999 remake and revel in the original—but by all means make sure the lights are turned on and you're not home alone! Makes a great double feature with *The Innocents*.

The Conqueror Worm (1968)

American International Pictures

Director: Michael Reeves; **Producers:** Louis M. Hayward, Arnold Miller, and Philip Waddilove; **Music:** Paul Ferris; **Running time:** 86 minutes

Cast: Vincent Price (Matthew Hopkins); Ian Ogilvy (Richard Marshall); Rupert Davies (John Lowes); Hilary Dwyer (Sarah Lowes)

Although largely overlooked during its American release, the merits of *The Conqueror Worm* have long been appreciated in Europe, where it was released as the more appropriately titled *The Witchfinder General*. However, due to star Vincent Price's recent string of successful films based on the works of Edgar Allan Poe, U.S. distributor AIP changed the title and added a brief prologue and epilogue based on a Poe story. The new title implied a monster film when, in fact, this is a gory but superbly made story that provides Price with one of the great roles of his career. He's terrific as a sadistic witchfinder who roams the towns of old England shaking down prospective victims for money and sex, lest he sentences them to a torturous death. Price clashed creatively with young director Michael Reeves, who initially wanted Donald Pleasence for the role. Ironically, Reeves died shortly after the film was released and so was never able to capitalize on his truly inspired achievement.

Gone with the Wind

The film was recut for censorship reasons in England and the United States. The recent British DVD restores the "European cut" that features topless bar wenches. The U.S. version also inexplicably replaced the musical score with one by Lex Baxter.

CHAPTER 11
ADVENTURE
"WE DON'T NEED NO BADGES!"

Always among the most popular of movie genres, the adventure film covers a wide canvas. It's fairly subjective as to what constitutes a movie in this category, thus I've tried to select a diverse group of titles ranging from obvious early classics such as *The Adventures of Robin Hood* to more esoteric choices like Cornel Wilde's superb, but not widely known, 1966 film *The Naked Prey.* Like the movie musical and the western, great adventure films seem to be largely relegated to the distant past. The kinds of sweeping swashbucklers that enthralled audiences in the 1930's ultimately gave way to stories of survival and exploration. By the 1960s, most adventure-oriented films weren't particularly memorable.

The films included in this chapter have merits that have allowed them to stand the test of time in extraordinary ways. It's worth noting that when many of these films were released, most people didn't travel as widely as they do today. Thus, for the average person, the prospect of journeying to exotic locales existed only on the silver screen. Audiences were captivated by the larger-than-life scenarios, despite the fact that most of the adventure films of this period were shot either in studios or in such "exotic" locales as Burbank. (Those notable exceptions that were actually shot on location, such as *The African Queen, The Treasure of the Sierra Madre,* and *Swiss Family Robinson,* benefited greatly from the authenticity this provided to the films.)

Perhaps the reason there is a dearth of traditional adventure films in the contemporary cinema is because the modern age has deprived us of much of our sense of wonder. When we can fly the Atlantic in a few hours, younger audiences may well find it difficult to relate to a film about the search for the Northwest Passage or the adventures of Foreign Legionnaires. Still, the films included in this chapter are much more likely to be held in high regard a century from now than the meager offerings being produced today.

Mutiny on the Bounty (1935)

MGM

Director: Frank Lloyd; **Producer:** Irving Thalberg (uncredited); **Writers:** Talbot Jennings, Jules Furthman, and Carey Wilson; **Music:** Herbert Stothart; **Running time:** 132 minutes

Cast: Charles Laughton (Capt. William Bligh); Clark Gable (Fletcher Christian); Franchot Tone (Roger Byam); Herbert Mundin (Smith)

Oscar nominations: Best Picture*, Score, Editing, Actor (Charles Laughton), Actor (Clark Gable), Actor (Franchot Tone), Screenplay, Director

The Oscar-winner for Best Picture of 1935 curiously won no other awards that year, the last time this has happened in Academy history. The film is a fairly faithful adaptation of the famed novel that was based on real-life events. Charles Laughton and Clark Gable provided the box-office sizzle though they despised working with each other. Laughton's performance is the main focus, as his sneering, menacing Captain Bligh is one of the screen's great villains. Trivia note: James Cagney and David Niven appeared as uncredited extras. Cagney was already a star but felt it would be fun to moonlight for a few hours.

 "Play It Again, Sam" _____

The Bounty saga had already been filmed twice before Frank Lloyd's version hit the screen: in a 1916 silent version and as *In the Wake of the Bounty* with Errol Flynn in 1933. In 1962, MGM remade the film as a magnificent but ill-fated mega budget production starring Marlon Brando. (See Chapter 16.) In 1984, Mel Gibson and Anthony Hopkins starred in the brilliant and underrated *The Bounty*, a historically accurate version that portrayed Bligh in a more human manner.

San Francisco (1936)

MGM

Director: W.S. Van Dyke; **Producers:** John Emerson and Bernard H. Hyman; **Writers:** Anita Loos and Robert Hopkins (story); **Music:** Herbert Sothart; **Running time:** 115 minutes

Cast: Clark Gable (Blackie Norton); Jeanette MacDonald (Mary Blake); Spencer Tracy (Father Tim Mullin); Jack Holt (Jack Burley)

Oscar nominations: Best Picture, Director, Sound*, Writing, Assistant Director, Actor (Spencer Tracy)

The granddaddy of all disaster films, *San Francisco* featured the powerhouse teaming of Gable, MacDonald, and Tracy as inhabitants of the city's bawdy Barbary Coast in the days before the devastating earthquake of 1906. Gable was reluctant to do the film, as he had been warned of MacDonald's reputation as a prima donna. Although he never warmed to her off the set, their chemistry onscreen is considerable. Tracy gained an Oscar nomination as a tough neighborhood priest. The highlight, of course, is the stunning depiction of the earthquake, brought to life by special effects that still seem remarkable today. D.W. Griffith is known to have directed one sequence in the film, but precisely which one is still debated.

The Prisoner of Zenda (1937)

United Artists

Director: John Cromwell; **Producer:** David O. Selznick; **Writers:** John L. Balderston, Wells Root, and Donald Ogden Stewart; **Music:** Alfred Newman; **Running time:** 101 minutes

Cast: Ronald Colman (Rudolf Rassendy/King Rudolf V); Madeleine Carroll (Princess Flavia); Douglas Fairbanks Jr. (Rupert); Mary Astor (Antoinette); David Niven (Fritz)

Oscar nominations: Score, Art Direction

The Prisoner of Zenda is a top swashbuckler with a sterling cast headed by Ronald Colman as an everyday man called upon to impersonate his identical cousin, the King, who has been kidnapped. To prevent the evil Rupert from taking the crown in his place, the King must make an appearance for his coronation. Colman agrees to the plot, hoping to buy time while rescuers search frantically for the real monarch. Viewers are treated to some marvelous fun, as Colman has to learn his alter-ego's personality quirks to avoid detection. The film made David Niven a star, and Douglas Fairbanks Jr. steals every scene as the most nefarious of villains. *Zenda* was shot three times in the silent era, and a 1952 remake with Stewart Granger is also well done. Peter Sellers starred in a slapstick comedy version in 1979.

The Adventures of Robin Hood (1939)

Warner Brothers

Directors: Michael Curtiz and William Keighly; **Producer:** Hal B. Wallis; **Writers:** Norman Reilly Raine and Seton I. Miller; **Music:** Erich Wolfgang Korngold; **Running time:** 102 minutes

Cast: Errol Flynn (Robin Hood); Olivia De Havilland (Maid Marian); Basil Rathbone (Sir Guy of Gisbourne); Claude Rains (Prince John)

Oscar nominations: Best Picture, Editing*, Score*, Art Direction*

One of the all-time great cinematic adventures, this film was originally designed for James Cagney! However, when Cagney became embroiled with a contract dispute, the role went to 28-year-old Errol Flynn, who had become a matinee idol four years earlier with *Captain Blood*. The role of Robin Hood fit Flynn so perfectly that it would be the part that defined his career. The film is drenched in glorious Technicolor and features a rousing score by Erich Wolfgang Korngold. Flynn gets outstanding support from his fellow cast members, with Olivia De Havilland enchanting as Maid Marian and Basil Rathbone superb as Flynn's nemesis. (Their climactic fencing sequence is truly thrilling thanks to both actors performing most of their own stunts.) The movie's budget was a (then) staggering $2 million, but the film became a box-office smash for Warner Brothers. Note: William Keighly was hired as director but was replaced by the studio shortly thereafter by Michael Curtiz.

Beau Geste (1939)

Paramount Pictures

Director and Producer: William Wellman; **Writer:** Robert Carson; **Music:** Alfred Newman; **Running time:** 112 minutes

Cast: Gary Cooper (Michael "Beau" Geste); Ray Milland (John Geste); Robert Preston (Digby Geste); Brian Donlevy (Sgt. Markoff); Susan Hayward (Isobel Rivers)

Oscar nominations: Supporting Actor (Brian Donlevy), Art Direction

Yet another classic film from the wondrous year of 1939, William Wellman's *Beau Geste* was actually the second screen version of Christopher Wren's novel. The first film adaptation was made in 1926 and starred Ronald Colman. The story was inspired by Wren's personal experiences in the French Foreign Legion, long a home for misfits and desperate men of all nations. The tale involves three British brothers who are driven from England in scandal. They join the Legion only to come under the thumb of a tyrannical master sergeant who terrorizes them more than the hordes of murderous Arab tribesman who are planning to butcher them. The film suffers from the old

Hollywood habit of casting American actors in European roles but never mandating that they even attempt to emulate the country they supposedly represent. Thus, Gary Cooper and his costars sound every bit the all-American boys. Brian Donlevy fares much better, earning an Oscar nomination for his superb performance as the sadistic Sgt. Markoff. The finale that finds the dwindling number of Legionaires trying to hold out against overwhelming odds is dramatically engaging and suspenseful. Remade by Universal in 1966 with Doug McClure and Telly Savalas. The film also inspired the nutty 1977 spoof *The Last Remake of Beau Geste*.

Drums Along the Mohawk (1939)

20th Century Fox

Director: John Ford; **Executive Producer:** Darryl F. Zanuck; **Writers:** Sonya Levien and Lamar Trotti; **Music:** Alfred Newman; **Running time:** 103 minutes

Cast: Claudette Colbert (Lana Martin); Henry Fonda (Gil Martin); Edna May Oliver (Mrs. McKlennar); Eddie Collins (Christian Reall); John Carradine (Caldwell)

Oscar nominations: Supporting Actress (Edna May Oliver), Cinematography (color)

It's long been said that most films attempting to portray the American Revolution are destined to be commercial and artistic failures. (Remember Al Pacino's portrayal of a colonist à la *Goodfellas* in - *Revolution?*) John Ford's *Drums Along the Mohawk* rises above the curse and remains a sweeping adventure that is often overlooked in discussions of the great films released in 1939. The trials and tribulations of New York farmers caught up in the on-going battles with the British and Indians is presented in a stunning Technicolor production. The film presents a simplified version of history (implying the entire conflict was started by a disreputable British officer), but the scenery and action benefits from the usual Fordian touches, primarily the showcasing of an eclectic group of character actors from his famed stock company. Edna May Oliver is hilarious as a feisty pioneer woman who is more dangerous than the Indian braves who confront her.

The Four Feathers (1939)

United Artists

Director: Zoltan Korda; **Producer:** Alexander Korda; **Writers:** R.C. Sherriff, Lajos Biro, and Arthur Wimperis; **Music:** Miklos Rosza; **Running time:** 130 minutes

Cast: John Clements (Harry Faversham); Ralph Richardson (John Durrance); C. Aubrey Smith (Gen. Burroughs); June Duprez (Ethne Burroughs)

Oscar nominations: Cinematography (color)

"Play It Again, Sam"

This classic story had been filmed previously in 1915, 1921, and 1959. A remake under the title of *Storm Over the Nile* with Laurence Harvey was released in 1955. More recently, it was remade as a 1977 TV movie and a 2002 theatrical release.

A young British army officer resigns his commission rather than ship out to Egypt to help quell a tribal insurrection. In doing so, he receives four feathers—a traditional branding of cowardice—from his fellow officers. He later decides to redeem himself by infiltrating enemy lines and extricating his former comrades from a potentially deadly situation. The film tells a moving story along with stunning action sequences that are enhanced by an outstanding cast and Georges Périnal's sweeping color cinematography.

Gunga Din (1939)

RKO Radio Pictures

Director and Producer: George Stevens; **Writers:** Joel Sayre and Fred Guiol; **Music:** Alfred Newman; **Running time:** 117 minutes

Cast: Cary Grant (Archibald Cutter); Victor McLaglen ("Mac" MacChesney); Douglas Fairbanks Jr. (Tommy Ballantine); Sam Jaffe (Gunga Din); Joan Fontaine ("Emmy")

Oscar nominations: Cinematography (b&w)

It's a mark of how many classic films were released in 1939 that this classic screen adventure only received one technical Oscar nomination. Rudyard Kipling's story is brought to the screen magnificently by George Stevens. Cary Grant, Victor McLaglen, and Douglas Fairbanks Jr. are superb as a trio of British soldier buddies fighting in India to put down the Thugee uprising. The chemistry and humor between the men is priceless. The most memorable performance, however, is by the great Sam Jaffe as the abused, but ever-loyal water boy, Gunga Din, who shows unexpected courage under fire. The final sequence, in which the soldiers finally pay him a belated tribute, is as moving as a film moment can be. Remade by director John Sturges (an editor on *Gunga Din*) as the 1962 Rat Pack western *Sergeants Three*.

Northwest Passage (1940)

MGM

Director: King Vidor; **Producer:** Hunt Stromberg; **Writers:** Laurence Stallings and Talbot Jennings; **Music:** Herbert Stothart; **Running time:** 125 minutes

Cast: Spencer Tracy (Major Robert Rogers); Robert Young (Landon Towne); Walter Brennan (Hunt Marriner); Ruth Hussey (Elizabeth Towne)

Oscar nominations: Cinematography (color)

This stirring adventure story is based on Kenneth Caldwell's novel—well, at least the first part of the novel dealing with Roger's Rangers, an elite group of soldier/scouts who fought for the British during the French and Indian Wars. Spencer Tracy and Robert Young head the revered group on their often-disastrous mission, facing fierce enemies, nasty weather, and starvation. There are some riveting action sequences including the desperate human chain across a raging river. King Vidor directed the movie, replacing W.S. Van Dyke, who had shot significant footage before being replaced. The color cinematography, which garnered an Oscar nomination, is outstanding. A planned sequel never materialized due to the hardships encountered in making this film, along with Spencer Tracy's exasperation with working with the strong-willed Vidor. *Passage* was remade as *Mission of Danger* (1959), which spawned a sequel, *Frontier Rangers*, released the same year. It was remade again as *Fury River* in 1961.

For Whom the Bell Tolls (1943)

Paramount Pictures

Director and Producer: Sam Wood; **Writer:** Dudley Nichols; **Music:** Victor Young; **Running time:** 156 minutes

Cast: Gary Cooper (Robert Jordan); Ingrid Bergman (Maria); Akim Tamiroff (Pablo); Arturo de Cordova (Agustin)

Oscar nominations: Best Picture, Actor (Gary Cooper), Actress (Ingrid Bergman), Supporting Actress* (Katina Paxinou), Art Direction-Interior Decoration (color), Cinematography, Supporting Actor (Akim Tamiroff), Editing, Score

This is a romanticized but enjoyable adaptation of Ernest Hemingway's novel. Hemingway himself had chosen Gary Cooper and Ingrid Bergman for the leads in this story of adventurers battling the fascist government of Franco during the Spanish Civil War. Sadly, the studio depoliticized most of the film's content, making it seem more or less like a generic adventure story. However, the film resonated with audiences when it was released in 1943 at the height of WWII—and it is still regarded as one of the best film adaptations of a Hemingway story. Akim Tamiroff steals the show with his Oscar-nominated performance. The film was released at 170 minutes then cut to 130. In recent years, 26 minutes of missing footage has been restored.

To Have and Have Not (1944)

Warner Brothers

Director and Producer: Howard Hawks; **Writers:** Jules Furthman and William Faulkner; **Music:** Franz Waxman; **Running time:** 100 minutes

Cast: Humphrey Bogart (Steve Morgan); Walter Brennan (Eddie); Lauren Bacall (Marie "Slim" Browning); Dolores Moran (Hellene de Bursac); Hoagy Carmichael (Cricket)

This memorable Howard Hawks production had an unusual genesis: Hawks had bet Ernest Hemingway that he could make a good movie from his worst novel. Hemingway took the bait, and Hawks managed to make good on his boast, though in fairness he added considerable new elements to the story. Humphrey Bogart gets embroiled in smuggling a fugitive from the Nazis into Martinique, all the while swapping classic double-entendres with rising star Lauren Bacall, with whom he would form a real life romance that led to marriage. The onscreen action is more exciting in the romantic scenes thanks to the sultry Bacall, of whom one critic said "Even her simplest remarks sound like jungle mating cries." Co-star Hoagy Carmichael was author Ian Fleming's original vision for the character of James Bond! Remade as *The Breaking Point* with John Garfield in 1950.

Scott of the Antarctic (1948)

Eagle-Lion Distributors

Director: Charles Frend; **Producer:** Michael Balcon; **Writers:** Walter Meade, Ivor Montagu, and Mary Haley Bell; **Music:** Vaughan Williams; **Running time:** 111 minutes

Cast: John Mills (Robert Falcon Scott); Diana Churchill (Kathleen Scott); Harold Warrender (Wilson); Anne Firth (Oriana Wilson)

In this criminally underrated adventure epic, John Mills plays the famed explorer who embarks on a disastrous expedition to be the first man to set foot on the South Pole. The movie, a top rate production from Britain's Ealing Studios, has been faulted in recent years for sanitizing Scott and making him into a hero when history suggests his bumbling decisions led to the story's tragic consequences. However, taken as an adventure story of man versus nature, the movie impresses on all levels. Good performances by Mills and the nonstar supporting cast (though Christopher Lee makes a brief early career appearance).

The Treasure of the Sierra Madre (1948)

Warner Brothers

Director and Writer: John Huston; **Producer:** Henry Blanke; **Music:** Max Steiner; **Running time:** 126 minutes

Cast: Humphrey Bogart (Fred C. Dobbs); Walter Huston (Howard); Tim Holt (Bob Curtin); Bruce Bennett (Cody)

Oscar nominations: Best Picture, Director*, Screenplay*, Supporting Actor* (Walter Huston)

A triumph for director/writer John Huston, *Madre* was the first American film to be shot largely on location outside of the United States. Huston insisted on filming in the harsh Mexican mountain terrain, and it lends great authenticity to this rugged tale of three penniless friends who discover treasure—and find it opens a Pandora's box of greed, deceit, and murder. Bogart gives the greatest performance of his career as Dobbs, a good man driven to insanity by his quest for wealth. His is matched by Walter Huston's (John Huston's dad) Oscar-winning performance as a crusty old miner—one of the most immortal acting accomplishments of the American cinema. Alfonso Bedoya is also unforgettable as the ruthless bandit.

Hollywood Confidential

John Huston makes cameo appearances as the American who sarcastically chastises Bogart in the beginning of the film. Robert Blake is the young boy who sells Bogart the lottery ticket.

The author of the source novel, B. Traven, was a legendary recluse who was never seen. However, Huston long suspected that Traven's representative who oversaw production on the film was Traven himself.

The African Queen (1951)

United Artists

Director: John Huston; **Producer:** Sam Spiegel; **Writers:** James Agee, John Huston, and Peter Viertel (uncredited); **Music:** Allan Gray; **Running time:** 105 minutes

Cast: Humphrey Bogart (Charlie Allnut); Katharine Hepburn (Rose Sayer); Robert Morley (Rev. Sayer); Peter Bull (Captain of the Louisa); Theodore Bikel (First Officer)

Oscar nominations: Actor* (Humphrey Bogart), Actress (Katharine Hepburn), Screenplay, Director

Humphrey Bogart's only Oscar came for his immortal performance as Charlie Allnut, a slovenly drunk who crosses paths with prim old maid Rosie Sayer (Katharine Hepburn), who is stranded in the deep Congo at the outbreak of WWII. The two attempt to find haven on Allnut's equally dilapidated river boat, *The African Queen*, and along the way encounter deadly rapids, natural disasters, and a German warship that they become determined to sink. The screenplay was originally written "straight" with little humor. However, the chemistry between Bogart and Hepburn (who proved she could hold her own among the hard-drinking crew) was so apparent that Huston advised his stars to improvise witticisms. Unexpectedly, the film works not only as a great screen adventure but also a timeless love story as this "odd couple" trade quips and develop a mutual admiration. Huston's insistence upon shooting in the Congo, Uganda, and Turkey adds immeasurably to the lush look of the production. The film was remade as a 1977 TV movie with Warren Oates and Mariette Hartley. The making of *The African Queen* inspired screenwriter Peter Viertel's semi-fictional book *White Hunter, Black Heart* based on his memories of Huston's obsession with the film. The novel was made into an under-rated 1990 production with Clint Eastwood giving a remarkable performance as the thinly-veiled Huston character.

Scaramouche (1952)

MGM

Director: George Sidney; **Producer:** Cary Wilson; **Writers:** Ronald Millar and George Froeschel; **Music:** Victor Young; **Running time:** 115 minutes

Cast: Stewart Granger (Andre Moreau); Eleanor Parker (Lenore); Janet Leigh (Aline); Mel Ferrer (Noel)

The definitive cinematic swashbuckler features Stewart Granger as the gentleman rogue and master swordsman intent on avenging the murder of his best friend who was killed by villainous nobleman Mel Ferrer. Rich production values enhance this lavish MGM costumer that boasts the longest swordfight ever staged on film, a spectacularly choreographed set piece that finds Granger and Ferrer traversing an entire theater in a fanatical quest to do each other in. Granger, who never quite achieved the stardom he deserved, makes this role a career high. Made previously as a silent film.

Mogambo (1953)

MGM

Director: John Ford; **Producer:** Sam Zimbalist; **Writer:** John Lee Mahin; **Running time:** 115 minutes

Cast: Clark Gable (Victor Marswell); Ava Gardner (Eloise); Grace Kelly (Linda Nordley); Donald Sinden (Donald Nordley)

Oscar nominations: Actress (Ava Gardner), Supporting Actress (Grace Kelly)

John Ford's remake of the 1932 adventure film *Red Dust* brought Clark Gable back to the role of a famous big game hunter he played in the original. Here, the wild life he has to contend with strides on two legs: he is the object of both Ava Gardner and Grace Kelly's passions. The catfight angle of the film is hokey but fun. Ford had a penchant for writing off exotic vacations as film projects (for example, *Donovan's Reef*), but he gets the most out of the African locations during an era in which most films taking place in the Heart of Darkness were shot within the confines of studios. Most of the drama took place on the set when Gardner's jealous hubby Frank Sinatra made a nuisance of himself trying to ensure that the game Gable bagged didn't include his notoriously promiscuous wife. The ploy worked—Gable entered an affair with her costar Grace Kelly.

The Wages of Fear (1953)

Distributors Corporation of America

Director: Henri Georges Clouzot; **Producers:** H.G. Clouzot and R. Borderie; **Writers:** H.G. Clouzot and Jerome Geronimi; **Music:** Georges Auric; **Running time:** 155 minutes

Cast: Yves Montand (Mario); Charles Vanel (M. Jo); Peter Van Eyck (Bimba); Vera Clouzot (Linda); Folco Lulli (Luigi)

H.G. Clouzot's gritty adventure is regarded as one of the seminal films of the French cinema. The story follows four financially desperate men who are hired by an American oil company to make a virtual suicidal delivery of nitroglycerin in two trucks across hazardous South American terrain. The first part of the movie builds slowly as we are introduced to the main characters, but once their ominous journey begins, the suspense is unrelenting. Yves Montand puts on a star-making performance. Remade in 1958 as the B movie *Violent Road* with Brian Keith and more effectively in 1977 as *Sorcerer* with Roy Scheider. Severely cut in its original U.S. release to eliminate unfavorable portrayals of U.S. oil companies (God forbid!), the film has now been restored to its initial length.

The Seven Samurai (1954)

Columbia Pictures

Director: Akira Kurosawa; **Producer:** Sojiro Motoki; **Writers:** Akira Kurosawa, Shinobu Hashimoto, and Hideo Oguni; **Music:** Fumiyo Hayasaka; **Running time:** 203 minutes

Cast: Takashi Shimura (Kambei Shimada); Toshiro Mifune (Kikuchiyo); Yoshio Inaba (Gorobei); Seiji Miyaguchi (Kyuzo)

Oscar nominations: Costume Design (b&w), Art Direction-Set Decoration (b&w)

Gone with the Wind

The Seven Samurai was butchered in its U.S. releases over a period of years. Its initial U.S. release under the title The Magnificent Seven cut 45 minutes from the original version! The film was remade as John Sturges's classic 1960 western under The Magnificent Seven title.

Akira Kurosawa's undisputed masterpiece stemmed from his fascination with the American western. He set his film in seventeenth-century Japan and focused on a small band of demoralized samurai who have been released as guardians of their royal masters and now find little purpose in life. They band together to defend a small village from vicious bandits and find their lives reinvigorated by taking on the seemingly impossible quest. Kurosawa manages to develop each of the samurai into a fascinating character, and the film is brilliantly enacted. The battle scenes are tremendous in their scope and excitement. By all means, skip the dubbed versions and view the film in Japanese with subtitles.

A Night to Remember (1958)

Rank Film Distributors

Director: Roy Ward Baker; **Producer:** William MacQuitty; **Writer:** Eric Ambler; **Music:** William Alwyn; **Running time:** 123 minutes

Cast: Kenneth More (Lightoller)Ronald Allen (Clarke); Robert Ayres (Peuchen); Honor Blackman (Mrs. Lucas)

It takes nothing away from James Cameron's blockbuster 1997 film that this modestly-budgeted recreation of the *Titanic* disaster ranks with many historians as the most definitive film version of the epic event. Based on Walter Lord's acclaimed book, *A Night to Remember* uses ingenuity to compensate for its lack of production value. Using a 35-foot model replica of the ship and intercutting footage from a 1943 German propaganda film, the movie is a stunning and emotionally riveting experience. The script wisely concentrates on the human drama as opposed to the spectacle. Shot at

England's Pinewood Studios, it boasts a cast of wonderful character actors headed by the great Kenneth More. Keep an eye out for other familiar faces such as David McCallum, Bernard Fox, Laurence Naismith, and a blink-and-you'll-miss-him Desmond Llewelyn, who would go on to play the gadget master "Q" in the 007 films.

The Vikings (1958)

United Artists

Director: Richard Fleischer; **Producer:** Jerry Bressler; **Writers:** Dale Wasserman and Calder Willingham; **Music:** Mario Nascimbene; **Running time:** 114 minutes

Cast: Kirk Douglas (Einar); Tony Curtis (Erik); Ernest Borgnine (Ragnar); Janet Leigh (Morgana)

A big, delightfully dumb epic that is so well made you actually accept Ernest Borgnine as Kirk Douglas's father (they were the same age) and Bronx Jewish guy Tony Curtis as Erik the Viking! Douglas and Borgnine are in a bloody rivalry for the hand of maiden Janet Leigh, but first they have to vanquish some mutual enemies. This is a lavishly produced film with outstanding action sequences. The climactic assault on the castle is a stunner, as are the enjoyable scenes of the characters walking across the oars of their ships. Coscripter Dale Wasserman would go on to write the play *Man of La Mancha*.

Swiss Family Robinson (1960)

Buena Vista Pictures

Director: Ken Annakin; **Producer:** Walt Disney; **Writers:** Lowell S. Hawley; **Music:** William Alwyn; **Running time:** 126 minutes

Cast: John Mills (Father Robinson); Dorothy McGuire (Mother Robinson); James MacArthur (Fritz); Janet Munro (Roberta); Tommy Kirk (Ernst); Kevin Corcoran (Francis)

This adaptation of Jonathan Wyss's classic novel is good, rollicking fun done in the impeccable Disney style. The lush Tobago locations and rich cinematography add immeasurably to the timeless tale of a family who find themselves castaways in a tropical paradise—but threatened by marauding pirates. Some minor gripes: for a remote locale, there seems to be an awful lot of human traffic, the tree house they build seemingly overnight rivals anything erected in ancient Rome, the cast members bear no physical resemblance to one another, and the boys sound more like Eddie Haskell and Ward and Beaver Cleaver than the strapping Swiss youths of the novel. Yet, it's all so stylishly directed by Ken Annakin that it's impossible not to sit back and relish the fun. Filmed previously in 1940, and a Disney remake is currently in the works.

Yojimbo (1961)

Seneca International

Director and producer: Akira Kurosawa; **Writers:** Ryuzo Kikushima and Akira Kurasawa; **Music:** Masaru Sato; **Running time:** 75 minutes

Cast: Toshiro Mifune (Sanjuro Kawabatke); Tatsuya Nakadai (Unosuke); Yoko Tsukasa (Nui); Isuza Yamada (Orin)

Oscar nominations: Costume Design (b&w)

Master Japanese director Akira Kurosawa strikes gold again in this cynically amusing, rousing adventure tale of a nineteenth-century samurai, Toshiro Mifune, who drifts into a small town experiencing a turf war between two crime factions. He opportunistically rents himself out to each of the competing sides with the ultimate goal of destroying both of his employers. Marvelously witty and excitingly staged, the film would be remade by Sergio Leone as *Fistful of Dollars*, the first of his "spaghetti western" trilogy with Clint Eastwood.

Billy Budd (1962)

Allied Artists

Director and Producer: Peter Ustinov; **Writers:** Peter Ustinov and DeWitt Bodeen; **Music:** Antony Hopkins; **Running time:** 119 minutes

Cast: Terence Stamp (Billy Budd); Robert Ryan (Claggart); Melvin Douglas (The Sailmaker); Paul Rogers (Seymour); David McCallum (Wyatt)

Oscar nominations: Supporting Actor (Terence Stamp)

Herman Melville's novel was adapted for the screen with excellent results by Peter Ustinov, who directed, produced, starred, and cowrote the gripping screenplay. Terence Stamp made his film debut as the young man who is gangpressed into the British Navy. Although his gentle nature and desire to see the good in everyone endears him to his shipmates, he finds himself the object of sadism on the part of a superior officer (Robert Ryan in one of the great performances of his career). Their ultimate clash brings tragic results for both men in the emotionally devastating conclusion. Stamp won an Oscar nomination, and there is fine support from Melvyn Douglas as an old salt who befriends him, and David McCallum as an officer racked by conscience versus duty.

Lord of the Flies (1963)

Continental Distributing

Director and Writer: Peter Brook; **Producer:** Lewis M. Allen; **Running time:** 92 minutes

Cast: James Aubrey (Ralph); Tom Chapin (Jack); Hugh Edwards (Piggy); Roger Elwin (Roger)

Lord of the Flies is director Peter Brook's bare bones but ambitious adaptation of William Golding's disturbing novel about a planeload of schoolboys who are marooned on a desert island with no surviving adults. Left to their own wits and resources to survive, their initial cooperative spirit rapidly degenerates into a caste society dominated by the physically adept who delight in persecuting the intellectuals. The film's ugly tone is often difficult to tolerate, but it paints a sadly accurate portrayal of human instincts. The film features remarkable performances from a cast of amateurs, most of whom did not stay in the acting profession. Skip the pointless, glossy Americanized 1990 remake.

The Naked Prey (1966)

Paramount Pictures

Director and Producer: Cornel Wilde; **Writers:** Clint Johnston and Don Peters; **Running time:** 96 minutes

Cast: Cornel Wilde (The Man); Gert Van Den Bergh (Man #2); Ken Gampu (Warrior Leader); Bella Randles (Little Girl)

Oscar nominations: Screenplay

One of the great adventure films of the 1960s is also one of the most unheralded. Cornel Wilde's film is a personal triumph on three levels: as actor, producer, and director. Wilde plays a guide on an African safari hired by two elitist Dutch hunters in the late 1800s. When his employers ignore his advice and insult the local tribesmen, the warriors capture them and subject the white men to horrendous torture and death. Wilde's character (who is never named) is made the object of a gruesome game of catch: he is released naked and unarmed and given a short head start before the warriors hunt him down. Wilde's cunning and ability to survive, however, turn the tables, and the warriors find themselves taxed to their physical limits in pursuit of their desperate prey. The film's pace is breakneck, and the atmosphere is enhanced by the fact it was shot entirely on location. Wilde also presents the warriors in a dignified and courageous manner, though the torture sequences are harrowing and quite upsetting. A brilliant look at man in his most primal state.

Chapter 12

DETECTIVE FILMS
"The Stuff That Dreams Are Made Of!"

Almost since the inception of the motion picture, audiences have embraced the detective story as one of the most popular film genres. There is something irresistible about attempting to match wits with celluloid gumshoes. The best detective movies, of course, are those that throw the audience an unexpected curve or two by introducing red herrings and adding a twist to the ending. Certainly no detective series in history has a prouder history of accomplishing this than Sherlock Holmes. Arthur Conan Doyle's legendary hero made his first film appearance in 1903 and has rarely been off cinema screens for an extended period of time since then.

By the 1940s, American cinema had introduced a new type of cinematic sleuth that was the polar opposite of the sophisticated British detective. The American detectives, such as Sam Spade and Philip Marlowe, tended to be cynical, moody men who seemed to have fallen into detective work rather than having chosen it. These characters defined the genre in ways every bit as important and influential as Sherlock Holmes. Films such as *The Maltese Falcon* and *The Big Sleep* were so influential that their style was immortalized decades later in movies like *Tony Rome*, *Harper*, and *Bullitt*. Some of these films are so confusing in their story lines that even multiple screenings fail to render them comprehensible to my feeble brain. (I confess to often being stymied by the meaning of Bazooka bubble gum cartoons.) However, the detective film is a perfect representation of style over substance. If the main hero is charismatic enough and the villains are larger-than-life, they can make for riveting entertainment—even if you can't figure out any of the key plot points. For example, no one associated with *The Big Sleep* could ever adequately explain the plot. However, few would deny it's one of the great detective films of all time. Besides, if Bogart couldn't solve the main plot issues, who are we to even try?

The Thin Man (1934)

MGM

Director: W.S. Van Dyke; **Producer:** Hunt Stromberg; **Writers:** Albert Hackett and Frances Goodrich; **Music:** William Axt; **Running time:** 93 minutes

Cast: William Powell (Nick Charles); Myrna Loy (Nora Charles); Maureen O'Sullivan (Dorothy Wynant); Nat Pendleton (Nat Guild)

Oscar nominations: Best Picture, Writing, Actor (William Powell), Director

Upon its release, *The Thin Man* proved a hit with depression-era audiences who were enthralled by the unapologetic excesses of the husband and wife detective team that debuted in Dashiell Hammett's novel. As played by the irresistible Powell and Loy, the pair gleefully introduced all sorts of amusing eccentricities as they matched wits with each other while solving crimes. Amazingly, the film was shot in about two weeks by workhorse director W.S. Van Dyke.

After the Thin Man (1936)

MGM

Director: W.S. Van Dyke; **Producer:** Hunt Stromberg; **Writers:** Frances Goodrich and Albert Hackett; **Music:** Herbert Stothart and Edward Ward; **Running time:** 112 minutes

Cast: William Powell (Nick Charles); Myrna Loy (Nora Charles); James Stewart (David Graham); Elissa Landi (Selma)

Oscar nominations: Screenplay

The irresistible coupling of William Powell and Myrna Loy in *The Thin Man* made the film a smash hit with the public. MGM would team them for five more sequels: *After the Thin Man, Another Thin Man, Shadow of the Thin Man, The Thin Man Goes Home,* and *Song of the Thin Man.* Of all the sequels, however, *After the Thin Man* remains the most enjoyable. Nick and Nora return from New York to San Francisco for a New Year's Eve party and immediately get embroiled in solving a case of murder and blackmail involving Nora's cousin. The Powell/Loy chemistry is at its peak here, and even their famous dog Asta gets some memorable screen moments. James Stewart impresses in an early film role.

The Hound of the Baskervilles (1939)

20th Century Fox

Director: Sidney Lanfield; **Producer:** Darryl F. Zanuck (uncredited); **Writer:** Ernest Pascal; **Running time:** 80 minutes

Cast: Richard Greene (Sir Henry Baskerville); Basil Rathbone (Sherlock Holmes); Wendy Barrie (Beryl Stapleton); Nigel Bruce (Dr. Watson); Lionel Atwill (Dr. Mortimer); John Carradine (Barryman)

The fact that Basil Rathbone's Sherlock Holmes gets second billing to Richard Greene in this classic Arthur Conan Doyle mystery indicates that 20th Century Fox did not immediately recognize the potential for a lucrative series. Yet, it's Rathbone who steals the show in his initial, immortal portrayal of Holmes. It's been said that this story is the most filmed of any novel and indeed it seems to have been brought to the screen countless times. It's still a crackling good yarn, even if solving the mystery now seems, well, elementary.

Gone with the Wind

The film's final line, "Watson, the needle!" was a daring reference to Holmes's cocaine addiction. It was ultimately cut for censorship purposes but was reinserted when the film was restored in the 1970s.

The Adventures of Sherlock Holmes (1939)

20th Century Fox

Director: Alfred L. Werker; **Producer:** Darryl F. Zanuck; **Writers:** Edwin Blum and William A. Drake; **Running time:** 85 minutes

Cast: Basil Rathbone (Sherlock Holmes); Nigel Bruce (Dr. Watson); Ida Lupino (Ann Brandon); George Zucco (Prof. Moriarty)

The success of *The Hound of the Baskervilles* led 20th Century Fox to fast track another Sherlock Holmes screen adventure. The public response to the pair of Basil Rathbone and Nigel Bruce made a sequel inevitable, and *The Adventures of Sherlock Holmes* (loosely based on William Gilette's 1899 play) actually improves upon the first film. For one, Rathbone doesn't have to suffer second billing to a flash-in-the-pan heart throb as he had to with Richard Greene in *Hound*. Second, the chemistry between Rathbone and Bruce is more refined and comfortable. Lastly, the film has an engaging plot that finds the evil genius, Prof. Moriarty (wonderfully played by

George Zucco), attempting to steal the crown jewels. Sadly, this would be the last Fox production; the series would be revived at Universal, albeit with lower production values.

The Maltese Falcon (1941)

Warner Brothers

Director and Writer: John Huston; **Executive Producer:** Hal B. Wallis; **Music:** Adolph Deutsch; **Running time:** 101 minutes

Cast: Humphrey Bogart (Sam Spade); Mary Astor (Brigid O'Shaughnessy); Peter Lorre (Joel Cairo); Sydney Greenstreet (Kasper Guttman); Elisha Cook Jr. (Wilma)

Oscar nominations: Best Picture, Screenplay, Supporting Actor (Sydney Greenstreet)

Arguably the greatest detective movie ever made, *The Maltese Falcon* is a rare example of letter-perfect filmmaking and yet another case in which the cast is "There but for the grace of God." Initially George Raft was offered the role of Sam Spade but turned it down because he was reluctant to work with newcomer director John Huston. The role fit Humphrey Bogart like a glove, and his performance redefined the detective movie genre. This was actually the third version of the film—it was released in 1931 with Ricardo Cortez, and Bette Davis starred in a 1936 adaptation of the Dashiel Hammett classic titled *Satan Met a Lady*. Few films have boasted a finer supporting cast, from Mary Astor's back-stabbing femme fatale to Peter Lorre's fey killer to Sidney Greenstreet (in his film debut) as the unforgettable Fat Man. Even Huston's dad Walter has an unbilled cameo as the sea captain who delivers the famed falcon. The film cemented a bond between John Huston and Bogart, and they would team for other classics over the years. Inspired the comedic 1975 sequel of sorts, *The Black Bird*.

Laura (1944)

20th Century Fox

Director and Producer: Otto Preminger; **Writers:** Jay Dratler, Samuel Hoffenstein, Elizabeth Reinhardt, and Ring Lardner Jr. (uncredited); **Music:** David Raksin; **Running time:** 88 minutes

Cast: Gene Tierny (Laura Hunt); Dana Andrews (Mark McPherson); Clifton Webb (Waldo Lydecker); Vincent Price (Shelby Carpenter); Judith Anderson (Ann Treadwell)

Oscar nominations: Director, Cinematography* (b&w), Screenplay, Supporting Actor (Clifton Webb), Art Direction-Interior Decoration (b&w)

A trouble-plagued production to bring to the screen, *Laura* is the classic mystery about a detective who becomes romantically obsessed with the woman whose murder he is attempting to solve. The film was the brainchild of Otto Preminger, who had secured rights to the novel. Fox production chief Darryl F. Zanuck allowed Preminger to produce but wanted Rouben Mamoulian to direct. Zanuck also envisioned the film as a B movie quickie. Ultimately, Mamoulian was fired and his footage was scrapped and reshot by Preminger, who secured approval to direct. Although Preminger delivered a great film, the meddlesome Zanuck insisted on shooting an epilogue that made the story appear to be a dream. This was scrapped only when columnist Walter Winchell sided with Preminger's original vision. The film boasts a great cast with outstanding performances by Clifton Webb and Vincent Price. The theme song became a classic.

Murder My Sweet (1944)

RKO Radio Pictures

Director: Edward Dmytryk; **Producer:** Adrian Scott; **Writer:** John Paxton; **Music:** Roy Webb; **Running time:** 95 minutes

Cast: Dick Powell (Philip Marlowe); Claire Trevor (Helen Grayle); Ann Shirley (Ann Grayle); Otto Kruger (Jules Amthor)

Dick Powell stars as Philip Marlowe in the screen debut of Raymond Chandler's famed sleuth. Based on the novel *Farewell, My Lovely* the film was quickly retitled when it became clear audiences thought the title implied a musical, which is a genre Powell was primarily associated with. This film proved to be his deliverance, and Chandler himself said Powell made a superb Marlowe. *Murder My Sweet* is loaded with all the prerequisite ingredients for a classic film noir: moody black and white cinematography, two-timing dames, and plenty of plot twists. It was remade quite well in 1975 under the original title with Robert Mitchum playing a convincing Marlowe.

The Scarlet Claw (1944)

Universal Pictures

Director and Producer: Roy William Neill; **Writers:** Edmund L. Hartman and Roy William Neill; **Music:** Paul Sawtell (uncredited); **Running time:** 74 minutes

Cast: Basil Rathbone (Sherlock Holmes); Nigel Bruce (Dr. Watson); Gerald Hamer (Ramson); Paul Cavanaugh (Penrose)

Three years after the teaming of Rathbone and Bruce proved a hit in two 1939 Sherlock Holmes films for 20th Century Fox, Universal brought the actors back for a series of highly popular films loosely (*very* loosely) based on elements of the original Conan Doyle stories. This time the series was set in contemporary London, which not only helped keep the budget low, but also allowed anti-Axis propaganda to be introduced in several films in which Holmes battled Nazis. All of these films were good, but *The Scarlet Claw* rises above most with Holmes and Watson trying to solve a series of hideous murders in a small country village. This, along with *The Voice of Terror*, had the strongest screenplay and some genuine surprises and thrills—and yes, at the risk of outraging Holmes purists, we even love Bruce's bumbling Dr. Watson.

The Big Sleep (1946)

Warner Brothers

Director and Producer: Howard Hawks; **Writers:** William Faulkner, Leigh Brackett, and Jules Furthman; **Music:** Max Steiner; **Running time:** 114 minutes

Cast: Humphrey Bogart (Philip Marlowe); Lauren Bacall (Vivien Rutledge); John Ridgley (Eddie Mars); Martha Vickers (Carmine Sternwood)

Given the tortured history of bringing Raymond Chandler's novel to the screen, it's somewhat amazing *The Big Sleep* turned out to be even moderately watchable, let alone a genuine classic. Notorious for its confusing plotline (even Chandler couldn't explain a key plot element to director Howard Hawks), this is one of those films that makes viewers throw up their hands and simply relish the exquisite dialogue between Bogart and Bacall. Warner Brothers was so enthused over public response to their pairing in *To Have and Have Not* that major portions of this film were reshot and revoiced to add suggestive repartee between the two. The best bit is a suggestive chat about horseracing that virtually borders on the pornographic! Bogart seems to be having a blast in this film, and his disguise as a fey book collector is a classic. There are so many extensive changes between the original cut and a revised definitive version that the DVD release features both versions of the film.

"Play It Again, Sam"

Director Michael Winner remade the film in 1978 but despite an all star cast headed by Robert Mitchum and James Stewart, the film was as confusing as the original version.

The Blue Daliah (1946)

Paramount Pictures

Director: George Marshall; **Producer:** John Houseman; **Writer:** Raymond Chandler; **Running time:** 96 minutes

Cast: Alan Ladd (Johnny Morrison); Veronica Lake (Joyce Harwood); William Bendix (Buzz); Howard Da Silva (Eddie Harwood); Doris Dowling (Helen Morrison)

Oscar nominations: Screenplay

A good, solid film noir with Alan Ladd as a Navy veteran who returns home to find his wife in the midst of a torrid affair. After they break up, she is murdered, and Ladd is framed for the crime. Good chemistry between Ladd and Veronica Lake and a solid screenplay by Raymond Chandler. Unfortunately, the studio meddled with the film and changed a key plot device because there was concern it reflected badly on a character who was a U.S. war veteran. In the immediate aftermath of WWII, this was considered to be too distasteful for mainstream audiences. Nevertheless, the film features plenty of atmosphere and a good supporting cast with bits by Hugh Beaumont of *Leave It to Beaver* fame and Noel Neill, Superman's Lois Lane, as an unbilled hat check girl. An intriguing and genuinely engrossing entry in the detective film genre.

Hollywood Confidential

The title refers to the name of a nightclub. Shortly after the film was released, a young woman was murdered in L.A., and the crime—still unsolved—was dubbed *The Black Daliah Murder* due to similarities with the film.

Out of the Past (1947)

RKO Radio Pictures

Director: Jacques Tourneur; **Producer:** Warren Duff; **Writer:** Geoffrey Homes; **Music:** Roy Webb; **Running time:** 97 minutes

Cast: Robert Mitchum (Jeff Bailey); Jane Greer (Kathie Moffat); Kirk Douglas (Whit Sterling); Rhonda Fleming (Meta Carson)

This moody, atmospheric film noir is directed under the steady hand of Jacques Tourneur. Robert Mitchum is a private dick hired by Kirk Douglas to track down his long-missing girlfriend, Jane Greer. When Mitchum finds her, she seduces him, and this leads to the perfect story ingredients for a film noir: deceit, double-crosses, and shootouts. The great teaming of Mitchum and Douglas makes one regret they would only make one other film together (*The Way West*, 1967).

Bad Day at Black Rock (1955)

MGM

Director: John Sturges; **Producer:** Dore Schary; **Writers:** Don McGuire and Millard Kaufman; **Music:** Andre Previn; **Running time:** 81 minutes

Cast: Spencer Tracy (John MacReedy); Robert Ryan (Reno Smith); Anne Francis (Liz Wirth); Dean Jagger (Tim Horn); Walter Brennan (Doc); Ernest Borgnine (Coley); Lee Marvin (Hector)

Oscar nominations: Actor (Spencer Tracy), Director, Screenplay

John Sturges sparse, intense mystery thriller is a textbook example of superb minimalist filmmaking. Spencer Tracy becomes a de facto detective when he arrives at a desolate desert town to give an award to the father of a Japanese American soldier killed in WWII. When he finds the man is missing, the mystery he tries to uncover leads to deadly consequences. Tracy is outstanding as a one-armed tough guy who cracks heads and witticisms with equal aptitude. (The scene where he beats up tough guy Ernest Borgnine is a classic.) A great supporting cast features everyone in top form, and the widescreen cinematography adds to Tracy's feeling of desolation and desperation. This film served as an early attempt to address the racism that afflicted many Japanese Americans during the war.

The Hound of the Baskervilles (1959)

United Artists

Director: Terence Fisher; **Producer:** Anthony Hinds; **Writer:** Peter Bryan; **Music:** James Bernard; **Running time:** 87 minutes

Cast: Peter Cushing (Sherlock Holmes); Andre Morell (Dr. Watson); Christopher Lee (Sir Henry Baskerville); Marla Landri (Cecile Stapleton)

Twenty years after Basil Rathbone made his debut as Sherlock Holmes in *The Hound of the Baskervilles*, Britain's famed Hammer Studios revived the story for the big screen, making this the first Holmes movie to be shot in color. Studio perennial Peter Cushing was cast as the master detective, and he makes for a dynamic Holmes: lean, quick-witted, and very much a man of action. Andre Morell's Watson is far removed from Nigel Bruce's bumbling character—he's actually an *asset* to Holmes. The film benefits from lush production design and rich cinematography and provided a rare romantic lead for Christopher Lee as the cursed Henry Baskerville. Envisioned as a new franchise, the failure of this film at the box office derailed a follow-up, though Cushing did portray the detective years later in a British TV series. In many ways, this remains the best film version of the classic Arthur Conan Doyle story.

Harper (1966)

Warner Brothers

Director: Jack Smight; **Producers:** Jerry Gershwin and Elliott Kastner; **Writer:** William Goldman; **Music:** Johnny Mandel; **Running time:** 121 minutes

Cast: Paul Newman (Lew Harper); Lauren Bacall (Elaine Sampson); Julie Harris (Betty Frayley); Arthur Hill (Albert Graves); Janet Leigh (Susan Harper); Shelley Winters (Fay Estabrook); Robert Wagner (Allan Taggart); Pamela Tiffin (Miranda)

Paul Newman succeeds in capturing the Bogart style as down-and-out private detective Lew Harper, who is called in to find a missing millionaire by the man's narcissistic wife. As with all good detective yarns, the plot soon becomes as tangled as a bowl of spaghetti, but director Jack Smight keeps the action moving at a fast clip and the all-star cast of supporting players adds a great deal of style and fun. (Particularly good are Shelley Winters as a frumpy one-time sex symbol and Pamela Tiffin, who virtually ignites the screen as a teen temptress of loose morals.) Newman is great as the weary, cynical PI who seems to take more beatings than he can dish out.

Hollywood Confidential

Harper was based on Ross MacDonald's novel *The Moving Target* and was released in England under that title. The character of Lew Archer was changed to Harper because Newman had good luck with films beginning with "H". (*Hud* and *The Hustler. Hombre* would follow the next year.) He would revive the character in the underrated 1975 sequel, *The Drowning Pool.*

Tony Rome (1967)

20th Century Fox

Director: Gordon Douglas; **Producer:** Aaron Rosenberg; **Writer:** Richard L. Breen; **Music:** Billy May; **Running time:** 110 minutes

Cast: Frank Sinatra (Tony Rome); Jill St. John (Ann Archer); Richard Conte (Dave Santini); Gena Rowlands (Rita Kosterman); Simon Oakland (Rudy Kosterman)

After years of drifting through mostly lazy acting jobs, Frank Sinatra regained his mojo in *Tony Rome*, a hardboiled detective thriller that was favorably compared to the best of Bogart's work. Sinatra is perfectly cast as the cynical, hard-drinking Rome, who lives on a boat and makes time with the local hussies. A routine case to retrieve a millionaire's wayward teenage daughter leads to murder and blackmail. *Tony Rome* boasts a great supporting cast and clever dialogue combined with liberal doses of sex (the film had a daring take on lesbianism). Director Gordon Douglas wrapped up production in only 28 days thanks to Sinatra's allergic reaction to second takes. Excellent use of the Miami locations, especially the Fountainbleu Hotel where Sinatra performed to packed houses after filming during the day. Nancy Sinatra sings the swingin' title song. An entertaining sequel, *Lady in Cement*, was released in 1968.

Bullitt (1968)

Warner Brothers

Director: Peter Yates; **Producer:** Philip D'Antoni; **Writers:** Alan R. Trustman and Harry Kleiner; **Music:** Lalo Schifrin; **Running time:** 113 minutes

Cast: Steve McQueen (Frank Bullitt); Robert Vaughn (Walter Chalmers); Jacqueline Bisset (Cathy); Don Gordon (Delgetti); Robert Duvall (Weissberg); Simon Oakland (Capt. Bennett)

Oscar nominations: Editing*, Sound

The quintessential Steve McQueen movie, *Bullitt* was a box office blockbuster in its day and has only grown in stature since then. (In 2005, Ford's TV spots for Mustang included footage from the film.) The movie is so identified with the superbly filmed car chase through the hills of San Francisco that many of its other pleasures are often overlooked. The film features great, realistic performances by a dream cast of supporting actors, Lalo Schifrin's hip jazz score, and a plot so deep that even after seeing the film dozens of times, I still can't say for certain I know what its all about. McQueen has never been cooler, and his decision to do much of the stunt driving (alternating with his long-time friend, stunt driver Bud Elkins) gave the famed car chase a sense of authenticity lacking in previous screen car chases. They should have outlawed all screen car chases after this one (okay, we'll make exceptions for *The French Connection* and *Ronin*). Warner Brothers is promising (threatening?) a remake.

Hollywood Confidential _____

McQueen wanted his old friend Robert Vaughn to play his political nemesis in the film, but Vaughn kept refusing because he couldn't understand the script. Thinking Vaughn was playing hard to get, McQueen kept raising his salary offer until it reached an absurd level, and Vaughn joked that suddenly the script made perfect sense! Vaughn's superb performance as the oily D.A. earned him a British Oscar nomination.

Coogan's Bluff (1968)

Universal Pictures

Director and Producer: Don Siegel; **Writers:** Herman Miller, Dean Reisner, and Howard Rodman; **Music:** Lalo Schifrin; **Running time:** 93 minutes

Cast: Clint Eastwood (Walt Coogan); Lee J. Cobb (McElroy); Susan Clark (Julie Roth); Tisha Sterling (Linny Raven); Don Stroud (Ringerman)

The historic first teaming of Clint Eastwood with director Don Siegel had a rocky start. Eastwood was told director Alex Segal would be at the helm and was reluctant to work with the other Siegel. The script had gone through ten drafts, and Siegel and Eastwood locked horns quite a bit before they developed a mutual respect and long-term friendship. The film is a terrific piece of action filmmaking, tightly edited in the Siegel style with nary a wasted frame. Eastwood would be greatly influenced by Siegel's methods when he took up directing himself. The film casts Eastwood as a fish-out-of-water Arizona lawman sent to New York City to extradite a thug (played with slimy efficiency by Don Stroud). When Eastwood blows the assignment, he has to team with crusty police lieutenant Lee J. Cobb to recapture his quarry. Great witty dialogue and a terrific score by Lalo Schifrin (why has it never been released on CD?). The poolroom fight is one of the best choreographed action scenes you'll ever see. *Coogan's Bluff* inspired Dennis Weaver's hit TV series *McCloud*.

The Detective (1968)

20th Century Fox

Director: Gordon Douglas; **Producer:** Aaron Rosenberg; **Writer:** Abby Mann; **Music:** Jerry Goldsmith; **Running time:** 114 minutes

Cast: Frank Sinatra (Joe Leland); Lee Remick (Karen Leland); Jacqueline Bisset (Norma); Ralph Meeker (Curran); Jack Klugman (Schoenstein); Horace McMahon (Capt. Farrell)

Released the same year as *Bullitt* and *Coogan's Bluff*, *The Detective* made 1968 a banner time for hip celluloid sleuths. This film reunited Frank Sinatra with *Tony Rome* director Gordon Douglas, but this is a far more somber and realistic affair. The plot centers on Sinatra's Det. Joe Leland, a New York cop who has to crack a particularly gruesome murder in the sordid underbelly of the city's gay community. This was the most shocking depiction of gay life ever seen on film, and although it presents the lifestyle as vulgar, the script was ahead of its time by also showing a degree of sympathy for the way gays were treated by society. Sinatra was supposed to star with wife Mia Farrow, but when she chose instead to do *Rosemary's Baby*, the hot-tempered star cast Jacqueline Bisset and served Farrow with divorce papers. This is a tough, realistic police drama and, sadly, it represents the last time Sinatra would give a great performance on film. Henceforth, he would merely be coasting as he lost interest in his screen career. (Though he did find some degree of inspiration for the 1981 thriller *The First Deadly Sin*.)

Hollywood Confidential

The novel by Roderick Mann on which *The Detective* was based bore a sequel with Det. Leland battling terrorists. Curiously, it was changed dramatically but became the basis for the first *Die Hard* movie.

Madigan (1968)

Universal Pictures

Director: Don Siegel; **Producer:** Frank P. Rosenberg; **Writers:** Abraham Polonsky and Howard Rodman (under pseudonym Henri Simoun); **Music:** Don Costa; **Running time:** 101 minutes

Cast: Richard Widmark (Dan Madigan); Henry Fonda (Commissioner Russell); Inger Stevens (Julia Madigan); Harry Guardino (Rocko Bonaro); James Whitmore (Charles Kane)

Yet another outstanding detective film released in 1968, *Madigan* was an unpleasant project for most of the principals. The story combines soap opera-like aspects of the failing marriage of New York detective Dan Madigan as he obsessively tracks an escaped convict while in conflict with the police commissioner. Many problems plagued the production as well. Director Don Siegel fought constantly with the producer; locations had to move from Harlem to L.A. when local gangs menaced the cast and crew; Henry Fonda was dismayed that the original script was changed so his character was no longer the central figure; and screenwriter Howard Rodman took his name off the film in protest of the rewrite. Yet, *Madigan* still manages to be a top-notch film in the tradition of Siegel's other urban thrillers. Outstanding work from the principals and a great supporting cast including Susan Clark, Michael Dunn, and Don Stroud. Inspired Widmark's 1972 TV series of the same name.

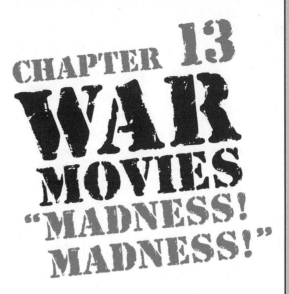

CHAPTER 13
WAR MOVIES
"MADNESS! MADNESS!"

War has played a significant factor in the evolution of the cinema. Mankind never seems to exhaust suitable real life experiences from which filmmakers draw their inspiration. War films generally fall into two categories: propaganda designed to impassion the public in support of a specific war and antiwar films designed to illustrate just how foolish the aforementioned conflict actually was. Both have played important roles in forming society's opinions about the validity of any conflict. It's probably safe to say that the antiwar films have aged better than those designed to propagate a contemporary cause. However, the impact or worthiness of the latter should not be discarded. Films such as *In Which We Serve* and *Sergeant York* played crucial roles in bolstering public morale during the early days of WWII when the tide seemed turned against the Allied cause. Their value as cinematic gems should not be compromised by the fact they may have been motivated by a political purpose.

Yet, the films that continue to resonate most are those that take a dim view of war and examine the emotional damage done to fighting men on an individual basis. Few films illustrate this point more eloquently than *Paths of Glory*, *All Quiet on the Western Front*, and *Grand Illusion*. During WWII, the last of the so-called "popular wars," Hollywood ground out endless patriotic epics and B movies. Most were harmless fluff designed to reinforce the fact that we were fighting the good cause. Some went notoriously over the top, such as the absurd pro-Soviet major studio releases *Song of Russia* and *Mission to Moscow*, made at the behest of the U.S. government to soften Stalin's image when he became our reluctant Ally against Hitler.

Curiously, as the wars of the 20th century became more complex and controversial, fewer studios were willing to take on the subject matter at all. In the aftermath of Vietnam, there were dozens of films that dealt with the conflict, generally in a critical way. Yet, when the seemingly endless war was taking place, the only major studio production to deal with it was Warner Brothers' *The Green Berets*. Although a box office hit, the film generated so much controversy that studios became less daring in presenting on-going wars onscreen. One truth is sadly inevitable: there will never be a lack of fresh material for the next generation of war films.

All Quiet on the Western Front (1931)

Universal Pictures

Director: Lewis Milestone; **Producer:** Carl Laemmle Jr.; **Writers:** Del Andrews, Maxwell Anderson, and George Abbott; **Running time:** 131 minutes

Cast: Louis Walheim (Katczinsky); Lew Ayres (Paul Baumer); John Wray (Himmelstoss); Arnold Lucy (Kantorek)

Oscar nominations: Best Picture*, Director*, Screenplay, Cinematography

Erich Maria Remarque's landmark antiwar novel traced the horrors of battle through the eyes of idealistic young German schoolboys who find the trench battles in WWI to be a terrifying and dehumanizing experience. The film version caused shockwaves around the world. Arguably not until Kubrick's *Paths of Glory* has the futility of war been so remarkably demonstrated on screen. Although critically praised, the film was denounced by some as being sympathetic to the rising Third Reich, while Hitler (still on the verge of power) thought it anti-Nazi and had screenings disrupted by his supporters. The battle scenes are stunning and the final, famous scene is still heartbreaking in its emotional intensity.

Hollywood Confidential

Famous screen comedienne Zasu Pitts had a poignant role as the mother of a young soldier, but her identification with comedy caused her scenes to be reshot with Beryl Mercer. The film was extensively cut after its initial release though it has largely been restored in recent years.

A silent version was made immediately prior to this early sound version. A 1939 release included scenes of anti-Nazi propaganda. The film was remade in 1979 as a TV movie with Richard Thomas and Ernest Borgnine.

The Charge of the Light Brigade (1936)

Warner Brothers

Director: Michael Curtiz; **Producer:** Hal B. Wallis (uncredited); **Writers:** Michael Jacoby and Rowland Leigh; **Music:** Max Steiner **Running time:** 115 minutes

Cast: Errol Flynn (Vickers); Olivia De Havilland (Elsa); Patrick Knowles (Perry Vickers); Henry Stevenson (Macefield)

Oscar nominations: Assistant Director*, Sound, Score

Tennyson's legendary poem about the courageous but futile British cavalry charge into the midst of Russian gun batteries during the Crimean War is turned on its head in this rousing but historically inaccurate action epic. Nevertheless, the cast (including a young David Niven) is dashing, and the final charge sequence is stupendous. Remade in 1968 by Tony Richardson as a far more cynical diatribe against war.

Grand Illusion (1937)

Continental Distributing

Director: Jean Renoir; **Producers:** Frank Rollmer and Albert Pinkovitch (uncredited); **Writers:** Jean Renoir and Charles Spaak; **Music:** Joseph Kosma; **Running time:** 114 minutes

Cast: Jean Gabin (Lt. Marechal); Pierre Fresnay (de Boldieu); Eric von Stroheim (Rauffenstein); Marcel Dalio (Rosenthal)

Oscar nominations: Best Picture

Jean Renoir's masterpiece is one of the great antiwar films. The movie traces the relationship between two aristocratic WWI officers—one a French POW, the other his German captor—as a metaphor for the decline of the social elite in Europe brought on by the advent of the world war. Gabin and von Stroheim give stunning performances. The first foreign film to be nominated for Best Picture, it was despised by the Nazis who confiscated and destroyed most of the prints when they occupied France. There are several cut versions of the film floating about—spring for the unedited original on DVD.

Sergeant York (1941)

Warner Brothers

Director: Howard Hawks; **Producers:** Howard Hawks, Jesse L. Lasky, and Hal B. Wallis; **Writers:** Abem Finkel, Harry Chandlee, John Huston, and Howard Koch; **Music:** Max Steiner; **Running time:** 134 minutes

Cast: Gary Cooper (Alvin York); Walter Brennan (Pastor Pile); Joan Leslie (Gracie); George Tobias ("Pusher" Ross)

Oscar nominations: Best Picture, Actor* (Gary Cooper), Editing*, Supporting Actor (Walter Brennan), Screenplay, Director, Art Direction-Interior Decoration (b&w), Sound, Cinematography (b&w), Score, Supporting Actress (Margaret Wycherly)

In days when America used to revere its war heroes, Sgt. Alvin York became the toast of the nation. A simple backwoods boy who was a pacifist by nature, York was the most decorated soldier of WWI, capturing and killing approximately 150 enemy troops single-handedly. York, a shy man, would only allow his story to be brought to the screen if he were played by Gary Cooper. The actor gave an immortal perform-ance, winning an Academy Award in the process. Director Howard Hawks handles the epic battle scenes with great flair, but it's the human side depicting this unassum-ing man in his country element that makes the movie an emotionally satisfying expe-rience.

In Which We Serve (1942)

United Artists

Directors: Noel Coward and David Lean; **Producer, Writer, and Music:** Noel Coward; **Running time:** 115 minutes

Cast: Noel Coward (Capt. Kinross); John Mills (Blake); Bernard Miles (Hardy); Celia Johnson (Alix)

Oscar nominations: Best Picture, Screenplay, Special Oscar awarded to Noel Coward for his out-standing work on this film.

A harrowing and unforgettable WWII saga filmed during the early days of the war when victory seemed anything but assured. The great Noel Coward brought the film to the screen after consultation with Churchill in order to boost the morale of the British public. The story unfolds as the survivors of a downed ship cling to a raft and recall their personal memories of events leading up to the incident. The film marked the directorial debut (in conjunction with Coward) of David Lean. Richard Attenborough made his first screen appearance in this film.

Thirty Seconds Over Tokyo (1944)

MGM

Director: Mervyn LeRoy; **Producer:** Sam Zimbalist; **Writer:** Dalton Trumbo; **Music:** Herbert Sothart; **Running time:** 138 minutes

Cast: Van Johnson (Lawson); Spencer Tracy (James Doolittle); Robert Walker (Thatcher); Scott McKay (Jones); Robert Mitchum (Bob Gray)

Oscar nominations: Special Effects*, Cinematography (b&w)

A gripping depiction of the planning of the famous Doolittle Raid over Tokyo. In the early months of WWII, the demoralized Americans were desperate for a victory. Colonel Doolittle devised the audacious plan of launching long range bombers from aircraft carriers to attack Japan, despite the fact that limited fuel capabilities would mean many pilot's fates would be left to chance. A reverent and exciting celebration of true American heroes. (Spencer Tracy has a rare supporting role as Doolittle.)

Henry V (1945)

United Artists

Director: Laurence Olivier; **Producers:** Laurence Olivier and Filipo Del Giudice; **Writers:** Dallas Bower, Alan Dent, and Laurence Olivier; **Music:** William Walton; **Running time:** 137 minutes

Cast: Laurence Olivier (Henry V); Leslie Banks (Chorus); Felix Aylmer (Archbishop of Canterbury); Robert Helpmann (Bishop of Ely)

Oscar nominations: Best Picture, Actor (Laurence Olivier), Art Direction-Interior Decoration (color), Score, Special Award to Olivier for "his outstanding achievement as actor, producer, and director."

Anyone who has ever wondered whether Laurence Olivier's reputation as one of the true masters of the acting profession has been exaggerated needs only to consider *Henry V.* Aside from his masterful leading performance as the British King whose outnumbered army defeated the French at Agincourt, Olivier had a hand in every other major aspect of the production. (This was the first film he directed.) Filmed in war-torn Britain, the movie also served as a valuable propaganda piece to boost sagging British morale. With film stock and other supplies scarce, Olivier still managed to pull together a $2 million production, though the constant air raids required him to shoot the battle scenes in Ireland. A stunning color production made at a time when the world itself seemed buried under the ashen clouds of war, Olivier's triumph is no less moving and impressive today.

Open City (1945)

Arthur Mayer and Joseph Burstyn, Inc.

Director: Roberto Rossellini; **Producers:** Roberto Rossellini, Giuseppe Amato, and Ferruccio De Martino (uncredited;) **Music:** Renzo Rossellini; **Running time:** 100 minutes

Cast: Aldo Fabrizi (Don Pietro Pellegrini); Anna Magnani (Pina); Marcello Pagliero (Luigi Ferrari)

Oscar nominations: Screenplay

Roberto Rossellini's acclaimed account of the fight to liberate Rome was shot in the immediate aftermath of the Allies' arrival in the city. The film was innovative in its technique of combining a quasi-documentary look with more traditional aspects of action filmmaking. The shoestring production (Rossellini reputedly sold some of his clothes to raise money for filming) is remarkable in capturing a significant historical event virtually as it was happening.

They Were Expendable (1945)

MGM

Director and Producer: John Ford; **Writer:** Frank Wead; **Music:** Herbert Sothart; **Running time:** 135 minutes

Cast: Robert Montgomery (John Brickley); John Wayne (Rusty Ryan); Donna Reed (Sandy Davys); Jack Holt (Gen. Martin); Ward Bond (Mulcahey)

Oscar nominations: Special Effects, Sound

This is John Ford's outstanding depiction of the dark early days of the war in the Pacific, which found an outgunned U.S. Navy turning to the small P.T. boats as offensive weapons. The film was based on the real-life experiences of Frank "Spig" Wead, who fought Naval brass in order to bring the P.T. boats into action. They proved crucial to the war effort, despite being virtual deathtraps for the crews. Robert Montgomery, who plays the lead role, was actually a P.T. boat captain during the war. The film's battle sequences are superbly directed, but the movie failed at the box office, as it was released in the immediate aftermath of the Japanese surrender and audiences were hungry for lighter entertainment.

Sands of Iwo Jima (1949)

Republic Pictures

Director: Allan Dwan; **Writers:** James Edward Grant and Harry Brown; **Music:** Victor Young; **Running time:** 100 minutes

Cast: John Wayne (Sgt. John Stryker); John Agar (Conway); Adele Mara (Allison); Forrest Tucker (Al Thomas)

Oscar nominations: Actor (John Wayne), Sound, Writing, Editing

Although clichéd by today's standards, *Sands of Iwo Jima* was an enormous success upon its release only a few scant years after the actual bloody battle took place. Iwo Jima had a special resonance for the American people—the nondescript dot of sand was defended with fanatical determination by Japanese troops—and thousands of men on both sides died. The film skillfully combined studio footage with actual newsreels of the conflict, while telling the story of a hard-ass sergeant who is in conflict with the men in his command. John Wayne won an Oscar nomination for his performance, and he gets able support from Forrest Tucker and John Agar as his antagonists. The three Marines who famously hoisted the flag on the island have cameos in the film.

Twelve O'Clock High (1949)

Director: Henry King; **Producer:** Darryl F. Zanuck; **Writers:** Sy Bartlett and Beirne Lay Jr.; **Music:** Alfred Newman; **Running time:** 132 minutes

Cast: Gregory Peck (Frank Savage); Hugh Marlowe (Gately); Gary Merrill (Davenport); Dean Jagger (Stovall)

Oscar nominations: Best Picture, Actor (Gregory Peck), Supporting Actor* (Dean Jagger), Sound*

This was one of the first major WWII films to forsake blatant propaganda and present the horrors of the conflict—and the resulting psychological damage on its participants—in a painfully realistic light. Gregory Peck is superb as the hard-as-nails new Brigadier General whose no-nonsense policies alienate him from his men—until they see his policies are the ones that will keep them alive. The aerial combat footage is stunning as is the opening stunt—an actual crash landing of a bomber. The movie spawned a 1965 TV series.

From Here to Eternity (1953)

Columbia Pictures

Director: Fred Zinnemann; **Producer:** Buddy Adler; **Writer:** Daniel Taradash; **Music:** Maurice Stoloff and George Duning; **Running time:** 118 minutes

Cast: Burt Lancaster (Sgt. Warden); Montgomery Clift (Robert E. Lee Prewitt); Deborah Kerr (Karen Holmes); Frank Sinatra (Maggio); Donna Reed (Lorene); Ernest Borgnine (Fatso Judson)

Oscar nominations: Best Picture*, Supporting Actor* (Frank Sinatra), Cinematography* (b&w), Screenplay*, Director*, Sound*, Editing*, Supporting Actress* (Donna Reed), Actor (Montgomery Clift, Burt Lancaster), Actress (Deborah Kerr), Score, Costume Design

Fred Zinnemann's screen adaptation of James Jones' spicy bestseller is cinematic perfection. The novel was said to be too steamy to bring to the screen in the uptight 1950s, but despite some watering down of the overt sexuality, the movie remains as sensuous as it is compelling. (The beach scene with Lancaster and Kerr is more erotic than anything seen onscreen today.) The lives of a diverse group of soldiers and their women are transformed by the attack on Pearl Harbor. This is not actually a war movie per se, as the battle doesn't come until near the end of the film, but it completely affects the lives and destinies of the characters in the most unpredictable ways. A brilliant cast with Clift's quirky, loser Prewitt a career high. Sinatra made his famed comeback in this film, though he was only paid $8,000! *Eternity* was remade as a TV mini series in 1979 and a short-lived TV series in 1980.

Stalag 17 (1953)

Paramount Pictures

Director and Producer: Billy Wilder; **Writers:** Billy Wilder and Edwin Blum; **Music:** Franz Waxman; **Running time:** 120 minutes

Cast: William Holden (Sefton); Don Taylor (Dunbar); Otto Preminger (von Scherbach); Robert Strauss (Kasava); Peter Graves (Price)

Oscar nominations: Actor* (William Holden), Supporting Actor (Robert Strauss), Director

William Holden won an Oscar for his portrayal as a cynical, self-consumed scrounger suspected by his fellow POWs of collaborating with their Nazi captors. Holden was reluctant to play a character this unlikable, but director Billy Wilder refused to soften the part. The film was shot in sequence, thus the cast was ultimately surprised by the unveiling of the real traitor in the climax. Otto Preminger is unforgettable as the sadistic camp commandant. The film so obviously inspired the *Hogan's Heroes* TV series that a lengthy lawsuit ensued.

The Dam Busters (1954)

Warner Brothers

Director: Michael Anderson; **Writer:** R.C. Sherriff; **Music:** Eric Coates and Leighton Lucas; **Running time:** 105 minutes

Cast: Richard Todd (Gibson); Michael Redgrave (Wallis); Ursula Jeans (Mrs. Wallis); Basil Sydney (Harris)

Oscar nominations: Special Effects

The Dam Busters is a terrifically exciting British war epic about the audacious mission of low-flying bomber planes to blow up the German Ruhr dam using experimental weaponry. The film is tightly edited and directed with a cast of nonglamorous but always reliable British actors who convey the tension and high stakes surrounding the mission. Look for young Robert Shaw in an early role. Beware: some American versions are cut by as much as 15 minutes from the film's British running time. Director Peter Jackson is rumored to be considering a remake.

Attack! (1956)

United Artists

Director and Producer: Robert Aldrich; **Writer:** James Poe; **Music:** Frank DeVol; **Running time:** 107 minutes

Cast: Jack Palance (Joe Costa); Eddie Albert (Erskine Cooney); Lee Marvin (Bartlett); Robert Strauss (Bernstein); Richard Jaeckel (Snowden); Buddy Ebsen (Tolliver)

Robert Aldrich's gritty and realistic WWII drama centers on a cowardly officer whose failure to provide support for a besieged company of men results in disastrous consequences. Jack Palance excels as a survivor who swears revenge on his superior officer, excellently played by Eddie Albert (who was ironically a decorated war hero in real life). The U.S. Army was so disturbed by the nature of the film that they refused to provide equipment or support, forcing Aldrich to be innovative with his scarce resources. A riveting wartime drama.

Friendly Persuasion (1956)

Allied Artists

Director and Producer: William Wyler; **Writer:** Michael Wilson; **Music:** Dimitri Tiomkin; **Running time:** 137 minutes

Cast: Gary Cooper (Jess Birdwell); Dorothy McGuire (Eliza Birdwell); Anthony Perkins (Josh Birdwell); Richard Eyer (Little Jess)

Oscar nominations: Best Picture, Director, Screenplay, Song (*Friendly Persuasion—Thee I Love*), Supporting Actor (Anthony Perkins), Sound

William Wyler's moving and often humorous film portrays an Indiana Quaker family conflicted by the outbreak of the Civil War. Although they try to honor their religious commitment to nonviolence, when Confederate troops pose a menace, their son (winningly played by Anthony Perkins) is motivated to take up arms. A charming and often delightful film with a fine performance by Gary Cooper as the likeable patriarch. Enhanced by a good Dimitri Tiomkin score. Remade as a 1975 TV movie.

The Bridge on the River Kwai (1957)

Columbia Pictures

Director: David Lean; **Producer:** Sam Spiegel; **Writers:** Michael Wilson and Carl Foreman (originally uncredited); **Music:** Malcolm Arnold; **Running time:** 161 minutes

Cast: William Holden (Shears); Jack Hawkins (Warden); Alec Guinness (Nicholson); Sessue Hayakawa (Saito); James Donald (Clipton)

Oscar nominations: Best Picture*, Actor* (Alec Guinness), Director*, Music*, Screenplay*, Cinematography*, Editing*, Supporting Actor (Sessue Hayakawa)

Alec Guinness's immortal performance in this film has been such an important part of cinematic lore that it's startling to realize he actually received third billing. So towering is Guinness's performance that one tends to overlook the fine work of other cast members. The story casts Guiness as a stubborn British POW officer whose determination to build a magnificent bridge as a symbol of English superiority causes him to lose site of the fact that the project will benefit his Japanese captors. David Lean's masterpiece contains so many classic sequences they are impossible to summarize, but none are as wonderful as Guinness leading his ragtag men into camp proudly strutting to the *Colonel Bogey March*. Gigantic in scope, yet poignant and moving on a personal level, *Kwai* is one of the great cinematic achievements of all time. It inspired a little-seen unofficial 1989 sequel *Return to the River Kwai*.

Hollywood Confidential

In one of the great Hollywood scandals, *The Bridge on the River Kwai* screenwriters Carl Foreman and Michael Wilson could not get screen credit or pick up the Oscar for their script as they were blacklisted. (The award was given to Pierre Boulle, who wrote the source novel.) It was not until the 1980s that the Academy awarded the men their Oscars (Wilson posthumously) and the restored film prints added their names to the credits.

Paths of Glory (1957)

United Artists

Director: Stanley Kubrick; **Producers:** Kirk Douglas, Stanley Kubrick, and James B. Harris; **Writers:** Stanley Kubrick, Calder Willingham, and Jim Thompson; **Music:** Gerald Fried; **Running time:** 87 minutes

Cast: Kirk Douglas (Col. Dax); Adolphe Menjou (Gen. Broulard); Ralph Meeker (Cp. Paris); George MacReady (Gen. Moreau)

It's hard to believe that the greatest antiwar movie ever made garnered nary a single Oscar nomination. Additionally, Stanley Kubrick's stunning denouncement of elitism in the French military brass during WWI was considered so provocative that the movie was banned in France until 1975. Kirk Douglas gives a powerful performance as a harried Colonel trying to save his men from being made sacrificial lambs to cover the gross incompetence of his superior officers. The opening battle for "The Anthill" is one of the most harrowing action sequences ever filmed. The movie was shot in Germany, using a local farm as the setting for the battle sequence. *Paths of Glory* seems to grow in stature with every viewing.

The Young Lions (1958)

20th Century Fox

Director: Edward Dmytryk; **Producer:** Al Lichtman; **Writer:** Edward Anhalt; **Music:** Hugo Friedhofer; **Running time:** 158 minutes

Cast: Marlon Brando (Christian Diestel); Montgomery Clift (Noah Ackerman); Dean Martin (Michael Whitacre); Hope Lange (Hope); Barbara Rush (Margaret)

Oscar nominations: Sound, Score, Cinematography (b&w)

The Young Lions is a generally underrated and highly ambitious screen version of Irwin Shaw's book about the lives of three young men—two Allied soldiers and a reluctant German soldier—whose lives interweave during the course of WWII. A stellar cast with good support from May Britt, Maximillian Schell, and Lee Van Cleef. Montgomery Clift's role as the oppressed GI is similar to his part as Prewitt in *From Here to Eternity*. Brando impresses as a Nazi who begins to doubt his political beliefs, and Dean Martin shocked critics with his impressive dramatic performance (the part came shortly after his split with Jerry Lewis).

The Guns of Navarone (1961)

Columbia Pictures

Director: J. Lee Thompson; **Producer and Writer:** Carl Foreman; **Music:** Dimitri Tiomkin; **Running time:** 158 minutes

Cast: Gregory Peck (Mallory); Anthony Quinn (Stavros); David Niven (Miller); Stanley Baker (Brown); Anthony Quayle (Franklin)

Oscar nominations: Best Picture, Director, Special Effects*, Screenplay, Editing, Music, Sound

One of the great WWII epics, *The Guns of Navarone* was based on Alistair MacLean's bestseller about a small group of commandos sent to Greece on a seemingly impossible mission to blow up massive Nazi gun emplacements that have been wreaking havoc on Allied ships. This was a troubled film to get off the ground: Alexander Mackendrick was the original director and William Holden and Kenneth More were to star in the roles eventually played by Gregory Peck and David Niven. What emerged was a masterful adventure story, ably directed by the underrated J. Lee Thompson and featuring an edge-of-the-seat finale. Dimitri Tiomkin's score is superb. The great supporting cast includes James Darren, Irene Papas, Gia Scala and, very briefly, Richard Harris. It inspired the awful 1978 sequel *Force Ten From Navarone*.

The Great Escape (1963)

United Artists

Director and Producer: John Sturges; **Writers:** James Clavell and W.R. Burnett; **Music:** Elmer Bernstein; **Running time:** 172 minutes

Cast: Steve McQueen (Hilts); James Garner (Hendley); Richard Attenborough (Roger); James Donald (Ramsey); Charles Bronson (Danny); James Coburn (Sedgwick); Donald Pleasence (Colin); David McCallum (Ashley-Pitt)

Oscar nominations: Editing

A textbook example of superb filmmaking, *The Great Escape* is a fictionalized account of a legendary breakout from a German POW camp. Masterfully directed by John

Sturges, the film boasts a dream cast of superstars and soon-to-be superstars topped by Steve McQueen's cynical wise guy. Outstanding German locations are made all the more impressive when backed by Elmer Bernstein's triumphant score. Ferris Webster's seamless editing miraculously gives each of the burgeoning cast their own individual special moments. McQueen did most of his own motorcycling, though his famous "hop the barbed wire" stunt was performed by his friend Bud Ekins. The film inspired the so-so TV movie sequel *The Great Escape II: The Untold Story* starring Christopher Reeve. In 2004, the Imperial War Museum in London dedicated an impressive exhibit to both the actual escape and Sturges's film. Incredibly, this timeless masterpiece was nominated for only a single Oscar.

Zulu (1964)

Embassy Pictures Corporation

Director: Cy Endfield; **Producers:** Stanley Baker and Cy Endfield; **Writers:** John Prebble and Cy Endfield; **Music:** John Barry; **Running time:** 138 minutes

Cast: Stanley Baker (Chard); Michael Caine (Bromhead); Jack Hawkins (Witt); Ulla Jacobsen (Margarita); James Booth (Hook)

Ranking with the all-time great war films, *Zulu* is a letter-perfect depiction of the stand a small group of British soldiers made against an overwhelming force of Zulu warriors at Roarke's Drift in Natale. The battle sequences are truly stunning, and they do not detract from the human elements of the story as the soldiers nervously await what they believe will be their ultimate destruction. The film features brilliant performances by all, with young Michael Caine leaping to stardom in his first major role. John Barry's score, one of his best, adds immeasurably to the film's numerous qualities. It spawned a little-seen but highly impressive 1979 prequel, *Zulu Dawn*.

The Battle of Algiers (1965)

Rizzoli

Director: Gillo Pontecorvo; **Producers:** Antonio Musu and Yacef Saadi; **Writers:** Gillo Pontecorvo and Franco Solinas; **Music:** Ennio Morricone and Gillo Pontecorvo; **Running time:** 117 minutes

Cast: Brahmim Haggiag (Ali La Pointe); Jean Martin (Col. Mathieu); Saadi Yacef (Djafar)

Oscar nominations: Best Foreign Language Film, Director, Screenplay

This visually striking film documents the Algerian revolt against the French in the mid to late 1950s. Director Gillo Pontecorvo's Marxist leanings are well known, but refreshingly he attempts to present both sides of the conflict. The French government is personalized through the character of a single colonel who ultimately realizes that his government's victory can only be temporary. The movie won wide acclaim for its outstanding presentation of documentary-style filmmaking that led many people to believe Pontecorvo had used footage from the actual insurgency. Pentagon brass screened the film prior to the 2003 invasion of Iraq.

In Harm's Way (1965)

Paramount Pictures

Director and Producer: Otto Preminger; **Writer:** Wendell Mayes; **Music:** Jerry Goldsmith; **Running time:** 165 minutes

Cast: John Wayne (Rockwell Torrey); Kirk Douglas (Eddington); Patricia Neal (Maggie); Tom Tryon (Mac); Paula Prentiss (Bev)

Oscar nominations: Cinematography (b&w)

Otto Preminger's large scale WWII soap opera is one of the last major b&w studio productions. A long, leisurely paced, but always interesting film that looks at the lives of Navy personnel in the wake of the attack on Pearl Harbor. *In Harm's Way* boasts a stellar cast of esteemed Hollywood veterans—including Burgess Meredith, Dana Andrews, Henry Fonda, Sterling Holloway, and Bruce Cabot—along with young talent such as Brandon DeWilde, Jill Haworth, and Barbara Bouchet. The film benefits from strong chemistry between John Wayne and Kirk Douglas, who had opposing and outspoken political beliefs in real life but were respectful of each other's talents on the set. A great score by Jerry Goldsmith accompanies the film's impressive cinematography. The shoddy model work in the battle scenes has long been criticized, but in the aggregate, the film is one of the best war movies of its era.

The Train (1965)

United Artists

Director: John Frankenheimer; **Producer:** Jules Bricken; **Writers:** Franklin Coen and Frank Davis; **Music:** Maurice Jarre; **Running time:** 133 minutes

Cast: Burt Lancaster (Labiche); Paul Scofield (von Waldheim); Jeanne Moreau (Christine); Michel Simon (Papa Boule)

Oscar nominations: Screenplay

John Frankenheimer's masterful film with Burt Lancaster as a reluctant but heroic French Resistance fighter who must stop a corrupt German general (Paul Scofield) from absconding with a train loaded with France's great art masterpieces in the final days of the war. Featuring thrilling action setpieces capped by a colossal train wreck done without miniatures. This is a moving and highly exciting production with glorious black and white cinematography. The film's original director was Arthur Penn, but he was quickly replaced after artistic differences with Lancaster.

 Hollywood Confidential

Lancaster and Frankenheimer were on location in France when they were asked by Paramount Pictures to reshoot the last sequence of their just-completed previous collaboration, *Seven Days in May*. The brief scene was shot with Lancaster inside a car that actually belonged to Frankenheimer.

Von Ryan's Express (1965)

20th Century Fox

Director: Mark Robson; **Producer:** Saul David; **Writers:** Wendell Mayes and Joseph Landon; **Music:** Jerry Goldsmith; **Running time:** 117 minutes

Oscar nomination: Effects/Sound Effects

Cast: Frank Sinatra (Ryan); Trevor Howard (Fincham); Rafaella Carra (Gabriella); Brad Dexter (Bostick); Edward Mulhare (Costanzo)

In this first-rate action film, Frank Sinatra is a highly unpopular commanding officer leading a large group of escaped Allied POWs on a stolen train in Italy. Their goal is to reach Switzerland against overwhelming odds. Highlights include the atmospheric European locations and excellent chemistry between Sinatra and Trevor Howard as officers in conflict with each other as well as with the enemy. The final scene is gut wrenching.

Closely Watched Trains (1966)

Sigma III Films

Director: Jiri Menzel; **Producer:** Dr. Zdenek Oves; **Writers:** Bohumil Hrabal and Jiri Menzel; **Running time:** 91 minutes

Cast: Vaclav Neckar (Milos Hrma); Josef Somr (Hubicka); Vlastimil Brodsky (Zednicek)

Oscar nominations: Best Foreign Language Film*

This acclaimed Czech comedy/drama was representative of the brief but glorious period of freedom enjoyed by the nation prior to the Soviet invasion of 1968. The film tells the slight tale of a young man who is so determined to lose his virginity that he is all but oblivious to the fact that his country is under Nazi occupation—a revelation that becomes all too real in the film's surprising climax. Funny, sad, and consistently engaging, the movie's sexual content was considered hot stuff in its day.

It Happened Here (1966)

Lopert Pictures Corporation

Directors, Producers, and Writers: Kevin Brownlow and Andrew Mollo; **Music:** Jack Beaver (uncredited); **Running time:** 93 minutes

Cast: Pauline Murray (Pauline); Sebastian Shaw (Dr. Fletcher); Bart Allison (Skipworth); Reginald Marsh (Medical Officer)

This amazing but little seen film was shot over a period of eight years by its teenage directors, producers, and writers, Kevin Brownlow and Andrew Mollo. The movie speculates on what life in England would have been like had Hitler successfully launched his long-planned invasion and managed to vanquish British forces. Deprived of any substantial budget for their black and white production, Brownlow and Mollo scrounged film stock wherever they could and were forced to forego shooting for extended periods when funds completely dried up. Their perseverance paid off, however, as this is one of the most compelling amateur films ever made.

Gone with the Wind

Seven minutes of footage showing real life, contemporary Nazi anti-Semites at a rally was excised from most prints and has only recently been restored.

The Dirty Dozen (1967)

MGM

Director: Robert Aldrich; **Producer:** Kenneth Hyman; **Writers:** Nunnally Johnson and Lukas Heller; **Music:** De Vol; **Running time:** 145 minutes

Cast: Lee Marvin (Maj. Reisman); Ernest Borgnine (Gen. Worden); Robert Ryan (Col. Breed); John Cassavetes (Franko); Charles Bronson (Wladislaw); Jim Brown (Jefferson)

Oscar nominations: Supporting Actor (John Cassavetes), Sound Effects*, Sound, Editing

This is the quintessential "anti-chick flick" with Lee Marvin leading a squad of rugged convicts on a virtual suicide mission to blow up a French chateau housing top Nazi brass. The film's barbaric premise horrified some reviewers, including the

New York Times, because the Dozen slaughter innocent civilians as well as military men. However, if you want sensitivity, see a Robin Williams movie—this one explodes with excitement right up to its suspense-drenched finale. You know you're in good hands when the *supporting* cast includes George Kennedy, Telly Savalas, Richard Jaeckel, and Donald Sutherland. The magnificent chateau was constructed at MGM Studios in England.

"Play It Again, Sam"

There were several sequels to *The Dirty Dozen*, all of them made for TV: *The Dirty Dozen: The Next Mission* (with Marvin, Borgnine, and Jaeckel reunited), *The Deadly Mission*, and *The Fatal Mission* both starring Borgnine and Savalas (in the role of a different character).

The Bridge at Remagen (1969)

United Artists

Director: John Guillerman; **Producer:** David L. Wolper; **Writers:** Richard Yates and William Roberts; **Music:** Elmer Bernstein; **Running time:** 115 minutes

Cast: George Segal (Hartman); Robert Vaughn (Kruger); Ben Gazzara (Angelo); Bradford Dillman (Barnes); E.G. Marshall (Shinner); Peter Van Eyck (Von Brock)

This criminally underrated WWII epic tells the fascinating story of the Allies' race to capture the last remaining bridge over the Rhine in the final days of the conflict. The film boasts outstanding battle sequences and cinematography along with a top-notch cast. Robert Vaughn is excellent as the German commander conflicted by his orders to destroy the bridge, thus stranding the remnants of the German army on the wrong side of the Rhine. This was the last film of noted German actor Peter Van Eyck. Elmer Bernstein's magnificent score has surprisingly never been released as a soundtrack.

Hollywood Confidential

Filming for *The Bridge at Remagen* took place in Czechoslovakia in the summer of 1968. When the Soviets invaded, the film crew was in chaos. Robert Vaughn and Ben Gazzara made a daring escape by car, ultimately traveling 24 hours nonstop to avoid arrest.

Where Eagles Dare (1969)

MGM

Director: Brian G. Hutton; **Producer:** Elliott Kastner; **Writer:** Alistair MacLean; **Music:** Ron Goodwin; **Running time:** 158 minutes

Cast: Richard Burton (Major Smith); Clint Eastwood (Lt. Schaffer); Mary Ure (Mary); Patrick Wymark (Turner); Michael Hordern (Rolland)

From the opening credits, which are set against Ron Goodwin's magnificent score, you know *Where Eagles Dare* is going to be one helluva ride—and it doesn't disappoint. This was the first screenplay written by Alistair MacLean directly for the screen, and it's a complicated but fascinating tale of an Allied commando group sent to rescue a captured American general from a mountaintop Nazi castle. There are twists, turns, and head-scratching plot devices, but the action is so superbly staged and enacted with great gusto by Burton and Eastwood that you just throw up your hands and enjoy the show. Expert direction by Brian G. Hutton and a great supporting cast including Darren Nesbitt and Ingrid Pitt. This is Steven Spielberg's favorite war movie.

Chapter **14**
WESTERNS

"When the Legend Becomes Fact,
Print the Legend."

There are very few uniquely American art forms. In the world of music, jazz bears the unmistakable stamp of its American roots, while onscreen, the western film represents a genre that is solely based upon the American experience. Many of the earliest Hollywood icons were known for their work in western films. It's hard to estimate the impact that actors like William Boyd and Tom Mix had on audiences during the early days of cinema. Such western heroes were virtually one-man industries with fanatically loyal audience support. None of their films can be called classics on an individual basis, thus they are not covered in this book; however, their contributions to the emergence of the western film genre cannot be overestimated. Indeed, the early western serials whet audience appetites, leaving them eager to see the increasingly elaborate and more sophisticated stories brought to the screen. One must remember that as distant as the Old West may seem to us now, it is still relatively recent history, and many of the filmmakers from decades ago actually recalled or lived the experiences they depicted onscreen. (John Ford was told about the gunfight at the O.K. Corral by Wyatt Earp himself!) Like all American success stories, the western has been exported to other countries, though this appears to be one film genre that has not been successfully exploited overseas. Aside from the works of Akira Kurosawa and Sergio Leone, most westerns made outside of America have proven to be largely forgettable, quickly made horse operas designed to make a fast buck then fade away. Thus, it is all the more curious why the western genre has all but faded from the American conscience. Since the release of the disastrous box office flop *Heaven's Gate* in 1981, Hollywood has steered clear of one of its most lucrative genres. There have been the occasional anomalies: Kevin Costner's *Dances with Wolves* and *Open Range* and Clint Eastwood's triumphant *Unforgiven*. Yet, these successes did not pave the way for a big screen renaissance of this great American art form. Perhaps it's because we lack the type of star power that traditionally enhanced westerns. Indeed, it's difficult to imagine Matt Damon as Rooster Cogburn in *True Grit* or Brad Pitt in *High Noon*. One day this will hopefully change, but until then, revel in the great westerns you'll find in this chapter.

Stagecoach (1939)

United Artists

Director: John Ford; **Producer:** Walter Wanger; **Writer:** Dudley Nichols; **Music:** Gerard Carbonara (uncredited); **Running time:** 96 minutes

Cast: Claire Trevor (Dallas); John Wayne (The Ringo Kid); Thomas Mitchell (Doc Boone); John Carradine (Hatfield); George Bancroft (Curly); Andy Devine (Buck)

Oscar nominations: Best Picture, Art Direction, Director, Editing, Cinematography (b&w), Supporting Actor* (Thomas Mitchell), Score*

Considered to be the first "adult" western, *Stagecoach* marked the return of John Ford to the genre that would define him, having made only silent westerns many years before this. The film also elevated John Wayne to leading man status after toiling in B westerns for a decade. The wonderful script by Dudley Nichols fleshes out the "nine strange people" (as the ads proclaimed the characters), each embellished by an equally adept actor. This was Ford's first film in his beloved Monument Valley, Utah—an isolated locale of great beauty where the director is still revered at the same modest resort he and the crew stayed at in 1938. A 1966 remake isn't as bad as conventional wisdom says it is, but it is no threat to the original. Remade again as a TV movie in 1986 with Johnny Cash.

The Ox Bow Incident (1943)

20th Century Fox

Director: William Wellman; **Producer and Writer:** Lamar Trotti; **Music:** Cyril J. Mockridge; **Running time:** 75 minutes

Cast: Henry Fonda (Gil Carter); Dana Andrews (Donald Martin); Mary Beth Hughes (Rose); Anthony Quinn (Juan Martinez)

Oscar nominations: Best Picture

Although a box-office failure due to its grim storyline and claustrophobic atmosphere, this masterful screen adaptation of the classic novel has earned its place as an undisputed classic. A rare western that also made sociological observations, the story concerns a lynch mob that rushes to judgment to execute three men they suspect to be rustlers—over the protestations of more level-headed folks who argue for the sanctity of law. This is a powerful film that has not been diminished by the years. It was originally developed as a possible screen vehicle for Mae West!

My Darling Clementine (1946)

20th Century Fox

Director: John Ford; **Producer:** Samuel G. Engel; **Writers:** Samuel G. Engel and Winston Miller; **Music:** Cyril Mockridge; **Running time:** 97 minutes

Cast: Henry Fonda (Wyatt Earp); Linda Darnell (Chihuahua); Victor Mature ("Doc" Holliday); Kathy Downs (Clementine); Walter Brennan (Old Man Clanton)

Despite an awful title that makes this seem like a Judy Garland musical, the film is actually a rousing and engrossing western done in the usual grand John Ford style. You can almost taste the dust. Henry Fonda gives one of his most memorable portrayals as Wyatt Earp. The screenplay is largely fictionalized, though the staging of the gunfight at the O.K. Corral in Tombstone was related to Ford as a young man by Earp himself.

Fort Apache (1948)

RKO Radio Pictures

Director: John Ford; **Producers:** Merian C. Cooper and John Ford; **Writer:** Frank S. Nugent; **Music:** Richard Hageman; **Running time:** 125 minutes

Cast: John Wayne (Kirby York); Henry Fonda (Owen Thursday); Shirley Temple (Philadelphia Thursday); Pedro Armendariz (Beaufort); Ward Bond (O'Rourke)

The first of John Ford's "cavalry trilogy" (with *She Wore a Yellow Ribbon* and *Rio Grande*) is the best of the lot. Loosely based on the exploits of George Custer, Henry Fonda is a martinet captain who takes control over a U.S. Cavalry post and proceeds to alienate both his own men and the hostile Indian tribes. Despite the star power of first-billed John Wayne, this is Fonda's show. He gives a remarkable performance as the stubborn Captain Thursday whose pride leads to tragedy for him and his men. Despite his flaws, Fonda still imbues the character with a degree of humanity and admirable traits. The absence of the usual Hollywood happy ending is a welcome and sobering development.

Red River (1948)

United Artists

Director and Producer: Howard Hawks; **Writers:** Borden Chase and Charles Schnee; **Music:** Dimitri Tiomkin; **Running time:** 133 minutes

Cast: John Wayne (Tom Dunson); Montgomery Clift (Matt); Joanne Dru (Tess); Walter Brennan ("Groot")

Oscar nominations: Writing, Editing

Howard Hawks's epic western can be described as *Mutiny on the Bounty*—on hooves. John Wayne is the hard-as-nails cowman on a massive cattle drive with his right-hand man—his adopted son (Montgomery Clift). When Wayne's methods become too tyrannical and brutal, Clift takes over the heard, thus setting up an inevitable revenge scenario in which Wayne threatens to hunt him down and kill him. The film is outstanding on every level, but Wayne and Clift command all the attention in roles envisioned for Gary Cooper and Cary Grant. Wayne in particular is superb, playing a role much older than his actual years. TV prints routinely cut 8 minutes of footage, but it has been restored on the DVD version. One of the top-rated of all westerns.

The Gunfighter (1950)

20th Century Fox

Director: Henry King; **Producer:** Nunnally Johnson; **Writers:** William Bowers and William Sellers; **Music:** Alfred Newman; **Running time:** 85 minutes

Cast: Gregory Peck (Jimmy Ringo); Helen Westcott (Peggy Walsh); Millard Mitchell (Marshall Strett); Jean Parker (Molly); Karl Malden (Mac)

Oscar nominations: Writing

One of the most intelligent westerns ever made, Henry King's *The Gunfighter* was also a controversial one. The story of the last sad day in the life of a notorious gunslinger trying to escape his past was written for John Wayne. However, when a salary for The Duke could not be agreed upon, Gregory Peck ended up in the role. (Wayne would masterfully play a similar role in his last film, *The Shootist*.) The film is beautifully written and features Peck in an outstanding performance as a man weary of having to prove he's the fastest draw in the west. The tragic ending packs a wallop even today. Studio mogul Darryl F. Zanuck raised hell over the decision to have Peck wear a thick black mustache, which was correct for the period. He claimed it would alienate his female fans. Zanuck was right: the film was a box office flop, but Peck had the last laugh because it long ago entered the ranks of the most highly acclaimed westerns.

High Noon (1952)

United Artists

Director: Fred Zinnemann; **Producer:** Stanley Kramer; **Writer:** Carl Foreman; **Music:** Dimitri Tiomkin; **Running time:** 85 minutes

Cast: Gary Cooper (Will Kane); Grace Kelly (Amy Fowler Kane); Katy Jurado (Helen Ramiriz); Lloyd Bridges (Harvey Pell)

Oscar nominations: Best Picture, Director, Actor* (Gary Cooper), Editing*, Score*, Song* (*Do Not Forsake Me; Oh, My Darlin'*), Screenplay

Originally offered to Gregory Peck (who turned it down because the lead role was too similar to *The Gunfighter*), Gary Cooper eagerly accepted the part of marshall Will Kane and won a second Oscar. The story finds Kane about to leave on his honeymoon with Quaker wife Amy (Grace Kelly in her first major role), when he learns that a band of outlaws are enroute to the town to exact revenge for Kane having jailed them years ago. When the marshall finds the men of the town are too cowardly to back him up, he opts to face the gang himself. The film is presented in (almost) real time with close-ups of the clock adding suspense as it ticks toward the arrival of the noon train with the gang aboard. Cooper is wonderful as the weary, disillusioned lawman, and the able supporting cast included Harry Morgan, Lon Chaney, and Lee Van Cleef (in his first film). The title song sung by Tex Ritter is a classic. *High Noon* spawned a TV movie sequel, and is President Clinton's favorite film.

Hollywood Confidential

High Noon's screenwriter Carl Foreman had been an uncooperative witness at the McCarthy hearings, and some say the film's story is a criticism of those who didn't stand up to the controversial Senator's witch hunts. Foreman fell out with producer Stanley Kramer over the political issues, and was later blacklisted. He moved to Europe but still wrote classic films—albeit without screen credit.

Shane (1953)

Paramount Pictures

Director and Producer: George Stevens; **Writer:** A.B. Guthrie Jr.; **Music:** Victor Young; **Running time:** 118 minutes

Cast: Alan Ladd (Shane); Van Heflin (Joe Starrett); Jean Arthur (Marian Starrett); Brandon De Wilde (Joey Starrett); Jack Palance (Jack Wilson); Ben Johnson (Calloway)

Oscar nominations: Best Picture, Director, Supporting Actor (Jack Palance), Screenplay, Supporting Actor (Brandon De Wilde), Cinematography* (color)

George Stevens's meticulously produced western remains riveting in its emotional impact. Alan Ladd stars as a mysterious ex-gunfighter trying to escape his past. He befriends a farm family who, along with their neighbors, are being terrorized by gunslingers hired by a cattleman to drive them off their land. Although the title role would probably have been more appropriate for John Wayne, Ladd gave the performance of his career here (even if he is saddled with a buckskin outfit that makes him look like an extra from *Seven Brides for Seven Brothers*). The superb supporting cast includes Jack Palance's star-making performance as the assassin with ice in his veins. The finale will still bring a lump to your throat as young Brandon De Wilde tries to induce his idol Shane to "come back!" Inspired a short-lived TV series and was unofficially remade by Clint Eastwood in 1985 as *Pale Rider*.

The Searchers (1956)

Warner Brothers

Director: John Ford; **Producer:** C.V. Whitney; **Writer:** Frank S. Nugent; **Music:** Max Steiner; **Running time:** 119 minutes

Cast: John Wayne (Ethan Edwards); Jeffrey Hunter (Martin Pawley); Vera Miles (Laurie); Ward Bond (Rev. Clayton); Natalie Wood (Debbie)

Reputed to be Steven Spielberg's favorite film, John Ford's *The Searchers* has influenced numerous movies including the original *Star Wars*. John Wayne gives a magnificent performance—certainly the most intense of his career—as Ethan Edwards, a racist man with a dubious past who is intent on tracking down a niece kidnapped by the Indians who slaughtered his brother's family. As the years pass, Edwards's mission transforms from a rescue attempt to a determination to kill the girl because she has now been soiled by her life with the Indians. The characters and their motives are far more complex than would originally appear (there is an insinuation that Ethan had an affair with his sister-in-law) and the film has been debated and analyzed for decades. Winton Hoch's cinematography compliments the aching beauty of Monument Valley, all set to a wonderful Max Steiner score. The finale is as emotionally satisfying as it is unexpected, and the final frames of Ethan are haunting and legendary. A true American masterpiece that did not receive a single Oscar nomination.

Gunfight at the O.K. Corral (1957)

Paramount Pictures

Director: John Sturges; **Producer:** Hal Wallis; **Writer:** Leon Uris; **Music:** Dimitri Tiomkin; **Running time:** 122 minutes

Cast: Burt Lancaster (Wyatt Earp); Kirk Douglas (Doc Holliday); Rhonda Fleming (Laura); Jo Van Fleet (Kate); John Ireland (Johnny Ringo)

Oscar nominations: Sound, Editing

A lot of artistic license is apparent in this acclaimed western purporting to tell the events leading up to the infamous showdown between Wyatt Earp and the Clantons at the nondescript O.K. Corral in Tombstone, Arizona. However, who needs facts when you have the pleasure of watching Burt Lancaster and Kirk Douglas squaring off against the bad guys? Douglas has the meatier role and makes the most of it as the manic-depressive "Doc" Holliday, one of the most flawed heroes imaginable. This highly stylized movie is expertly directed by John Sturges—and the final shootout is worth the wait. You won't be able to get the corny but catchy Frankie Laine theme song out of your head.

Rio Bravo (1959)

Warner Brothers

Director and Producer: Howard Hawks; **Writers:** Jules Furthman and Leigh Brackett; **Music:** Dimitri Tiomkin; **Running time:** 141 minutes

Cast: John Wayne (John T. Chance); Dean Martin (Dude); Ricky Nelson (Colorado); Angie Dickinson (Feathers); Walter Brennan (Stumpy)

Rio Bravo may not be Howard Hawks's greatest western (it lacks the gravitas of *Red River*) but it's undeniably the most fun. John Wayne is a sheriff who finds himself against an army of hired guns trying to free a rich man's brother from his jail. His only allies are a motley group of eccentrics who somehow manage to summon the cunning and courage to gain the upper hand. The film is like a western Rat Pack movie in that everyone appears to be having a hell of a grand time. The running time is a leisurely 141 minutes, but somehow you wish it went on longer. Walter Brennan steals the show as the cantankerous deputy Stumpy. Remade as *Assault on Precinct 13*.

The Magnificent Seven (1960)

United Artists

Director and Producer: John Sturges; **Writer:** William Roberts; **Music:** Elmer Bernstein; **Running time:** 128 minutes

Cast: Yul Brynner (Chris); Eli Wallach (Calvera); Steve McQueen (Vin); Charles Bronson (O'Reilly); Robert Vaughn (Lee); James Coburn (Britt); Horst Bucholz (Chico); Brad Dexter (Harry)

Oscar nominations: Score

"Play It Again, Sam"

The success of *The Magnificent Seven* inspired several follow-ups films, though only the first sequel, *Return of the Seven* (1966), had an original cast member (Yul Brynner). The other films were *Guns of the Magnificent Seven* (1969) and *The Magnificent Seven Ride* (1972). The film also bred a 1998 TV series that cleverly featured Robert Vaughn in a recurring role as a judge.

One of the all-time great action adventure films, *The Magnificent Seven* is as impressive as Kurosawa's *The Seven Samurai*, the film upon which it is based. Yul Brynner leads the ragtag group of down-on-their-luck gunmen to defend a small Mexican village from Eli Wallach's bandits. Along the way, they regain their self-respect, but at a tragic loss. You will never see a cast like this again, with each actor embellishing his character with unforgettable traits. Most would reach stardom based on their appearance in this film. The film was a patchwork production that was rewritten as shooting was underway, but what emerged was a macho masterpiece. Oh, and the actor's name you keep forgetting in barroom trivia is Brad Dexter. Elmer Bernstein's score is possibly the most famous ever from a nonmusical, except for the James Bond theme.

One Eyed Jacks (1961)

Paramount Pictures

Director: Marlon Brando; **Producer:** Frank P. Rosenberg; **Writers:** Guy Trosper and Calder Willingham; **Music:** Hugo Friedhofer; **Running time:** 141 minutes

Cast: Marlon Brando (Rio); Karl Malden (Dad Longworth); Katy Jurado (Maria); Pina Pellicer (Louisa)

Oscar nominations: Cinematography (color)

This big budget western bears the distinction of being the only film Marlon Brando ever directed. Although he acquitted himself well with this story of a bankrobber who is intent on taking revenge on a partner who double-crossed him, Brando had little respect for the studio's money. His final cut ran over five hours! Paramount brass carved the film into a still leisurely 141 minutes. The troubled production history makes for an occasionally uneven, but always compelling and interesting, morality tale with excellent chemistry between antagonists Brando and Karl Malden, who previously costarred in *A Streetcar Named Desire*.

Lonely Are the Brave (1962)

Universal Pictures

Director: David Miller; **Producer:** Edward Lewis; **Writer:** Dalton Trumbo; **Music:** Jerry Goldsmith; **Running time:** 107 minutes

Cast: Kirk Douglas (Jack Burns); Gena Rowlands (Jerry Bondi); Walter Matthau (Sheriff Johnson); Michael Kane (Paul Bondi)

Yet another magnificent screen performance by Kirk Douglas that was denied recognition by the Academy. Douglas is superb as a modern cowboy unwilling to accept that his way of life is fading fast. When he escapes from jail for a minor offense, he is pursued by a sheriff (Walter Matthau) who comes to admire his prey for the ingenious way he uses only his wits and horse to outmaneuver modern pursuit vehicles. The excellent supporting cast includes George Kennedy and Carroll O'Connor. The film is emotionally moving on every level, even as we recognize that the Douglas character's quest to remain pure to the cowboy ethic is doomed to failure.

The Man Who Shot Liberty Valance (1962)

Paramount Pictures

Director: John Ford; **Producer:** Willis Goldbeck; **Writers:** James Warner Bellah and Willis Goldbeck; **Music:** Cyril Mockridge; **Running time:** 123 minutes

Cast: James Stewart (Ransom Stoddard); John Wayne (Tom Doniphon); Vera Miles (Hallie); Lee Marvin (Liberty Valance); Edmond O'Brien (Dutton Peabody)

Oscar nominations: Costume Design (b&w)

John Ford's last great film is appropriately a poetic, low-key, and somber look at the tail end of the Wild West era. James Stewart is the tenderfoot lawyer who rides to fame as the man who slays notorious gunfighter Liberty Valance (Lee Marvin in one of the great villain roles of all time). However, he is haunted by a secret he has been hiding for many years. A dream cast, including great contributions from John Carradine, Woody Strode, Strother Martin, Lee Van Cleef, and Andy Devine, offer expert support. The top-selling theme song by Gene Pitney does not appear in the film!

Ride the High Country (1962)

MGM

Director: Sam Peckinpah; **Producer:** Richard E. Lyons; **Writer:** N.B. Stone Jr.; **Music:** George Bassman; **Running time:** 94 minutes

Cast: Randolph Scott (Gil Westrum); Joel McCrea (Steve Judd); Marietta Hartley (Elsa); Ron Starr (Heck)

This modestly budgeted western allowed Sam Peckinpah to rise from directing TV to feature films, though the transition would not be a happy one. Peckinpah's film about two aging, ex-lawmen hired to guard a gold shipment contained many wonderful touches and nuances about friendship, greed, and corruption—not to mention superb performances by Randolph Scott and Joel McCrea. However, MGM released the film as a bottom of the bill "B" movie, resulting in the first of seemingly endless battles Peckinpah would have with blind, deaf, and dumb studio executives in the years to come. However, the film (released in Europe as *Guns in the Afternoon*) was a major success abroad and over the years has been rightly recognized as a major work by a major American director.

Fistful of Dollars (1964)

United Artists

Director: Sergio Leone; **Producers:** Arrigo Colombo and George Pappi; **Writers:** Victor Andres Catena, Jamie Comas, and Sergio Leone; **Music:** Ennio Morricone; **Running time:** 99 minutes

Cast: Clint Eastwood (The Stranger); Marianna Koch (Marisol); Gian Maria Volante (Ramon Rojo); Wolfgang Lukschy (John Baxter)

With the release of this western in the United States in 1967, the western genre was revitalized in a most unexpected way. Italian director Sergio Leone (credited originally as "Bob Robertson" in order to hide the film's European origins) was so enamored of westerns that he created this (unauthorized) remake of Akira Kurosawa's *Yojimbo* as a western. However, the screen had never seen a hero like Clint Eastwood's Man with No Name: a ruthless, emotionless individual whose actions only look heroic because the people he interacts with epitomize overt villainy. Crude and under-budgeted but mesmerizing, *Fistful of Dollars* lived up to the marketing team's boast of being an entirely new brand of cinematic entertainment. This film launched the "spaghetti western," a genre in its own right. It spawned two sequels: the very good *For a Few Dollars More* and the masterpiece *The Good, the Bad, and the Ugly*.

Hollywood Confidential _____

When the ultra violent *Fistful of Dollars* was shown on ABC TV, the network commissioned a prologue directed by Monte Hellman with a contrived plot in which the Stranger is sent on a virtual humanitarian mission to kill the bad guys! This scenario was created to justify the hero's violent actions. Harry Dean Stanton appeared in this scene, though the Stranger was seen from behind because he was played by another actor. This absurd scene appears on the U.K. DVD edition.

For a Few Dollars More (1965)

United Artists

Director: Sergio Leone; **Producers:** Arturo Gonzalez and Albert Grimaldi (uncredited); **Writers:** Sergio Leone and Luciano Vincenzoni; **Music:** Ennio Morricone; **Running time:** 130 minutes

Cast: Clint Eastwood (The Man with No Name); Lee Van Cleef (Col. Mortimer); Gian Maria Volonte (El Indio); Mara Krup (Mary)

After the surprising box office success of *Fistful of Dollars*, Sergio Leone immediately attempted to catch lightning in a bottle twice—and succeeded with this intriguing sequel. Although Leone—like Howard Hawks and John Ford—prided himself on using a stock company of actors, his increased budget did allow the casting of another American opposite Clint Eastwood: the inimitable Lee Van Cleef. Van Cleef was a familiar character actor, but his role here launched him to stardom playing a competing bounty hunter who ultimately teams with Eastwood. Their chemistry together was so enjoyable that it's a shame they made only one other film together. Incidentally, Eastwood's character *is* referred to fleetingly as "Manco," which is Spanish for "one-armed"—a reference to his always keeping his right hand on his gun.

The Good, the Bad, and the Ugly (1966)

United Artists

Director: Sergio Leone; **Producer:** Alberto Grimaldi; **Writers:** Agenore Incrocci, Furio Scarpelli, Luciano Vincenzoni, and Sergio Leone; **Music:** Ennio Morricone; **Running time:** 161 minutes

Cast: Clint Eastwood ("Blondie"); Eli Wallach (Tuco); Lee Van Cleef (Sentenza); Aldo Giufrre (Union Captain)

Dismissed as Eurotrash by most critics when it opened in the United States, Sergio Leone's third film in the Man with No Name series is his greatest cinematic achievement—and many of those who bashed the film when it came out would later

"Well, Nobody's Perfect!"

The film contains a glaring blooper: when Blondie and Tuco see Sentenza ("Angel Eyes") they talk about him as though he were an old acquaintance. Yet, the film never shows them meeting previously. A scene that explained the connection was either cut at the last minute or was never filmed.

sing the praises of the legendary Italian director. A long but beautifully constructed epic involving three greedy men in a deadly quest for a hidden treasure, *GBU* boasts superb performances (primarily from Eli Wallach), an epic battle sequence, and more stylized action sequences than in any dozen American westerns. The film was not originally envisioned as a continuation of the Eastwood/Leone series. Before its release, it was cut severely and some of those scenes have recently been restored. Ennio Morricone provides one of the greatest of all film scores.

The Professionals (1966)

Columbia Pictures

Director, Producer, and Writer: Richard Brooks; **Music:** Maurice Jarre; **Running time:** 117 minutes

Cast: Burt Lancaster (Bill Dolworth); Lee Marvin (Fardan); Robert Ryan (Ehrengard); Claudia Cardinale (Maria); Ralph Bellamy (Grant); Jack Palance (Raza); Woody Strode (Jake)

Oscar nominations: Director, Screenplay, Cinematography

Pauline Kael likened this expertly filmed western with "the expertise of a cold, old whore with practiced hands and no thoughts of love." Indeed, if you're looking for male heroes in touch with their feminine sides, rent the latest Richard Gere movie. This is a three-way triumph for director, producer, and writer Richard Brooks—a slam-bang, no-nonsense adventure about four tough guys who are hired to go to Mexico to rescue a millionaire's kidnapped wife. The four male leads are as charismatic as any of *The Magnificent Seven*, and Claudia Cardinale is perhaps the sexiest vision imaginable in her perennially sweat-soaked shirt. Maurice Jarre's score is as thrilling as the onscreen action. Great all the way to the cynical finale.

Hombre (1967)

20th Century Fox

Director: Martin Ritt; **Producers:** Martin Ritt and Irving Ravetch; **Writers:** Irving Ravetch and Harriet Frank, Jr.; **Music:** David Rose; **Running time:** 111 minutes

Cast: Paul Newman (John Russell); Fredric March (Dr. Favor); Richard Boone (Grimes); Diane Cilento (Jessie); Martin Balsam (Mendez)

In this outstanding western, Paul Newman stars as a white man who must enter back into "civilization" after being raised by Indians. When his stagecoach is robbed and the passengers are left to die in the desert, he finds himself the reluctant rescuer of people who despise him because of his Indian past. A marvelous supporting cast and a low-key but memorable score by David Rose add to the impressive elements. The final shootout is a classic, suspense-drenched sequence. Richard Boone makes an unforgettable villain.

Once Upon a Time in the West (1968)

Paramount Pictures

Director: Sergio Leone; **Producer:** Fulvio Morsella; **Writers:** Sergio Leone and Sergio Donati (English translation by Mickey Knox); **Music:** Ennio Morricone; **Running time:** 165 minutes

Cast: Henry Fonda (Frank); Claudia Cardinale (Jill); Jason Robards (Cheyenne); Charles Bronson (Harmonica); Gabriele Ferzetti (Morton)

Considered by many to be Sergio Leone's ultimate masterpiece, *West* suffered an undignified fate in its American release when Paramount chopped up this lyrical and beautifully made film because the pace was too slow, thus eliminating the distinctive touches that defined Leone's style. Fortunately, saner heads have restored the version to its original European cut, and this story of greed and vengeance can now be enjoyed in all its glory. An impossibly handsome Henry Fonda turns in one of his greatest performances in a rare villainous role. Ennio Morricone's score is a true work of art, as is the cinematography by Tonino Delli Colli. Leone intended to cast *The Good, the Bad, and the Ugly* stars Clint Eastwood, Eli Wallach, and Lee Van Cleef as the three ill-fated gunslingers in the opening sequence, but alas, Eastwood could not be persuaded to participate.

Will Penny (1968)

Paramount Pictures

Director and Writer: Tom Gries; **Producers:** Walter Seltzer and Fred Engel; **Music:** David Raksin; **Running time:** 108 minutes

Cast: Charlton Heston (Will Penny); Joan Hackett (Catherine Allen); Donald Pleasence (Preacher Quint); Lee Majors (Blue); Bruce Dern (Rafe)

An unusually mature and emotionally moving story about an aging cowboy who reluctantly becomes the savior of a down-and-out woman and her young son. Together they not only face the elements but the unexpected terror of being captured by a crazed preacher (wonderfully played by Donald Pleasence) and his bloodthirsty sons. Heston gives one of his finest performances under Tom Gries's impressive direction. Just when you think the story is getting too predictable, it takes a sharp turn, and the ending is as satisfying as it is frustrating. Young Horace is well played by the director's son Jon, who was not a professional actor.

The Stalking Moon (1968)

National General Pictures

Director: Robert Mulligan; **Producer:** Alan J. Pakula; **Writers:** Wendell Mayes and Alvin Sargent; **Music:** Fred Karlin; **Running time:** 109 minutes

Cast: Gregory Peck (Sam Varner); Eva Marie Saint (Sarah Carver); Robert Forster (Nick); Ned Nolan (Boy)

Never heard of this film? It's no wonder because it only had a limited VHS release and was not successful in its original theatrical run. Yet, it's an inventive and highly unusual western—one that avoids shootouts in favor of suspense. Gregory Peck reteamed with *To Kill a Mockingbird* director Robert Mulligan to star as a scout who rescues a white woman who has long been the captive wife of a ruthless Indian warrior. Along with her son, they accompany Peck to his isolated cabin—unaware that the Indian brave is following them in a one-man rampage of brutality and murder. The film wisely avoids showing us Peck's almost ghostly antagonist until the very end, thus making us fear the unknown as much as Peck does. A great, atmospheric film that will have you on edge.

Butch Cassidy and the Sundance Kid (1969)

20th Century Fox

Director: George Roy Hill; **Producer:** John Foreman; **Writer:** William Goldman; **Music:** Burt Bacharach; **Running time:** 110 minutes

Cast: Paul Newman (Butch Cassidy); Robert Redford (Sundance Kid); Katharine Ross (Etta Place); Strother Martin (Garris); Jeff Corey (Bledsloe)

Oscar nominations: Best Picture, Director, Score*, Song* (*Raindrops Keep Fallin' on My Head*), Screenplay*, Cinematography*, Sound

The year 1969 was a great one for westerns, having seen *The Wild Bunch* and *True Grit* released in the summer and *Butch Cassidy and the Sundance Kid* a major year-end release. In keeping with the new wave of youth-oriented film making, William

Goldman's script emphasized one-liners and cynical humor. The film made the teaming of Newman and Redford legendary even though they would only make one other film together, *The Sting*, in 1973. Conrad Hall's cinematography and Burt Bacharach's classic score add to the timeless appeal of this classic that is loosely based on the lives of the titular outlaws. A marvelous supporting cast includes a particularly funny Strother Martin in his standard grumpy old geezer role. The final shootout is a wonder of superb editing and direction. Inspired the 1970s TV movies *Mrs. Sundance* and *Wanted: The Sundance Woman* as well as the ill-fated big screen prequel *Butch and Sundance: The Early Years*.

True Grit (1969)

Paramount Pictures

Director: Henry Hathaway; **Producer:** Hal B. Wallis; **Writer:** Marguerite Roberts; **Music:** Elmer Bernstein; **Running time:** 128 minutes

Cast: John Wayne (Rooster Cogburn); Glen Campbell (La Bouef); Kim Darby (Mattie Ross); Robert Duvall (Ned Pepper); Jeremy Slate (Quincy); Dennis Hopper (Moon)

Oscar nominations: Actor* (John Wayne), Song (*True Grit*)

For those who maintain that John Wayne couldn't really act because he couldn't play Shakespearean roles, remind them that Lord Olivier would have been just as inept playing Rooster Cogburn, the role that won Wayne his long-denied acting Oscar. His is a triumphant performance, playing against type as a boozy, self-centered, seemingly washed up lawman who helps a young girl track down her father's killers. Glen Campbell and Kim Darby hold their own in what is essentially Big Duke's show, and there is a wonderful cast of supporting actors each playing a memorably eccentric character. The Elmer Bernstein score and title theme are classics, but the most memorable aspect of *True Grit* is the climactic confrontation between Wayne and the bad guys. Holding the reins of his horse between his teeth, he charges them wielding a pistol in one hand and a rifle in the other. It was enough for critic Kathleen Carroll to refer to it as "John Wayne's finest moment." A 1975 sequel *Rooster Cogburn* was an amusing but lightweight affair, as was a TV movie with Warren Oates as Rooster.

The Wild Bunch (1969)

Warner Brothers

Director: Sam Peckinpah; **Producer:** Phil Feldman; **Writers:** Walon Green, Roy N. Sickner, and Sam Peckinpah; **Music:** Jerry Fielding; **Running time:** 14 minutes

Cast: William Holden (Pike); Ernest Borgnine (Dutch); Robert Ryan (Deke Thornton); Edmond O'Brien (Sykes); Warren Oates (Lyle); Ben Johnson (Tector); Jamie Sanchez (Angel)

Oscar nominations: Screenplay, Score

So much has been written about Sam Peckinpah's *The Wild Bunch* that it seems inconceivable movie fans don't know at least some of the fascinating stories behind this legendary film. *The Wild Bunch* centers on a group of aging outlaws out of step with the changing times, yet determined to adhere to a bastardized code of honor. The cast is filled with withered veteran actors who wouldn't stand a chance of being employed today by the very studio that has made a fortune from re-releasing the film over the decades on video and theatrically. *The Wild Bunch* caused a firestorm in its day for breaking down barriers in terms of screen violence, but it's hard to imagine the movie having the same raw edge without Peckinpah's penchant for bloodletting. The climatic shootout is arguably the best directed and choreographed action sequence in the history of the cinema. *The Wild Bunch* improves with every viewing. A modern day version is in the works, and somehow Mark Wahlberg has escaped this latest pointless remake.

 Gone with the Wind

Upon its American release, Warner Brothers severely cut Peckinpah's version of the film against his wishes. Many of the nuances and important motivations of the characters were lost. Fortunately, most of the cuts were restored in 1995, and this is the version available on DVD. Don't miss producers Paul Seydman and Nick Redman's Oscar-nominated documentary *The Wild Bunch: An Album in Montage* on the DVD set. It features rare footage taken on the set.

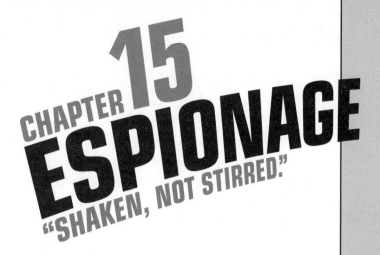

CHAPTER 15
ESPIONAGE
"SHAKEN, NOT STIRRED."

The intrigue and suspense that define the espionage film genre would seem to provide fertile ground for directors and producers. Yet, for many years, spy movies were woefully ignored as mainstream entertainment. There were some exceptions: Alfred Hitchcock seemed particularly drawn to the subject through films such as *Saboteur*, *The Man Who Knew Too Much*, *The Thirty Nine Steps*, and *North by Northwest*. However, most of these stories concerned the adventures of an innocent man caught up in a nightmare of mistaken identity rather than dwelling on the espionage elements of the stories.

The spy movie genre exploded in 1962 with the release of the first James Bond film, *Dr. No*. The Bond films went beyond being box office hits—they redefined popular culture. The 007 movies were the first to introduce fantastic sets, villains, and production values to what had initially been a drab genre. By the mid 1960s, seemingly every actor old enough to legally order a Martini was playing a spy. Some were inspired choices (James Coburn as Derek Flint) while others were seemingly tailor-made for future ridicule on *Mystery Science Theater* (for example, Neil Connery's big screen debut and farewell in the Eurotrash vehicle *Operation Kid Brother*). Ironically, from a return-on-investment perspective, the most profitable spy movies of this time period weren't movies at all. Eight feature films (only three of which were released in the United States) were cobbled together from episodes of the red hot TV hit *The Man From U.N.C.L.E.*, starring Robert Vaughn and David McCallum. Released in theaters, these films drew huge paybacks on their minimal marketing costs and in England several actually broke house records!

The spy movie genre continues to maintain its popularity through a new age of secret agent heroes, brooding, anti-establishment types like Jack Ryan and Jason Bourne. Yet, the granddaddy of all spies, Agent 007, remains very much relevant today. He has survived the most dangerous threat to any cinematic movie hero: fickle audiences.

The 39 Steps (1935)

Gaumont British Picture Corporation of America

Director: Alfred Hitchcock; **Producers:** Michael Balcon and Ivor Montagu (uncredited); **Writer:** Charles Bennett; **Running time:** 86 minutes

Cast: Robert Donat (Richard Hannay); Madeline Carroll (Pamela); Lucie Mannheim (Annabelle Smith); Godfrey Terle (Prof. Jordan)

Hitchcock's first major spy movie is a lighthearted suspense story set in the U.K. Robert Donat is wonderfully charismatic as a young man mistaken for a murderer. His attempts to clear his name embroil him in a wild chase on foot across the Scottish moors while handcuffed to an unwilling accomplice, Madeline Carroll. It all culminates in a complex riddle that unveils a deadly espionage scheme climaxing at the London Palladium. Regarded as one of the master director's best films of this era, the movie holds up well today—even if the finale seems a bit rushed and abrupt. Remade in 1978 with another version in production as of this writing.

The Lady Vanishes (1938)

Gaumont British Picture Corporation of America

Director: Alfred Hitchcock; **Producer:** Edward Blac (uncredited); **Writers:** Sidney Gilliat and Frank Launder; **Music:** Louis Levy and Charles Williams (uncredited); **Running time:** 97 minutes

Cast: Margaret Lockwood (Iris Henderson); Michael Redgrave (Gilbert Redmond); Paul Lukas (Dr. Hartz); Dame May Whitty (Miss Froy); Naunton Wayne (Caldicott); Basil Radford (Charters)

Alfred Hitchcock directed this superior British thriller with Agatha Christie overtones. Margaret Lockwood is a young woman who befriends a kindly old lady on a trans-European train only to find she has vanished in the course of the journey—and all other passengers deny any knowledge of her existence. The ensuing story has plenty of suspense coupled with the usual Hitchcock penchant for dry humor.

Michael Redgrave gives an excellent performance as the leading man despite the fact that he and Hitchcock grew to loathe each other during production. Supporting actors Naunton Wayne and Basil Radford were so acclaimed for their hilarious performances as a team of eccentric British buddies that they repeated their *schtick* in many other films to follow. Remade in 1979 as one of the final Hammer Films productions.

Foreign Correspondent (1940)

United Artists

Director: Alfred Hitchcock; **Executive Producer:** Walter Wanger; **Writers:** Charles Bennett and Joan Harrison; **Music:** Alfred Newman; **Running time:** 120 minutes

Cast: Joel McCrae (Johnny Jones); Laraine Day (Carol Fisher); Herbert Marshall (Stephen Fisher); George Sanders (Scott ffolliott)

Oscar nominations: Best Picture, Supporting Actor (Albert Bassermann), Screenplay, Special Effects, Art Direction (b&w), Cinematography (b&w)

Don't be fooled by the drab title, *Foreign Correspondent* is one of Alfred Hitchcock's most exciting thrillers. Shot on the brink of the Nazi blitz over London, the story was updated from a script that was originally set in the Spanish Civil War. Joel McCrae is an American newspaper reporter who gets more than he bargained for when a Dutch diplomat he is going to interview is assassinated. In true Hitchcockian fashion, he is soon embroiled in a frantic race to prevent German spies from damaging the Allied cause. The film contains many classic sequences including the murder of the diplomat by use of a gun hidden in a camera, and the thrilling chase through a windmill.

Saboteur (1942)

Universal Pictures

Director: Alfred Hitchcock; **Producer:** Frank Lloyd; **Writers:** Peter Viertel, Joan Harrison, and Dorothy Parker; **Music:** Frank Skinner; **Running time:** 108 minutes

Cast: Priscilla Lane (Pat Martin); Robert Cummings (Barry Kane); Otto Kruger (Charles Tobin); Alan Baxter (Mr. Freeman); Norman Lloyd (Frank Fry)

Although not among the top ranks of Hitchcock thrillers, this popular spy film is enormously entertaining. Released only months after America's entry into the war, the script played up concerns about Nazi infiltration and sabotage within U.S. borders. Robert Cummings is the everyday airplane plant worker who becomes embroiled in an outlandish plot of blackmail and terrorism. The cross-country chase that follows culminates in the classic sequence in which he grapples with Norman Lloyd while dangling from atop the Statue of Liberty.

The Man Who Knew Too Much (1956)

Paramount Pictures

Director and Producer: Alfred Hitchcock; **Writers:** John Michael Hayes; **Music:** Bernard Hermann; **Running time:** 120 minutes

Cast: James Stewart (Ben McKenna); Doris Day (Jo McKenna); Brenda de Banzie (Lucy Drayton); Bernard Miles (Edward Drayton); Daniel Gelin (Louis Bernard)

Oscar nominations: Song* (*Que Sera, Sera*)

Alfred Hitchcock's 1934 version of this film was a terrific suspense film in its own right, but although most critics would disagree, I've always preferred this 1956 remake largely on the basis that James Stewart and Doris Day exude wonderful chemistry and the fact that Hitchcock makes good use of atmospheric locations in and around London. Stewart and Day find their son kidnapped and held hostage by a spy ring intent on killing a foreign head of state. The plot is complex, but the action moves quickly to the brilliantly directed, suspense-drenched conclusion in Albert Hall. Day allegedly hated the theme song *Que Sera, Sera* but it ended up winning the Oscar and becoming her most popular standard.

North by Northwest (1959)

MGM

Director and Producer: Alfred Hitchcock; **Writer:** Ernest Lehman; **Music:** Bernard Hermann; **Running time:** 136 minutes

Cast: Cary Grant (Roger Thornhill); Eva Marie Saint (Eve Kendall); James Mason (Phillip Vandamm); Jessie Royce Landis (Clara Thornhill); Leo G. Carroll (The Professor)

Oscar nominations: Art Direction-Set Decoration (color), Editing, Screenplay

Alfred Hitchcock called this film the epitome of his work in the American cinema. *North by Northwest* comes close to achieving pure cinematic perfection. The wonderfully witty script by the incredibly versatile Ernest Lehman and the frantic yet intoxicating score by Bernard Hermann combine to make this madcap spy chase arguably the best film of Hitchcock's career. Cary Grant, in the type of wonderful performance that was traditionally overlooked by the Academy, is a Madison Avenue executive mistaken for a spy and is plunged into a bizarre plot involving murder, sex, and international spy rings. There are many classic sequences, but Grant being pursued by a crop dusting plane and the climax atop Mount Rushmore stand as seminal moments in motion picture history. Relish the great supporting cast from Saint's quintessential Hitchcockian "cool blonde" to Mason's erudite fiend to Leo G. Carroll's droll intelligence chief (a part that inspired his role as Alexander Waverly in *The Man From U.N.C.L.E.* TV series). Curiously, another legendary TV "chief" appears in the film: Edward Platt of *Get Smart!* Jessie Royce Landis, who gives a delightfully daft performance as Grant's mother, was actually the same age as him!

 "Well, Nobody's Perfect!"

In the sequence in which Cary Grant is shot by Eva Marie Saint in the cafeteria at Mount Rushmore, observe the little boy at a nearby table. He uses his fingers to plug his ears *before* Saint fires the pistol.

The Counterfeit Traitor (1962)

Paramount Pictures

Director and Writer: George Seaton; **Producers:** George Seaton and William Perlberg; **Music:** Alfred Newman; **Running time:** 140 minutes

Cast: William Holden (Eric Erickson); Lilli Palmer (Marianne); Hugh Griffith (Collins); Carl Raddatz (Otto Holtz)

This thrilling and intelligently scripted spy story set in WWII is based on the true experiences of Swedish industrialist Eric Erickson, who was reluctantly dragooned into acting as a spy for the Allies. In order to gain access to top secret Nazi information, he ingratiates himself with the enemy by acting as a collaborator and traitor to his country. In doing so, he must endure the frustration of being disowned by his friends and colleagues without confiding in them the heroic acts he is performing. William Holden gives an excellent performance in the lead role. The occasional slow moving story builds up considerable suspense as Erickson attempts to flee the Nazis before he can be exposed.

Dr. No (1962)

United Artists

Director: Terence Young; **Producers:** Albert R. Broccoli and Harry Saltzman; **Writers:** Richard Maibaum, Johanna Harwood, and Berkely Mather; **Music:** Monty Norman; **Running time:** 110 minutes

Cast: Sean Connery (James Bond); Ursula Andress (Honey Ryder); Joseph Wiseman (Dr. No); Jack Lord (Felix Leiter); Bernard Lee ("M")

It's difficult to recall the cinematic experience without the influences of James Bond. Until Bond appeared onscreen for the first time in *Dr. No*, the British post-war cinema had largely been defined by grim "kitchen sink" dramas that reflected the morose atmosphere of economically depressed post-war England. Bond brought back vestiges of pride in the old British Empire. Here was an antihero who was difficult to admire but impossible to not like. Bond was aloof, opaque about his personal life, and indulged in all sorts of promiscuous vices. Yet, he was an honorable throwback to the age of chivalry. The success of *Dr. No* revolutionized the film world. Peter Hunt's innovative, fast-paced editing set the trend for all action movies that followed. Ken Adam's ingenious production designs would set the mold for all Bond films to follow. The emergence of Ursula Andress from the surf in a white bikini is an iconic screen image. The most influential ingredient was the inclusion of cynical humor, played with a straight face by the incomparable Sean Connery, who fit the role of Bond perfectly. The early Bond films have influenced virtually every action movie made since 1962. Few have come close to achieving their level of enduring success.

From Russia with Love (1963)

United Artists

Director: Terence Young; **Producers:** Albert R. Broccoli and Harry Saltzman; **Writers:** Richard Maibaum and Johanna Harwood; **Music:** John Barry; **Running time:** 115 minutes

Cast: Sean Connery (James Bond); Daniela Bianchi (Tatiania Romanova); Pedro Armendariz (Kerim Bey); Lotte Lenya (Rosa Klebb); Robert Shaw (Red Grant)

The second James Bond film is the only entry in the series to address the Cold War in a serious fashion. It's also Sean Connery's personal favorite among his 007 movies.

Hollywood Confidential

Pedro Armendariz, who plays Bond's charismatic ally, Kerim Bey, was terminally ill with cancer during shooting. He barely finished his scenes and had to be doubled in long shots during the gypsy camp fight. Weeks after leaving the set, Armendariz shot himself in his hospital bed.

Made before the series became awash with spectacle, *FRWL* stays relatively faithful to Ian Fleming's novel. Bond is knowingly sent into a death trap on the pretense of retrieving a decoding machine from a sexy Soviet defector. The film has many outstanding elements including the introduction of the first Bond gadget—the lethal attaché case—and Desmond Llewelyn's introduction as Q. Lotte Lenya's villainess, Rosa Klebb, is a classic embodiment of evil as is Robert Shaw's chilling assassin Red Grant. His fight with Bond in a compartment aboard the Orient Express is one of the best-choreographed and edited action sequences ever filmed.

Goldfinger (1964)

United Artists

Director: Guy Hamilton; **Producers:** Albert R. Broccoli and Harry Saltzman; **Writers:** Richard Maibaum and Paul Dehn; **Music:** John Barry; **Running time:** 112 minutes

Cast: Sean Connery (James Bond); Honor Blackman (Pussy Galore); Gert Frobe (Auric Goldfinger); Shirley Eaton (Jill Masterson); Tania Mallet (Tilly Masterson); Harold Sakata (Oddjob)

Oscar nominations: Sound*

This is the film that transformed the James Bond series into a pop culture phenomenon. With more emphasis on humor, the nature of the series found a perfect balance under Guy Hamilton's direction, though Hamilton would later be guilty of bringing broad slapstick elements to the series. There's no point in recounting the plot because unless you are under age ten, the only question is how many times you've seen the film. Ken Adam's amazing production design of Ft. Knox is still a marvel to behold, and John Barry's score combined with Shirley Bassey's warbling of the title song are classics. The film boasts two of the most memorable villains in movie history with Gert Frobe as the jovial but evil Goldfinger and Harold Sakata as his mute manservant Oddjob who has a penchant for using a lethal derby to decapitate his targets. The film introduced another Bond star: the amazing Aston Martin DB5, the popularity of which remains undiminished (it appears in the 2006 version of *Casino Royale*).

Hollywood Confidential

When German actor Gert Frobe arrived on the set, the director was horrified to find he didn't speak English! Frobe learned to mouth his lines phonetically, and he was dubbed in the final cut by British actor Michael Collins.

The Ipcress File (1965)

Universal Pictures

Director: Sidney J. Furie; **Producer:** Harry Saltzman; **Writers:** Bill Canaway and James Doran; **Music:** John Barry; **Running time:** 109 minutes

Cast: Michael Caine (Harry Palmer); Nigel Green (Dalby); Guy Doleman (Ross); Sue Lloyd (Jean Courtney); Gordon Jackson (Carswell)

Designed as the antidote to the Bond movies (ironically produced by 007 movie mogul Harry Saltzman), *The Ipcress File* showed the seamy side of the espionage business. Based on Len Deighton's novel, the film presents the first screen appearance of Michael Caine's bespectacled antihero Harry Palmer, a hip, cynical Bizarro version of

"Play It Again, Sam"

There were two Harry Palmer big screen sequels, *Funeral in Berlin* (1966) and *Billion Dollar Brain* (1967). The character was resurrected in the 1990s for two middling TV movies, *Bullet to Beijing* and *Midnight in Saint Petersburg.*

007 who loathes authority and seems anything but dedicated to the missions to which he is assigned. Palmer becomes embroiled in a complex plot involving missing scientists, brainwashing, and double agents. The film gained high praise, especially in England where it was awarded the Best Film prize by BAFTA. Bond veteran John Barry provides the atmospheric musical score and fellow 007 alumni Ken Adam created the non-Bondian sets. One of the top spy thrillers of the 1960s.

Morituri (1965)

20th Century Fox

Director: Bernhard Wicki; **Producer:** Aaron Rosenberg; **Writer:** Daniel Taradash; **Music:** Jerry Goldsmith; **Running time:** 123 minutes

Cast: Marlon Brando (Robert Crain); Yul Brynner (Capt. Mueller); Janet Margolin (Esther Levy); Trevor Howard (Col. Statter)

As with most of Marlon Brando's work in the 1960s, critics and audiences were non-responsive to his performance in *Morituri*, and the film failed at the box office. The confusing title (taken from a Latin salute given by gladiators who were about to die) didn't enhance its prospects. However, this is a well-made, if somber, spy story with Brando as a double agent attempting to scuttle a Nazi cargo ship helmed by Yul Brynner. More a human drama than a spy thriller, the film showcases good screen chemistry between the two acting titans along with an interesting supporting cast including Wally Cox, who was Brando's roommate in their early days. The studio attempted to boost audience interest by retitling the movie with the even more cumbersome: *The Saboteur: Code Name Morituri.*

The Spy Who Came in from the Cold (1965)

Paramount Pictures

Director and Producer: Martin Ritt; **Writers:** Paul Dehn and Guy Trosper; **Music:** Sol Kaplan; **Running time:** 102 minutes

Cast: Richard Burton (Alec Leamas); Claire Bloom (Nan Perry); Oskar Werner (Fiedler); Sam Wannamaker (Peters)

Oscar nominations: Actor (Richard Burton), Art Direction-Set Decoration (b&w)

When it came to the Oscars, Richard Burton was always a bridesmaid and never a bride. Although nominated many times, Burton never received so much as an honorary award. One of his finest performances is in this dark, depressing look at the world of Cold War espionage based on John Le Carre's bestseller. Burton is a worn-out, disillusioned British agent coerced into pretending he's defected as part of an elaborate and dangerous plot to undermine an East German intelligence chief. Claire Bloom is his love interest, a woman inadvertently swept up in the cat-and-mouse game between men who use innocent people like pawns. Superb cinematography by Oswald Morris enhances the suspenseful conclusion set at the Berlin Wall. Keep an eye out for Bernard Lee ("M" in the Bond films) as a shopkeeper.

Thunderball (1965)

United Artists

Director: Terence Young; **Producer:** Kevin McClory; **Presented by:** Albert R. Broccoli and Harry Saltzman; **Writers:** Richard Maibaum and John Hopkins; **Music:** John Barry; **Running time:** 130 minutes

Cast: Sean Connery (James Bond); Claudine Auger (Domino); Adolfo Celi (Largo); Luciana Paluzzi (Fiona Volpe); Rik Van Nutter (Felix Leiter)

Oscar nominations: Special Visual Effects*

Although *Thunderball* is the most successful James Bond film ever (in terms of the number of tickets sold), it has often been criticized for marking the point at which James Bond's gadgetry threatened to eclipse all other aspects of the series. Still, this is a visually stunning film with exotic locations ranging from Paris to the Bahamas and the type of grandiose action sequences that can never be imagined today. The underwater battle is a masterpiece of choreography and cinematography, all greatly enhanced by John Barry's exciting score. This was to be the first Bond film, but legal wrangling about story rights led to the producers choosing *Dr. No* for 007's big screen debut. A 1983 remake titled *Never Say Never Again* was made outside the control of Eon Productions, which produces the "official" Bond movies. It starred Sean Connery, but despite some good sequences, the film paled compared to its predecessor. *Thunderball* marked the pinnacle of Bondmania with some theaters staying open 24 hours to accommodate the crowds. Many of the cast and crew were reunited at a 40th anniversary reunion screening in London in 2005.

Gone with the Wind

In the film, Largo invites Bond to tour his yacht, the *Disco Volante*. A sequence was shot with Bond aboard the vessel, but it was cut and is lost presumably forever, though some stills of the scene survive.

Our Man Flint (1966)

20th Century Fox

Director: Daniel Mann; **Producer:** Saul David; **Writers:** Hal Fimberg and Ben Starr; **Music:** Jerry Goldsmith; **Running time:** 108 minutes

Cast: James Coburn (Derek Flint); Lee J. Cobb (Cramden); Gila Golan (Gila); Edward Mulhare (Malcolm Rodney)

Inspired by the success of Bondmania, 20th Century Fox hopped on the bandwagon and quickly put *Our Man Flint* into production, top lining James Coburn as an almost superhuman operative who works solo and only needs a cigarette lighter with a seemingly endless array of gadgets to combat the forces of the evil organization Z.O.W.I.E. Unlike most Bond rip-offs, *Flint* was praised for its witty script and emphasis on overt humor. Derek Flint never loses his cool, whether bedding a bevy of beauties, learning how to communicate with dolphins, or taking on entire armies single-handedly. The film raised Coburn from supporting actor ranks to leading man status. He gets excellent support from Lee J. Cobb as the intelligence chief who is perpetually exasperated by Flint's refusal to be a "team player." The film features an excellent Jerry Goldsmith score.

"Play It Again, Sam"

Our Man Flint inspired one sequel, the highly entertaining *In Like Flint* (1967) before Coburn moved on to greener pastures. A bizarre 1976 ABC TV movie *Our Man Flint: Dead on Target* starred Ray Danton, though the character bore absolutely no resemblance to the film hero and was more akin to Peter Falk's Columbo!

The Quiller Memorandum (1966)

20th Century Fox

Director: Michael Anderson; **Producer:** Ivan Foxwell; **Writer:** Harold Pinter; **Music:** John Barry; **Running time:** 105 minutes

Cast: George Segal (Quiller); Alec Guinness (Pol); Max Von Sydow (Oktober); Senta Berger (Inge); George Sanders (Gibbs)

This unusually intelligent espionage drama benefits from a deliberately-paced but engrossing script by playwright Harold Pinter. George Segal is an agent sent by MI6 to Berlin to investigate the deaths of two operatives. He uncovers a neo-Nazi organization and finds himself marked for assassination. Some good plot twists ensue, with Segal's character refreshingly vulnerable and occasionally inept. The production makes excellent use of the West German locations.

The Silencers (1966)

Columbia Pictures

Director: Phil Karlson; **Producer:** Irving Allen; **Writer:** Oscar Saul; **Music:** Elmer Bernstein; **Running time:** 102 minutes

Cast: Dean Martin (Matt Helm); Stella Stevens (Gail Hendrix); Daliah Lavi (Tina); Victor Buono (Tung Tze); James Gregory (MacDonald)

No film series epitomizes the concept of "guilty pleasures" as much as the Matt Helm movies. The first in the series, *The Silencers*, is the best of the lot. That may sound like feint praise, but at least here Martin makes an attempt to stay awake and read his cue cards. Despite—or perhaps *because*—of the cheesy production values, there is something irresistible about the 60s pop culture element of the film—it's a cinematic time capsule for the grooviest of all decades. All of Helm's female acquaintances have bra sizes that eclipse their I.Q.s, and most find ways to end up parading about in lingerie and garter belts. No complaints from this corner.

"Play It Again, Sam"

The series consisted of three sequels to this film: *Murderer's Row* (1967), *The Ambushers* (1967), and *The Wrecking Crew* (1969). A planned production of *The Ravagers* never took place. Tony Franciosa starred in the 1975s TV movie and flop series that followed, but the character bore little resemblance to Dean Martin's interpretation.

Torn Curtain (1966)

Universal Pictures

Director and Producer: Alfred Hitchcock; **Writer:** Brian Moore; **Music:** John Addison; **Running time:** 128 minutes

Cast: Paul Newman (Michael Armstrong); Julie Andrews (Sarah Louise Sherman); Lila Kedrova (Countess)

When this film was released, it was universally derided by critics as an ill-fated attempt by Hitchcock to exploit the spy movie craze. Indeed, Hitchcock later criticized the casting of the movie himself, saying there was no chemistry between Paul Newman and Julie Andrews, whom he cast because they were the "it" stars of the moment. The criticism seems overly harsh. While *Torn Curtain* isn't one of the director's top efforts, it's an interesting and intriguing story with Newman as an academic pretending he has defected to East Germany in order to obtain a secret formula.

Hitchcock's penchant for inexcusably lousy backscreen projection is on display here, but some good action sequences, including a painstakingly choreographed murder sequence set in a kitchen, resonate long after the film's flaws have been forgotten. Hitchcock's longtime collaborator Bernard Hermann wrote the original score, but when the director caved to studio pressure to replace him with John Addison, the two men never spoke again.

Casino Royale (1967)

Columbia Pictures

Directors: Val Guest, Joseph McGrath, John Huston, Kenneth Hughes, and Robert Parrish; **Producer:** Charles K. Feldman; **Writers:** Wolf Mankiewicz, John Law, and Michael Sayers; **Music:** Burt Bacharach; **Running time:** 131 minutes

Cast: Peter Sellers (Evelyn Tremble); Ursula Andress (Vesper Lynd); David Niven (Sir James Bond); Woody Allen (Jimmy Bond); Orson Welles (Le Chiffre)

Oscar nominations: Song (*The Look of Love*)

What?! *That* version of *Casino Royale?* No, I haven't taken leave of my senses—this film's inclusion is intentional. I admit this at the risk of being tossed into Blofeld's piranha pool. This is an admittedly messy, overblown production based on—well, inspired by—the only Ian Fleming James Bond novel not controlled by Eon Productions. The decision was made to make it into a spoof rather than try to compete with the Sean Connery Bond films. The production quickly spiraled out of control with five directors working simultaneously, but never in conjunction with each other. For all that, the film is a *glorious* mess that seems to have been the primary inspiration for the Austin Powers films. An all-star cast, outstanding production design, groovy music from Burt Bacharach, and that great Herb Alpert theme song combine to make this a guilty pleasure. You only have to start doubting your sanity when it begins to make sense to you.

"Play It Again, Sam"

Fleming's novel was first filmed as a live TV production for CBS in 1954 with American actor Barry Nelson in the role. Daniel Craig, the sixth actor cast as the big screen version of 007, starred in the 2006 "real" Bond version of the story, though Fleming's claustrophobic setting had to be compromised for major action sequences.

You Only Live Twice (1967)

United Artists

Director: Lewis Gilbert; **Producers:** Albert R. Broccoli and Harry Saltzman; **Writer:** Roald Dahl; **Music:** John Barry; **Running time:** 117 minutes

Cast: Sean Connery (James Bond); Donald Pleasence (Blofeld); Akiko Wakabayashi (Aki); Tetsuro Tamba (Tanaka); Mie Hama (Kissy Suzuki)

By the time Sean Connery made this fifth James Bond film, the actor had tired of the role and the maniacal following he had built among fans. He announced this would be his final Bond film (though he would be induced back twice more in the future). Connery does indeed look bored in *You Only Live Twice*, the first Bond film to completely discard all elements of an Ian Fleming source novel. The production stresses opulence and gadgetry, and if you can get past the absurdities of Roald Dahl's script, the film is a feast for the ears and the eyes. Ken Adam's mammoth volcano lair for SPECTRE chief Blofeld (seen onscreen for the first time in a memorably creepy performance by Donald Pleasence) is the real star of the movie. The massive set is literally jawdropping to behold, yet Adam was denied an Oscar nomination for Art Direction (the living room set for *Guess Who's Coming to Dinner?* got the honor!). The movie features a magnificent and beautiful score and theme song by John Barry and imaginative use of Japanese locations. Following Connery's departure from this film, the producers had the unenviable task of finding someone to succeed the actor.

On Her Majesty's Secret Service (1969)

United Artists

Director: Peter Hunt; **Producers:** Albert R. Broccoli and Harry Saltzman; **Writers:** Richard Maibaum and Simon Raven (additional dialogue); **Music:** John Barry; **Running time:** 140 minutes

Cast: George Lazenby (James Bond); Diana Rigg (Tracy); Telly Savalas (Blofeld); Gabriele Ferzetti (Draco); Ilsa Steppat (Irma Bunt)

Largely dismissed by critics at the time of its release, *OHMSS* has grown in stature over the years, and many consider it to be the best of all Bond movies. Don't be misled by conventional wisdom that George Lazenby made a poor James Bond. Although he had the unenviable task of succeeding Sean Connery, Lazenby—who had no prior acting experience—acquits himself well on all counts, particularly the action sequences. The film boasts the best script of the series, the finest musical score, and inspired direction by the series former editor Peter Hunt, who succeeded in making the film more believable than recent entries had been. Diana Rigg is the perfect Bond girl (she can act!) and the downbeat ending is as inspired as it is daring. The script stays close to Ian Fleming's source novel, one of his best, though the filmmakers liven things up with some incredible action and stunt sequences, including a prolonged toboggan chase that cameraman Willy Bogner managed to film while skiing backwards!

Hollywood Confidential

Perceptions that *OHMSS* was a box office failure are false. The film was quite successful, but its grosses were below those of the Connery era. Lazenby stunned producers by announcing this would be his only Bond film. After his departure, Connery was lured back for *Diamonds Are Forever* (1971), a film that restored Bond's box office mojo to full strength—but also began the era of over-the-top comedy that would characterize the series for the entire Roger Moore era that followed.

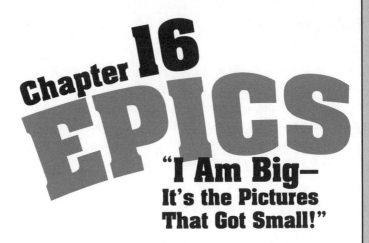

Chapter 16
EPICS

"I Am Big— It's the Pictures That Got Small!"

From the earliest inception of motion pictures, producers and directors have attempted to make films as grandiose as possible in order to lure customers out of their easy chairs and into theaters. From the early silent films by D.W. Griffith and Cecil B. DeMille to the stunning color productions of David Lean, the motion picture epic has been a mainstay of the industry.

In this chapter, you will find a number of epic films that most critics do not generally regard as classic movies. These productions have been victimized by what I refer to as "The *Cleopatra* Syndrome"—movies whose productions have been so fraught with problems that they became synonymous with waste and budgetary overruns. Few critics, however, have reflected on their value as *films*. The background story of clashing egos and wasted money may make for interesting reading in scandal sheets; however, many of the most maligned films actually deserve ranking as classic productions. Although several of the films listed here are indisputably flawed in some way, I strongly defend the many merits to be found in epic productions such as *The Alamo*, *Mutiny on the Bounty* and, yes, even the much-criticized *Cleopatra*.

Sadly, as George Lucas recently stated, the era of the true epic film is pretty much over. When we see a cast of thousands today, it's probably four actors who have been replicated by CGI a hundred times over. Additionally, we have seen the demise of the "all-star" production such as *The Longest Day*. Soaring costs, largely attributed to overpaid talent, have relegated such films to the past—though, truth be told, studios would have a difficult time finding enough "stars" today to warrant the term "all star" production. There are the occasional exceptions but they are few and far between. Yet, we can revel in the classics of the past, made by filmmakers the likes of whom we may never see again. When it comes to movie epics, moreso than any other genre, the term "They don't make 'em like that anymore" seems appropriate.

Around the World in 80 Days (1956)

United Artists

Director: Michael Anderson; **Producer:** Michael Todd; **Writers:** James Poe, John Farrow, and S. J. Perelman; **Music:** Victor Young; **Running time:** 175 minutes

Cast: David Niven (Phileas Fogg); Cantinflas (Passepartout); Robert Newton (Mr. Fix); Shirley MacLaine (Princess Aouda)

Oscar nominations: Best Picture*, Score*, Cinematography* (color), Screenplay*, Editing*, Director, Costume Design (color), Art Direction-Set Decoration (color)

Producer Michael Todd's penchant for "over the top" projects was exemplified by this big budget adaptation of Jules Verne's adventure story about an aristocrat in Victorian England who wagers he can find a way to circle the globe in, well, 80 days. Todd insured the film would get maximum buzz by casting virtually every major star available for highly publicized cameos. Some of these roles were substantial, others were of the "blink-and-you-miss-him" type. The real fun is seeing the great David Niven in wonderful form as the priggish gentleman who endures every hardship without displacing his top hat. The biggest laugh-getter proved to be the famed Mexican comedian Cantinflas, who gave an extraordinary performance as Niven's long-suffering but loyal valet. The DVD special edition of this overstuffed but enjoyable production contains interesting extras that amply show how Todd made this film *the* movie event of 1956. Remade as a 1989 TV series with Pierce Brosnan and an ill-fated 2004 feature film with Jackie Chan!

Ben-Hur (1959)

MGM

Director: William Wyler; **Producer:** Sam Zimbalist; **Writer:** Karl Tunberg; **Music:** Miklos Rosza; **Running time:** 212 minutes

Cast: Charlton Heston (Judah Ben-Hur); Jack Hawkins (Quintus Arrius); Haya Harareet (Esther); Stephen Boyd (Massala); Hugh Griffith (Sheik Ilderim)

Oscar nominations: Best Picture*, Special Effects*, Supporting Actor* (Hugh Griffith), Actor* (Charlton Heston), Costume Design* (color), Art Direction-Set Decoration* (color), Sound*, Score*, Cinematography* (color), Editing*, Director*, Screenplay

MGM gambled a (then astonishing) $12.5 million—and the financial stability of the company—on this massive remake of the silent film classic. The payoff was the biggest grossing film ever released until that point, generating over $40 million in revenue. Unlike Charlton Heston's other Biblical epic, DeMille's cartoonish *The Ten Commandments*, William Wyler's production is both literate and well-acted with Heston perfectly cast as the ill-fated hero sold into slavery under false charges by a once trusted friend. The final portion of the film can be heavy going and somewhat ponderous as Ben-Hur undergoes a religious transformation. However, the famed chariot race still stands as arguably the most impressive action sequence ever filmed (it was directed by Andrew Marton and legendary stuntman Yakima Canutt and employed up to 15,000 extras). Beware of the "pan-and-scan" TV broadcasts and videos of the film that crop out 40 percent of the picture. This movie exemplifies the glory of widescreen video presentations.

The Alamo (1960)

United Artists

Director and Producer: John Wayne; **Writer:** James Edward Grant; **Music:** Dimitri Tiomkin; **Running time:** 202 minutes

Cast: John Wayne (Davy Crockett); Richard Widmark (Jim Bowie); Laurence Harvey (Col. William Travis); Frankie Avalon (Smitty); Richard Boone (Sam Huston); Chill Wills (Beekeeper)

Oscar nominations: Best Picture, Sound*, Cinematography (color), Editing, Score, Song (*The Green Leaves of Summer*), Supporting Actor (Chill Wills)

Despite longstanding rumors to the contrary, John Wayne's epic film (which he produced and directed) was not a box office disaster. Over time, it made a substantial profit, although Wayne didn't benefit as he had sold his interest in the film in order to finance budget overages. It was also *not* critically lambasted, as evidenced by its multiple Oscar nominations. The film did suffer from a notorious Oscar campaign by nominee Chill Wills that implied voting for anyone else would be anti-American, thus resulting in a negative backlash. However, there has always been a loyal fan base for the film, which is indisputably magnificent in its production values. The script is heavy handed at times, with grizzled mountain men emoting like Lord Olivier about freedom and patriotism, but the spectacle is impressive—especially the final battle that ranks with the greatest action sequences ever. The same praise is also extended to

Dimitri Tiomkin's superb score, one of the best ever heard in a dramatic film. If the epilogue doesn't move you emotionally, then—in the words of Davy Crockett—"you may be walkin' around, but you're dead as a beaver hat."

 Gone with the Wind _____

Shortly after *The Alamo's* premiere engagements, the studio forced Wayne to cut almost a half hour to allow for more daily showings. The footage was thought lost forever but was found and restored on home video in the early 1990s. Inexplicably, the current MGM DVD reverts back to the truncated version! The running time listed refers to the uncut version.

Exodus (1960)

United Artists

Director and Producer: Otto Preminger; **Writer:** Dalton Trumbo; **Music:** Ernest Gold; **Running time:** 208 minutes

Cast: Paul Newman (Ari Ben Canaan); Eva Marie Saint (Kitty Fremont); Ralph Richardson (Gen. Sutherland); Peter Lawford (Caldwell); Sal Mineo (Dov)

Oscar nominations: Score*, Cinematography (color), Supporting Actor (Sal Mineo)

Otto Preminger's big budget adaptation of Leon Uris's bestseller about the founding of Israel would almost certainly never be made in today's climate of political friction in the Middle East. It's a reverent look at the conflict from the Israeli point-of-view but makes up in scale what it lacks in subtlety. The all-star cast compensates for the meandering screenplay, and the soundtrack of Ernest Gold's great score was a mainstay in family record collections during the 1960s.

Spartacus (1960)

Universal Pictures

Director: Stanley Kubrick; **Producer:** Edward Lewis; **Executive Producer:** Kirk Douglas; **Writer:** Dalton Trumbo; **Music:** Alex North; **Running time:** 196 minutes

Cast: Kirk Douglas (Spartacus); Laurence Olivier (Marcus Licinius Crassus); Jean Simmons (Varinia); Charles Laughton (Sempronius Gracchus); Peter Ustinov (Lentulus Batiatus); John Gavin (Julius Caesar)

Oscar nominations: Art Direction-Set Decoration* (color), Cinematography* (color), Supporting Actor* (Peter Ustinov), Costume Design* (color), Editing, Score

Determined to avoid the "tits and togas" reputation of many Roman empire epics, Kirk Douglas hired writer Dalton Trumbo to pen the screenplay for *Spartacus*, and thereby valiantly broke the McCarthy era blacklist that had victimized Trumbo and others. Yet, this was a troubled production. Anthony Mann was the original director but left in a squabble with producer Douglas. He was replaced by Stanley Kubrick who so resented Douglas's vision of the film that he vowed to keep total control over his future projects, a promise he managed to keep. For all that, *Spartacus* is a solid achievement not only as a spectacular retelling of the man who led the slave rebellion against Rome, but also as a compelling story of cruelty, love, and tragedy. Remade as a 2004 TV movie.

Gone with the Wind

After its premiere, the studio bowed to censorship pressure and removed a suggestive bath sequence with homosexual overtones between Laurence Olivier and Tony Curtis. When the film received a high profile restoration in 1991, the scene was restored but the soundtrack was missing. Curtis revoiced his part and Anthony Hopkins dubbed the voice of the late Olivier.

El Cid (1961)

Allied Artists Pictures Corp.

Director: Anthony Mann; **Producer:** Samuel Bronston; **Writers:** Philip Yordan and Frederic M. Frank; **Music:** Miklos Rosza; **Running time:** 182 minutes

Cast: Charlton Heston (El Cid); Sophia Loren (Jimina); Raf Vallone (Count Ordolez); Genevieve Page (Princess Urraca)

Oscar nominations: Art Direction-Set Decoration(color), Score, Song (*The Falcon and the Dove*)

Acclaimed as one of the most intelligent period epics of the 1960s, *El Cid* tells the story of the legendary Spanish leader Rodrigo Diaz, who drove the Moors from Spain. Anthony Mann crafts a fine spectacle without losing the human element, and there is considerable chemistry between Charlton Heston and Sophia Loren. The film never attained the status it deserves, though the restoration of 16 minutes of missing footage for video was a welcome development.

How the West Was Won (1962)

MGM

Directors: John Ford, Henry Hathaway, and George Marshall; **Producer:** Bernard Smith; **Writer:** James R. Webb; **Music:** Alfred Newman; **Running time:** 162 minutes

Cast: James Stewart (Linus Rawlings); Debbie Reynolds (Lily Prescott); George Peppard (Zeb Rawlings); Karl Malden (Zebulon Prescott); Richard Widmark (Mike King); Henry Fonda (Jethro Stewart); John Wayne (Gen. Sherman); Gregory Peck (Cleve); Spencer Tracy (Narrator)

Oscar nominations: Best Picture, Sound*, Screenplay*, Editing*, Cinematography (color), Art Direction-Set Decoration (color), Costume Design (color), Score

The last Cinerama production to be filmed with the traditional three camera process, MGM's *How the West Was Won* is outstanding entertainment on every level. The screenplay succeeds in personalizing the story of the settling of the west through the eyes of one pioneer family. Politically incorrect by today's standards (it implies all the heavy lifting was done without any minority presence), the film is nonetheless a triumph. Three directors collaborated, but the story is told seamlessly. The buffalo stampede and ride down the rapids lose much of their power on TV, but they still never fail to impress. Alfred Newman's thundering score adds immeasurably to the overall excitement. Inspired the hit 1970s TV series starring James Arness.

Hollywood Confidential

Most of the major stars worked for a paltry $25,000 saying they considered it an honor to tell the story of America's heritage.

Lawrence of Arabia (1962)

Columbia Pictures

Director: David Lean; **Producer:** Sam Spiegel; **Writers:** Robert Bolt and Michael Wilson; **Music:** Maurice Jarre; **Running time:** 216 minutes

Cast: Peter O'Toole (T.E. Lawrence); Alec Guinness (Prince Feisal); Anthony Quinn (Auda abu Tayi); Jack Hawkins (Allenby); Omar Sharif (Sherif Ali)

Oscar nominations: Best Picture*, Director*, Cinematography* (color), Art Direction-Set Decoration* (color), Editing*, Sound*, Score*, Screenplay, Actor (Peter O'Toole), Supporting Actor (Omar Sharif)

Considered by many to be the greatest motion picture ever made, David Lean's masterwork is a film that cries out to be seen on the big screen. Peter O'Toole, previously an unknown, skyrocketed to stardom with his sensitive portrayal of the British adventurer who tried to unite warring Arab tribes to bring stability to the Middle East. Of O'Toole's impossibly good looks, Noel Coward noted that if he were any prettier, he'd have to be called "Florence of Arabia." Despite the flawless supporting cast (curiously devoid of any women), the real star of the film is cinematographer Freddie Young, whose camerawork ensures the status of *Lawrence* as the most beautifully photographed film of all time.

Gone with the Wind

Over the years, *Lawrence of Arabia* had been cut substantially. In 1989, film historian Robert Harris, in conjunction with David Lead, presided over an ambitious restoration of the movie. Most of the missing footage was restored, but some dialogue had to be revoiced by O'Toole, and Charles Gray had to dub dialogue for the late Jack Hawkins.

The Longest Day (1962)

20th Century Fox

Directors: Ken Annakin, Andrew Marton, Bernhard Wicki, and Darryl F. Zanuck (uncredited); **Producer:** Darryl F. Zanuck; **Writers:** Cornelius Ryan, Romain Gary, James Jones, David Pursall, and Jack Seddon; **Music:** Maurice Jarre; **Title Song:** Paul Anka; **Running time:** 178 minutes

Cast: John Wayne (Col. Vandervoot); Henry Fonda (Theodore Roosevelt Jr.); Robert Mitchum (Norman Cota); Curt Jurgens (Gen. Blumentritt); Peter Lawford (Lord Lovatt); Red Buttons (John Steele); Richard Burton (Campbell)

Oscar nominations: Best Picture, Cinematography* (b&w), Special Effects*, Editing, Art Direction-Set Decoration (b&w)

Producer Darryl F. Zanuck succeeded in this highly personal "dream project" of paying homage to the men who fought during the Allied invasion of Normandy. Zanuck's production captures not only the sweep of the massive military operation, but also manages to give ample time to the individual characters, portrayed by the ultimate all-star cast. Zanuck had to stave off Fox studio executives who were tempted to rush the film into release as a run-of-the-mill war movie to gain a quick cash infusion that would help stem the red ink being incurred by the spiraling costs of *Cleopatra*. The outraged mogul prevailed and, in doing so, literally took control of the studio he had run previously. His film remains a testament to the bravest fighting men of all time and, despite Steven Spielberg's excellent *Saving Private Ryan*, *The Longest Day* will always stand as the definitive tribute to the men who freed Europe from tyranny.

Mutiny on the Bounty (1962)

MGM

Director: Lewis Milestone; **Producer:** Aaron Rosenberg; **Writer:** Charles Lederer; **Music:** Bronislau Kaper; **Running time:** 178 minutes

Cast: Marlon Brando (Fletcher Christian); Trevor Howard (Capt. Bligh); Richard Harris (Mills); Hugh Griffith (Smith); Richard Haydn (Brown); Tarita (Maimiti)

Oscar nominations: Best Picture, Art Direction-Set Decoration (color), Special Effects, Score, Song (*Follow Me*), Editing, Cinematography (color)

Like *Cleopatra*, MGM's remake of *Mutiny on the Bounty* proved to be another lavish, out-of-control production that has been largely dismissed by critics but not by fans of epic films who have long recognized this as the superior of the two versions. Brando's much-criticized portrayal of Fletcher Christian as an elitest fop was far more daring and effective than Clark Gable's run-of-the-mill Americanized portrayal. Trevor Howard is equally compelling as Bligh. The cinematography is beautiful as is the score, though *Mutiny's* bad press ensured it was shut out of Oscar wins. Brando's allegedly bizarre and costly off-screen antics also helped put his career in a decade-long slump. However, this is one of his finest screen performances.

Gone with the Wind

The original version of the film featured a prologue in which a ship lands at Pitcairn Island and learns the story of the mutiny from the one surviving crew member, the botanist Brown. This scene has been removed from virtually all versions of the film seen today.

Cleopatra (1963)

20th Century Fox

Director: Joseph L. Mankiewicz; **Producer:** Walter Wanger; **Writers:** Joseph L. Mankiewicz, Sidney Buchman, and Randall MacDougall; **Music:** Alex North; **Running time:** 192 minutes

Cast: Elizabeth Taylor (Cleopatra); Richard Burton (Marc Antony); Rex Harrison (Julius Caesar); Roddy McDowell (Octavian); Hume Cronyn (Sosigenes)

Oscar nominations: Best Picture, Cinematography* (color), Art Direction-Set Decoration* (color), Costume Design* (color), Special Effects*, Sound, Actor (Rex Harrison), Score, Editing

Although a financial boondoggle on such a massive scale that it almost sunk 20th Century Fox, *Cleopatra* is one of the most inappropriately maligned films of all time. This is a prime example of a troubled production whose background story dwarfed any on-screen dramatics. The film was so ineptly produced and prone to disaster that a major portion of the movie had to be scrapped and filmed anew with different actors! In today's dollars, the production would have cost almost $300 million. Its ultimate failure at the box office wasn't due to lack of audience interest (it pulled in big crowds), but the insurmountable cost of bringing this remake of the 1934 Claudette Colbert version to the screen. If you can get past the waste, this is spectacle on an unprecedented scale and filled with visuals that are still eye-popping today. The acting honors go to Burton and Harrison, each outstanding. The weak link is Liz's interpretation of Cleopatra. She looks stunning but emotes like a spoiled Beverly Hills High School homecoming queen. The entrance of Cleopatra into Rome is a jaw-dropping spectacle. Remade as a TV movie in 1999.

55 Days at Peking (1963)

Allied Artists Picture Corp.

Director: Nicholas Ray; **Producer:** Samuel Bronston; **Writers:** Bernard Gordon and Philip Yordan; **Music:** Dimitri Tiomkin; **Running time:** 150 minutes

Cast: Charlton Heston (Matt Lewis); Ava Gardner (Natalie Ivanoff); David Niven (Sir Arthur Robertson); Flora Robson (Empress); John Ireland (Sgt. Harry)

Oscar nominations: Score, Song (*So Little Time*)

Unfairly maligned as a dud, Samuel Bronston's epic recounts China fighting against foreign influences during the Boxer Rebellion. This is a sweeping and impressive film, with Bronston recreating the city of Peking on Spanish soil. However, the enormous sets drove the production costs sky-high. Still, there is an admirable quality to Bronston's mad ambitions, and they represent the kind of epic moviemaking that characterized the Golden Age of Hollywood. A first rate cast is marred only by the old racist ploy of having western actors portray major Asian characters, and none too convincingly at that. The battle sequences are stunning in their scope, and Dimitri Tiomkin's score adds a distinguished touch.

The Fall of the Roman Empire (1964)

Paramount Pictures

Director: Anthony Mann; **Producer:** Samuel Bronston; **Writers:** Ben Barzman, Basilio Franchina, and Philip Yordan; **Music:** Dimitri Tiomkin; **Running time:** 188 minutes

Cast: Sophia Loren (Lucilla); Stephen Boyd (Livius); Alec Guinness (Marcus Aurelius); James Mason (Timonides); Christopher Plummer (Commodus)

Oscar nominations: Score

Producer Samuel Bronston's penchant for making epic films reached its zenith with *The Fall of the Roman Empire*, the title of which suggests a historical story of such magnitude it would not be equaled in ambition until Mel Brooks's *The History of the World–Pt. 1.* Yet, the film does a credible job of condensing some of history's highlights while simultaneously presenting an engrossing love story. On a Bronston map one inch equaled one inch, and the massive scale of the production comes close to rivaling *Cleopatra.* A fine cast helps compensate for the prolonged running time that will occasionally make you think you're reliving the title event in real time.

Doctor Zhivago (1965)

MGM

Director: David Lean; **Producers:** Carlo Ponti and David Lean; **Writer:** Robert Bolt; **Music:** Maurice Jarre; **Running time:** 197 minutes

Cast: Omar Sharif (Zhivago); Julie Christie (Lara); Geraldine Chaplin (Tonia); Rod Steiger (Komarovsky); Alec Guinness (Yevgraf Zhivago)

Oscar nominations: Best Picture, Director, Sound, Editing, Supporting Actor (Tom Courtenay), Score*, Costume Design* (color), Cinematography* (color), Art Direction-Set Decoration* (color), Screenplay*

David Lean's sprawling adaptation of Boris Pasternak's legendary novel (it was banned in his native Russia), *Doctor Zhivago* was a crowd-pleaser from the moment it premiered and became one of MGM's top-grossing films of all time. It's a flawed production in many ways: The script is too ambitious in its attempt to combine the sweep of the Russian Revolution with the lives of the story's protagonists. There is little historical context, so audiences not attuned to Russian history may be bewildered. Omar Sharif's Zhivago is another misstep: he looks handsome, but he's an empty vessel. The acting honors go to a superb supporting cast, and the production design is magnificent. Maurice Jarre's score is a classic for the ages. David Lean's misses are more interesting than most directors' hits. Remade as a TV movie in 2002.

Khartoum (1966)

MGM

Director: Basil Dearden; **Producer:** Julian Blaustein; **Writer:** Robert Ardry; **Music:** Frank Cordell; **Running time:** 128 minutes

Cast: Charlton Heston (Gen. Gordon); Laurence Olivier (The Mahdi); Richard Johnson (Stewart); Ralph Richardson (Gladstone)

Oscar nominations: Screenplay

This epic retelling of the fall of Khartoum, despite a gallant defense by British General Gordon, was probably too alien to American sensibilities. The film failed at the box office, but it doesn't diminish the fact that it's a grand show, literately and intelligently told. Charlton Heston gives one of his best performances as Gordon, and Laurence Olivier is mesmerizing as his nemesis, the religious fanatic The Mahdi (though the meeting between he and Gordon seen in the film never occurred in real life). *Khartoum* benefits from outstanding cinematography and a sweeping score by Frank Cordell. Trivia note: the film was originally going to star Burt Lancaster and be directed by Lewis Gilbert.

The Sand Pebbles (1966)

20th Century Fox

Director and Producer: Robert Wise; **Writer:** Robert Anderson; **Music:** Jerry Goldsmith; **Running time:** 179 minutes

Cast: Steve McQueen (Jake Holman); Richard Attenborough ("Frenchy"); Richard Crenna (Capt. Collins); Candice Bergen (Shirley Eckert); Mako (Po-hahn)

Oscar nominations: Best Picture, Actor (Steve McQueen), Sound, Score, Art Direction-Set Decoration (color), Cinematography (color), Supporting Actor (Mako), Editing

Steve McQueen received his only Oscar nomination for his portrayal of an alienated, disillusioned sailor stuck aboard a U.S. Navy gunship in China during the height of the 1926 revolution. A major career achievement for the esteemed Robert Wise (who was inexplicably denied his own Oscar nomination), the film was seen as having parallels to the on-going Vietnam crisis. The movie boasts magnificent visuals and outstanding supporting performances, as well as one of Jerry Goldsmith's best scores. A letter perfect production, though the story it relates is steeped in tragedy. The film was cut by 17 minutes after its premiere engagements. Some of the footage exists in various foreign prints, but the film has never been fully restored.

Battle of Britain (1969)

United Artists

Director: Guy Hamilton; **Producers:** Harry Saltzman and S. Benjamin Fisz; **Writers:** Wilfred Greatorex and James Kennaway; **Music:** Ron Goodwin; **Running time:** 133 minutes

Cast: Laurence Olivier (Sir Hugh Dowding); Michael Caine (Canfield); Christopher Plummer (Colin Harvey); Suzanna York (Maggie Harvey); Robert Shaw (Squadron leader); Ralph Richardson (Sir David Kelly)

Vastly under-rated and often overlooked in discussions of great war movies, *Battle of Britain* is an imperfect but visually stunning depiction of the unsuccessful Nazi blitz in the skies over London. The production, masterminded by 007 producer Harry Saltzman and director Guy Hamilton, amassed a huge array of vintage aircraft and replicated amazing battle sequences over England. The script bogs down a bit with an irrelevant and out of place love story, but the cast is truly impressive and features some of Britain's most acclaimed actors. Be aware of the fact that various versions of the film are floating about, some of which alter the main titles by Maurice Binder and some that credit only William Walton and eliminate the credit for composer Ron Goodwin, who scored most of the film.

The American Film Institute's Top 100 Films of All Time

The American Film Institute surveyed 1,500 noted film professionals and historians to choose the top 100 American films of all time. Here are their selections.

1. *Citizen Kane* (1941)

2. *Casablanca* (1942)

3. *Godfather, The* (1972)

4. *Gone with the Wind* (1939)

5. *Lawrence of Arabia* (1962)

6. *Wizard of Oz, The* (1939)

7. *Graduate, The* (1967)

8. *On The Waterfront* (1954)

9. *Schindler's List* (1993)

10. *Singin' in the Rain* (1952)

11. *It's a Wonderful Life* (1946)

12. *Sunset Boulevard* (1950)

13. *Bridge on the River Kwai, The* (1957)

14. *Some Like It Hot* (1959)

15. *Star Wars* (1977)

16. *All About Eve* (1950)

17. *African Queen, The* (1951)

18. *Psycho* (1960)

19. *Chinatown* (1974)

20. *One Flew Over the Cuckoo's Nest* (1975)

21. *Grapes of Wrath, The* (1940)

22. *2001: A Space Odyssey* (1968)

23. *Maltese Falcon, The* (1941)

24. *Raging Bull* (1980)

25. *E.T. The Extra-Terrestrial* (1982)

26. *Dr. Strangelove* (1964)

27. *Bonnie and Clyde* (1967)

28. *Apocalypse Now* (1979)

29. *Mr. Smith Goes to Washington* (1939)

30. *Treasure of the Sierra Madre* (1948)

31. *Annie Hall* (1977)

32. *Godfather Part II, The* (1974)

33. *High Noon* (1952)

34. *To Kill a Mockingbird* (1962)

35. *It Happened One Night* (1934)

36. *Midnight Cowboy* (1969)

37. *Best Years of Our Lives, The* (1946)

38. *Double Indemnity* (1944)

39. *Doctor Zhivago* (1965)

40. *North By Northwest* (1959)

41. *West Side Story* (1961)

42. *Rear Window* (1954)

43. *King Kong* (1933)

44. *Birth of a Nation, The* (1915)

45. *Streetcar Named Desire, A* (1951)

46. *Clockwork Orange, A* (1971)

47. *Taxi Driver* (1976)

48. *Jaws* (1975)

49. *Snow White and the Seven Dwarfs* (1937)

50. *Butch Cassidy and the Sundance Kid* (1969)

51. *Philadelphia Story, The* (1940)

52. *From Here to Eternity* (1953)

53. *Amadeus* (1984)

54. *All Quiet on the Western Front* (1930)

55. *Sound of Music, The* (1965)

56. *M*A*S*H* (1970)

57. *Third Man, The* (1949)

58. *Fantasia* (1940)

59. *Rebel Without a Cause* (1955)

60. *Raiders of the Lost Ark* (1981)

61. *Vertigo* (1958)

62. *Tootsie* (1982)

63. *Stagecoach* (1939)

64. *Close Encounters of the Third Kind* (1977)

65. *Silence of the Lambs, The* (1991)

66. *Network* (1976)

67. *Manchurian Candidate, The* (1962)

68. *American in Paris, An* (1951)

69. *Shane* (1953)

70. *French Connection, The* (1971)

71. *Forrest Gump* (1994)

72. *Ben-Hur* (1959)

73. *Wuthering Heights* (1939)

74. *Gold Rush, The* (1925)

75. *Dances with Wolves* (1990)

76. *City Lights* (1931)

77. *American Graffiti* (1973)

78. *Rocky* (1976)

79. *Deer Hunter, The* (1978)

80. *Wild Bunch, The* (1969)

81. *Modern Times* (1936)

82. *Giant* (1956)

83. *Platoon* (1986)

84. *Fargo* (1996)

85. *Duck Soup* (1933)

86. *Mutiny on the Bounty* (1935)

87. *Frankenstein* (1931)

88. *Easy Rider* (1969)

89. *Patton* (1970)

90. *Jazz Singer, The* (1927)

91. *My Fair Lady* (1964)

92. *Place in the Sun, A (1951)*

93. *Apartment, The* (1960)

94. *Goodfellas* (1990)

95. *Pulp Fiction* (1994)

96. *Searchers, The* (1956)

97. *Bringing Up Baby* (1938)

98. *Unforgiven* (1992)

99. *Guess Who's Coming to Dinner* (1967)

100. *Yankee Doodle Dandy* (1942)

The American Film Institute's Top 100 Film Quotes

The American Film Institute surveyed film scholars and critics to arrive at a definitive listing of the most famous movie quotes in history. We present them here in the order in which they were ranked by those who voted in the survey.

1. "Frankly, my dear, I don't give a damn." *Gone with the Wind* 1939

2. "I'm going to make him an offer he can't refuse." *The Godfather* 1972

3. "You don't understand! I coulda had class. I coulda been a contender." *On the Waterfront* 1954

4. "Toto, I've got a feeling we're not in Kansas anymore." *The Wizard of Oz* 1939

5. "Here's looking at you, kid." *Casablanca* 1942

6. "Go ahead, make my day." *Sudden Impact* 1983

7. "All right, Mr. DeMille, I'm ready for my closeup." *Sunset Boulevard* 1950

8. "May the Force be with you." *Star Wars* 1977

9. "Fasten your seatbelts. It's going to be a bumpy night." *All About Eve* 1950

10. "You talking to me?" *Taxi Driver* 1976

11. "What we've got here is failure to communicate." *Cool Hand Luke* 1967

12. "I love the smell of napalm in the morning." *Apocalypse Now* 1979

13. "Love means never having to say you're sorry." *Love Story* 1970

14. "The stuff that dreams are made of." *The Maltese Falcon* 1941

15. "E.T. phone home." *E.T. The Extraterrestrial* 1982

16. "They call me *Mister* Tibbs!" *In the Heat of the Night* 1967

17. "Rosebud." *Citizen Kane* 1941

18. "Made it, Ma! Top of the world!" *White Heat* 1949

19. "I'm as mad as hell, and I'm not going to take this anymore!" *Network* 1976

20. "Louis, I think this is the beginning of a beautiful friendship." *Casablanca* 1942

21. "A census taker once tried to test me. I ate his liver with some fava beans and a nice Chianti." *The Silence of the Lambs* 1991

22. "Bond. James Bond." *Dr. No* 1962

23. "There's no place like home." *The Wizard of Oz* 1939

24. "I am big! It's the pictures that got small!" *Sunset Boulevard* 1950

25. "Show me the money!" *Jerry Maguire* 1996

26. "Why don't you come up sometime and see me?" *She Done Him Wrong* 1933

27. "I'm walking here! I'm walking here!" *Midnight Cowboy* 1969

28. "Play it, Sam. Play 'As Time Goes By.'" *Casablanca* 1942

29. "You can't handle the truth!" *A Few Good Men* 1992

30. "I want to be alone." *Grand Hotel* 1932

31. "After all, tomorrow is another day." *Gone with the Wind* 1939

32. "Round up the usual suspects." *Casablanca* 1942

33. "I'll have what she's having." *When Harry Met Sally* 1989

34. "You know how to whistle, don't you, Steve? You just put your lips together and blow." *To Have and Have Not* 1944

35. "You're gonna need a bigger boat." *Jaws* 1975

36. "Badges? We ain't got no badges! We don't need no badges! I don't have to show you any stinking badges!" *The Treasure of the Sierra Madre* 1948

37. "I'll be back." *The Terminator* 1984

38. "Today, I consider myself the luckiest man on the face of the earth." *The Pride of the Yankees* 1942

39. "If you build it, he will come." *Field of Dreams* 1989

40. "Mama always said life was like a box of chocolates. You never know what you're gonna get." *Forrest Gump* 1994

41. "We rob banks." Bonnie and Clyde 1967

42. "Plastics." *The Graduate* 1967

43. "We'll always have Paris." *Casablanca* 1942

44. "I see dead people." *The Sixth Sense* 1999

45. "Stella! Hey, Stella!" *A Streetcar Named Desire* 1951

46. "Oh, Jerry, don't let's ask for the moon. We have the stars." *Now, Voyager* 1942

47. "Shane. Shane. Come back!" *Shane* 1953

48. "Well, nobody's perfect." *Some Like It Hot* 1959

49. "It's alive! It's alive!" *Frankenstein* 1931

50. "Houston, we have a problem." *Apollo 13* 1995

51. "You've got to ask yourself one question: 'Do I feel lucky?' Well, do ya, punk?" *Dirty Harry* 1971

52. "You had me at 'hello.'" *Jerry Maguire* 1996

53. "One morning I shot an elephant in my pajamas. How he got in my pajamas, I don't know." *Animal Crackers* 1930

54. "There's no crying in baseball!" *A League of Their Own* 1992

55. "La-dee-da, la-dee-da." *Annie Hall* 1977

56. "A boy's best friend is his mother." *Psycho* 1960

57. "Greed, for lack of a better word, is good." *Wall Street* 1987

58. "Keep your friends close, but your enemies closer." *The Godfather Part II* 1974

59. "As God is my witness, I'll never be hungry again." *Gone with the Wind* 1939

60. "Well, here's another nice mess you've gotten me into!" *Sons of the Desert* 1933

61. "Say 'hello' to my little friend!" *Scarface* 1983

62. "What a dump." *Beyond the Forest* 1949

63. "Mrs. Robinson, you're trying to seduce me. Aren't you?" *The Graduate* 1967

64. "Gentlemen, you can't fight in here! This is the War Room!" *Dr. Strangelove* 1964

65. "Elementary, my dear Watson." *The Adventures of Sherlock Holmes* 1939

66. "Get your stinking paws off me, you damned dirty ape!" *Planet of the Apes* 1968

67. "Of all the gin joints in all the towns in all the world, she walks into mine." *Casablanca* 1942

68. "Here's Johnny!" *The Shining* 1980

69. "They're here!" *Poltergeist* 1982

70. "Is it safe?" *Marathon Man* 1976

71. "Wait a minute, wait a minute. You ain't heard nothin' yet!" *The Jazz Singer* 1927

72. "No wire hangers, ever!" *Mommie Dearest* 1981

73. "Mother of mercy, is this the end of Rico?" *Little Caesar* 1930

74. "Forget it, Jake, it's Chinatown." *Chinatown* 1974

75. "I have always depended on the kindness of strangers." *A Streetcar Named Desire* 1951

76. "Hasta la vista, baby." *Terminator 2: Judgment Day* 1991

77. "Soylent Green is people!" *Soylent Green* 1973

78. "Open the pod bay doors, HAL." *2001: A Space Odyssey* 1968

79. Striker: "Surely you can't be serious." Rumack: "I am serious … and don't call me Shirley." *Airplane* 1980

80. "Yo, Adrian!" *Rocky* 1976

81. "Hello, gorgeous." *Funny Girl* 1968

82. "Toga! Toga!" *National Lampoon's Animal House* 1978

83. "Listen to them. Children of the night. What music they make." *Dracula* 1931

84. "Oh, no, it wasn't the airplanes. It was Beauty killed the Beast." *King Kong* 1933

85. "My precious." *The Lord of the Rings: The Two Towers* 2002

86. "Attica! Attica!" *Dog Day Afternoon* 1975

87. "Sawyer, you're going out a youngster, but you've got to come back a star!" *42nd Street* 1933

88. "Listen to me, mister. You're my knight in shining armor. Don't you forget it. You're going to get back on that horse, and I'm going to be right behind you, holding on tight, and away we're gonna go, go, go!" *On Golden Pond* 1981

89. "Tell 'em to go out there with all they got and win just one for the Gipper." *Knute Rockne: All American* 1940

90. "A martini. Shaken, not stirred." *Goldfinger* 1964

91. "Who's on first." *The Naughtie Nineties* 1945

92. "Cinderella story. Outta nowhere. A former greenskeeper, now, about to become the Masters' champion. It looks like a mirac … It's in the hole! It's in the hole! It's in the hole!" *Caddyshack* 1980

93. "Life is a banquet, and most poor suckers are starving to death!" *Auntie Mame* 1958

94. "I feel the need—the need for speed!" *Top Gun* 1986

95. "Carpe diem. Seize the day, boys. Make your lives extraordinary." *Dead Poets Society* 1989

96. "Snap out of it!" *Moonstruck* 1987

97. "My mother thanks you. My father thanks you. My sister thanks you. And I thank you." *Yankee Doodle Dandy* 1942

98. "Nobody puts Baby in a corner." *Dirty Dancing* 1987

99. "I'll get you, my pretty, and your little dog, too!" *The Wizard of Oz* 1939

100. "I'm king of the world!" *Titanic* 1997

The Top Ten Box Office Stars 1950–1969

1950

John Wayne
Bob Hope
Bing Crosby
Betty Grable
James Stewart
Abbott and Costello
Clifton Webb
Esther Williams
Spencer Tracy
Randolph Scott

1951

John Wayne
Martin and Lewis
Betty Grable
Abbott and Costello
Bing Crosby
Bob Hope
Randolph Scott
Gary Cooper
Doris Day
Spencer Tracy

1952

Martin and Lewis
Gary Cooper
John Wayne
Bing Crosby
Bob Hope
James Stewart
Doris Day
Gregory Peck
Susan Hayward
Randolph Scott

1953

Gary Cooper
Martin and Lewis
John Wayne
Alan Ladd
Bing Crosby
Marilyn Monroe
James Stewart
Bob Hope
Susan Hayward
Randolph Scott

1954

John Wayne
Martin and Lewis
Gary Cooper
James Stewart
Marilyn Monroe
Alan Ladd
William Holden
Bing Crosby
Jane Wyman
Marlon Brando

1955

James Stewart
Grace Kelly
John Wayne
William Holden
Gary Cooper
Marlon Brando
Martin and Lewis
Humphrey Bogart
June Allyson
Clark Gable

1956

William Holden
John Wayne
James Stewart
Burt Lancaster
Glenn Ford
Martin and Lewis
Gary Cooper
Marilyn Monroe
Kim Novak
Frank Sinatra

1957

Rock Hudson
John Wayne
Pat Boone
Elvis Presley
Frank Sinatra
Gary Cooper
William Holden
James Stewart
Jerry Lewis
Yul Brynner

1958

Glenn Ford
Elizabeth Taylor
Jerry Lewis
Marlon Brando
Rock Hudson
William Holden
Brigitte Bardot
Yul Brynner
James Stewart
Frank Sinatra

1959

Rock Hudson
Cary Grant
James Stewart
Doris Day
Debbie Reynolds
Glenn Ford
Frank Sinatra
John Wayne
Jerry Lewis
Susan Hayward

1960

Doris Day
Rock Hudson
Cary Grant
Elizabeth Taylor
Debbie Reynolds
Tony Curtis
Sandra Dee
Frank Sinatra
Jack Lemmon
John Wayne

1961

Elizabeth Taylor
Rock Hudson
Doris Day
John Wayne
Cary Grant
Sandra Dee
Jerry Lewis
William Holden
Tony Curtis
Elvis Presley

1962

Doris Day
Rock Hudson
Cary Grant
John Wayne
Elvis Presley
Elizabeth Taylor
Jerry Lewis
Frank Sinatra
Sandra Dee
Burt Lancaster

1963

Doris Day
John Wayne
Rock Hudson
Jack Lemmon
Cary Grant
Elizabeth Taylor
Elvis Presley
Sandra Dee
Paul Newman
Jerry Lewis

1964

Doris Day
Jack Lemmon
Rock Hudson
John Wayne
Cary Grant
Elvis Presley
Shirley MacLaine
Ann-Margaret
Paul Newman
Richard Burton

1965

Sean Connery
John Wayne
Doris Day
Julie Andrews
Jack Lemmon
Elvis Presley
Cary Grant
James Stewart
Elizabeth Taylor
Richard Burton

1966

Julie Andrews
Sean Connery
Elizabeth Taylor
Jack Lemmon
Richard Burton
Cary Grant
John Wayne
Doris Day
Paul Newman
Elvis Presley

1967

Julie Andrews
Lee Marvin
Paul Newman
Dean Martin
Sean Connery
Elizabeth Taylor
Sidney Poitier
John Wayne
Richard Burton
Steve McQueen

1968

Sidney Poitier
Paul Newman
Julie Andrews
John Wayne
Clint Eastwood
Dean Martin
Steve McQueen
Jack Lemmon
Lee Marvin
Elizabeth Taylor

1969

Paul Newman
John Wayne
Steve McQueen
Dustin Hoffman
Clint Eastwood
Sidney Poitier
Lee Marvin
Jack Lemmon
Katharine Hepburn
Barbra Streisand

Source: *The Motion Picture Herald*

How the Web Was Won: Useful Internet Sites

The following are useful and recommended websites pertaining to classic movies, genre films, and cult classics.

www.imdb.com   The International Movie Database is an indispensable resource for anyone researching film-related data. In addition to the most extensive cast and credits listings found anywhere, the site provides an amazing amount of useful and entertaining information, including box office details, links to reviews, information about varying versions of films, major awards, and many other fascinating facts. The basic service is free, but it's worth buying a subscription for the deluxe package. This will upgrade your service and provide you with other key information including contact addresses for actors and filmmakers.

www.oscars.org   The official website for the Academy of Motion Picture Arts and Sciences is filled with priceless trivia, news on Oscar-oriented events and public screenings of classic films, and a wealth of other useful data.

www.afi.com   The American Film Institute's excellent site affords movie fans valuable information about the organization and the films they honor and preserve. You can also find out about events pertaining to classic movies.

www.greatestfilms.org   A well-researched site that provides analysis of classic movies including breakdowns by genre and insightful reviews.

www.flickhead.com   An eclectic but highly entertaining combination of movie reviews, interviews with cult filmmakers, and links to offbeat sites pertaining to both mainstream and cult cinema.

www.briansdriveintheater.com   A fun-filled romp through "B" movie heaven with tributes to kitsch films and stars ranging from the Hercules movies to those loveable old sci-fi clinkers.

www.wildestwesterns.com   A tribute site for all manner of western movies ranging from silent horse operas to more contemporary films. The site features up-to-date information on the most obscure book and soundtrack releases as well as an opportunity to subscribe to their print magazine.

www.In70mm.com   A site that celebrates widescreen movies in all their glory. Includes valuable links to a plethora of other sites devoted to the subject.

www.mi6.co.uk   The most ambitious of a seemingly endless number of sites dedicated to the James Bond phenomenon. Up-to-the-minute information about new film developments, interviews with series alumni, and extensive archives of interesting facts. A "must" for all Bond fans.

www.learnaboutmovieposters.com   A thoroughly entertaining site dedicated to the hobby of collecting vintage movie posters. (You remember when posters were created by *artists* and not kids with a scanner and scissors?) Ed and Sue Poole have amassed a wealth of information about the hobby as well as resources and advice for buying and selling.

www.clinteastwood.net   A long-standing site dedicated to the iconic screen legend. Film clips, stills, rare audio tapes, and other resources guaranteed to make your day.

www.cineramaadventure.com   A fun and informative site dedicated to the preservation of the old Imax forerunner, Cinerama. Interesting insights about the history of the format as well as news about international screenings.

www.fulvuedrive-in.com   Fun sight packed with well-written DVD reviews as well as interviews with cult moviemakers and essays on classic movies.

members.tripod.com/keesstam/harrypalmer.html   If you can bear typing the long-winded web address, you'll find this a rewarding site devoted to Michael Caine's Harry Palmer films. The site offers everything from production information to recent photos of film locations.

www.whereeaglesdare.com   A site dedicated to the classic 1969 Clint Eastwood/ Richard Burton war movie *Where Eagles Dare*. Packed with interesting insights and photos.

www.petercushing.co.uk   Christopher Gullo, the biographer of the late esteemed British actor Peter Cushing, provides a "Museum" dedicated to the star of numerous horror film classics as well as Cushing's often neglected other works.

members.tripod.com/~stvmcqueen   The most elaborate site dedicated to Steve McQueen is chockfull of photos, interviews with McQueen colleagues, and trivia about the life and career of the superstar.

www.thesandpebbles.com   A site entirely devoted to Robert Wise's epic 1966 war film, *The Sand Pebbles*. There's always new information about cast and crew as well as the latest video release information. Additionally, there's a wealth of interesting facts about scenes that were deleted from the movie.

www.turnerclassicmovies.com   The best TV network for classic movies (one of the only places you can see them widescreen and uncut) also offers an informative and fun website packed with information about the stars and films of yesteryear. There's also a cool function that allows you to play old original film trailers.

www.thrillville.net   A site dedicated to the love of B movies and 1960s icons. Here you can find everyone from Elvis to the Rat Pack to obscure sex goddesses from cult movies.

www.johnbarry.org.uk   An officially endorsed site dedicated to the Oscar-winning composer of so many classic movie themes.

www.schifrin.com   The official website of film composer Lalo Schifrin whose memorable works include the classic themes from *Mission: Impossible* and *Bullitt*. Schifrin also has his own CD label, and you can order his classic soundtracks online.

www.moviehunter.tv   Looking for a movie that has never been released on home video? Try this site. They do not mass-produce films, but they will find you one copy of virtually any film you may need for purposes of research.

www.moviegoods.com   A good source for vintage movie material from all over the world. Original lobby cards, posters, stills, and other interesting artifacts.

www.the-cinema-store.com   London's famed retail outlet for all things movie related is a great place to find European books and videos that have not been released in the United States.

www.filmscoremonthly.com   The acclaimed magazine dedicated to the art of film music composition ceased publication as a traditional print issue. However, it exists as a subscription-based website where new content and interviews with famed composers are updated regularly.

www.sixtiescinema.com   Fun-filled site hosted by Tom Lisanti, author of numerous books about cult movies of the 1960s. This is the place to be if you want to revel in lore relating to beach movies, B horror films, and other cult favorites.

www.classicmovies.org   Brad Lang's excellent tribute site to great movies complete with an extensive links section with references to other useful sites.

www.badmovies.org   No, it's not a site devoted to your Uncle Herman's old 8mm vacation movies of his trip to Miami. This is a cynical, fun look at all the golden oldie turkeys we love to complain about but can't stop watching.

www.cinematreasures.org   A good site devoted to the worthwhile cause of preserving and promoting old-time movie theaters (an endangered species!) throughout the United States.

www.driveinmovie.com   A useful resource for anyone who wants to locate an operating drive-in movie theater. The site gives you the ability to search by geographical area.

www.cinema.ucla.edu   The website of UCLA's film preservation division gives insights about screening rare films as well as public events revolving around classic cinema.

www.uib.no/herrmann   This site is a tribute to the famed film composer Bernard Hermann, who was best known for his collaborations with Alfred Hitchcock.

www.leonardmaltin.com   The noted film critic and historian provides a wealth of interesting information about Hollywood's Golden Age on his official website.

www.rogerebert.com   The legendary film critic's official site not only reviews the latest movies but also presents links to some of Ebert's original reviews from classics of the past.

www.bafta.com   The British Academy of Film and Television Arts official website with databases showing all previous nominees and winners. Provides good insight into British movie classics.

Further Reading

Recommended Books

In the course of doing research for this book and the film magazine I publish, I've found the following books to be quite helpful.

Annakin, Ken. *So You Wanna Be a Director?* Tomahawk Press (2001)

Bayer, William. *The Great Movies.* Grosset and Dunlap (1973)

Bogdanovich, Peter. *Who the Hell's in It?: Conversations with Hollywood's Legendary Actors.* Ballantine Books (2005)

Bona, Damiena and Mason Wiley. *Inside Oscar (10th Anniversary Edition).* Ballantine (1996)

Bray, Christopher. *Michael Caine: A Class Act.* Faber (2005)

Britton, Wesley. *Spy Television.* Praeger (2004)

Canby, Vincent, et. al. *The New York Times Guide to the Best 1,000 Movies Ever Made.* Three Rivers Press (1999)

Chandler, Charlotte. *The Girl Who Walked Home Alone: Bette Davis, a Personal Biography.* Simon and Schuster (2006)

Clark, Donald and Christopher Andersen. *The Alamo: The Making of John Wayne's Epic Film.* Carol Publishing (1993)

Coleman, Terry. *Olivier.* Henry Holt (2005)

Earnshaw, Tony. *Beating the Devil: The Making of Night of the Demon.* Tomahawk Press (2005)

Ebert, Roger. *The Great Movies.* Broadway (2003)

Frayling, Christopher. *Ken Adam: the Art of Production Design.* Faber (2005)

Frayling, Christopher. *Once Upon a Time in Italy.* Harry Abrams (2005)

Giblin, Gary. *James Bond's London.* Daleon Publishing (2001)

Gullo, Christopher. *In All Sincerity, Peter Cushing.* Xlibris Corp. (2004)

Hall, Sheldon. *Zulu: With Some Guts Behind It—The Making of the Epic Movie.* Tomahawk Press (U.K.) (2005)

Halliwell, Leslie. *Halliwell's Guide to Who's Who in Movies.* Collins (2003)

Harryhausen, Ray and Tony Dalton. *Ray Harryhausen: An Animated Life.* Billboard Books (2005)

Hunter, Jack. *House of Horror: The Complete Hammer Films Story.* Creation Books (2000)

Hunter, Tab and Eddie Muller. *Tab Hunter Confidential: The Making of a Movie Star.* Algonquin Books (2005)

Kay, Eddie Dorman. *Boxoffice Champs.* Portland House (1990)

Kiel, Richard. *Making It Big in the Movies.* Reynolds and Hearn (2001)

Knox, Mickey. *The Good, the Bad and the Dolce Vita.* Nation Books (2005)

Lee, Christopher. *Lord of Misrule: The Autobiography of Christopher Lee.* Orion Publishing (2004)

Lewis, Jerry and James Kaplan. *Dean and Me: A Love Story.* Doubleday (2005)

Lisanti, Tom. *Hollywood Surf and Beach Movies: The First Wave 1959–1969.* McFarland (2005)

Maltin, Leonard. *Leonard Maltin's Classic Movie Guide.* Plume (2005)

Martin, Mick and Marsha Porter. *DVD and Video Guide.* Ballantine (2006)

Mazursky, Paul. *Show Me the Magic: My Adventures in Life and Hollywood.* Simon and Schuster (1999)

McCarty, John. *The Modern Horror Film.* Citadel Press (1990)

McFarlane, Brian (ed.). *The Cinema of Britain and Ireland.* Wallflower Press (U.K.) (2005)

National Society of Film Critics. *The A List: The National Society of Film Critics 100 Essential Films.* Da Capo Press (2002)

Nollen, Scott Allen. *The Cinema of Sinatra.* Luminary Press (2003)

Owen, Gareth and Oliver Bayan. *Roger Moore: His Films and Career.* Robert Hale (U.K.) (2005)

Poole, Ed and Susan. *Learn About Movie Posters.* Iguide Media (2002)

Rothel, David. *Richard Boone: A Knight Without Armor in a Savage Land.* Empire Publishing (2000)

Schneider, Steven Jay. *1001 Movies to See Before You Die (2nd Edition).* Barron's Educational Series (2005)

Sellers, Robert. *Sean Connery: A Celebration.* Robert Hale (U.K.) (1999)

Server, Lee. *Robert Mitchum: Baby, I Don't Care.* St. Martin's Press (2001)

Silver, Alaine and Elizabeth Ward. *Film Noir: An Encyclopedic Reference to the American Style.* Overlook (1993)

Slifkin, Irv. *Video Hound's Groovy Movies: Far Out Films of the Psychedelic Era.* Visible Ink Press (2004)

Steinbruner, Chris and Norman Michaels. *The Films of Sherlock Holmes.* Citadel Press (1991)

Stevens Jr., George. *Conversations with the Great Moviemakers of Hollywood's Golden Age: At the American Film Institute.* Knopf (2006)

Sweet, Matthew. *Shepperton Babylon.* Fabre and Fabre (2005)

Thomas, Bob. *Walt Disney: An American Original.* Disney Editions (1994)

Thomson, David. *Hollywood: A Celebration.* Dorling Kindersley (2001)

Vaughn, Robert. *Only Victims: A Study of Show Business Blacklisting* (*Revised edition*). Limelight Editions (1996)

Wallach, Eli. *The Good, the Bad and Me.* Harcourt Books (2005)

Williams, Lucy Chase. *The Complete Films of Vincent Price.* Citadel Press (1995)

Winner, Michael. *Winner Takes All: A Life of Sorts.* Robson Books (U.K.) (2005)

Worrall, Dave. *The Most Famous Car in the World: James Bond's Aston Martin DB5.* Solo Publishing (U.K.) (1993)

Wood, Lana. *Natalie: A Memoir by Her Sister.* Putnam (1984)

Recommended Magazines

There are very few film-related magazines of any consequence to fans who want to study classic cinema. Virtually all of the best-regarded periodicals on the subject are from grass roots publishing houses. Yet, these magazines contain some of the best freelance writing on the subject of classic and cult movies.

The Big Reel   For decades this has been the Bible for collectors of 16mm and 35mm feature films. The newspaper format also provides interviews with stars of the past as well as appreciations of niche market movies. (www.collect.com)

Cineaste   One of the most enduring and respected magazines dedicated to film criticism, *Cineaste* has been on the scene since 1967 covering "the art and politics of cinema." The wide range of subject matter includes foreign films, film noir classics, and avante-garde efforts by international moviemakers. Don't expect to see an appreciation of Jerry Lewis in these pages, but their essays do make for compelling reading. (www.cineaste.com)

Cinema Retro   In the interest of full disclosure, I hereby confirm I am the Editor-in-Chief and co-publisher of this magazine. If you can't indulge in shameless self-promotion in your own book, what value is there to being a writer? My co-publisher Dave Worrall and I have dedicated this magazine solely to films of the 1960s and 1970s, the last Golden Age of cinema. Every issue features interviews with legendary actors and filmmakers, rare stills and movie poster art, celebrity columnists, and DVD and movie book reviews. (www.cinemaretro.com)

Classic Images: Films of the Golden Age   This tabloid-style periodical is dedicated primarily to films of the 1930s and 1940s. Well-written and entertaining with good insights into the making of many movies that have been obscured with the passage of time. (www.classicimages.com)

Movie Collectors World   Having been around seemingly forever, this ever-popular newspaper covers all aspect of collecting movie memorabilia, with good articles about older movies as well as celebrity updates and interviews. (www.collect.com)

Shock Cinema   A magazine that proudly extols the virtues of B movies and cult classics. Where else can you read in-depth analyses of *Jerkbeast* and *Kamikaze Girls* in a single issue? Excellent interviews with actors and filmmakers, including many individuals you probably thought had entered the Hereafter decades ago. (members.aol.com/shockcin)

Video Watchdog   Long regarded as one of the best written magazines about cult movies, Tim Lucas's addictive publication concentrates on horror and sci-fi films as well as spaghetti westerns and kung fu epics. The joy of the magazine is that it does not treat these films in a condescending manner but evaluates them with the same in-depth analysis most critics would apply to *Citizen Kane*. There are also insightful DVD, CD soundtrack, and movie book reviews. (www.videowatchdog.com)

Wildest Westerns   A highly enjoyable celebration of vintage western movies features well-written and informative analysis of both B westerns and major studio releases along with interviews with leading and supporting actors. (www.wildestwesterns.com)

Actors Index

H-I

J

X–Y–Z

Directors Index

Movies Index

X-Y-Z